A Grammar of Southern Pomo

A Grammar of Southern Pomo

NEIL ALEXANDER WALKER

UNIVERSITY OF NEBRASKA PRESS | LINCOLN

This book is published as part of the Recovering Languages and Literacies of the Americas initiative. Recovering Languages and Literacies is generously supported by the Andrew W. Mellon Foundation.

Library of Congress Cataloging-in-Publication Data
Names: Walker, Neil Alexander, author.
Title: A grammar of Southern Pomo / Neil Alexander Walker.
Description: Lincoln: University of Nebraska Press, [2020] | Based on the author's dissertation (doctoral)—University of California, Santa Barbara (2013). | Includes bibliographical references and index. | Summary: "A Grammar of Southern Pomo is the first comprehensive published description of the Southern Pomo language, one of seven Pomoan languages once spoken in the vicinity of Clear Lake and the Russian River drainage of California"—Provided by publisher.
Identifiers: LCCN 2019015766 | ISBN 9781496217653 (cloth) | ISBN 9781496218919 (pdf) | ISBN 9781496218902 (mobi) | ISBN 9781496218896 (epub)
Subjects: LCSH: Southern Pomo language—Grammar.
Classification: LCC PM1601.Z9 S6893 2020 | DDC 497/.574—dc23
LC record available at https://lccn.loc.gov/2019015766

Set in Merope by Tseng Information Systems, Inc.

CONTENTS

ILLUSTRATIONS AND TABLES

ILLUSTRATIONS

TABLES

PREFACE

The present work builds on research I began as undergraduate student and continued through graduate school.[1] In my preparation of this work I have avoided the temptation to incorporate the vast amount of Robert L. Oswalt's unpublished notes on Southern Pomo, which are now available at the Survey of California and Other Indian Languages, in the Language Archive at the University of California at Berkeley. I knew Oswalt personally when I was an undergraduate at Berkeley, and he gave me the copy of his unfinished Southern Pomo dictionary before I began graduate school. He instructed me not to use anything therein without his permission because he reckoned the dictionary contained many errors. Sadly, Oswalt passed away not long after I began my graduate work. I therefore used Oswalt's unpublished Southern Pomo dictionary with great care in my 2013 dissertation, and I made sparing use of his other field notes.

Oswalt's field notes include descriptions of a multitude of linguistic phenomena, some of which are not dealt with in great depth in this work. I have resisted the temptation to delve too deeply into these notes for additional material for the present work because it is often impossible to be sure of the grammaticality of forms listed in the notes. Indeed, Oswalt's style of fieldwork often involved his creating possible words in Southern Pomo by using his knowledge of Kashaya Pomo and his understanding of Proto Pomo phonology. When eliciting verbs, for example, he would create a plausible instrumental prefix+root combination and ask a speaker whether it was a felicitous verb in Southern Pomo. As might be expected, Oswalt often received negative responses when he created a plausible Southern Pomo word; he also found that different speakers would disagree about the grammaticality of such words, and even the same speaker would later deny that a word she had accepted earlier was truly grammatical.

Oswalt zealously went back over large portions of these notes with speakers and added annotations indicating that forms had been denied as grammatical by speakers. Though his process is certainly open to modern criticism, he never published any Pomoan forms that he could not confirm were really a part of speakers' language use. I believe his understanding of the problematic nature of his private notes explains his reticence to have me reference anything therein without his prior permission. Oswalt's notes do, of course, play a role in this work; however, I view anything outside his publications and draft dictionary as tentative material if it lacks corroboration in Abraham M. Halpern's work.

Much has changed in the relatively short period since I completed my graduate work on the language: the Southern Pomo language program that I coordinated for the Dry Creek Rancheria Band of Pomo Indians ended, and the last truly fluent speaker of Southern Pomo passed away. Wedged into that period between the completion of my dissertation and the death of the last fluent speaker of Southern Pomo was a single day when I and some of my Southern Pomo language students, all of whom were members of the Dry Creek Rancheria, visited Olive Fulwider, their relative and the last fluent speaker, in order to elicit some Southern Pomo words and phrases.

Mrs. Fulwider—Aunt Helen to many of her family members—had dementia by the time of our visit, and for this reason neither I nor any of my students had made any attempts to visit her for the purposes of gaining linguistic knowledge. But after more than a year of weekly classes, two of my students, who were both close relatives of Mrs. Fulwider, decided it would be appropriate to visit her and ask questions.

That visit would be the last time I would hear Southern Pomo roll off the lips of a fluent speaker. And though the dementia prevented Mrs. Fulwider from fully engaging with her visitors or all of their questions, her ability to manipulate the phonological and morphological complexities of her native language was unaffected. I have added the handful of words and phrases we gained from that visit as appendix 1 in the present work, but I shall share a true and depressing statement she made to us on that day:

ʔayha	*ʔom:i=t̪^{h}oṭ'*	*p^{h}al:aʔčay*	*ya:la*	*ʔom:i-w*
Indian	understand=NEG	white.man	only	understand-PFV

'(You) don't understand the Indian (language); (you) only understand the whiteman's (language)'

Though no one now speaks Southern Pomo fluently and some aspects of its grammar are understood only in fragmented form, we know more than we do not know. And I can attest that several of my former students have a sophisticated grasp of Southern Pomo phonology, basic sentence structure, and a large portion of the lexicon. In fact, enough tribal members have progressed in the language to allow me to compose the following prediction without providing a translation—there are Southern Pomo people who can understand it without my help: *ʔayha čahnu ʔo:mik^{h}:eʔwaʔmaya.*

This project would not have been possible without the patient help and kindness of so many people. It has been almost twenty years since I first heard Southern Pomo spoken and began the quest to study the language that led me to a career in linguistics. First and foremost, I wish to thank my lovely wife, Jenny (Kic:idu), for introducing me to her family and their unique history and language. She has been patient and supportive throughout my journey to document and share Southern Pomo. I wish to thank the late Olive Fulwider (Na:hoʔmen) for being so kind to me and my young family. I know she shared so much with us because she wanted my family to feel connected to those who had gone before. I hope I have done some small amount to repay her by learning and sharing all I can about her language. I would also like to thank her daughter, Dorothy, and her late stepdaughter, Gwen, for their unfailing kindness to us on each visit to their home.

I am grateful to the late Robert L. Oswalt for inviting me into his home, sharing his precious data, and caring so deeply about Pomoan people. Thanks also go to my undergraduate mentor, Leanne Hinton, for supporting my work on Pomoan as I began my study of linguistics at UC Berkeley. I am especially thankful to my dissertation chair, Marianne Mithun. I would never have been able to make any headway into the complexities of the language without her assistance. Thanks go to a host of other linguists who have had some role in the completion of this project, whether through work as committee members for the earlier dissertation or as support in the years thereafter. Thank you to Bernard Comrie, Dirk Elzinga, Matthew Gordon, Timothy Henry-Rodriguez, Uldis Balodis, Andrea Berez-Kroeker, Rebekka Siemens, Edmundo Luna, Carmen Jany, Conor Quinn, and Janie Lee.

Thanks go also to my friends and in-laws at the Dry Creek Rancheria Band of Pomo Indians and to my former Southern Pomo language students: Joe Gonzales (ʔač:ay Man:ed:u), Michael Racho (Ko:t̪olo), Joseph Byron, Ramón (Šahčoŋhk^{h}le) and Jasmine Billy, Cheryl Bowden, Silver Galleto, Tieraney Giron, Anthony England, and many others who supported our efforts to teach and preserve the language. Gus Pina, former tribal administrator for the Dry Creek Rancheria Band of Pomo Indians, supported my work on the language for years, and he passed away shortly before I finished this manuscript. I wish to thank him and acknowledge the major contribution he made to the completion of this grammar as my mentor and benefactor.

Finally, I wish to acknowledge my own family members: my mother, Christine, and my late maternal grandmother, Helen, deserve special mention for the years they spent listening to me ramble on about languages. And, of course, I wish to thank my children, Joshua (Biʔdu), Christopher (Bu:ṭaka), Nathan (K^{h}aʔbe), and Maayu (Ma:yu), all of whom have patiently endured their father's research obsessions and the many moves those obsessions have required. I sincerely hope y'all will appreciate the gift of knowledge that has been left for you.

INTRODUCTION

Southern Pomo is no longer a spoken language. It has not been a language of daily use during this century, and there are no fluent speakers now living. Less than sixty miles separate San Francisco, the seat of wealth and education in California since statehood, and Santa Rosa, the city which grew up on Southern Pomo lands. It is difficult to explain how a language could die within a morning's drive of the most populous part of Northern California without a single published book (grammar or dictionary) devoted to it. Generations of scholars have come and gone in the Bay Area, but only a handful seem to have taken notice of Southern Pomo. As noted by Sally McLendon, the lack of published work on the language "is unfortunate, since a clear understanding of Southern Pomo is especially important for the reconstruction of Proto Pomo" (2009: 879). This academic neglect is inexplicable, if not criminal.

A great debt is owed to those few intrepid investigators who chose to work on Southern Pomo without hope of advancement or compensation for so doing. An even greater debt is owed to the Southern Pomo speakers who patiently worked with the various academics who passed through their ancient homeland in an effort to record their language.

What should be covered in a description of a language that has only recently lost the last of its fluent speakers? Everything, of course, would seem the obvious answer. However, time, ability, and available data constrain what can be covered. In this grammar I seek to describe the language to such a degree that future scholars and heritage learners should be able to work through surviving texts and stories with confidence. To this end, I have taken care to provide sources for individual example words, and most examples include a more detailed phonological and morphological breakdown than is usually provided in descriptive grammars. I have adopted a three-part organization for this grammar.

Chapter 1 gives a detailed overview of the culture and history of Southern Pomo speakers. Languages evolve in a specific context, and a knowledge of the Southern Pomo homeland is critical to appreciating the forces which shaped the grammar of the language. This section also lays out the data sources upon which this study is built.

Chapter 2 introduces the sound system of Southern Pomo. Great care has been taken to clarify phonetic details, where relevant, and to back up the decisions I have made in crafting a working orthography for the language. This section also introduces the word classes of Southern Pomo. I have included morpheme-by-morpheme listings, where useful, for each major word class.

Chapter 3 covers sentence-level phenomena, including clause types, clause combining, and grammatical relations. I have focused on those features which are most important to an understanding of the monologic texts. These texts form the data bedrock upon which my current understanding of sentence-level grammar is based. Thus topics such as case marking, switch-reference, and clause nominalization strategies have been given special emphasis.

The orthography used through this work is identical to the alphabet used by the Dry Creek Rancheria Band of Pomo Indians in their language revitalization program, for which I was the coordinator from 2011 to 2014. Though this grammar is aimed toward an academic audience, it is my hope that the large number of examples and the consistent use of the current orthography will make this work useful to language revitalization efforts. To this end, a Southern Pomo narrative that has been transcribed into the current orthography is included in the appendixes. These resources have never been published before and otherwise exist only as archived manuscripts recorded in divergent orthographies.

ABBREVIATIONS

Ø	nought; zero allomorph
1	first person
2	second person
3	third person
3C	third person coreferential
A	transitive subject
ABL	ablative
AGT	agentive
ALL	allative
AUX	auxiliary
C	consonant
CAUS	causative
COLL	collective
COM	comitative
COND	conditional
COP	copula
DEFOC	defocus
DENOM	denominalizer
DEM	demonstrative
DET	determiner
DIR	directional
D.IRR	different subject irrealis
DISTR	distributive
D.SEQ	different subject sequential
D.SIM	different subject simultaneous
EMPH	emphatic
EVID	evidential
F	feminine
FUT	future
GOAL	goal
GS	generational suffix
H	laryngeal increment
HAB	habitual
IMP	imperative
INCH	inchoative
INSTR	instrumental
INTENT	future intentive
INTER	interrogative
IPA	International Phonetic Alphabet
IPFV	imperfective
ITER	iterative
LOC	locative
M	masculine
NEG	negative
NP	noun phrase
O	direct object of transitive verb
OBJ	object
OBL	oblique
PAT	patient
PFV	perfective
PL	plural
PL.ACT	plural act
POSS	possessive
PROH	prohibitive
Ps	Southern Pomo

QUOT quotative
ř reduplication of preceding root
R reduplication of preceding stem
RECIP reciprocal
REFL reflexive
S single argument of an intransitive verb
SG singular
S.IRR same subject irrealis
S.SEQ same subject sequential
S.SIM same subject simultaneous
SUBJ subject
TAM tense, aspect, mood
V vowel; default vowel
VOC vocative
VOT voice onset time

Citing Unpublished Data
(See table 5 for fuller detail)

H I–XI Halpern unpublished narratives, Annie Burke
H EA Halpern data, Elsie Allen
H EA:REC Halpern audio data, Elsie Allen
H ms. Halpern data, Annie Burke
O I Oswalt data, Elizabeth Dollar
O II Oswalt data, Elsie Allen
O III Oswalt data, Laura Somersal
O D Oswalt's unpublished Southern Pomo dictionary
O D: EA Oswalt's unpublished Southern Pomo dictionary, Elsie Allen
O D: ED Oswalt's unpublished Southern Pomo dictionary, Elizabeth Dollar
O ms. Oswalt's unpublished notes
T Molino data, Tony Pete
T:REC Molina audio data, Tony Pete
S:REC Siniard audio data, Maggie Woho and Laura Fish Somersal
W: OF Walker data, Olive Fulwider

Rendering and Symbols in Transcriptions

< > angle brackets = original orthography from another source
|| || double pipes = morphophonemic transcriptions
/ / single slashes = phonemic transcriptions

[ ]	square brackets = narrow phonetic transcriptions in IPA; also, material that was not in original source
( )	parentheses = present in original source but better omitted
*	reconstructed forms; length in Oswalt's electronic Ps dictionary files
#	word boundary
σ	syllable

A Grammar of Southern Pomo

ONE

The Cultural, Ecological, and Sociolinguistic Context of the Language

1.1. THE NAME OF THE LANGUAGE

George Gibbs collected the first known linguistic material from Pomoan languages in 1851 in the form of word lists, and the name Hulanapo, one of the titles of these lists, was used by Powell (1891) to form the name Kulanapan to refer to all the Pomoan languages. It was Barrett (1908) who first identified seven distinct Pomoan languages and proposed that they be designated with geographically based terms, all of which used the term Pomo: Northern Pomo, Northeastern Pomo, Central Pomo, Eastern Pomo, Southern Pomo, Southwestern Pomo (now known as Kashaya), and Southeastern Pomo (McLendon and Oswalt 1978: 274).[1]

The word Pomo comes from two different Northern Pomo sources, both of which contain words which are cognate with Southern Pomo forms (McLendon and Oswalt 1978: 277). The first source, *pʰo:mo:* 'at red earth hole', contains the Northern Pomo words *pʰo:* 'magnesite' and *mo-:* 'hole-at'. The Southern Pomo cognate forms are *pʰo:ʔo* and *hi:mo* respectively.[2] This form, *pʰo:mo*, was the original source of the English term Pomo. The second source, *pʰoʔmaʔ*, contains the Northern Pomo morpheme *pʰo-* 'reside, live in a group' and was affixed to place names. It is cognate with the root of the Southern Pomo word *nopʰ:o* 'village'. This second source came into English as Poma, a term that remained interchangeable with Pomo for a time until Barrett chose to use Pomo to refer to the whole family of languages (McLendon and Oswalt 1978: 277).

Though Barrett's geographic designation works well enough for Southern Pomo, the choices he made in assigning geographic terms to the other Pomoan languages are somewhat idiosyncratic: Southeastern Pomo is northeast of Southern Pomo and due east of Eastern Pomo, and the Pomoan language that might have been named Western Pomo is instead Central Pomo. Since Barrett's popularization of the geographically based names, Southern Pomo has been the preferred term used by linguists.

A native term for the language, if one existed, might be preferable to the name Southern Pomo. With the exception of Kashaya (*k̓ahšá:ya*) and Northeastern Pomo (*č̓ʰéʔe: fóka:*),[3] self-identified ethnic communities and Pomoan languages were not coextensive and thus most Pomoan languages were not known by specific names in aboriginal times; rather, speakers from specific villages might refer to the relevant place name in order to distinguish between speakers from different speech communities. Thus there is no Southern Pomo word for the Southern Pomo language or its speakers.

McLendon and Oswalt (1978: 279–80) suggest that 'Chamay' might be used as a native-based term to replace the name Southern Pomo. It is based on the morpheme *-(h)čamay* 'people' used in the formation of Southern Pomo group names like *ʔaš:ohčamay* 'Wappo' (literally 'east people') and *wiš:ahčamay* 'Ridge People' (an extinct branch of possible Southern Pomo speakers). However, this morpheme does not appear to have been a free-standing word, and the compound words in which it occurs do not refer to Southern Pomo speakers in particular. For these reasons the Anglicization 'Chamay' does not seem to be a suitable replacement for the established name of the language.

Some modern rancherias have adopted the controversial practice of referring to the Southern Pomo language with the name of a specific village or dialect. For example, the Dry Creek Band of Pomo Indians uses 'Mihilakhawna', which is an Anglicization of *mih:ilaʔkʰawna* (*mih:ila* 'west' + *-ʔkʰawna* 'river, creek') 'Dry Creek', in its literature to refer to the language. This practice is not adopted herein for two reasons: (1) it is inaccurate—the same language was spoken in many villages and not just Dry Creek, and materials from other villages, such as Cloverdale, form a large part of the corpus on which all studies of the language are based; and (2) there is no evidence that the original speech communities identified the language with a local place name.

If Southern Pomo communities were to choose a native term for their language, one possible choice would be *ʔay:a:kʰe čahnu* 'our speech', which Elsie Allen, who spoke the dialect of Cloverdale, used at least once to reference Southern Pomo (H EA: 10a; see table 5 later in this chapter for how unpublished items are cited).[4] This term has in its favor a clear history of usage by native speakers, but there is no reason to believe that 'our speech' meant anything more than it does in English. And it is likely that anyone with a different mother tongue might have used 'our speech' to refer to languages other than Southern Pomo. The potential ambiguity notwithstanding, posters, language apps, and other media produced or maintained for and by the Dry Creek Rancheria Band of Pomo Indians between 2011 and the present use *ʔay:a:k^{h}e čahnu* as a Southern Pomo term for the language. Another possible option would be *ʔayha čahnu* 'Indian (thing or culture-related) language', though like 'our language' this term did not refer to Southern Pomo specifically in the past.

I shall not attempt to introduce a replacement for the name Southern Pomo, but the door is open, and there is at least one good reason why a change in terminology should be considered in the future: Barrett's geographical terms incorrectly imply that the seven Pomoan languages are merely dialects of one another, an unfortunate reality which might have negative effects on Southern Pomo tribes' future attempts to apply for language revitalization funding.[5]

1.2. PREVIOUS RESEARCH

No one appears to have focused a great deal of attention on Southern Pomo during the nineteenth century. Samuel Barrett (1908: 56–68) provides a comparative word list of the seven Pomoan languages, and this word list includes many Southern Pomo words. Barrett's transcription is quite good for the time, but it omits so many necessary phonemic contrasts that it is impossible to convert his Southern Pomo words into a phonemically accurate transcription unless the words can be recognized. Table 1 gives examples of Barrett's transcription together with the modern orthography.

As can be seen in table 1, Barrett fails to indicate vowel length and ejectives consistently. He also fails to distinguish different voiceless coronal plosives, all of which he transcribes with <t>. Barrett's word list, however, is an important source against which later records can be compared to establish lexical continuity. His lists include a surprisingly diverse number

Table 1. Sample of Barrett's 1908 Southern Pomo records

Barrett	**Barrett's Gloss**	**Modern orthography**
atcai	'man'	ʔač:ay
baai	'woman'	baʔ:ay
tc!aa	'one'	č̓a:ʔa
a-tcen	'mother' [1-mother-AGT]	ʔa:č̓en
a-batsen	'father's brother' [1-father's father-AGT]	ʔa:baċen
kawi	infant [child]	ka:wi
wo ′to	'dirty, ashes' [roiled]	wo:ṭo
tca-co ′to	'10'	č̓a: šoṭ̓:o

of Southern Pomo words, and the Southern Pomo numerals he includes therein might be the only extant record of the higher numbers. Some of Barrett's examples can be matched with known words but appear unusual. For example, he lists the form <hamūtcakan> 'they', which is quite similar to the well-attested pronoun *ham:uhča* 'they (AGENT)', but the final syllable in Barrett's form is unexpected and has not yet been identified with any known morphemes. Another unexpected form is Barrett's <kītcidū> 'small' for *kic:idu* [kitsˈsiɾu] 'small (SINGULAR)'; Barrett's <tc> is otherwise used only for the post-alveolar affricates.

Dialect mixing is one possible explanation for some of the observable differences between Barrett's record and later records. The upheavals of the nineteenth century saw the destruction of Pomo sovereignty and the forced relocation of Pomoan peoples, and there were no government reservations till the decade after the publication of Barrett's work. This is not, however, an ultimately satisfying explanation. Barrett carefully flags any Southern Pomo words in his list that have a substantially different form in the speech of some consultants.

Specifically, his list gives the forms that were in use in the communities north of Healdsburg, and differing forms in use from Healdsburg south to Santa Rosa are given in his notes. Since the speakers who survived to be recorded in greatest detail (and from whom came the vast majority of the data upon which this grammar is based) were from the regions from which

Barrett collected his primary data, it seems unlikely that dialectal differences can be invoked as a valid explanation for discrepancies between more recent records and his 1908 publication; rather, the differences most likely come from language change (i.e., Barrett's consultants might have used more conservative words) or idiolectal differences in lexical choices. In the case of 'small', Barrett's transcription does not appear to be an error, and it might be the case that the comparatively rare Southern Pomo phoneme /c/ [ts] had been lost in the speech of certain speakers.

Barrett's Southern Pomo contribution is most important because he was among the last American scholars to interact with Southern Pomo speakers from the Healdsburg and Santa Rosa areas. His notes on differences in pronunciation and lexical choice between the more northern varieties of Southern Pomo and those further south constitute some of the best evidence of the character of the southern Southern Pomo dialects, all of which died out before the more northerly Southern Pomo dialects.

The next interested party to collect substantial amounts of Southern Pomo data was C. Hart Merriam. In the fall of 1922 Merriam collected hundreds of plant and animal names from Cloverdale speakers. Around the same time he also collected the equivalent words from Healdsburg speakers.

Merriam was not a formally trained linguist, and his method of transcribing Southern Pomo sounds was beyond inadequate. Though Barrett's work, which predated Merriam's by two decades, did lack the sophistication in transcription practices that linguists now employ, his transcriptions are much closer to the actual phonemes of the language than are those of Merriam. Table 2 gives samples of Merriam's transcription of both Cloverdale and Healdsburg dialect forms together with their phonemic representation in the modern orthography.

As is apparent from table 2, Merriam's transcription practices leave much to be desired. Table 2 also highlights the unique nature of Merriam's Healdsburg dialect data, much of which shows unique or unexpected forms for scores of words. Sadly, it is impossible to assign the correct (or even potentially correct) phonemes on the basis of Merriam's records.[6] For example, the Healdsburg form of 'barn owl', which he records as <Tah´-lahk>, could represent any of the following possible strings of phonemes:

Table 2. Merriam's transcriptions

Merriam's gloss	**Cloverdale**	**Modern orthography**	**Healdsburg**	**Modern orthography**
'Wood rat, round-tail (*Neotoma*)'	Me´-he-yōk	*mihyok̓*	Yoo´-loo	???
'Barn owl (*Strix*)'	Wĕ´-chĕ	*wec̆:e*	Tah´-lahk[7]	???
'Screech owl (*Megascops*)'	Dah-to´-to	*daʔṭ̓oṭ̓o*	Mo-kŏ´-to	???
'Bald eagle (*Halioeetus*)'	Kah´-li	???	O´-te	ʔo:ṭʰiy[8]

/t̪a:lak̓/, /t̪al:ak̓/, /t̪ahlak̓/, /t̪aʔlak̓/, /t̪ʰa:lak̓/, /t̪ʰal:ak̓/, /t̪ʰaʔlak̓/, /t̪̓a:lak̓/, /t̪̓al:ak̓/, /t̪̓ahlak̓/, /ṭa:lak̓/, /ṭal:ak̓/, /ṭahlak̓/, /ṭaʔlak̓/, /ṭʰa:lak̓/, /ṭʰal:ak̓/, /ṭʰaʔlak̓/, /ṭ̓a:lak̓/, /ṭ̓al:ak̓/, /ṭ̓ahlak̓/

Merriam's records are a valuable source of information when it is necessary to verify the species to which an otherwise attested word refers. His records of Southern Pomo also offer a tantalizing glimpse at the lost Southern Pomo speech communities south of Dry Creek. His records are not, however, a trustworthy source of data for any other purposes.

Edward W. Gifford collected kinship data from Southern Pomo speakers around the same time as Merriam's fieldwork was being conducted. His description of the Southern Pomo kinship system (Gifford 1922) remains the only detailed source of information on the workings of that system. His transcription of Southern Pomo words was better than Merriam's work but no more phonetically accurate than Barrett's earlier work. However, Gifford's detailed data include important details about the way the language handled kinship terms, and thanks to Gifford's fieldwork on Southern Pomo, it is now known that the language was unique within the Pomoan family with regard to its handling of cross-cousin terms.[9] Gifford's small contribution to Southern Pomo research also includes the names of four Southern Pomo consultants, two of whom were from Healdsburg, two of whom were from Cloverdale. These data represent both the northern and southern Southern Pomo dialects, and Gifford's data therefore join Barrett's and Merriam's data as the best evidence still extant of the Healdsburg dialect.

The first systematic work on Southern Pomo began with Abraham M.

Halpern. Halpern made a whirlwind tour of all seven Pomoan languages between the late 1930s and 1940 after having cut his teeth on the Yuma language of Southeastern California. He collected traditional stories, phrases, and individual words from all seven languages. His Southern Pomo consultant, Annie Burke, spoke the Cloverdale dialect and provided him with several texts. These texts constitute the only examples of Coyote tales in the Cloverdale dialect (Halpern 1964; Oswalt 2002: 312–13). Later, after a career spent away from Pomoan studies, Halpern returned to work on Southern Pomo in 1982. During this second period of fieldwork, Halpern worked with Elsie Allen, the daughter of Annie Burke, his earlier consultant. Elsie also spoke the Cloverdale dialect. Halpern did not work with any speakers of the Dry Creek or Healdsburg dialects—whether this was because of time constraints is not known—and no linguist after him had the opportunity to work with the Healdsburg dialect.

Halpern was trained in the best practices of phonetic transcription for his time, and his experience with the Yuma language had prepared him well for his work with the Pomoan languages. His transcriptions of Southern Pomo are therefore the first accurate records of the language, and as covered in §1.9 of the present volume, Halpern's notes, audio recordings, and publications are crucial to this grammar.

Robert Oswalt, who completed a grammar and a book of texts for Kashaya Pomo (Southwestern Pomo) by 1963, began working on Southern Pomo around the same time. Oswalt's principal consultants were Elizabeth Dollar, a Dry Creek dialect speaker, and Elsie Allen, a speaker of the Cloverdale dialect (the same consultant with whom Halpern worked in the 1980s). He collected Southern Pomo data from these speakers from the 1960s through the 1980s (Oswalt 2002: 313). Oswalt also collected a small amount of data from Laura Fish Somersal, who learned the Dry Creek dialect of Southern Pomo from her father and was also one of the last speakers of Wappo.

Kashaya and Southern Pomo have similar sound inventories, and Oswalt's ear was well prepared for work on the language. His unpublished field notes, audio recordings, and publications with Southern Pomo data, which are listed in §1.9, constitute the best records of the Dry Creek dialect.[10]

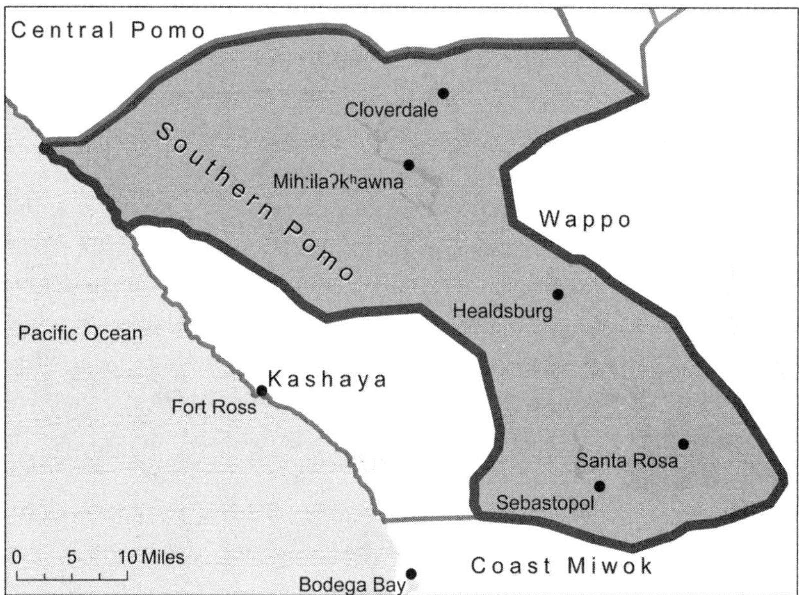

Fig. 1. Map of Southern Pomo area. Courtesy of the author.

1.3. DEMOGRAPHY AT CONTACT

Estimates of the total number of Pomoan language speakers at the time of European contact vary between eight thousand and twenty-one thousand (Oswalt 2002: 311). Kroeber considers the lower figure, eight thousand, to be appropriate, though he accepts the possibility of an even lower total (1925: 237–38). The Southern Pomo–speaking communities constituted about a third of that total (Oswalt 2002: 312).

Southern Pomo speakers lived in villages from as far south as present-day Santa Rosa and Sebastopol north to the greater Cloverdale area. To the west of Cloverdale, speakers lived along Dry Creek, and a small number lived along the highlands west of the Russian River valley and in the redwood forests and coastal land along the Pacific between the Kashaya and the Central Pomo speakers.[11]

Southern Pomo speakers were not organized into a single political unit, though larger villages could serve as political and ceremonial centers for smaller villages (Fredrickson, Peri, and Lerner 1984: 13). The villages south of Healdsburg were closest to the last of the California missions and the Rancho Petaluma adobe, both of which were built and maintained with the use of Southern Pomo and other Indigenous laborers, and were therefore the first Southern Pomo speech communities to be negatively affected by European colonization (Silliman 2004: 65). It is therefore difficult to find reasonable estimates of the population of those southernmost Southern Pomo communities.

The communities situated around Dry Creek and the present-day Cloverdale area, which were less heavily affected by Europeans prior to American colonization, included several villages for which reasonable population estimates do exist. The largest Dry Creek village was <Amalako> 'rabbit field', which served as the cultural center; the smaller village of <Ahkamodot> 'where cold water is' lay nearby and was within the sphere of influence of the larger village.[12] The two villages had an estimated combined population of 500 at the time of European contact. There were an estimated 600–1,000 people living in the greater Cloverdale area. The principal Cloverdale towns were <Makahmo> (*ma:k^{h}a-hmo*) 'salmon-hole', with an estimated pre-contact population of 300–500; the rest lived in <Amakho> (*ʔam:a-k:o*) 'dirt-field', which was politically independent of <Makahmo>, and several smaller towns, including <Mayumo> (*ma:yu-hmo*) 'dove-hole', that were under the political leadership of <Makahmo> (Fredrickson, Peri, and Lerner 1984: 11–13).

1.3.1. History after Contact

In 1812 the Russians founded Fort Ross on the coast in Kashaya territory.[13] The Russians and their Aleut allies from Alaska had not come to settle Pomoan territory in the manner of subsequent European invaders; rather, Fort Ross existed solely to support the Russians' lucrative fur trade network. However, the effects of Russia's small settlement did reach the nearby Southern Pomo communities: there was intermarriage between some members of the Russian contingent and Southern Pomo speakers from the Healdsburg area (Fredrickson, Peri, and Lerner 1984: 50). It was during this time that some Russian words were borrowed (Russian > Aleut > Kashaya) into Southern Pomo (Oswalt 1958). The Southern Pomo experience with Russians was, no doubt, not completely indirect and benign; however, the Fort Ross period, by any measure, affected the Pomoan speakers less severely than the following period, which saw the coming of the Spanish (later Mexicans) and the Americans.

The first Spanish expedition into Southern Pomo territory was led by Luis Arguello in 1821. This expedition was the beginning of the end of native sovereignty. In 1823 Mexico, which had freshly won its independence from Spain, established Mission Solano, the last and northernmost of the California missions (Fredrickson, Peri, and Lerner 1984: 49–50).[14] Southern Pomo speakers were among those whom the Mexicans forced into service, and Indigenous labor built the mission and other structures (Silliman 2004: 65).

What followed was cataclysmic: settlements were set up throughout Pomoan territory, and Pomoan speakers were constantly raided to be sold as slave labor. By 1836 the slave trade in California Indians reached "critical levels," a crisis which was worsened by the smallpox epidemic of 1838–39 (Bean and Theodoratus 1978: 299). In 1840 the Russian presence effectively ended with the abandonment of Fort Ross—at a time when increasing numbers of Kashaya had begun to move there—and the Mexican government became the sole non-Indigenous power in the region (Oswalt 1961: 6).

The Mexican period ended with America's successful war for territory and the 1848 Treaty of Guadalupe Hidalgo, but the change in overlords did nothing to improve the lot of suffering Pomoan peoples. California law came to recognize the rights of non-Indigenous land owners to indenture Indians who were deemed prisoners of war—a suspicious categorization when one considers that there were no real native polities with which to engage in true war—or who had no settled habitation or means of livelihood (i.e., all Indigenous persons living traditional lifestyles). The wages earned by such indentured Indians were to remain in the custody of the non-Indian overseer, though the Indigenous servants were ostensibly provided with clothes and basic necessities as part of the relationship. In reality, however, the law had legalized slavery for Indians, almost all of whom fell into the two broad categories of prisoners of war or transients. Southern Pomo speakers thus became the legal property of the new land owners (Fredrickson, Peri, and Lerner 1984: 58).

Decades of murder, disease, and displacement took an awful toll on all Indigenous communities in California, but the fruits of genocide were especially visible among Pomoan communities: only three Indian children are recorded as living in the Southern Pomo homelands in the United States census records of 1860. A traveler who visited the remaining Cloverdale Pomo noted that the survivors had begun to practice infanticide occasionally in order to spare their offspring the suffering they then endured (Fredrickson, Peri, and Lerner 1984: 58). Less than forty years after the first Spanish expedition to the Southern Pomo homelands—half a lifetime!—all the Southern Pomo villages which were once filled with children's voices had fallen silent.

Once America had moved beyond the assignment of de facto slavery for California's Indians, the status of Indigenous peoples in the state hovered in a dark limbo. Bereft of any land rights or other benefits, Southern Pomo speakers were eventually force-marched to the Round Valley reservation after its creation in 1858. Round Valley was not a well-administered reservation, and once it became possible for them to do so, some Southern Pomo speakers began to trickle back down to their riverine homeland in the south. For a time there was an effort by the government to make treaties with Pomoan groups and provide them with reservation lands; however, all attempts to provide the Pomo and other California Indians with sizable (if inferior) reservation lands were thwarted by protesting California citizens who feared the Indians might end up with gold-rich land (Fredrickson, Peri, and Lerner 1984: 55–57).

It was not till the twentieth century that Southern Pomo speakers were granted official reservation lands (termed 'rancherias' in California parlance) on which to live. More than a dozen such rancherias were created for Pomoan people, at least five of which included sizable Southern Pomo populations: Dry Creek (1915–present), Graton (1915–66), Mark West (1916–61), Cloverdale (1921–65), and Lytton (1926/27–61) (Fredrickson, Peri, and Lerner 1984: 51). All these rancherias were small; none approached the size of reservations commonly encountered in other states bordering California. After the period of termination began with the Rancheria Act of 1958, only the Dry Creek Rancheria (75 acres) remained as sovereign territory for Southern Pomo speakers (Fredrickson, Peri, and Lerner 1984: 62; Bean and Theodoratus 1978: 302).[15] Some of these terminated rancherias have been reconstituted in recent times.

1.4. THE NATURAL SETTING

The Southern Pomo homeland contains a diverse range of habitats set within varied topography. The Russian River and its tributaries provide ample amounts of water year-round. Kroeber summarized the Pomoan landscape succinctly:

> It is typical California land: arid to the eye once the winter rains are over, yellow and gray in tone, but fertile; monotonous in the extreme to the stranger, yet endlessly variegated to those familiar with it and its resources. (Kroeber 1925: 225)

The river valleys and gently rolling hills were populated with several species of oak tree (*biʔdu kʰa:le*) from which the Pomo collected acorns, their most important food item. In places the open oak woodland gave way to the *ši:yo*, dense redwood forests. As Kroeber mentioned, the Pomo homeland enjoys California's famous temperate climate. Winters rarely bring freezing weather (snow is virtually unknown), and summers are rainless and sunny.

The native fauna of the Pomoan homeland has much in common with that in the rest of California, though it is in many respects different from that of much of North America. The largest flying bird was the magnificent California condor (*ʔihsun*), a bird which figured in the mythology and rituals of Pomoan groups. The California quail (*šak:a:ka*) was the most important woodland game bird, and its topknot was used in basketry. Reptiles included lizards (*mut̪ʰ:u:nu*), several species of snake (*mus:a:la*), including rattlesnakes (*moht̪ʰi*), gopher snakes (*č̓o:ṭi*), and the California king snake (*ʔoh:od:u*). The sole freshwater turtle, the western pond turtle (*kʰa:wana*), was commonly encountered in the wetlands. The mammalian fauna included mule deer (*hint̪ilku behše*)[16] and elk (*k̓as:i:si*), both of which were important sources of food, and the more dangerous cougar (*yamhoṭ̓*), bobcat (*do:lon*), wolf (*ce:me:wa*),[17] and coyote (*ʔohkoʔše*).[18]

Southern Pomo speakers were familiar with Clear Lake, and they seem to have visited the lake frequently in order to fish.[19] Clear Lake and the Russian River once contained a unique freshwater fish assemblage that was related to the one found in the Central Valley to the east. Clear Lake contained the Sacramento perch, the hardhead, and its own subspecies of splittail, in addition to other fish. None of these year-round freshwater fish was found outside California, and, sadly, the first researchers to collect Southern Pomo data were ignorant of these unique species. It is therefore often impossible to know which species is being referenced in earlier records because all fish are glossed with names for fish east of the Rockies (e.g., 'perch' in these glosses could refer to the Sacramento perch, or the tule perch, or perhaps another fish that appeared perch-like to the researcher). By the mid-twentieth century it was too late to obtain correct forms because non-native species of freshwater fish had overtaken the native ones—a heartbreaking pattern that mirrored the fate of the Southern Pomo speakers—and most native fish became rare or, as in the case of the Clear Lake splittail, extinct. However, some fish, such as salmon (*ma:k^{h}a*) and trout (*le:wen*), which had appropriate counterparts in the eastern part of the United States, were recorded accurately.

The only domesticated animal in pre-European times was the dog (*hay:u*), the word for which was shared in similar phonological form across six of the seven Pomoan languages (see §1.8.2).

1.5. MATERIAL CULTURE

Southern Pomo speakers practiced a hunter-gatherer culture with comparatively few durable material goods, at least by modern Western standards. Men's clothing consisted of a skin wrapped around the hips, if present at all. Women would wear a double skirt of deerskin or shredded bark and some ornamentation. Unlike some tribes further north, the Pomo did not wear basket caps. Some workbaskets, however, were supported by means of a tumpline (Kroeber 1925: 240).

House construction varied by climate, but the majority of Southern Pomo speakers, who lived along the Russian River and its tributaries, likely constructed their homes according to the manner recorded by Kroeber for the 'Russian River Pomo', who "erected a framework of poles, bent together at the top, and thatched [it] with bundles of grass" (1925: 241). The type of construction recorded by Kroeber closely matches the description of a seasonal traditional structure recorded by Elsie Allen, the last known speaker of the Cloverdale dialect of Southern Pomo: she describes a "house made of leaves put over willow frames" (Allen 1972: 9).

In addition to domiciles, Southern Pomo speakers built sweathouses and ceremonial dance houses (a.k.a. round houses), of which the latter were substantial structures. The dance house was circular with a large post providing support in the center. These dance houses, according to Kroeber, had two entrances: an entrance was placed at the south of the structure, passing "through a long, descending tunnel," and there was a smoke hole above the fire (1925: 242).[20]

Boats (*čuhse*) were known to Southern Pomo speakers, though they were most fully developed among the Pomoan communities of Clear Lake. The tribes along the lakeshore made a balsa boat of tules that included a prow, stern, and raised sides to prevent water washing over into the boat. Boats of this sort might have been used further south (by Southern Pomo speakers?) on Santa Rosa lagoon (Kroeber 1925: 243).

At least two stone tools, the pestle (*dok:o*) and the mortar (*kʰaʔbet̯'le*), were manufactured by Southern Pomo speakers (see fig. 9 in appendix 1). These were used for preparing acorns and other foodstuffs which needed to be ground.[21]

The Pomo were famed as the money makers of Northern California.[22] They produced money from Bodega Bay shells, which their artisans "ground round on sandstone, bored, strung, and . . . rolled on slab," a form of wealth that was reckoned to be of less value than special magnesite beads, which were "ground down, perforated, baked, and polished" (Kroeber 1925: 248–49).

By far the most famous material goods produced by the Pomoan people were their baskets. Pomoan basket weavers employed several types of basket construction: different types of baskets were made with coiling or twining, and certain forms were constructed by use of wickerwork and lattice twining, the latter of which was unique to the Pomo among California Indians (Kroeber 1925: 244). Another unusual (and possibly unique) aspect of Pomo basketry art was the creation of small, sometimes tiny feathered baskets, which had no use other than as art or gifts. These baskets were coiled and made use of colorful feathers from woodpeckers, orioles, ducks, and other birds (Allen 1972: 37). Some of these baskets included polished abalone shell ornaments and topknots from California quail, with a clamshell string attached to the rim so that such baskets could be hung from the ceilings of Pomoan houses (Bibby 1996: 80–81).

1.6. GENETIC AND AREAL AFFILIATIONS

Pomoan languages have been placed in the Hokan superfamily, which includes a number of North American languages, most of which were spoken in California (Campbell 1997: 290). The validity of the Hokan hypothesis has not been confirmed by recent inquiry (Mithun 1999: 303–4). Whether or not Southern Pomo and its Pomoan sister tongues are genetically related to any known language, it is the case that no researcher has claimed that the languages immediately neighboring the Pomoan languages have any genetic relation to them. The seven Pomoan languages differ substantially and have clearly been in the vicinity of Clear Lake for thousands of years, during which time—in an area that scarcely fills a few counties—they have separated more fully than the Romance languages of Europe. If, therefore, there are extant languages to which Pomoan is related, their shared parent language would have been spoken very deep in the past indeed, perhaps too far in the past to allow modern scholars to distinguish between genetic relatedness and past contact between unrelated languages.

1.7. DIALECTS

Barrett recognized different dialects within the Southern Pomo speech area early in the twentieth century, including a significant difference between the dialects north of present-day Healdsburg and those of Healdsburg and points southward (1908: 87). Though Barrett made special note of lexical differences between the southern dialects and those farther north, and Merriam (1979: 96, 237) also recorded flora and fauna names from Healdsburg (in addition to Cloverdale), neither Halpern nor Oswalt collected data from speakers from Healdsburg and communities south of there. This grammar, therefore, is based almost entirely on the dialects of Dry Creek and Cloverdale. The differences between these northernmost Southern Pomo dialects appear to have been slight, and there does not appear to have been any barrier in communication between speakers of the two dialects. The most obvious shibboleth that distinguishes Cloverdale from Dry Creek is the raising of /a/ to /e/ before /y/ (which is generally the surface form of ||č||) in certain words, especially the words for 'Indian, person', Dry Creek *ʔahčahčay* versus Cloverdale *ʔahčahčey*, and 'White person', Dry Creek p^{h}*al:aʔčay* versus Cloverdale p^{h}*al:aʔčey*.[23]

1.8. SOCIOLINGUISTIC SITUATION

As already discussed, the nineteenth century saw drastic changes in the lives of Southern Pomo speakers. It was into this fragmented world of suffering that the last Southern Pomo speakers were born, and none of the speakers from whom substantial amounts of accurate data were recorded learned the language outside this awful situation. The upheavals—murder, rape, forced relocation, loss of power—destroyed native forms of government and traditional patterns of marriage and childbirth. Most of the last speakers, all of whom were raised in the first three decades of the twentieth century, attended schools where Southern Pomo (and all other Indigenous languages) could not be spoken without the threat of punishment. The pressures and dangers of the period in which the last speakers learned the language directly caused the functional death of Southern Pomo when it ceased to be learned by any children (circa 1930).

There is some evidence for how this situation affected the use of Southern Pomo within families. Elsie Allen narrated biographical information (in Southern Pomo) wherein she recalled that she and her mother would not speak Southern Pomo loudly when in public and usually did not speak it at all in front of others. The family's fear of whites was so great in the first decades of the twentieth century that Elsie's mother would tell the children to run and hide at the sight of an approaching white person. These fears were reinforced by Elsie's experience in school: she was sent to school as a non-English speaker and faced whipping for speaking her native language. It was for these reasons that Elsie Allen ultimately chose not to teach her children the culture and language (H EA: 9a–10a).

A similar situation played out in the early decades of the twentieth century for most Southern Pomo families, and it is for this reason that the last speakers who were born in this era often failed to learn certain things. No traditional Coyote stories were recorded from Elsie Allen or any younger speakers, and speakers born after Elsie lack full mastery of the complex kinship system and higher numbers.

1.8.1. Viability

Southern Pomo has no living fluent speakers. No child born after 1920 learned the language fully. Though no living person is fluent in the language, there are scores of tribal members who learned dozens of words as children, and a subset of these words have been passed down to subsequent generations.[24] Between the fall of 2011 and the spring of 2014 the Dry Creek Rancheria Band of Pomo Indians held weekly language classes. Students with Southern Pomo ancestry from up to five different federally recognized tribes attended these classes, which I taught.

Toward the end of the spring of 2014, the Western Institute for Endangered Language Documentation in partnership with the California Indian Museum and Cultural Center continued the classes for a brief period. Students from all tribes with historic Southern Pomo connections were allowed to attend. In 2016 and 2017 monthly classes were restarted by the Dry Creek Rancheria and facilitated by Tieraney Giron and taught by me via video conferencing, but these meetings stopped after the horrific 2017 fires which ravaged Santa Rosa and disrupted many tribal members' lives.

Roughly a half dozen or more tribal members learned a number of words and phrases in these classes, and a few students mastered the phonology and acquired an admirable amount of grammatical and syntactic knowledge. There are still heritage speakers who are striving to learn the language, and perhaps someday the extant Coyote stories will be read aloud and understood by both reader and listener.

1.8.2. Loan Words

Most identifiable borrowings in Southern Pomo postdate the coming of Europeans; however, a number of non-European borrowings can be identified, and they provide some clues to past cultural changes. Halpern identified the stems *yomt̪a* 'doctor' and *ʔelši-* 'to sell' as borrowings into the Pomoan languages from non-Pomoan languages on the basis of their unusual consonant clusters and almost invariable shape across Pomoan languages, but the source language for these words is not known (Halpern 1984: 5). The words for 'doctor' and 'sell' both appear to be fairly recent borrowings into Pomoan, and though it might be the case that they replaced native Pomoan forms for these concepts (in each language), these borrowings hint at the possibility that Pomoan culture encountered a new type of doctor and the concept of selling at a rather late date.[25]

Another word that might be a borrowing into Pomoan is *hay:u* 'dog', as it is shared across six of the seven Pomoan languages with virtually the same phonological shape, including languages where Southern Pomo /h/ should correspond to zero in word-initial position.[26] Though I considered this word a clear borrowing in my 2013 dissertation on Southern Pomo, I now believe the existence of this seemingly anomalous h-initial word across the Pomoan family and among other California languages is an example of culturally specific onomatopoeia: the syllables approximate the sound of a howling hound. If this be the case, then my earlier claims that the unique family-wide pronunciation of 'dog' is evidence for a late date for the introduction of domestic dogs into the Pomoan world must be rejected. It might still be the case that dogs arrived relatively recently, but they need not have done so in order to explain the areal distribution of the cognates for Southern Pomo *hay:u*.[27]

There are other words for animals which sound similar to forms in neighboring non-Pomoan languages and might be borrowings, but they too are most likely onomatopoeic in origin. They are exemplified by the word for 'western scrub-jay' (*Aphelocoma californica*): its name is *ċa:yi* in Southern Pomo and *ċáy* in Wappo (Sawyer 1965: 12). (Compare the Pomoan and Wappo words for 'scrub jay' with the English word <jay> /džeɪ/, which ultimately comes from the same attempt at capturing the raucous call of small corvids.) The word for 'mourning dove', *ma:yu,* is among this number, and something similar to it is found across unrelated languages in Northern California.

A small number of Russian words came into neighboring Kashaya Pomo during the Fort Ross period, some of which possibly came into the language via Aleuts who had accompanied the Russians (Oswalt 1958). Some of these, such as the word for 'bottle', made their way into Southern Pomo (Oswalt 1971a: 189; 1971b).[28]

Many loan words come from Spanish, some of which might have passed through other native languages first. Spanish words were borrowed for new domestic animals (e.g., *kawa:yu* 'horse' < Sp. *caballo, kayi:na* 'chicken' < Sp. *gallina* 'hen', *wese:lu* 'calf' < Sp. *becerro*); new material goods (*kapo:t̪e* 'coat' < Sp. *capote* 'cape', *lame:sa* 'table' < Sp. *la mesa* 'the table', *nawa:ha* 'pocketknife' < Sp. *navaja* 'small knife'); and new food items (*ma:yiš* 'corn' < Sp. *maíz, na:wus* 'turnips' < Sp. *nabos*). Some Spanish loan words maintain the non–Southern Pomo sounds /f/ and /r/, though it is unclear whether these sounds were used by monolingual Southern Pomo speakers.

There are comparatively few attested borrowings from English. The last speakers were fluent in English, and English words that they produced were therefore not obviously assigned as borrowings into Southern Pomo. One clear example of an English borrowing, however, comes from Elsie Allen's autobiographical narrative in which she uses the word *t̪ʰiča=yčon* 'teacher=PATIENT', a word that has clearly been changed to accommodate Southern Pomo phonology and to which native morphology has been encliticized (H EA: 12b–12a).[29]

1.9. THE CORPUS

The data corpus from which examples in this grammar come includes both written and audio data collected by several scholars over the last 110 years. These scholars have been covered in §1.2 and are not covered further. The majority of the data come from Abraham Halpern's unpublished notes and transcribed texts and Robert Oswalt's unpublished notes and partial dictionary manuscript. All these data are now housed at the Survey of California and Other Indian Languages (SCOIL) at the University of California at Berkeley. Additional data come from a handful of published articles which are cited throughout this grammar. Tables 3 and 4 summarize the nature of the unpublished materials.

1.9.1. Consultants and Other Sources

The bulk of the data upon which this grammar is based comes from three speakers: Annie Burke, Elsie Allen, and Elizabeth Dollar. Following is basic biographical information for each of these speakers. Information, where it

Table 3. Quality and quantity of Oswalt's unpublished materials

SCOIL number	Size	Summary of contents	Quality	Usefulness
Oswalt .004.050	30+ pages	drafts of a paper on the causative	High	Moderate
Oswalt .003.007	45+ pages	Letters and comments regarding Halpern's Southern Pomo paper	High	High
Oswalt .002.027	8 pages	Loanwords from Spanish	High	Moderate
Oswalt .001.023	1 page	Lullaby	High	High
Oswalt .001.018	15 pages	Two short texts (both dialects)	High	High
Oswalt .001.015	40 pages	Elicited words	High	High
Oswalt .001.014	5 pages	100 word list	Low	Low
Oswalt .001.013	4 pages	100 word list	Low	Low
Oswalt .001.012	4 pages	100 word list, Effie Luff speaker (only record of her?)	Moderate	Moderate
Oswalt .001.011	4 pages	100 word list	Low	Low
Oswalt .001.010	4 pages	100 word list	Low	Low
Oswalt .001.009	13 pages	Partial verb paradigms	High	High
Oswalt .001.007	20 pages	Halpern's retranscription of Oswalt's notes	Moderate	Low
Oswalt .001.008	10 pages	Word list, Lucy Andrews Macy (only record of her?)	Low	High
Oswalt .001.006	35+ pages	Re-elicitations of Merriam data	High	High
Oswalt .001.005	17 pages	Biographical info on Elizabeth Dollar	High	High
Oswalt .001.005	7 pages	Work with Olive Fulwider	High	High
Oswalt .001.001	110+ pages	Notes, family names, a text	High	High
Oswalt .001.002	300 pages	Verb paradigms, prayers	High	High
Oswalt .001.003	33 pages	Elicited sentences, place names, verb paradigms	High	High
Oswalt electronic dictionary	265 KB (would print out as hundreds of pages)	Lexical entries arranged by the second consonant of the stem with example phrases, incomplete	High	High

Table 4. Quality and quantity of unpublished materials

Group	Speaker(s)	Size	Quality	Usefulness
Mythic texts	Annie Burke	9 texts	High (some transcription errors in earlier versions)	High (provides the best examples of dependent clause marking)
First-person narratives	Elsie Allen	300+ pages	Very high	High (provides the most complex affixing on verbs in running discourse)
Verb and kinship phrases and paradigms	Annie Burke, Elsie Allen	500+ pages	High	Very high (it might be impossible to understand the kinship system without these Halpern materials)
Individually elicited words (mainly nouns)	Annie Burke, Elsie Allen	500+ pages	Moderate	Moderate (data were mainly collected early in Halpern's field work and lack phonetic accuracy and show incorrect word breaks)

exists, is also given for several other speakers from whom some data in this work come or whose names are mentioned in previous published works.

Annie Burke (1876–1960) spoke the Cloverdale dialect as her first language. She and her family eventually settled in the Hopland Reservation, a Central Pomo–speaking rancheria, where both she and her daughter, Elsie Allen, learned that language (Oswalt 2002: 313). Annie served as Halpern's first consultant, and all unpublished Halpern data not cited as (H EA) come from her.

Elsie Allen (1899–1990), Annie Burke's daughter, spoke Southern Pomo as her first language and did not begin learning English till her eleventh year (Allen 1972: 10). She was Halpern's sole consultant during his second round of field work in the 1980s. Elsie also worked extensively with Oswalt, and it appears that she was the only informant with whom both Oswalt and Halpern worked extensively.

Elizabeth Dollar (1895?–1971) was raised with Southern Pomo as her first language and did not begin learning the English language till her second decade. Unlike Annie Burke and Elsie Allen, Elizabeth Dollar spoke the Dry Creek dialect and was affiliated with a Southern Pomo–speaking reservation, the Dry Creek Rancheria. Oswalt collected traditional stories from Mrs. Dollar; however, only one (Oswalt 1978) is known to have been translated and transcribed; the others exist as audio records.

Laura Fish Somersal (1890?–1990)[30] was raised to be bilingual in Southern Pomo, her father's language, and Wappo, her mother's language and the language of the family with whom she had the most contact. Mrs. Somersal's mother was blinded with rattlesnake poison by a shaman, and as her mother's caretaker she avoided being sent to school, where her use of the Wappo language would have been curtailed; however, it does not appear that she used Southern Pomo to the same extent as Wappo, as she "did not interact much with her father's side of the family" (Thompson et al. 2006: xiii–xv). There is no doubt that her Southern Pomo was fluent enough to allow for conversation and that her phonology was native. Roy Siniard recorded Maggie Woho speaking Southern Pomo and used Mrs. Somersal as an interpreter. These recordings include several instances of the two women conversing in Southern Pomo. Laura Somersal's ability to communicate in Southern Pomo notwithstanding, there are reasons to separate language data produced by her from that produced by all other speakers born before 1920. Oswalt found that Mrs. Somersal's use of case in Southern Pomo was influenced by Wappo. Southern Pomo has an agent/patient case system; Wappo has a nominative/accusative system, and Mrs. Somersal's Southern Pomo apparently used the agentive case as though it were the nominative case of Wappo (Oswalt .001.003). Data from Laura Somersal are therefore given less weight in this grammar than data from other speakers.

Olive Fulwider (1918–2014) was born to a Southern Pomo-speaking mother from Dry Creek. When she was still a child her mother died, and she was raised by her grandmother.[31] Mrs. Fulwider and her grandmother spoke Southern Pomo with each other while doing many traditional activities, including gathering and preparing various kinds of acorns. Oswalt worked with her briefly in the early 1990s. I met Mrs. Fulwider in 2000 (before I studied linguistics), and between 2000 and 2006 she met with me on several occasions and shared bits and pieces of language. Though her command of the language was complete (she could and did express anything with her grandmother), certain things—some kinship terms, numbers above five, names for recently extirpated fauna (condor, elk, etc.)—did not survive in her Southern Pomo.

Tony Pete (1919–2019) was not officially affiliated with any rancheria as a young man, though in later life he became a member of the reconstituted Graton Rancheria. He spoke the Dry Creek dialect as a child, but he was unable to use the language for much of his adult life. I could not confirm his status as a fluent speaker in the sense that Olive Fulwider was fluent. Tony Pete's nephew, Tim Molino, worked a great deal to record and preserve examples of the Southern Pomo words and phrases his uncle did recall.[32] As the only data spoken by a male and recorded with modern devices, Tony Pete's examples are extremely important.

Several other speakers' names have been recorded by Pomoan scholars. Oswalt, for example, recorded a small number of words from Lucy Andrews Macy and Effie Luff, speakers about whom little is known and from whom came little in the way of unique data, if any. As already mentioned, there exist recordings of the Southern Pomo speaker Maggie Woho made by Roy Siniard in the 1960s. Mrs. Woho's speech was not transcribed—a task that demands working with a native, fluent speaker and the recordings—by Siniard or any subsequent scholar, and the time to do so has now passed. Other speakers, such as those who served as consultants to Barrett (1908) and Gifford (1922), are also comparatively unknown, though Gifford lists the names of his Southern Pomo consultants together with their dialect affiliation: Clara Felis, Cloverdale, Sonoma Co.; Charles Ramon, Cloverdale, Sonoma Co.; Henry Maximilian Sr., Healdsburg, Sonoma Co.; and Mamie Brown, Healdsburg, Sonoma Co. (Gifford 1922: 13).

1.9.2. Presentation of Data

References which come from published sources are cited in the standard manner. References to unpublished works (written or audio) are cited in the manner summarized in table 5.

Table 5. Citing conventions for unpublished data

Citation	Collector	Consultant	Dialect	Genre
(H I–IX)	Halpern	Annie Burke	Cloverdale	Narrative texts
(H ms.)	Halpern	Annie Burke	Cloverdale	Elicited words and phrases
(H EA)	Halpern	Elsie Allen	Cloverdale	First-person narratives; elicited words
(H EA:REC)	Halpern	Elsie Allen	Cloverdale	Audio recording of (H EA)
(O I)	Oswalt	Elizabeth Dollar	Dry Creek	Published narrative text
(O II)	Oswalt	Elsie Allen	Cloverdale	Short narrative text
(O III)	Oswalt	Laura Somersal	Dry Creek (Wappo influenced)	Short narrative text
(O D) (O D: EA) (O D: ED)	Oswalt	Elsie Allen (EA), Annie Burke (rare), & Elizabeth Dollar (ED)	Cloverdale & Dry Creek	My printed copy of Oswalt's electronic dictionary
(T)	Tim Molino (transcribed by me)	Tony Pete	Dry Creek	Elicited words and phrases
(T:REC)	Tim Molino	Tony Pete	Dry Creek	Audio recording of (T)
(S:REC)	Roy Siniard	Maggie Woho and Laura Fish Somersal	Dry Creek	Audio recordings
(W: OF)	Neil Alexander Walker	Olive Fulwider	Dry Creek	Words and phrases

(H I–IX), (O I–III), and (H EA) can be found (retranscribed into the current orthography) in the appendixes to Walker (2013). Items in this work sourced from (H EA) include page numbers (e.g., 7a, 20b). However, these page numbers exist only in the transcribed version of (H EA) included in the appendixes to Walker (2013).

TWO

Word Structure

2.1. TYPOLOGICAL SKETCH

Southern Pomo is a morphologically complex language with AOV (SV & OV) constituent order. It is primarily suffixing, though almost all verb stems have one instrumental prefix and a handful of verbs may take up to two prefixes. The two most robust word classes are nouns and verbs. There are also a small number of morphologically distinct adjectives and adverbs, and small classes of pronouns, auxiliaries, and other function words.

Nouns can be divided into distinct subclasses on the basis of morphological patterns: common nouns, personal names, kinship terms, and pronouns. Common noun morphology includes suffixes and enclitics for case and number. In actual usage, however, common nouns may appear without any affixes or enclitics. Personal names include gender-specific morphology, but the data are too few in number to provide a thorough summary of this small subclass. Kinship terms are the most morphologically complex subclass of nouns: they consist of a root, a possessive prefix, and are marked for case and plurality, among other things. The case-marking system is of the agent/patient type on pronouns, kinship terms, and animate common nouns; subject/object (nominative/accusative) case-marking morphemes are optionally applied to noun phrases regardless of animacy.

Verbal morphology can be quite complex: verb roots are all bound and must be combined with an instrumental prefix and at least one TAM suffix, in addition to other optional inflectional and derivational affixes. Southern Pomo, like some of its sister languages, does not have pronominal affixes on the verb. Long sentences in Southern Pomo make use of dependent verbs that take switch-reference suffixes. For some events there are completely different verbs depending on whether the agent(s) is or are collective or distributive.

Adjectives generally follow the nouns they modify. There may be completely different adjectives depending upon whether the noun phrase being modified is collective or distributive.

Pronouns are marked for case and, in the third person, for gender. There is a special third-person coreferential pronoun. Pronouns have phonologically reduced forms when encliticized to other words as second-position clitics.

There are other words that do not fit into the classes listed in the preceding description, including adverbs, which might be distinguished by a complete lack of morphological complexity, and a small number of function words (e.g., non-numeral quantifiers).

2.2. PHONOLOGICAL INVENTORY AND ORTHOGRAPHY

Both International Phonetic Alphabet (IPA) and Americanist symbols are used in §2.2–§2.3.2 to describe the sounds of Southern Pomo. Thereafter, only the Americanist system is used for all Southern Pomo examples. This system is also the current practical orthography of the Dry Creek Rancheria Band of Pomo Indians.

Throughout this text angled brackets < > enclose original orthography from another source; double pipes || || enclose morphophonemic transcriptions; single slashes / / enclose phonemic transcriptions; square brackets [ ] enclose narrow phonetic transcriptions in the IPA. Thus the word *ʔahčanhk^{h}ay* 'homeward' might be represented as <ahǯáŊkay>, ||ʔahča-n-k^{h}ač||, /ʔahča-nh=k^{h}ay/, or [ʔahˈʧaŋ͡ŋ̊k^{h}aj].[1]

Within examples which are set off from the body of text, transliterations of other researchers' transcriptions are not set off by brackets, slashes, or italicization. In such transliterations, square brackets [ ] indicate not narrow phonetic transcription but material missing in the original source that I think should be supplied; parentheses ( ) are used to indicate material present in the original source that I think should be omitted. Italics are used for Southern Pomo words, but the morphological breakdown, if any, is not italicized. Each morpheme is glossed with English words or (in the case of bound morphemes and certain function words) with small caps. A free translation is provided within single quotes. Thus the same word from the previous paragraph, *ʔahčanhkʰay* 'homeward', might be given in a separate example as follows:

[ʔ]ahčáŋhkʰay (H VIII)
ʔahčanhkʰay
/ʔahča-nh-kʰay/
house-to-DIR
'homeward'

Free translations of (W: OF), (T), isolated words without referenced sources, and those enclosed in [ ] are my own. All others are unchanged from the original sources.

2.2.1. Consonants

Southern Pomo, at least in its pre-European-contact form, had no fewer than twenty-eight consonantal phonemes.[2] This minimum set, which is the number accepted in this grammar, is given in both the IPA and the Americanist system in tables 6 and 7.

The inventory of consonants given in the tables 6 and 7 agrees with the analyses of Oswalt (1978) and Halpern (1984). This, however, does not mean that it is clearly the only possible analysis. Kashaya Pomo, the nearest Pomoan language to Southern Pomo (in both proximity and phonological similarities), has been described with two competing analyses of its consonantal phonemes, one proposed by Oswalt (1961), which is virtually iden-

Table 6. Southern Pomo consonants in IPA

	Bilabial	Dental	Alveolar	Post-alveolar	Palatal	Velar	Glottal
Unaffricated stops	pʰ p b p'	t̪ʰ t̪ t̪'	tʰ t d t'			kʰ k k'	ʔ
Affricated stops			ts ts'	t̠ʃʰ t̠ʃ t̠ʃ'			
Nasals	m		n				
Fricatives			s	ʃ			h
Central approximant	(w)				j	(w)	
Lateral approximant			l				

Table 7. Southern Pomo consonants in Americanist orthography

	Bilabial	Dental	Alveolar	Post-alveolar	Palatal	Velar	Glottal
Unaffricated stops	p^{h} p b p̓	t̯^{h} t̯ t̯̓	ṭ^{h} ṭ d ṭ̓			k^{h} k k̓	ʔ
Affricated stops			c c̓	č^{h} č č̓			
Nasals	m		n				
Fricatives			s	š			h
Central approximant	(w)				y	(w)	
Lateral approximant			l				

tical to the inventory listed in the preceding tables for Southern Pomo, and one proposed by Buckley (1994), which acknowledges the same sound contrasts as Oswalt (1961) but fits them into a more abstract (if elegant) analysis of the consonantal phonemes of Kashaya. Specifically, Buckley treats the two voiced plosives of Kashaya, [b] and [d], as underlying glottalized nasals, /m̓/ and /n̓/, an analysis which neither adds to nor subtracts from the total number of consonants, and he adds eight additional sonorant phonemes not found in Oswalt's (1961) analysis (Buckley 1994: 12–15). Buckley's inventory of Kashaya Pomo consonantal phonemes is given in table 8 using the Americanist orthography of this work (consonants not treated as phonemes in Oswalt (1961) are in bold).[3]

Though Buckley's analysis adds additional phonemes in comparison to Oswalt's analysis, his handling of Kashaya's sonorants actually simplifies the phonotactic description of the language. In Kashaya, [d] and [n̓] are in complementary distribution, as seen in the following examples adapted from Buckley (1994: 48):

(1) Allophonic alternation of [d] and [n̓] in Kashaya

/čan̓-u/	/čan̓-p^{h}i/
[ʧa'du]	['ʧan̓p^{h}i]
'look!'	'if he sees'

Though Kashaya does not have any phonological alternations that confirm [b] and [m̓] as allophones of one phoneme, both phones are in com-

Table 8. Kashaya consonant phonemes according to Buckley (1994)

	Bilabial	Dental	Alveolar	Post-alveolar	Palatal	Velar	Uvular	Glottal
Unaffricated stops	pʰ p b p̓	t̪ʰ t̪ t̪̓	ṭʰ ṭ d ṭ̓			kʰ k k̓	qʰ q q̓	ʔ
Affricated stops			c̓	čʰ č č̓				
Nasals	**mʰ** m **m̓**		**nʰ** n **n̓**					
Fricatives			s	š				h
Central approximant	(**wʰ**)(w) (**w̓**)				**yʰ** y **y̓**	(**wʰ**)(w) (**w̓**)		
Lateral approximant			**lʰ** l **l'**					

plementary distribution, and Buckley was thus able to describe the distribution of all four phones with a single rule (1994: 49):[4]

N' → C / [σ__

This analysis elegantly captures the synchronic distribution of all four phones ([d], [n̓], [b], and [m̓]) in Kashaya and it also establishes glottalized sonorants as phonemes in the language. The total number of consonants is larger in Buckley's analysis than in Oswalt's, as he adds a full set of glottalized and aspirated sonorants (/y̓/, /yʰ/, /l'/, /lʰ/, /w̓/, /wʰ/, /mʰ/, /nʰ/) in addition to the glottalized nasals /m̓/ and /n̓/. This increase in the total number of phonemes, however, reduces rather than increases the complexity of Kashaya phonotactics. In Buckley's analysis the two-consonant codas (leading to tri-consonantal consonant clusters) of Oswalt's analysis are replaced by one-consonant codas, as exemplified in the following Kashaya words in table 9, from Buckley (1994: 45), each of which is listed with Oswalt's phonemicization and Buckley's system (all converted to the regularized transcription system of this work).

As Buckley observes, there are no three-consonant clusters in Oswalt's transcriptions of Kashaya which are not composed of a sonorant+glottal pair (1994: 45). By treating these clusters as unitary phonemes, Buckley removes the would-be exception to a simpler analysis of Kashaya syllable structure.

Table 9. Comparison of Kashaya sonorants by Oswalt and Buckley

Oswalt	**Buckley**	**Gloss**
lanhk^{h}o	lan^{h}k^{h}o	‘seven’
mo:nʔ	mo:n̓	‘is running’
q^{h}ayhč^{h}i	q^{h}ay^{h}č^{h}i	‘pelican’
wolʔwo	wol’wo	‘badger’

Buckley’s analysis also simplifies the phonological description of Kashaya roots. Unless a small number of exceptions transcribed by Oswalt with a final /lh/ or /nh/ cluster should be accepted, all roots in Kashaya may end with no more than a single consonant. Buckley removes these exceptions by converting these sonorant+glottal root-final clusters to the phonemes /l^{h}/ and /n^{h}/ (1994: 44).

At first glance there appear to be reasons to adapt Buckley’s analysis of Kashaya sonorants to Southern Pomo. Tri-consonantal clusters in Southern Pomo may be composed of a sonorant+glottal+consonant combination, as in the following examples:

(2) Southern Pomo words with sonorant+glottal+consonant clusters[5]

(a) /mʔd/
hi:lamʔda ‘nose’

(b) /mhč/
k^{h}omhča ‘eight’

(c) /wʔd/
hniwʔdu ‘always says’

(d) /nhk^{h}/ [ŋ͡ŋ̊k^{h}]
ʔahčanhk^{h}ay ‘homeward’

(e) /lhk^{h}/
mih:ilhk^{h}a ‘ocean’

(f) /yʔm/
muhwayʔmi ‘strawberry’

(g) /yhč/
p^{h}al:aʔčayhča ‘white people’

In addition to a large number of tri-consonantal clusters where the first member is a sonorant and the second a glottal, the voiced plosives /b/ and /d/ of Southern Pomo pattern in a way that differs from all other plosives in the language, a way that is similar to the patterns seen in Kashaya and used to justify Buckley's analysis of that language with voiced glottalized nasals /ṁ/ and /ṅ/ as the underlying phonemes for surface [b] and [d]. Southern Pomo has synchronically productive alternations between [d] and [n], as seen in the following examples with the kinship root ||-dakʰad-|| 'spouse':

(3) synchronic alternations between [d] and [n] in Ps

miy:aṭʰkʰan	*maʔdakʰden*
||miy:a-dakʰad-Ø||	||maH-dakʰad-en||
/miy:a-ṭʰkʰan-Ø/	/ma-ʔdakʰd-en/
3-spouse-AGT	3C-spouse-PAT
'his/her spouse'	'his/her own spouse'

As shown in example (3), Southern Pomo /d/ has the morpheme-final allophone [n] when the morpheme boundary places the /d/ in coda position. Though /d/ can never surface as [d] in morpheme-final coda position in the language, /n/ can surface as [n] in onset position. This allophonic distribution is reminiscent of that seen between [d] and [ṅ] in Kashaya.

Although this allophonic pattern does not include a glottalized nasal as one of the allophones, there are two phonological patterns involving both voiced stops and [ʔ] that hint at a past glottalized component to the phonemes from which synchronic /d/ and /b/ in Southern Pomo descend.

Southern Pomo word stems, with rare exceptions, must include one of three segments as an augment (hereafter termed laryngeal increment, abbreviated as H), the purpose of which is to prevent words from beginning with a light syllable. It is premature to discuss the complexities of laryngeal increment distributions and movement in Southern Pomo phonology at this point. What follows is necessarily an incomplete overview of a subset of details regarding laryngeal increment distribution and movement, which bears upon the question at hand, namely, whether or not the Southern Pomo consonant inventory should be changed and expanded to include aspirated and glottalized sonorants, as has been done for its closest sister language, Kashaya.

The vast majority of Southern Pomo word stems are disyllabic with one of three segments, [ʔ], [h], or [:] (lengthening of a preceding vowel or consonant) as an obligatory laryngeal increment on the second consonant of the stem (not counting the laryngeal increment, of course); this second consonant is generally the onset of the synchronic verb root.[6] The distribution of these three laryngeal increments is in partial complementary distribution: [h] may not occur with ejective consonants as a laryngeal increment; [ʔ] may not occur with aspirated consonants as a laryngeal increment; only sonorants may take any one of the three laryngeal increments.

The two voiced stops [b] and [d] do not pattern with the sonorants in their ability to take any of the three laryngeal increments; rather, they may not take [h] as their laryngeal increment, which is the pattern seen with the true ejective consonants. However, if the laryngeal increment follows, then the voiced stops, unlike the ejective consonants, may only take [ʔ], whereas all other consonants, aspirated, ejective, and voiced sonorants, may take [:] as a post-consonantal increment.

This unique characteristic of the voiced stops is apparent when certain affixes are added to verb stems with [b] and [d] as the second non-increment consonant. A subset of verbal affixes cause change or movement of the laryngeal increment. For example, some directional suffixes trigger a change whereby a laryngeal increment that precedes the second consonant of the stem is replaced by gemination of the incremented consonant.[7] This phonological alternation can be schematized as follows:

CVHCV(C)- + -DIR → CVC:V(C)-DIR-
(H = the laryngeal increments /h/, /ʔ/, and /:/; DIR = directional suffixes which trigger the change)

However, when the same suffixes are added to verb stems with [b] or [d] as their second non-laryngeal increment consonant, the increment, which may only be [ʔ], is not replaced with [:] to the right of the second consonant; rather, the laryngeal increment is moved to the right of the second consonant unchanged.

CVʔDV(C)- + -DIR → CVDʔV(C)-DIR-
(D = [b] or [d]; DIR = directional suffixes which trigger the change)

Examples (4) and (5) present these phonological alternations on the verb *huʔċak-* 'to be stingy', which has the ejective /ċ/ as the root consonant around which the laryngeal increment changes, and on the verb *šuʔdi-* 'to take (by pulling)', which has the voiced stop /d/ as the root consonant around which the laryngeal increment moves.

(4) Increment movement with the verb *huʔċak-* 'to be stingy'

<table>
<tr><td>huʔċak̓waʔt̪o (O D: AB)[8]</td><td>huċ:a:kayʔdu (O D: EA)</td></tr>
<tr><td>||hu-ʔċa-ak=ʔ=wa=ʔat̪:o||</td><td>||hu-ʔċa-ak-kač-wadu||</td></tr>
<tr><td>/huʔċak=wa=ʔt̪o/</td><td>/huċ:a:-kay-ʔdu/</td></tr>
<tr><td>to.be.stingy=COP.EVID=
1SG.PAT</td><td>to.be.stingy-DIR-HAB</td></tr>
<tr><td>'I'm stingy with it'</td><td>'always stingy'</td></tr>
</table>

(5) Increment movement around voiced stops[9]

<table>
<tr><td>šoʔdimʔduy (H V: 17)</td><td>šudʔeduy (O I: 9)</td></tr>
<tr><td>||šu-ʔdi-maduč-w||</td><td>||šu-ʔdi-aduč-w||</td></tr>
<tr><td>/šoʔdi-mʔduy-Ø/</td><td>/šudʔe-duy-Ø/</td></tr>
<tr><td>take.by.pulling-DIR-PFV</td><td>take.by.pulling-DIR-PFV</td></tr>
<tr><td>['brought (them)']</td><td>['led (someone) away']</td></tr>
</table>

Another peculiar feature of the voiced stops in Southern Pomo is their tendency to cause a glottal stop to appear to separate them from a preceding sonorant after the intervening vowel is lost to regular syncopation rules.

(6) sonorant+vowel+voiced stop → sonorant+[ʔ]+voiced stop

<table>
<tr><td>mi:mayʔdu (O I: 25)</td><td>hač̓:owʔdu (O I: 2)</td></tr>
<tr><td>||mi-:mač-wadu||</td><td>||ha-č̓:o-wadu||</td></tr>
<tr><td>/mi:may-ʔdu/</td><td>/hač̓:o-wʔdu/</td></tr>
<tr><td>cry-HAB</td><td>arrive-HAB</td></tr>
<tr><td>['always crying']</td><td>['used to arrive']</td></tr>
</table>

These three phenomena, a nasal allophone for /d/, obligatory incrementing of voiced stops with the glottal stop, and glottal stop insertion between a sonorant and a voiced stop, lend support to an interpretation of

Southern Pomo voiced stops as having a glottalized component to them, even if only in a fossilized form that is no longer true of these sounds in isolation; it also hints that /d/ might have been a nasal in the past.

In summary, if the Southern Pomo consonant inventory were to be changed and expanded as has been done for Kashaya by Buckley, such a change would be based on the aforementioned facts: the Southern Pomo sonorants /m/, /w/, /n/, /l/, and /y/ may combine with the glottals /h/ and /ʔ/ to form complex clusters that might be more parsimoniously analyzed as unitary phonemes in their own right (i.e., the aspirated or glottalized sonorants /m^h/, /mʔ/, /w^h/, /wʔ/, /n^h/, /nʔ/, /l^h/, /lʔ/, /y^h/, /yʔ/); the voiced stops /b/ and /d/ uniquely pattern with [ʔ] in certain phonological alternations; and /d/ also has the nasal allophone [n] in coda position at the end of a morpheme, which might warrant an abstract analysis of these voiced stops as the underlying glottalized nasals /ṁ/ and /ṅ/.

Though there are reasons to change and expand the consonant inventory along the lines of Buckley's analysis of Kashaya, such a reanalysis is not advocated in this work. The more traditional Southern Pomo inventory has been retained and the expanded sonorant inventory has been rejected for three reasons:

(1) Glottalized and aspirated sonorants have a defective distribution

Most instances of sonorant+glottal clusters are synchronically explainable as the result of vowel syncope after separate morphemes have come together (whether through affixation or compounding), and none of these sonorant+glottal clusters may surface in onset or coda position within a phonological word. If the sample words with sonorant+glottal clusters given in example (7) are more closely scrutinized, the majority of them are synchronically parsable with a morpheme break separating the sonorant from the glottal consonant or a sonorant+glottal cluster that is the outcome of syncopated vowels within compounds:

(7) Morphological breakdown of words with sonorant+glottal clusters

(a)	*hi:lamʔda*	'nose'	(not synchronically segmentable)[10]
(b)	*hw-adem-ʔdu*	'always goes about'	||hu:w-aded-wadu||
(c)	*k^{h}o-mhča*	'eight'	< *ʔak^h:o* 'two' + *mihča* 'four'

(d)	*hni-wʔdu*	'always says'	‖nih:i-wadu‖
(e)	*ʔahča-nh-kʰay*	'homeward'	‖ʔahča=li=kʰač‖
(f)	*mih:ilhkʰa*	'ocean'	< *mih:ila* 'west' + *ʔahkʰa* 'water'
(g)	*muhway-ʔmi*	'strawberry'	< *muhway* 'fawn' + *ʔim:i* 'blackberry'
(h)	*pʰal:aʔčay-hča*	'white people'	< *pʰal:aʔčay* 'white person' + *=hča* COLL

(2) There is no synchronic evidence that both of the voiced stops are nasals

Only /d/ has a synchronic nasal allophone, and that allophone is identical to the allophones of the phoneme /n/—word-final [ṁ] and [ṅ] in Kashaya correspond to /n/ in Southern Pomo, and there are thus no data to support an analysis of /b/ as a nasal. In Kashaya it is the allophonic alternations between [d] and [ṅ] and the fact that [b] and [ṁ], though they do not participate in obvious allophonic alternations, are in complementary distribution that warrants an analysis collapsing the voiced stops and the glottalized nasals into two phonemes. In Kashaya the more abstract analysis of the voiced stops is only possible if nasal+glottal stop clusters are reanalyzed as glottalized nasals. In Southern Pomo if nasal+glottal stop clusters were reanalyzed as glottalized nasals, [d] and [n]—not [ṅ]—would still participate in allophonic alternations; [d] would not alternate with a glottalized nasal, and there would still be no evidence that [d] and [m] should be considered allophones of /ṅ/ and /ṁ/; rather, there would be additional evidence against such an analysis because [d] would still alternate with [n] and not [ṅ].[11]

(3) Not enough is gained by changing the inventory

The addition of a large number of sonorant phonemes, none of which may begin or end a phonological word and most of which are astride morpheme boundaries, might simplify a schematized description of one corner of Southern Pomo phonotactics, but it would do so at the cost of common sense: language is messy, and there is no reason to disallow that Southern Pomo sonorants may form complex clusters with glottals which are not otherwise to be found in the language.

The inventory of consonants listed in table 7 is therefore the one used throughout the rest of this grammar.

The pseudo-consonant /:/ might be added to the phonemic inventory of

Southern Pomo: length in Southern Pomo functions in a way that warrants its being treated as something separate and not merely a part of the vowel or consonant that is long or geminate. Halpern (1984: 4) recognizes this and chooses to represent Southern Pomo length in a different way than he does for the other six Pomoan languages:

> Length in Ps has a unique phonological role: it closes the syllable; it occurs as an augment [=laryngeal increment] of root-initial consonants, with a distribution parallel to that of the other augments, h and ʔ ; and it occurs as an allomorphic alternant of several other consonants.

The first unique property of /:/ listed by Halpern, its closing the syllable, appears at first blush to be an odd way of describing what would otherwise be termed long vowels. Specifically, Halpern views vowel+/:/ combinations as accomplishing the same phonological requirements as vowel+consonant combinations: they result in a heavy syllable. The second, that of /:/ serving as one of three laryngeal increments, supports pseudo-consonantal status for /:/ because some words have /:/ as their underlying laryngeal increment—length is not merely the product of phonological changes. In the case of words with /:/ as their underlying laryngeal increment, /:/ moves around the second consonant of the stem in exactly the same manner as the laryngeal increments /ʔ/ and /h/ do, as in example (8) following:

(8) Movement of /:/ laryngeal increment

kʰa:ma	'foot'	*kʰam:a=wi*	['with foot']	(Halpern 1984: 18)
t̪ʰa:na	'hand'	*t̪ʰan:a=wi*	['with hand']	(H EA: 4a)

Halpern's third observation regarding /:/, its occurrence as an "allomorphic alternant," relates to the frequency with which consonants are replaced by or reduced to length on a preceding vowel or consonant. This process is extremely common in the verb paradigms, and it is examined in greater detail in later sections. Example (9) provides a snapshot of this process with two allomorphs of the directional suffix *-aduč-* 'away':

(9) Allomorphic alternates with /:/ (H ms.)

[ʔ]ap[ʰ]:eč:in	[ʔ]ap[ʰ]:edu:le
ʔapʰ:eč:in	*ʔapʰ:edu:le*

‖ha-hp^{h}e-aduč-Vn‖	‖ha-hp^{h}e-aduč-le‖
/ʔap^h:e-č:-in /	/ʔap^h:e-du:-le/
carry.on.back-DIR-SG.IMP	carry.on.back-DIR-PL.IMP
['carry it away!']	['y'all carry it away!']

The instances of length in example (9) are the result of syncope and assimilation (in the case of the allomorph [-č:-]) and deletions combined with compensatory lengthening (in the case of the allomorph [-du:-]).

Perhaps the most persuasive argument in favor of granting /:/ special status as a separate segment in its own right is one not put forward by Halpern: several bound morphemes, both suffixes and enclitics, begin with /:/ as their first segment, though it only surfaces in such cases when the morphemes are attached to vowel-final morphemes. In some cases, it is possible to reconstruct the origin of the length at the beginning of morphemes. For example, the switch-reference suffix *-:li* most likely descends from a combination of the perfective suffix *-w* and the enclitic *=li, which carried the same (or similar) meaning as the modern suffix. The plausibility of such an origin for morpheme-initial /:/ in the suffix *-:li* is supported through language-internal evidence by a synchronically productive internal sandhi process of consonant deletion and replacement with compensatory lengthening (as seen in example (9) with the [-du:-] allomorph of the directional suffix *-aduč-*); such a process, if it happened in the past, would reduce the perfective suffix *-w* to length before a consonant-initial morpheme like *=li. Robust language-external evidence from Central Pomo, the sister language to the north of Southern Pomo, supports this theory of the origin of length in the length-initial suffix *-:li*. In Central Pomo the cognate morpheme is an enclitic and takes the shape *=li* and may be placed directly after the Central Pomo suffix *-w* (cognate with Southern Pomo *-w* PERFECTIVE) without any internal sandhi changes altering the consonants in the two morphemes (Mithun 1993: 132). Such comparative work could be done for many instances of /:/ in Southern Pomo morphemes; however, diachronic facts notwithstanding, the synchronic distribution of /:/ as a morpheme-initial segment does not include phonological alternations which allow a native speaker to assign any other segment in its place. In fact, it is not now possible to explain the origin of every instance of morpheme-initial /:/ by means of internal reconstruction and comparative data. Example (10) includes the length-initial morpheme *=:meṭ̓* '(to be) like', an enclitic (not a suffix like *-:li*) for which the ultimate origin of its initial length is not now known.[12]

(10) Length-initial enclitic *=:meṭ̓*

ʔahčahčay mahṭʰe:meṭ̓ (W: OF)[13]

ʔahčahčay ma-hṭʰe=:meṭ̓

Indian 3C-mother=like

'Indian like his own mother'

Some morphemes are only distinguished from others by the presence of a morpheme-initial /:/, as in the case of the conditional suffix *-:ba* (on the verb stem *mi:ṭi-* 'to lie down') versus the same subject sequential switch-reference suffix *-ba* (on the verb stem *čohṯi-* 'to write'), which are given in (11):

(11) Contrast between *-:ba* COND and *-ba* S.SEQ[14]

[ʔ]ay:áḱoʔwénṭoʔma mi:ṭí:ba (H ms.)

ʔay:aḱoʔwenṭoʔma mi:ṭi:ba

/ʔay:a=ḱo=ʔwen=ṭo=ʔma mi:ṭi-:ba/

1PL=COM=be?=EMPH=2SG.AGT lie.SG-COND

'you ought to lie w[ith] us'

miy:aṭʰe p[ʰ]al[:]aʔča:[č]on pa:pel čohṯiba ʔuhṯehṯew (H EA: 16a)

miy:aṭʰe pʰal:aʔča:čon pa:pel čohṯiba ʔuhṯehṯew

/miy:a-ṭʰe	pʰalaʔča:=čon	pa:pel čohṯi-ba	ʔuhṯehṯe-w/	/miy:a-ṭʰe
3-mother.AGT	white.folk=PAT	paper	write-S.SEQ	tell-PFV

['Her mother told the white person(s) in writing.']

Excluding the pseudo-consonant /:/, all of the consonantal phonemes of Southern Pomo are provided before front vowels with near-minimal contrasting words in table 10.

Table 10. Near-minimal contrasts of consonants before front vowels

Phoneme	Example	Gloss
/p/	*piʔni*	little (DISTRIBUTIVE)
/p^h/	*p^{h}iʔt̪̓aw*	to look (like)
/p̓/	*p̓eʔye*	fish scale
/b/	*biʔdu*	acorn (general term)
/t̪/	*t̪il:i*	killdeer
/t̪^{h}/	*t̪^{h}e:*	no
/t̪̓/	*t̪̓ek:e*	beaver
/ṭ/	*ṭil:emi*	sea fig
/ṭ^h/	*ṭ^{h}iw:i*	fork (in tree)
/ṭ̓/	*-ṭ̓iki-*	younger brother (root+generational suffix)
/d/	*dic̓:a-*	to break (with the body)
/č/	*čiʔba*	rush (n.)
/č^h/	*č^{h}i:lan*	net for burdens
/č̓/	*č̓i:wi*	acorns which have turned black and sour
/k/	*kic:idu*	little (COLLECTIVE)
/k^h/	*k^{h}i:k^{h}i*	fish gills
/k̓/	*k̓i:li*	black
/ʔ/	*ʔihsun*	California condor
/c/	*ceṭ̓*	how
/c̓/	*c̓iht̪a*	bird
/m/	*miʔdiš*	edible nut
/n/	*nih:i-*	to say
/s/	*si:lun*	acorn bread
/š/	*šiʔdo*	breast
/h/	*hiʔbu*	edible tuber ("Indian potato")
/l/	*lip^h:u*	leg
/w/	*wiʔc̓i*	Jerusalem cricket
/y/	*wi:yi*	acorn of Oregon oak

Table 11. Southern Pomo vowels

Short vowel	Example	Gloss	Long vowel	Example	Gloss
/i/	*hiʔda*	'road'	/i:/	*hi:mo*	'hole'
/e/	*heʔ:e*	'head hair'	/e:/	*he:ʔey*	'where?'
/a/	*haʔ:a*	'horn'	/a:/	*ha:meṭ*	'thus'
/o/	*hoʔ:o*	'tooth'	/o:/	*ho:li-*	'go, leave'
/u/	*huʔ:uy*	'face'	/u:/	*hu:lušbe*	'eyelashes'

2.2.2. Vowels

The Southern Pomo vowel inventory, in contradistinction to its inventory of consonants, is quite simple: there are five vowel qualities, each of which may be short or long, as listed in table 11:

The distinction between long and short vowels is an important one in the language; however, the status of long vowels as unitary phonemes is problematic. As has been discussed, the status of /:/ as a segment that moves between vowels and consonant in the same word stems forces a careful analysis of long vowels in Southern Pomo. Unlike many of the world's languages which have a phonemic contrast between long and short vowels (e.g., Thai, Khmer, Afrikaans), Southern Pomo does not have many minimal pairs which are distinguished solely by the length of the vowel. One possible minimal pair is *boṭ* 'flour' and *bo:ṭ* 'lungs'. However, this pair is problematic for at least three reasons: (1) monosyllabic phonological words are extremely rare; this applies even more to content words; (2) the word *boṭ* 'flour' appears to be most common as part of the compound *biʔduboṭ* 'acorn flour' (indeed, whether or not *boṭ* regularly occurs outside such a compound is an open question); (3) Halpern records the compound *biʔduboṭ* 'acorn flour' as *biʔdubot̪*—that is, he heard a dental rather than an alveolar final consonant (H I: 1).[15]

Though there can be no question that long versus short vowel qualities are phonemically distinct—their distribution cannot be predicted completely by an appeal to word class or surrounding phones—it is also true that the functional load (at least in terms of crucial avoidance of homophony) of length on vowels in Southern Pomo is not too great.

One reason for this is the preference in Southern Pomo for phonological words of not less than two syllables (only a handful of words, most of them function words, are monosyllabic). This preference complicates the possibility of minimal pairs between long and short vowels because of phonotactic requirements that the first syllable of any disyllabic (and, at least in careful speech, any polysyllabic) word be heavy; both CV: and CVC are heavy syllables in the language. Thus the pair *ʔa:ma* 'thou' and *ʔam:a* 'earth, ground, dirt, thing' and the pair *k*[h]*a:le* 'tree, plant' and *k*[h]*al:e* 'Healdsburg' (from *ʔahk*[h]*a* 'water' + *de:le* 'midst') are the closest things to minimal pair examples for the long vowel versus short vowel distinction in polysyllabic words. In the vast majority of recorded words, a long vowel in an initial syllable must be followed by a singleton-initial syllable; a short vowel in an initial syllable must be closed by a consonant, which may be part of a consonant cluster or a geminate.

The only polysyllabic words on record that break with this pattern have the shape CV:RHV(C)- ~ CV:HRV(C)- (where R stands for a sonorant). Halpern records a few words from the Cloverdale dialect of this shape, as given in example (12):

(12) CV:RHV- words from the Cloverdale dialect

šá:mhew (H V: 11)
/ša:mhe-w/
cut.up-PFV
'cuts up'

[ʔ]a:lhok̓oy (H EA: 8a)
/ʔa:lhok̓oy-Ø/
many.talk-PFV
'talked'

Such apparent exceptions to the otherwise canonical CV:CV(C)- ~ CVC:V(C)- ~ CVCCV(C)- shape are, however, problematic in their own right. Oswalt collected both of these words independently of Halpern. In the case of *ša:mhe-* 'to cut up', Oswalt does record the same word with a long vowel and /mh/ cluster from Elizabeth Dollar, a Dry Creek dialect speaker (for whom he also records a short vowel variant), but from Elsie Allen, the daughter of Annie Burke (the speaker from whom Halpern recorded *ša:mhew*), Oswalt only records *ša:me-*, which agrees in vowel length with her mother's form and one of Elizabeth Dollar's variants, yet it disagrees with both speakers' /h/ post-consonantal incrementing of the root consonant of the verbal stem (O D: ED and O D: EA).

The other example, *ʔa:lhok̓oy*, is even murkier: Oswalt only records this form from Elizabeth Dollar as *ʔalhok̓oy*—without the initial long vowel—but with the same /h/ post-consonantal incrementing of the root consonant (O D: ED). The long-vowel version of *ʔa:lhok̓oy* is recorded by Halpern from both Elsie Allen, as seen in example (12), and her mother, Annie Burke (H ms.).

Thus *ša:mhe-* ~ *šamhe-* ~ *ša:me-* shares a long vowel in the initial syllable across three speakers and two dialects (though optionally for Elizabeth Dollar's Dry Creek dialect), but only two speakers and both dialects share the /h/ (one being the mother of the speaker who lacks it!); and *ʔa:lhok̓oy* is recorded as such from two speakers (mother and daughter) of the Cloverdale dialect by Halpern, but Oswalt records *ʔalhok̓oy* from two speakers from two dialects, one of the speakers being the same as one of Halpern's consultants, namely Elsie Allen.

Halpern (1984: 17) also records some inflected verbs which shift from CVRCV- to CV:CRV- in certain instances:

(13) Example of inflected verbs with the shape CV:CRV-

[ʔ]ahlok̓o	[ʔ]a:lhot̪ak̓
ʔahlok̓o	*ʔa:lhot̪ak̓*
/ʔahlok̓-o/	/ʔa:lho<t̪a>k̓-Ø/
piece.to.fall-EVID	piece.to.fall<PL.ACT>-PFV
'one (piece) falls off'	'(pieces) drop off'

Halpern's consultants were Annie Burke and (much later) Burke's daughter, Elsie Allen; these forms in example (13) must have come from one or both of these speakers. Oswalt also recorded one of these from Elsie Allen, but he does not record a long vowel in the initial syllable, as in (14).

(14) Oswalt's transcription of verbs Halpern records as CV:CRV-

<ʔalhotak'> (O D: EA)

ʔalhot̪ak̓

/ʔalho<t̪a>k̓-Ø/
piece.to.fall<PL.ACT>-PFV
'sev. to fall'

The foregoing variations recorded by Oswalt are not all dialectal and are not the result of an inability on the part of Oswalt to hear length in such an environment. Oswalt did consistently hear length in such a phonological environment in other words from speakers of both the Cloverdale and Dry Creek dialects, as in the root *-:hmič-* 'do well, do carefully, do to perfection', which he recorded in several stems from both Elizabeth Dollar and Elsie Allen:

(15) Examples of CV:HCVC- stems recorded by Oswalt
do:hmiy (O D: ED)
||du-:hmič-Ø||
/do:hmiy-Ø/
prepare.well-PFV
'to prepare well and sufficiently'

ʔo:hmiy (O D: EA)
||hu-:hmič-Ø||
/ʔo-:hmiy-Ø/
comprehend-PFV
'to hear perfectly, to understand well what is said; to come to a verbal understanding, to make a date'

The forms in (15) confirm what has already been established; namely, that long vowels in Southern Pomo do contrast phonemically with short vowels. Yet the examples in (15) above also hint at the peculiar nature of /:/ in the language: the length on these long vowels, perhaps the only long vowels in closed syllables (in polysyllabic words) which Oswalt heard consistently from speakers of both dialects, is actually part of the root: these words do not really have underlying long vowels but short vowels abutting a /:/-initial root.[16]

Long vowels in Southern Pomo exist phonetically and bear a heavy functional load; however, their distribution is unlike that of other phonemes.

With the exception of the aforementioned monosyllabic words and, possibly, some stems of the shape CV:HCV(C)- ~ CV:CHV(C)-, long vowels seem to be short vowels combined with /:/ as a distinct segment (/:/ as a laryngeal increment, /:/ as the result of compensatory lengthening, /:/ as a morpheme-initial segment that only surfaces when preceded by a vowel). Because of these peculiarities, I treat /:/ as segment separate from the vowels or consonants with which it may be combined.

2.2.2.1. *Schwa [^{ə}]*

In addition to the five vowel qualities listed previously, some polysyllabic words in Southern Pomo have a schwa separating consonants. This schwa has not been regularly transcribed by Halpern or Oswalt, though in his dictionary files (O D) Oswalt does indicate the presence of schwa with notes in parentheses following a transcription, as shown in (16).

(16) Example of Oswalt's recording of schwa (O D: EA)[17]
</ham*i loh$oncwa (c schwa w)/>
ham:i lohšonč^{ə}wa
/ham:i lohšom-č-wa/
there stand.together-SEM-EVID
'They gathered together standing.'

A review of all instances of this method of recording schwa in (O D) produces not more than one hundred examples and reveals many duplicate entries. It also reveals some instances where Oswalt was unsure of whether a vowel was a schwa or a full vowel and where the speakers varied between a schwa and no vowel at all. The examples for which schwa is indicated in (O D) can be reduced to twenty-four consonantal environments (taking into consideration only the consonants immediately preceding and following the schwa). If the total number of surface syllables in each word is considered (excluding schwa), only trisyllabic and quadrasyllabic words are indicated as having schwa, though there is a single example of what may be described as a phonological word of five syllables (quadrasyllabic word + monosyllabic pronominal enclitic). In all cases, the schwa surfaces between the second and third syllables counting from the left edge of the

Table 12. Consonants before and after schwa with syllable count (O D)

_ə	ə_	σσ_σ	σσ_σσ	σσ_σσ =σ
p	l	✓		
p	y	✓		
m	h	✓		
t̯	m	✓		
t̯	l	✓	✓	
t̯̓	m	✓		
t̯̓	d	✓		
t̯^{h}	m	✓		
ṭ	l	✓		
ṭ̓	w	✓	✓	
l	m	✓		
č	m	✓		
č	w	✓	✓	
č	l	✓		
č̓	n	✓		
č̓	W	✓		
k	b	✓		
k	m	✓		
k	w	✓		✓
k	d	✓		
k	l	✓		
k^h	d	✓		
k̓	m	✓		
k̓	d	✓		

word (discounting the schwa as a syllable). And with only two exceptions, which are discussed later, the consonant immediately preceding the schwa is a voiceless obstruent and the one immediately following is a voiced consonant. These data are presented in table 12.

The first exception to the above generalization about the consonantal environments surrounding known occurrences of schwa, as shown in table 12, is the sequence /m^{ə}h/ in one word (O D):

(17) Example of schwa before a voiceless obstruent
<ˀa*ya ˀwa $i*ba*tʌhmhuy> <(m schwa b)> (O D: EA)
ʔa:yaʔwa ši:ba:t̺ʰmᵊhuy
||ʔa:ya=ʔwa ši:ba:t̺ʰa/i-mhuč̓-Ø||[18]
/ʔa:ya=ʔwa ši:ba:t̺ʰ-mᵊhuy-Ø/
1PL.AGT=COP.EVID poor-RECIP-PFV
'We feel sorry for e[ach].o[ther].'

Example (17) is aberrant for more than one reason: in addition to the presence of a schwa before a voiceless consonant, the schwa is separating two consonants within one morpheme. Oswalt notes that this is only one variant of the same word as produced by Elsie Allen. The other variant, *ši:ba:t̺ʰᵊmhuy,* conforms to the regular pattern of schwa occurring solely before a voiced consonant. Though both possibilities are counted in the table, the [mᵊh] variant appears to be unusual and, perhaps, an example of an idiolectal quirk or speech error. Oswalt notes that "E[lsie] A[llen] has trouble with [this] cluster" and shows variation between /t̺ʰᵊmh/ and / t̺ʰmᵊh/ (O D). This single possible counterexample to the otherwise straightforward distribution of schwa only before voiced consonants is therefore to be set aside. Note, however, that both variants of this word have the schwa inserted between the second and third surface syllables counting from the left.

The other example of schwa which breaks with an otherwise solid pattern is the presence of a schwa between /l/ and /m/—all other noted instances of schwa in Oswalt's dictionary (setting aside the aberrant *ši:ba:t̺ʰᵊmhuy ~ ši:ba:t̺ʰmᵊhuy* already discussed) follow voiceless obstruents. There is only one example of this in (O D):

(18) Schwa between /l/ and /m/ (O D: EA)
</s'a*lalmaw (l schwa m)/>
ċa:laləmaw
/ċa:lal-ma-w/
be.bruised-ESSIVE-PFV
'to get bruised'[19]

The phoneme /l/ has undergone some unique changes with respect to Pomoan: it has been replaced by /n/ in word-final position, but it can optionally resurface when followed by a vowel-initial suffix; it can also be replaced by /m/ when followed by a vowel-initial suffix (Oswalt 1976a: 21).[20] Word-internal /lm/ clusters are recorded elsewhere, as in (19) from Halpern:

(19) Example of /lm/ cluster from Halpern
[ʔ]ap[ʰ]:almé:le (H ms.)
ʔapʰ:alme:le
||ha-hpʰ-alameč̓-le||[21]
/ʔapʰ:-alme:-le/
carry-DIR-PL.IMP
['carry it down from above, y'all!']

Though there is only a single example of schwa preceded by /l/ in (O D), and though this example is also the only invariable example of a voiced consonant preceding schwa therein, this data poverty should be treated as the outcome of a poor sampling rather than evidence of another idiosyncratic speech or recording error. The phoneme /l/ has such synchronic instability—at least three sonorant allophones, some of which are allophones of other voiced consonants—that there are functional reasons for a speaker to keep /l/ distinct from a following voiced consonant. This reason, however, is not the most likely explanation. The syllable counting which holds true for all attested transcriptions of schwa in (O D) provides the best predictive power: a word of three or more surfacing syllables may have a schwa inserted after the second syllable from the left between any consonant and a voiced consonant. All other factors appear to be irrelevant, including morpheme boundaries: the schwa is recorded between an infix and the final consonant of word stem; between the first and second consonant of a reduplicated stem; between the final consonant of stem and a consonant in following suffix, and between the consonants within a suffix.

In fact, it is quite possible that some or all of the examples which both Oswalt and Halpern transcribe as sequences of C[+/-voice]C[+voice] two syllables from the left edge of trisyllabic or greater words were optionally pronounced with an intervening schwa. The word *optionally* is the key term: Oswalt also consistently records variation across speakers and uncertainty within individual speakers with regard to the presence or absence of a schwa. In a couple of instances Oswalt is unsure of whether a vowel is schwa or another unstressed vowel.

Following are examples of each these problematic instances of schwa as recorded in (O D):

(20) CəC ~ C'C variation by one speaker (O D: EA)
</lip∧h*u miz*ikbiy/> <(Note: k schwa b; later k' preferred)>
lip^{h}:u mic:ik^{ə}biy ~ mic:ik̓biy
'foot to go up when knee struck, reflex kick'

(21) CC ~ CəC variation between speakers (O D: ED, O D: EA)
</ki*likliw/> <(EA sometimes has k schwa l)>
ki:likliw ~ ki:lik^{ə}liw
'sound of fire blazing or motor running [ED]; sound of heater, earthquake, thunder [EA]'

(22) e ~ ə confusion by Oswalt (O D: ED)
</ham*uhca ho?k'o?c'eway./> <Perhaps -e- is a schwa>
ham:uhča hoʔk̓oʔč̓eway ~ hoʔk̓oʔč̓^{ə}way
'They're bragging.'

(23) a ~ ə confusion by Oswalt (O D: EA)
</mak∧h*ac*(a or schwa)law/>
mak^{h}:ač:alaw ~ mak^{h}:ač: ^{ə}law
'to scrape (leaves) off (limb) with hand'

Of the questionable cases of schwa listed, only the latter two (Oswalt's uncertainty about the presence of schwa) have any effect on interpretations of written Southern Pomo data—unstressed, unrounded, short vowels which are the nucleus of the third syllable from the left might actually be schwa, at least on the basis of Oswalt's admitted uncertainty with some forms. It seems unlikely, however, that such transcription mistakes are widespread in the extant records.[22] The schwa vowel in Southern Pomo is not an additional phoneme: no lexical weight rests upon it. It is also not clearly the allophone of any one vowel or vowels, nor is it mandatory for the breaking up of consonant clusters; it is optional. On the basis of the small sample of recorded instances in (O D), the possibility of its presence can be predicted according the number of syllables in a word (between the second and third surface syllables counting from the left edge of the word), but its actual presence is entirely optional, and speakers' preferences differ. Hereafter the schwa is transcribed in my phonemic transcriptions with the superscript symbol <^{ə}>, as has been done throughout this subsection, if it is indicated in some way in the written sources or, when working from an audio record, if it is clearly audible.

2.2.3. Stress

Stress in Southern Pomo is predictable: primary stress falls on the penultimate syllable of a phrase.[23] In a paper on Northern Pomo prosody, Eero Vihman states that among the seven Pomoan languages only Southern Pomo and Southeastern Pomo have predictable (non-phonemic) stress systems (1976: 55). Halpern confirms this for Southern Pomo and elaborates on the basic stress patterns in the language:

> The general rule, subject to some optionality, for non-phonemic accent in [Southern Pomo] is that loudest stress accompanied by raised pitch, both with falling contour, occurs on the penult of a breath-group, with secondary stress normally falling on every second syllable preceding the penult. In the sentence, the loudest and highest-pitched accent occurs on the final word or breath-group. Thus, using ˋ for secondary, ˊ for primary, and ˆ for loudest stress, sí:ma p^{h}ìʔt̯̓awâʔt̯o . . . 'I feel sleepy'. (Halpern 1984: 38 [Southern Pomo converted to my orthography])[24]

Walker (2008: 33–35) includes an investigation of Southern Pomo phrases and individual words (monomorphemic and polymorphemic) that corroborates Halpern's description of the distribution Southern Pomo stress — penultimate primary stress with secondary stress on every second syllable preceding the penultimate syllable — and his identification of pitch as the primary correlate of stress; it also analyzes a small number of monomorphemic trisyllabic nouns, a type not touched upon by Halpern, and

Table 13. Polymorphemic phrases analyzed for stress (Walker 2008)

kahmaṭ kaʔma	[ˌkah.maṭ' 'kaʔ.ma]	'are you angry?'
kac:i yokʰ:e	[ˌkat.tsi 'yok.kʰe]	'it will be cold'
ḱoʔdi biʔṭaw	[ˌk'oʔ.di 'biʔ.ṭ'aw]	'it tastes good'
pe:sa kamkʰe	[ˌpeː.sa 'kam.kʰe]	'have you any money?'
ma:li wadun	[ˌmaː.li 'wa.ɾun]	'come here!'

Table 14. Monomorphemic words analyzed for stress (Walker 2008)

ʔahkʰa	['ʔah.kʰa]	'water'
ʔahša	['ʔah.ʃa]	'fish'
hay:u	['haj.ju]	'dog'
haṭ:a	['hat.t'a]	'red'
kac:i	['kat.tsi]	'cold'
kahle	['kah.le]	'white'
ḱo:ʔo	['k'oː.ʔo]	'song'
ḱoʔdi	['k'oʔ.di]	'good'
čaʔća	['tʃaʔ.ts'a]	'green'
šaʔḱa	['ʃaʔ.k'a]	'black'
ćahkil	['ts'ah.kil]	'blue'
ćihṭa	['ts'ih.ṭa]	'bird'
pʰa:la	['pʰaː.la]	'also'
wa:yu	['waː.ju]	'yellow'
kic:idu	[ˌkit.'tsi.ɾu]	'small (COLL)'
muṭʰ:u:nu	[ˌmuṭ.'ṭʰuː.nu	'lizard'
mus:a:la	[ˌmus.'saː.la]	'snake'

finds that the initial syllable of such words also carries secondary stress, which causes stress clash with the primary stress of the penultimate syllable.[25] The words and phrases analyzed in Walker (2008) are reproduced in tables 13 and 14:

That the primary correlate of stress in Southern Pomo would be pitch rather than duration is not a surprise: penultimate short vowels may bear the primary stress in words with long vowels, as in *bu:ṭaka* [ˌbuː.'ta.ka] 'bear', and a great deal of additional homophony at the morpheme level might arise if concomitant lengthening of a stressed vowel (at least to a degree seen in a language like English) were the principal correlate of stress in Southern Pomo.

2.3. PHONETICS

2.3.1. Voicing Distinction in Obstruents

Halpern analyzes the consonants /t̪/ and /p/ as voiceless unaspirated stops; he treats the consonants /ṭ/, /c/, /č/, and /k/ separately as "intermediates" and describes them as having "voiceless onset and voiced release when initial or intervocalic . . . [and] fully voiced when in direct contact with the voiced sonorants m n l w y" (1984: 4). He therefore makes two striking claims: (1) there is a distinction between the voiceless unaspirated stops and the so-called intermediates (both of which must therefore differ from the voiceless aspirated stops and voiced stops he also lists in the same paragraph); and (2) the so-called intermediates are partially or fully voiced in certain environments.

In order to understand the reasons behind Halpern's analysis, it is important to note that he is alone among Pomoan scholars in treating the single voiced coronal plosive, /d/, as dental rather than alveolar (Walker 2008: 16). He therefore acknowledges a four-way contrast (voiced, voiceless unaspirated, voiceless aspirated, ejective) among bilabial plosives and dental plosives. Because he incorrectly assigns the voiced coronal plosive to a dental place of articulation, it appears he believes the voiceless unaspirated alveolar plosive /ṭ/ (his 'intermediate' <ḍ>) has no voiced counterpart at the same place of articulation with which it might be confused should it be voiced allophonically, and that the voiceless unaspirated dental plosive /t̪/ does not follow the same pattern as the so-called intermediates further back in the mouth in having allophonic voicing because the dental could be confused with the voiced plosive wrongly assigned to that place of articulation.

However, as has already been stated, the /d/ of Southern Pomo is not dental but alveolar, a place of articulation it shares with the other Pomoan languages. Thus if Halpern's analysis of possible voicing of the unaspirated stops were true, the voiceless unaspirated alveolar plosive would share an allophone with /d/ in some environments; it does not do so.

The voiceless unaspirated stops (plosives and affricates) of Southern Pomo have very short VOT (voice onset time), but are clearly voiceless and do not have a voiced release; they sound similar (if not identical) to the voiceless unaspirated plosives of Khmer, Thai, and White Hmong. In the case of Khmer and Thai, the voiceless unaspirated stops must contrast with voiceless aspirated and voiced (optionally implosive in Khmer) stops at two places of articulation; the voiceless unaspirated stops of Southern Pomo bear a similar load. Measurements of a handful of tokens reveal that the voiceless unaspirated stops of Southern Pomo have 8–18 ms of positive VOT, and the voiceless unaspirated stops have 60 ms or more of positive VOT (Walker 2008: 22). The voiceless unaspirated stops of Southern Pomo are therefore not voiced in the manner described by Halpern.

2.3.2. Phonemic Status of the Glottal Stop

Oswalt records no vowel-initial words in Southern Pomo; all words which do not begin with /h/ or a supralaryngeal consonant are consistently recorded with an initial /ʔ/in his notes and publications.[26] Halpern, however, does not consider the glottal stop to be phonemic in this position, though he acknowledges the possible phonetic presence of word-initial glottal stops:

> In my older (1940) hearing of Ps . . . I recorded many initial vowels. In my recent (1982) hearing of Ps I find that such vowels have an optional light glottal attack on the initial vowel. This glottal attack is most frequent when the word is initial in a breath-group or follows another word which ends in a vowel. The glottal attack is normally absent when the preceding form ends in a consonant. (Halpern 1984: 6)

The precise meanings of "normally" and "optional" in this context are not clear, but what is clear is the acknowledgment of the possibility of a phonetically present glottal stop in word-initial position in some instances. Halpern's Southern Pomo orthography shows no word-initial glottal stops in his published paper, but a review of his unpublished notes from both his early (1939–40) fieldwork and his later (1982) work reveal that he did hear the word-initial glottal stop in a number of words in several environments.

If Halpern's early work with Southern Pomo included recordings, they cannot be located. It is therefore impossible to know with any surety whether his consultant at that time, Annie Burke, produced word-initial glottal stops. It is, however, possible to go back to some of the earliest writ-

Table 15. Words with and without written word-initial glottal stop in (H I)

Written without ʔ	Written with ʔ		Total
	Following vowel	Following consonant	
147	9	8	**164**

ten versions of the texts Halpern collected from Burke, where he used a more phonetic transcription system.[27] The text (H I), the first (and presumably oldest) of the narrative texts collected by Halpern at this time, shows that he transcribed the majority of words which did not have an initial [h] or supralaryngeal consonant as being vowel-initial. However, he also transcribed several words with an initial [ʔ]. Some of the words written with an initial glottal stop are also written without one, for example 'house' appears as *ʔahča* (H I: 6) but also as *ahča* (H I: 23). The nature of the final segment of the preceding words, if any, does not seem to affect Halpern's use of word-initial glottal stops—the examples with 'house' above both follow vowel-final words in the text. Table 15 summarizes the presence or absence of word-initial glottal stops in the (H I) text. For those words that are written with an initial glottal stop in (H I), the table indicates whether the final consonant of the preceding word is a consonant or vowel.

As can be seen in table 15, those words Halpern transcribed with an initial glottal stop are almost evenly distributed between those following consonant-final words and those following vowel-final words. The total number of those following consonant-final words might be slightly misleading, however, because it is possible that some did not immediately follow the preceding word. It is impossible to know which, if any, might fit this scenario without access to the original speech event, but it is possible to make an educated guess on the basis of the presence or absence of a comma following the preceding consonant-final word in Halpern's text.[28] On the basis of this criterion, the total number of words with a written initial glottal stop that can be assumed to have immediately followed a consonant-final word in speech is reduced to five. Table 16 gives all five words, the consonants they follow, and their place in the (H I).

These data are few and must be handled with great care, but it is clear

Table 16. Glottal stop–initial words that immediately follow consonant-final words

Final consonant of preceding word	ʔ-initial words	Gloss	Location
[n]	ʔač^{h}:o-w	NEG.EXISTENTIAL-PFV	(H I: 3)
[n]	ʔač^{h}:o-w	NEG.EXISTENTIAL-PFV	(H I: 3) [second occurrence]
[n]	ʔohčo-w	give-PFV	(H I: 4)
[t̪ʼ]	ʔe:me:la=yey	flea=AGT	(H I: 5)
[j]	ʔač:a	in.house	(H I: 6)

that Halpern heard word-initial glottal stops following at least three different consonants ([n], [t̪ʼ], [j]) and preceding front, back, and low vowels ([e], [o], [a]).

The data from Halpern's early work confirm that he heard word-initial glottal stops, though he appears to have heard few of them, and that their distribution is not word-specific (i.e., the same word might be recorded with or without an initial glottal stop). A third (or more) of the word-initial glottal stops he did record immediately follow consonant-final words.

Halpern's transcriptions of his later work on Southern Pomo with Elsie Allen, the daughter of Annie Burke (his consultant for his 1939–40 work), give a similar distribution of word-initial glottal stops to that seen in his earlier records. Many more words in the Elsie Allen materials are written as vowel-initial than glottal stop–initial, though the proportion of word-initial glottal stops that are written is greater than that seen in the earlier (H I) data. Table 17 summarizes the total number of words written as vowel-initial or glottal stop–initial in Halpern's 1982 transcriptions of Elsie Allen's narratives (H EA).[29]

If the non-narrative pages of (H EA) are excluded, and only the transcription of Elsie Allen's actual discourse is consulted, there are 111 instances of glottal stop–initial or ostensibly vowel-initial words following consonant-final words. These are summarized in table 18.

It is clear that Halpern heard many more word-initial glottal stops in his later fieldwork. If there were no extant recordings for (H EA), it would

Table 17. Words with and without written word-initial glottal stop in (H EA)

Written without ʔ	Written with ʔ	Total
360	155	**515**

Table 18. Written word-initial glottal stops following C-final words in (H EA)

Written without ʔ	Written with ʔ	Total
31	80	**111**

be necessary to accept the tally in table 18 uncritically. However, Halpern's recordings of these narratives are accessible. The first 19 words of the 111 of table 18 were checked in the recording with Praat for two things:

1. Does the word immediately follow the preceding consonant-final word, or is there a pause between words?
2. For those words that do immediately follow a consonant-final word, is there phonetic evidence of a glottal stop?

A total of 15 of the 19 words were found to be immediately following the final consonant of the preceding word. Of these words, all were judged to have a phonetically present initial glottal stop on the basis of the observable acoustic record in the waveform or spectrogram (or both).

Figure 2 gives an example of the words *ham:u-n=hlaw ʔahk*^{h}*a* [3SG-PAT=also water]. This example comes from Abraham Halpern's recording of Elsie Allen, and his transcription of this string of morphemes omits the clearly audible word-initial glottal stop of *ʔahk*^{h}*a* 'water'.[30] (Halpern's original transcription is given in < > below the IPA transcription in figure 2.)

As can be seen in figure 2, the glottal stop is present word-initially after a consonant-final word (in this case the labiovelar approximant). If word-initial glottal stops were only inserted to avoid vowel hiatus, it seems unlikely that one would be inserted automatically following a w-final word—the consonant /w/ might be expected to resyllabify as the onset of 'water'

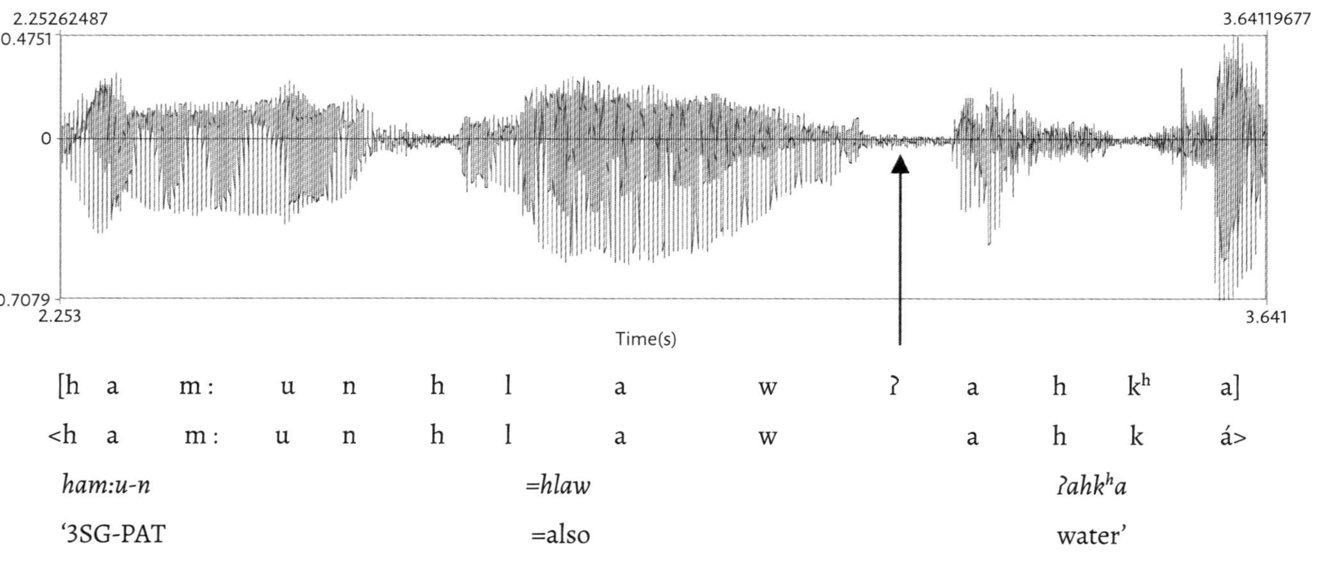

Fig. 2. Example of ʔ-initial word from Halpern’s recordings of Elsie Allen. Courtesy of the author.

instead. It is worth noting that Southern Pomo /w/ is a fully developed consonant in the language, one which may occur in any position within a word and may even follow /u/ as a coda consonant (e.g., *diʔbuw* 'buried').

On the basis of the evidence, Oswalt's analysis of zero vowel-initial words in Southern Pomo conforms most closely to the observable distribution of [ʔ] as phonetically present in word-initial position in Southern Pomo. The glottal stop as a phoneme in word-initial position is the most parsimonious explanation for the word-initial phonetic presence of [ʔ] in Southern Pomo after both vowels and consonants; the glottal stop is well-attested as a consonant in other positions: as a root consonant, as a laryngeal increment, in clusters with certain suffixes, and, at least in some records, as a final in certain vocative kinship terms. In other words, the glottal stop is clearly a consonantal phoneme in other environments in Southern Pomo, and it is clearly phonetically present in word-initial position, and there is no reason not to treat it as a phoneme in initial position. This grammar therefore follows Oswalt's analysis and treats all vowel-initial words in Halpern's records as glottal stop–initial words.

2.4. SYLLABLE STRUCTURE

The vast majority of Southern Pomo words begin with a single consonant; none begins with a vowel. There are, however, a small number of words which allow word-initial consonant clusters, all of them /h/+sonorant. The most common of these are contracted speech variants of a subset of the inflected allomorphs of the stem ||hu:w-|| 'to go (about; toward speaker; of one)', as in examples (24) and (25), following.

(24) Example of *hw*-initial word
hwadém̓ʔdu (H VIII: 1)
hwademʔdu
||hu:w-aded-wadu||
/hw-adem-ʔdu/
GO-DIR-HAB
'always goes around'

(25) Example of *hm*-initial word

[ʔ]ač:a hmayʔdu (H EA: 23a)

||ʔač:a hu:w-mač-wadu||

/ʔač:a	h-may-ʔdu/
house.in	go-DIR-HAB[31]

‘they come inside the house’

Another commonly attested word that may begin with an /h/+sonorant cluster is *nih:i-* ‘to say’, which has the unusual variant /hnihi-/ in rapid speech, as in example (26).

(26) Example of *hn*-initial word

hnihiw (H EA: 10a)

||nih:i-w||

/hnihi-w/

say-PFV

‘said’

In addition to the two verbs in (26), both of which only allow C+sonorant onsets as variants, there is another free-standing word which allows a C+sonorant onset cluster, *hla:li* ‘perhaps, might’, a word which appears to be unique and most likely a grammaticized variant of a verb like *dahla:li-* ‘to think’, one which has lost the otherwise obligatory instrumental prefix and now begins with a prefixless root, as shown in (27), which has both *dahla:li-* and *hla:li-* in the same excerpt.[32]

(27) *hla:li-* and *dahla:li-*

behšé dahlá:li. hé: [ʔ]ahšá dahlá:li, (H III: 3)

behše dahla:li he: ʔahša dahla:li

/behše	dahla:li	he:	ʔahša	dahla:li/
deer(meat)	think	or	fish	think

hiʔ[:]inwánṯin ċíyaw k̓óʔdi hla:líʔwen.

hiʔ:inwanṯin ċiyaw k̓oʔdi hla:liʔwen

/hiʔ:inwanṯin	ċi-ya-w	k̓oʔdi	hla:li=ʔwen/
either?	make-DEFOC-PFV	good	perhaps=BE?

['Deer, (I) think. Or fish, (I) think. Either (of them) would be good to make, perhaps.'][33]

There are perhaps additional words with limited distribution which also allow /h/+sonorant-initial clusters to begin them in special circumstance, but if so, they are not common. The foregoing forms discussed are restricted to three of the most common concepts in human language (saying, going, epistemic information), and as such can be expected to undergo unique phonological changes, and are therefore set aside hereafter.

There is also at least one function word that may begin with a consonant cluster according to some transcriptions: *k^{h}ma:yow* 'after, following'. This word, however, might be analyzed as an enclitic, a topic covered in greater detail in the subsequent section. Whether *k^{h}ma:yow* is a freestanding word or a rather large enclitic does not affect the fact that it grammaticized from *k^{h}a:ma* 'foot' and its derivative *k^{h}am:a* 'on foot' (i.e., the cluster is clearly a recent development via syncope of the initial vowel).

Laying aside these exceptions, all Southern Pomo words begin with a heavy syllable with a single consonant onset. Both CV: and CVC syllables are heavy in the language. Word-internally, it is possible to have a bi-consonantal onset if the coda of the immediately preceding syllable is a surface sonorant, as in (28).

(28) Example of CCVC syllable
hit̺ʼ:ank^{h}č̓in (H EA: 46a)
[hit̪.ˈt̪ʼaŋ.k^{h}ʧʼin]
'thinking'[34]

It is also possible that this example is actually an instance of a bi-consonantal coda and should be syllabified as [hit̪.ˈt̪ʼaŋk^h.ʧʼin]. The evidence is equivocal: it is not possible to conduct tests or otherwise make observations which would decide the matter. The complex onset has herein been chosen as the preferred analysis for two reasons: (1) convenience—the first of the three consonants in such clusters is always part of a separate morpheme; and (2) Pomoan family typology—neighboring Central Pomo and more distant Southeastern Pomo have developed complex onsets but not complex codas.

2.5. WORD STRUCTURE

Southern Pomo words are composed of roots, stems, affixes, and enclitics. Verb stems take the shape CV-XCV(C)- ~ CV-CXV(C)- (where X = /:/~/h/~/ʔ/) with the first syllable being an obligatory instrumental prefix and the second syllable being the root. Noun stems take the same shape as verbs, but there is no synchronic evidence that the disyllabic common noun stems can be segmented into roots and prefixes (kinship stems, a robust nominal subclass, can be segmented into prefixes and roots).[35]

The definitions of root and stem for Southern Pomo are the same as those provided by Payne: "a root is an unanalyzable form that expresses the basic lexical content . . . and does not necessarily constitute a fully understandable word in and of itself," whereas "a stem consists minimally of a root . . . [or] a root plus derivational morphemes" (1997: 24). Note that roots do not necessarily double as fully understandable words in Southern Pomo; common nouns, adjectives, adverbs, and numerals have roots which are also stems and valid grammatical and phonological words: verbs, kinship terms, and pronouns do not have roots which are also stems.

The precise definition of the word in Southern Pomo is not cut and dried. Indeed, one of the greatest differences between the transcription practices of Halpern and Oswalt lies in where they place spaces between morphemes: Halpern places fewer spaces between morphemes than Oswalt. A clear example of this difference is demonstrated by Oswalt's retranscription of a portion of (H VI) in the introductory pages to Oswalt's translation of the same text, which shows the two differ with regard to the status of *kʰma:yow* 'after' as a free-standing word (Oswalt 2002: 316). Examples (29) and (30) display Halpern's original transcription and Oswalt's retranscription of the same section from (H VI).

(29) Halpern's original transcription of (H VI: 3)
ha:mini:bakʰmá:yow hídʔa hwá:ba
ha:mini:bakʰma:yow hidʔa hwa:ba
/ha:mini:-ba=kʰma:yow hidʔa hw-a:-ba/
and.then-S.SEQ=after outside go-DIR-S.SEQ

[ʔ]ahčáŋhk^{h}ay hó:liw.
ʔahčanhk^{h}ay ho:liw
/ʔahča-nh=k^{h}ay   ho:li-w/
house-to-ward   Leave ~ go-PFV
'After having done so, having gone outside, he went off homewards.'

(30) Oswalt's retranscription of (H VI: 3) from (Oswalt 2002: 316)
<ha:mini-ba k^{h}ma:yow, hid'a hwa:-ba, 'ahca-n-hk^{h}ay ho:li-w>

As can be seen in (29) and (30), *k^{h}ma:yow* is written together with the preceding morphemes as a single phonological word by Halpern, and the otherwise unusual initial cluster seems to support such an analysis, whereas Oswalt writes *k^{h}ma:yow* as a separate word. This difference holds true throughout each scholar's work.

These two methods of word division in transcription fall roughly on either side of the divide between the morphological word in Southern Pomo (Oswalt's preference) and the phonological word (Halpern's preference). Precisely what constitutes a morphological word and a phonological word is, of course, a language-specific problem. Dixon (2010b: 7) defines the phonological word (as a useful crosslinguistic concept) as "a phonological unit larger than the syllable . . . which has at least one . . . phonological defining property" which comes from the following list he provides:

a. *Segmental features*—internal syllabic and segmental structure; phonetic realizations in terms of this; word boundary phenomena; pause phenomena.
b. *Prosodic features*—stress (or accent) and/or tone assignment; prosodic features such as nasalization, retroflexion, vowel harmony.
c. *Phonological rules*—some rules apply only within a phonological word; others (external sandhi rules) apply specifically across a phonological word boundary.

Contrasted with this list are the more eclectic diagnostic criteria he provides for identifying a grammatical word, only the first three of which are quoted here, as the others are not directly relevant to Southern Pomo (Dixon 2010b: 12–19):

a. [A morphological word] has as its base one or more lexical roots to which morphological processes (compounding, reduplication, shift of stress, change of tone, internal change, subtraction, affixation) have applied; and
b. has conventionalized coherence and meaning.
c. [When compounding or affixation are involved on the morphological word, they] always occur together, rather than scattered through the clause (the criterion of cohesiveness) . . .

Dixon's criteria can be used to distinguish morphological words which are not free phonological units from phonological words which are not single morphological words. However, the two types of word are not mutually exclusive: they may coincide (Dixon 2010b: 22).

In Southern Pomo the criteria for morphological wordhood and phonological wordhood are similar to but less complex than those laid out by Dixon, and in many cases the two do coincide. All three possibilities, which have been assigned type numbers (Type 1 = phonological word, Type 2 = morphological word, Type 3 = both), can be defined for Southern Pomo using table 19.

Verbs with TAM marking and kinship terms with case marking are specifically identified in the table 19 because they, unlike all other words, have roots and stems which do not coincide with phonological or morphological words. Southern Pomo verbs which are treated herein as morphological words are composed minimally of a root, at least one prefix, and at least one TAM affix.[36] Kinship terms which are likewise treated as morphological words are composed minimally of a root and a case-marking suffix.[37]

As table 19 makes clear, the single most important diagnostic question for morphological or phonological wordhood is whether the morpheme is a clitic or combined with morphemes of which one is a clitic. Thus the agentive case enclitic *=yey* is a morphological word but not a phonological word; the verb *hiʔduʔc̆̓edu=ʔka=ʔma* know=INTER=2SG.AGT 'do you know?' is a single phonological word made up of three morphological words (the first of which, the verb stem *hiʔduʔc̆̓edu-* 'to know', has a root and affixes);[38] the noun *nup*^{h}*:e* 'striped skunk' is a root, a stem, a morphological word, and a phonological word. The three types of word in Southern Pomo can only be defined on the basis of clitics; the identification of clitic-hood in

Table 19. Identifying phonological and morphological words in Southern Pomo

	Phonological word	Morphological word	Type
Words of any class with attached clitics	Yes	No	1
Clitics	No	Yes	2
Monomorphemic nouns, pronouns, adjectives, adverbs, numerals, function words, kinship terms with case marking, and verbs with TAM marking	Yes	Yes	3

Southern Pomo is therefore a crucial matter and is dealt with in great detail throughout the remainder of this section.

There is no shortage of potentially useful definitions and diagnostic tests for clitic-hood (such as Zwicky 1977; Zwicky 1985; Zwicky and Pullum 1983; Payne 1997: 22; Dixon 2010a: 221–25; Dixon 2010b: 20), all of which agree that clitics can be identified on the basis of at least three characteristics: (1) they do not fit language-specific categories of word or affix; (2) they are phonologically bound to an adjacent word in some way; and (3) they may attach to units larger than the word (phrase or clause level).

Zwicky (1985: 286–90) lists more specific tests for clitic-hood, four of which are especially useful to the formation of a definition of clitic-hood in Southern Pomo (listed 1–4 and not with original numbering):

1. Phonological: "[A] clitic . . . forms a phonological unit with an independent word."
2. Internal/external sandhi: "[A]n element affected by or conditioning a sandhi rule otherwise known to be internal should be a clitic, not an independent word . . . [whereas one] affected by or conditioning a sandhi rule otherwise known to be external should be an independent word, not a clitic."
3. Ordering: "[A]n element that is strictly ordered with respect to adjacent morphemes is almost surely a clitic (or an affix), while an element exhibiting free order with respect to adjacent words is certainly an independent word."
4. Distribution: "[C]litics typically behave like affixes in . . . having

> distributions describable by single principles like 'combines with the head verb of a clause', 'combines with the first constituent of a clause' . . . an element with [such] a simple distribution of this sort is probably a clitic (or an affix), and . . . [one] with a complex distribution is almost surely an independent word."

The first type of test, a phonological one, and the second type, one which takes into account sandhi rules, are related, obviously, with sandhi being more appropriately one specific corner of the phonological test for clitic-hood. Therefore in the discussion that follows, tests 1 and 2 are grouped together; 3 and 4 are discussed separately.

(1) Phonological and (2) sandhi test

The phonological tests for clitic-hood in Southern Pomo are not as straightforward as they are for a language such as English, where one clear symptom of clitic-hood is the absence of stress on certain morphemes (with syllabic segments) and their corresponding need to bind to an adjacent word with stress. Southern Pomo stress, as described earlier in §2.2.3, is completely regular: the penultimate syllable bears primary stress with every other syllable bearing secondary stress to the left of the penult. However, a matter not touched upon in §2.2.3 is the unit of which the stressed syllable is the penult. Halpern's description of Southern Pomo stress specifically defines the domain of stress as the "breath-group," and he notes that there are three levels of stress: (1) loudest primary, which he transcribes with ^ over the stressed vowel; (2) primary stress, which he transcribes with ´ over the stressed vowel; and (3) secondary stress, which he transcribes with ` over the stressed vowel (Halpern 1984: 38). This breath-group, at least in the example provided by Halpern, corresponds to a clause-level phrase. The assignment of stress in Southern Pomo, therefore, is not a word- or phrase-level phenomenon, but it is assigned at the level of a breath-group, a term for which a working definition for Southern Pomo is unavoidably circular: stress is applied at the level of a breath-group utterance; a breath-group utterance can be identified by the assignment of stress. This definition, whatever its logical faults, points to a stress domain in the language that is not easy to fix within clear bounds. This analysis is supported by an appeal to data from neighboring Kashaya Pomo, which also has a stress domain with no fixed bounds.

The specifics of the stress system of Kashaya are complicated and bear little resemblance to the Southern Pomo one, but the domain in which stress is assigned in Kashaya does appear to be similar. In Kashaya, "stress can fall on any of the first five syllables (out of *a phrasal domain with no fixed limit*)" (Buckley 1994: 171; italics mine). Southern Pomo stress therefore appears to have the same domain as that of Kashaya: stress is assigned at the level of a phrasal domain with no fixed limit.

All of this relates to the identification of clitics in Southern Pomo because stress is assigned after clitics are attached to words and the words are strung together with other words: clitics are not necessarily unstressed. In fact, it is possible for a clitic to bear all three types of stress described by Halpern (loudest primary, primary, and secondary). Though this might not be the expected case, Zwicky notes descriptions of Modern Greek, Bikol, Latin, and Sanskrit where clitics have been reported to take stress (1977: 14–15). Crucially, any Southern Pomo clitic that includes a vowel can bear stress if it is the penultimate or pre-antepenultimate (and so on) in a phrase-level domain, and that stress, as already stated, can be of any type allowed in the language. The cases of clitics with stress reported in Zwicky (1977) are not so broad in their application as the case of Southern Pomo, and in this detail, perhaps, Southern Pomo might prove to be typologically unusual.

If stress cannot be used as a phonological diagnostic for clitic-hood in Southern Pomo, sandhi rules are more useful tools for identifying clitics. Zwicky states that phonological words are the domain in which internal sandhi rules operate and that a morpheme which is not an affix but participates in such internal sandhi rules must be a clitic (1985: 286). This insight applies to Southern Pomo with some qualifications.

In Southern Pomo, within a grammatical word, two underlying consonants may not surface together across morpheme boundaries after affixation unless the first consonant is a nasal: the first must be deleted and replaced with compensatory lengthening of the vowel for which it had been a coda, as in examples (31) and (32).

(31) Consonant deletion within a grammatical word with *-ya*

kahsa:yaw[39] (H EA: 21a)

kahsa:yaw

||kahsak-ya-w||

/kahsa:-ya-w/

abandon-DEFOC-PFV

'left'

(32) Consonant deletion within a grammatical word with *-ba*

mi:má:ba (H VI: 6)

mi:ma:ba

||mi-:mač-ba||

/mi:ma:-ba/

cry-S.SEQ

'having cried'

Case-marking enclitics in Southern Pomo behave like affixes in this regard, as in examples (33), (34), and (35) with the enclitics *=t̪on* LOCATIVE ('on; over'), *=k̓o* COMITATIVE ('with'), and *=wi* INSTRUMENTAL ('with, at, in').[40]

(33) Consonant deletion within a phonological word with *=t̪on*

kahsa:=t̪on (O I: 17c)

kahsa:t̪on

||kahsak=t̪on||

/kahsa:t̪on/

desert=LOC

'leaving [gerund]'

(34) Consonant deletion within a phonological word with *=k̓o*

mi:má:k̓o (H VI: 7)

mi:ma:k̓o

||mi-:mač=k̓o||

/mi:ma:=k̓o/

cry=COM

'[with] weeping'

(35) Consonant deletion within a phonological word with =*wi*

mi:ma:wi (H EA: 6a)

mi:ma:wi

||mi-:mač=wi||

/mi:ma:=wi/

cry=INSTR

'w[ith] crying'

These examples confirm that these clitics do participate in internal sandhi rules when applied to verbs. The evidence shown proves that the aforementioned morphemes are, in fact, bound morphemes and not separate phonological words.

The case-marking enclitics in these examples may also attach phonologically to other word classes (a distributional fact covered later); however, when they do so, they do not obligatorily participate in the sandhi rules in which they participate when attached to verbs. In the examples already given, the verb stem ||mi-:mač-|| 'to cry' was shown to lose its final consonant to compensatory lengthening when the enclitics were bound to it. (The form *mi:may* shows a different final consonant because of a rule whereby morpheme-final /č/ and /č̓/ become /y/ before a word boundary.)

The examples that follow show the same enclitics from preceding examples attached to nouns which surface with the same final as 'to cry' (some of which underwent the same change of post-alveolar affricate to palatal approximant in an earlier stage of the language).[41]

(36) Enclitic =*t̪on* on nouns

ʔač:ay=t̪on (O I: 6)

ʔač:ayt̪on

/ʔač:ay=t̪on/

man=LOC

'over the man'

čún:am háyt̪on (H IV: 6)

čun:am hayt̪on

/čun:am hay=t̪on/

drift wood=LOC
'[on] driftwood'

(37) Enclitic =*wi* on noun
[ʔ]ah:aywi (H EA: 28a)
ʔah:aywi
/ʔah:ay=wi/
wood=INSTR
['with/on wood/stick']

Though the pattern seen in these examples is the most common in the narrative texts, there is at least one /y/-final noun that does participate in the sandhi rule already discussed for verbs. As given in example (38), the noun *huʔ:uy* 'face' does not preserve its final consonant as might be expected on the basis of the previous nominal examples.[42]

(38) =*t̪on* on ||huʔ:uč|| *huʔ:uy* 'face' with verb-like word-internal sandhi
huʔ:u:t̪on (H EA: 10a)
huʔ:u:t̪on
||huʔ:uč=t̪on||
/huʔ:u:=t̪on/
face=LOC
'in front of'

If the counterexample with 'face' from (38) is set aside, the clitics discussed thus far are like verbal affixes in their participating in word-internal sandhi rules when bound to verbs; however, they are unlike verbal affixes in their being able to combine with other word classes with which they do not obligatorily participate in sandhi rules. This distribution in itself sets them apart from affixes and strengthens the case for a separate clitic category.

There is another class of clitics within Southern Pomo, some of which can be treated as clitics only on the basis of phonological considerations. These clitics do not participate in any word-internal sandhi rules. Zwicky divides clitics into two broad classes: simple clitics and special clitics (1977: 5–6). Simple clitics are those which are merely phonologically reduced variants of full words and show no special semantics or syntax (e.g., the

[=l] allomorph of *will* ~ *shall* in English which carries the same meaning as the full forms); special clitics do not necessarily represent reduced forms of full words and can show specialized semantic and syntactic properties.[43] The clitics discussed thus far all qualify as special clitics (a claim that is bolstered in the subsequent discussion), but there is another set of phonological words in Southern Pomo that are astride the boundary between special and simple clitics: they show special phonological behavior at times that identifies them as bound morphemes; they may also stand alone or at the head of breath-group and have bound morphemes added to them.

The four most common morphemes which fall into this clitic class are *wa* ~ *=(ʔ)wa* COP.EVIDENTIAL, *ka* ~ *(ʔ)ka* INTERROGATIVE, *yo* ~ *=(ʔ)yo* AUXILLIARY, *t̪i* ~ *=t̪i* INCHOATIVE. The enclitic *=:met̪̓* 'like' might be added to this list, but the evidence of its ability to surface as a free phonological word is not as strong; however, its status as a clitic is predicated upon similar phonological criteria to those invoked for *wa* ~ *=(ʔ)wa*, *ka* ~ *(ʔ)ka*, and *yo* ~ *=(ʔ)yo*.

The first three of these morphemes are problematic because the glottal stop that may surface before the [wa], [ka], and [yo] was almost surely a separate morpheme in the past, and an analysis for this glottal stop's synchronic status as a separate morpheme when it precedes [wa] has been put forward by Oswalt (1978: 14). They are treated as single morphemes which each have at least one allomorph that descends from two morphemes throughout the rest of this section.[44]

These morphemes can stand alone (and have affixes and enclitics added to them) or they may bind to a preceding morpheme. Crucially, though, they need not be in different positions depending on whether or not they are bound. It is only through one phonological pattern that they can be identified as having enclitic allomorphs: when *wa*, *ka*, and *yo* come immediately after a vowel-final morpheme (without any pause), they surface as *=ʔwa* *=ʔka* and *=ʔyo*. When they come after a vowel-final morpheme but are not bound to it, they are not preceded by the glottal stop. There is no semantic difference between the free forms and the encliticized forms. Thus in the case of texts where there is no surviving audio record, the presence or absence of a glottal stop before one of these morphemes when they follow a vowel-final morpheme is the best evidence of clitic-hood.

Examples (39)–(44) provide attested illustrations of each of these grammatical words as both clitics and free morphemes (to which other morphemes may be bound). The morphemes under discussion are in bold and underlined.

(39) *=ʔwa* after a vowel-final word

ma?[:]ék̓oʔwáʔa (H ms.)

*maʔ:ek̓o**ʔwa**ʔa*

/maʔ:e=k̓o=ʔwa=ʔa/

father=COM=COP.EVID=1SG.AGT

'I have a father'

(40) *wa* after a vowel-final word

ham:u wa mahčuk̓unčon [. . .] ʔam:a k^{h}aṭ:ič̓aw hwalak^{h}:et̪^{h}ot̪̓ (H EA: 30a)

*ham:u **wa** mahčuk̓unčon ʔam:a k^{h}aṭ:ič̓aw hwalak^{h}:et̪^{h}ot̪̓*

/ham:u	wa	mahčuk̓un-čon	ʔam:a	k^{h}aṭ:ič̓aw	hw-ala-k^{h}:e=t̪^{h}ot̪̓/
3SG	COP.EVID	they-PAT	thing	bad	go-DIR-FUT=NEG

'so there won't be bad luck come down to them'

(41) *=ʔka* after a vowel-final word

ham:uʔkaʔmaʔt̪o he:menin (H EA: 13a)

*ham:u**ʔka**ʔmaʔt̪o he:menin*

/ham:u=ʔka=ʔma=ʔt̪o	he:menin-Ø/
3SG=INTER=2SG.AGT=1SG.PAT	how.do-PFV

'how is it that you never told me about that'

(42) *ka* after a vowel-final word

hé:meni:t̪i kaʔma k^{h}aʔbéʔwan ban:éduy (H ms.)

*he:meni:t̪i **ka**ʔma k^{h}aʔbeʔwan ban:eduy*

/he:meni:-t̪i	ka=ʔma	k^{h}aʔbe=ʔwan	ban:e-duy-Ø/
how.do-INTENT	INTER=2SG.AGT	rock=DET.OBJ	throw.non-long.obj.-DIR-PFV

'why did you throw the rock away[?]'

(43) *=ʔyo* after a vowel-final word

bút̪:eʔyómt̪o [ʔ]ahčáči[y] (H ms.)

*but̪:e**ʔyo**mt̪o ʔahčačiy*

/buṯ:e=ʔyo=mṯo ʔahčačiy-Ø/[45]
when=AUX=2SG.PAT awake-PFV
'when did you wake up'

(44) *yo* after a vowel-final word
ha:miní:li yódo miy[:]aṯ[=ṭ(ʰ)]kʰan bíʔdu čóhšin (H I: 1)
ha:mini:li ***yo****do miy:aṭʰkʰan biʔdu čohšin*
/ha:mini-:li yo-do miy:a-ṭʰkʰan-Ø biʔdu čohšin-Ø/
and.then-D.SEQ AUX-QUOT 3-spouse-AGT acorn pound-PFV
'Then, it is said, his wife was pounding acorns[.]'

These morphemes are treated as clitics at times (and therefore as a part of larger phonological words) because they show synchronic phonological alternations in the realization of segments (in these cases the glottal stop) *only* when bound to vowel-final morphemes. Each of these morphemes has a variant which may stand alone without the glottal stop surfacing even after a vowel-final preceding word, which supports such variants being analyzed as phonological and grammatical words in their own right and not clitics.

The clitic *=:meṭ́* 'like' shows a similar pattern to that seen for the clitics already discussed, namely, its first segment, /:/, can only surface after a vowel-final morpheme. Another clitic already mentioned, *=ṯi* INCHOATIVE, does not undergo or trigger any phonological changes, but it is consistently written as part of the preceding word when it occurs with no following clitics. It can also stand separately from any host word and carry its own bound morphemes. Of the non-case-marking clitics discussed thus far, *ṯi* ~ *=ṯi* is the least like a special clitic and the most like a simple clitic in showing little real variation between its bound and free forms and no special behaviors like those enumerated in the following discussion.

(3) Ordering test

Many of the clitics introduced thus far are enclitics which might be termed postpositions in an analysis less concerned with clitic-hood. Zwicky (1985) identifies strict ordering of a morpheme under consideration for clitic-hood with regard to "adjacent morphemes" as opposed to "free order" as one important piece of evidence in favor of clitic-hood, and many Southern Pomo clitics conform to this observation. The case-marking enclitics and additional clitics indicating location and direction may combine with one another on one word; however, they do so in a particular order. Perhaps the clearest example of this ordering is seen with *=li* 'at' + *=kʰač* 'ward' into *=nhkʰay* [ŋ͡ŋ̊kʰaj] 'toward' as in example (45):

(45) Combination of *=li* 'at' + *=kʰač* 'ward'
ʔahčanhkʰay (H EA: 9a)
ʔahčanhkʰay
||ʔahča=li=kʰač||
/ʔahča=nhkʰay/
house=ward
'[to] home'

The two encliticized morphemes in the combination in (45) cannot be reversed. When they are combined with the enclitic *=t̪on* LOCATIVE, they likewise must be in the fixed order *=t̪onhkʰay* [ˈt̪oŋ͡ŋ̊kʰaj] (where the final of *=t̪on* LOCATIVE either completely merges with the nasal allomorph of *=li* 'at' or the final nasal of *=t̪on* descends from *=li*), as in (46) following:

(46) Combination of *=t̪on* LOC + *=li* 'at' + *=kʰač* 'ward'
ʔaw:it̪onhkʰay (H EA: 1b)
ʔaw:it̪onhkʰay
||ʔaw:i=t̪on=li=kʰač||
/ʔaw:i=t̪onhkʰay/
1SG.OBL=toward
'towards me'

Thus far, in addition to the clitics like *=(ʔ)wa*, a specific type of case-marking special clitic has been discussed, namely, that of the type of morpheme Dixon suggests be called "non-inflectional case markers" (Dixon 2010a: 225).[46] There are, however, other clitics in the language, including one subset with very specific ordering properties.

As previously mentioned, Zwicky advocates a distinction between "special" and "simple" clitics (1977: 5–6). In Southern Pomo most clitics appear to be special clitics; however, there is an important division within this group. The case-marking enclitics (a.k.a. 'non-inflectional case markers') discussed thus far are not merely phonologically reduced forms of otherwise attested free phonological words in the language. This is not the case for the pronominal enclitics, which makes them more like the clitics *=(ʔ) wa*, *=(ʔ)ka*, and *=(ʔ)yo* with their unbound variants *wa*, *ka*, and *yo*.

Southern Pomo does not mark person on the verb, and it has a full complement of pronouns which are free phonological words (see §2.8.2 for a complete list). With a few possible exceptions (which might be the result of insufficient data), all pronouns have encliticized versions. These forms, however, are easily related to the full forms, and in that respect they superficially resemble the simple clitics of Zwicky's analysis. However, they do not show the same ordering as seen in clauses with full pronouns.

SOV is the expected ordering when two core arguments (as full NPs) are present in a clause, as seen in (47):

(47) Canonical word order with two full NPs in a clause
k^{h}áʔbek^{h}áč^{h}yey dó:lon čóh:on (H VI: 1)
k^{h}aʔbek^{h}ač̓yey do:lon čoh:on
/k^{h}aʔbek^{h}ač̓=yey do:lon čoh:on-Ø/
raptor.species=AGT bobcat marry-PFV
'Fish Hawk[47] married Wildcat'

The ordering of pronominal enclitics relative to one another when two come together is OS (VOS when they are attached to a verb), the opposite of the order seen in clauses with full NPs, as in (48) following:

(48) OS ordering of pronominal enclitics when combined
mihyanák^{h}:eʔwamt̪áʔa (H VIII: 6)
mihyanak^{h}:eʔwamt̪aʔa
/mihyana-k^{h}:e=ʔwa=mt̪a=ʔa/
kill-FUT=COP.EVID =2SG.PAT=1SG.AGT
'I'm going to kill you'

(4) Distribution

Whereas affixes in Southern Pomo are attached to words, clitics may be attached to larger constituents. The Southern Pomo special clitics mentioned thus far, case-marking enclitics, *=(ʔ)wa* type and pronominal enclitics, can be distinguished from affixes by their distributional qualities, though the clitics do not share all of the same distributional qualities with each other. Case-marking enclitics attach at the phrasal level, whereas affixes attach to stems.[48] Example (49) contains the PATIENT case enclitic attaching to multi-word NP (with a relative clause), and example (50) contains the INSTRUMENTAL case enclitic attached to a two-word phrase.

(49) Case-marking enclitic applied to phrasal constituent

mák:aċ ší:ba:t̪[ʰ]aw mát̪ʰ:i miṭ:í:čon [ʔ]uht̪éht̪ew (H IX: 8)

[mak:aċ ši:ba:t̪ʰaw mat̪ʰ:i miṭ:i]$_{NP}$*=:čon ʔuht̪eht̪ew*

/ma-k:a-ċ-Ø	ši:ba:t̪ʰaw	mat̪ʰ:i	miṭ:i=:čon	ʔuht̪eht̪e-w/
3C-mo.mo.-GS-AGT	poor	blind	one.lie=PAT	tell-PFV

'told their poor blind grandmother who was lying (there)'

(50) Case-marking enclitic applied to phrasal constituent

t̪[ʰ]a:na ʔakʰ:owi da:ṭʰow (H EA: 4a)

[t̪ʰa:na ʔakʰ:o]$_{NP}$*=wi da:ṭʰow*

/t̪ʰa:na	ʔakʰ:o=wi	da:ṭʰo-w/
hand	two=INSTR	scrape-pfv

'scrapes it off with both hands'

The distributional qualities exemplified—phrase-end encliticization—apply only to the case-marking clitics. The pronominal enclitics show very different behavior; they often appear to attach as second-position enclitcs (a.k.a. Wackernagel enclitics), especially in combination with *=(ʔ)wa* COP. EVIDENTIAL, and *=(ʔ)ka* INTERROGATIVE. However, it is not yet clear why these clitics are sometimes attached to the first word (of any word class) in a clause and sometimes to another word later in the clause (often a final verb). Thus far no appeal to semantics, verb transitivity, or any other reasonable criteria has elucidated the reasons for the varying patterns. Examples (51)–(57) show the pronominal enclitics (often in combination with the COP.EVID and INTER enclitics) attaching to a variety of word classes in various positions. The morphemes under discussion are in bold and underlined.

(51a) Pronominal enclitics attached to verbs
huw:aŋhk^{h}ét̪^{h}ot̪wáʔya (H V: 34)
*huw:anhk^{h}:et̪^{h}ot̪wa**<u>ʔya</u>***
||hu:w-ad-k^{h}:e=t̪^{h}ot̪=ʔwa=ʔya||
/huw:-anh-k^{h}:e=t̪^{h}ot̪=wa=ʔya/
go-DIR-FUT=NEG=COP.EVID=1PL.AGT
'we will not come'

(51b) huʔ[:]úk^{h}be [ʔ]ihna:káʔya (H VI: 8)
*huʔ:uk^{h}be ʔihna:ka**<u>ʔya</u>***
||huʔ:uč+k^{h}aʔbe hi-hnat̪-ka=ʔya||
/huʔ:uk^{h}be ʔihna:-ka=ʔya/
eye.rock try-CAUS=1PL.AGT
'let's try (to make) eyeballs'

(52a) Pronominal enclitics attached to nouns
č̓ú:ʔuʔ( )waʔya šuhnamhúk^{h}:e (H VIII: 1)
*č̓u:ʔuʔwa**<u>ʔya</u>** šuhnamhuk^{h}:e*
||č̓u:ʔu=ʔwa=ʔya šu-hnat̪-mhuč̓-k^{h}:e||
/č̓u:ʔu=ʔwa=ʔya šuhna-mhu-k^{h}:e/
arrow=COP.EVID=1PL.AGT try.by.pull=RECIP-FUT
'We'll try each other out in pulling arrows.'

(52b) nup[^{h}]:éʔ( )waʔya yók^{h}:e (H V: 37)
*nup^{h}:eʔwa**<u>ʔya</u>** yok^{h}:e*
/nup^{h}:e=ʔwa=ʔya yo-k^{h}:e/
striped.skunk=COP.EVID=1PL.AGT AUX-FUT
'We will be skunks[.]'

(53) Pronominal enclitic attached to a free pronoun
[ʔ]á:maʔwáʔyan béhše k̓óʔdi čuh:uká:t̪^{h}ot̪ (H V: 36)
*ʔa:maʔwa**<u>ʔyan</u>** behše k̓oʔdi čuh:uka:t̪^{h}ot̪*

/ʔa:ma=ʔwa=ʔyan behše ḱoʔdi čuh:u-ka-:=t̪ʰoṭ/[49]
2SG.AGT=COP.EVID=1PL.AGT meat good eat-CAUS-?=NEG
'You (are the one who) didn't let us eat good meat.'

(54) Pronominal enclitic attached to a kinship term
[ʔ]ákʰ:o má:ṭ́ikiyačó:ḱoʔwáʔa (H ms.)
*ʔakʰ:o ma:ṭ́ikiyačo:ḱoʔwa**ʔa***
/ʔakʰ:o ma-:ṭ́i-ki-ya-čo:=ḱo=ʔwa=ʔa/
two 3C-younger.sibling-GS-PL-OBL=COM=COP.EVID=1SG.AGT
'I have 2 y[ounger] siblings'

(55a) Pronominal enclitic attached to adverbs (manner, time, location)
sí:ṭoʔwáʔya ho:líkʰ:e (H V: 3)
*si:ṭoʔwa**ʔya** ho:likʰ:e*
/si:ṭo=ʔwa=ʔya ho:li-kʰ:e/
immediately=COP.EVID=1PL.AGT leave-FUT
'right now we'll go'

(55b) [ʔ]it̪[ʰ]:ín( )waʔya daʔṭ̪amhúkʰ:e (H VIII: 1)
*ʔit̪ʰ:inwa**ʔya** daʔṭ̪amhukʰ:e*
/ʔit̪ʰ:in=waʔya daʔṭ̪a-mhu-kʰ:e/
early=COP.EVID=1PL.AGT encounter-RECIP-FUT
'We will meet each other early.'

(55c) ma:liʔkaʔya das:ékʰ:e (H V: 11)
*ma:liʔka**ʔya** das:ekʰ:e*
/ma:li=ʔka=ʔya das:e-kʰ:e/
here=INTER=1PL.AGT wash-FUT
'shall we wash it here?'

(56a) Pronominal enclitic attached to numerals
[ʔ]akʰ:óhčaʔ( )waʔya čoh:ókʰ:e (H VI: 11)
*ʔakʰ:ohčaʔwa**ʔya** čoh:okʰ:e*
/ʔakʰ:o=hča=ʔwa=ʔya čoh:o-kʰ:e/
two=COLL=COP.EVID=1PL.AGT marry-FUT
'We'll both marry him.'

(56b) t̪ʰé: čʼá:hmaʔ( )wáʔya bat̪:íkʰ:e (H VI: 13)

*t̪ʰe: čʼa:hmaʔwa**ʔya** bat̪:ikʰ:e*

/t̪ʰe: čʼa:=hma=ʔwa=ʔya bat̪:i-kʰ:e/

no one=place=COP.EVID=1PL.AGT lie.PL-FUT

'No, we'll lie in one place.'

(57) Pronominal enclitic attached to pro-verb

ha:mini(:)p[ʰ]iʔwáʔ( )maya das:ekʰ:e (H V: 10)

*ha:minipʰiʔwa**ʔmaya** das:ekʰ:e*

/ha:mini-pʰi=ʔwa=ʔmaya das:e-kʰ:e/

and.then-S.IRR=COP.EVID=2PL.AGT wash-FUT

'After having done so, you will wash (them).'

The presence of a clitic is the defining feature of phonological words which are not also single grammatical words, and it is therefore imperative that clitics be identified correctly. In this study Southern Pomo clitics are analyzed as morphemes which are neither affixes nor independent phonological words; rather, they are phonologically dependent grammatical words. They can be distinguished from affixes by their ability to attach phonologically to words of various word classes at the phrasal level; they can be distinguished from phonological words by their participation in affix-like phonological alternations and unusual distributional properties. There are, however, differences among clitics as to their phonological and syntactic behavior. In reality Southern Pomo clitics are defined more by what they are not (free phonological words or affixes) than what they are.

This makes sense, of course, as the class of grammatical words that fit with any of the previously stated criteria for clitic-hood in the language descend from varied sources on the grammaticization path toward ever more grammatical usages. And it is not uncommon cross-linguistically to find sets of clitics within a language that behave in different ways. Sm'algyax, a polysynthetic Tsimshianic language, has clitics which are distinguished from words and affixes but may also be sorted into different types within the clitic class (Stebbins 2003).

Earlier in this section, in table 19, the three types of word in Southern Pomo were charted. Clitics (type 2) do not conform to any neat parame-

Table 20. Southern Pomo clitic types on a cline between affixes and free words

Affixes	**← Special clitics**	**Special/Simple**	**Simple clitics →**	**Free words**
-w PF	*=k̓o* COM	*=(ʔ)wa* COP.EVID	*=(ʔ)ya* 1PL.AGT	*ʔe:wen* 'fast'
-ya PL	*=yey* AGT	*=t̪i* INCHOATIVE	*=kʰma:yow* 'after'	*nupʰ:e* 'striped skunk'

ters, as has been demonstrated throughout this section. They are best seen as existing on a cline between affixes and clitic-less phonological words. Within this border region, some clitics are clearly more affix-like and like prototypical special clitics (and presumably well on their way to becoming affixes), some are more like stand-alone words and therefore like prototypical simple clitics, and most are in between. Table 20 summarizes this with two representative examples of each major morpheme class (note that none of the clitics is as close to simple clitic status as English [=m] for 'am', [=v] for 'have', etc.).

Only a sample of the morphemes which fit the criteria for clitic-hood in Southern Pomo has been introduced in this section. But the criteria for the remainder are the same. In the case of some enclitics, it is difficult to tell whether they are clitics or affixes when applied to certain word classes (especially the pronouns and kinship terms), and these difficulties are addressed in the relevant sections. Henceforth, any morpheme preceded by = in the glosses has been analyzed as a clitic because there is phonological, ordering, or distributional evidence for such an analysis.

2.6. MAJOR PHONOLOGICAL AND MORPHOPHONEMIC PROCESSES

This section focuses on those phonological alternations that apply to large parts of the lexicon; alternations that are restricted to one or two morphemes (e.g., the singular imperative) are covered more fully under later discussion of the individual morphemes. Each process is covered separately, but some are obviously related (e.g., deletion and assimilation often follow on the heels of syncope). Unlike both neighboring Kashaya and Central Pomo, Southern Pomo preserves glottal-initial syllables in both verbs and nouns (Kashaya only does so for nouns; Central Pomo has lost them in both word classes). If Southern Pomo is by far the most phonologically conservative Pomoan language in its handling of the first two syllables of a word, it is also by far the least conservative of any Pomoan language in its handling of final consonants and syllables beyond the first two of the word, and it is in this part of the Southern Pomo word that many of the most productive (and, perhaps, unusual) phonological alternations are to be observed.

2.6.1. Vowel Harmony

Southern Pomo displays regressive vowel lowering in which [+high] vowels in the initial syllable are lowered on the basis of the vowel of the second syllable from the left. In the first type, the vowel /i/ in an initial syllable becomes [e] when the vowel of the second syllable is /e/.

/i/ → [e] / #C_C(C)e(C)

This applies to verbs, pronouns, and kinship terms, word classes which have stems with synchronically segmentable roots and affixes, and at some point in the past it applied to all disyllabic stems, including common nouns for which there are no synchronic phonological alternations to indicate that the harmony process is still productive.[50] Examples of the three word classes for which this harmony rule still results in allomorphic alternations are given in examples (58)–(60).

(58) The verbal prefix *pʰi-* 'by sight' with and without vowel lowering

pʰiʔt̪ʼa- (W: OF)
||pʰi-ʔt̪ʼa-||
'to look (like)'

pʰey:e- (W: OF)
||pʰi-y:e-||
'to look for'

(59) The pronominal root *mi*-2SG- with and without vowel lowering

mi:t̯o (W: OF)
||mi:-t̯o||
2SG-PAT
'you'

me:kʰe (H ms: EA)
me:kʰe
||mi:-:kʰe||
2SG-POSS
['your']

(60) The kinship prefix *miH*-2SG- with and without vowel lowering

midʔíki (H ms.)	méʔ[:]en (H ms.)
midʔiki	*meʔ:en*
||miH-di-ki-Ø||	||miH-ʔe-n||
/mi-dʔi-ki-Ø/	/me-ʔ:e-n/
2-older.sister-GS-AGT	2-father-PAT
'your o[lder] sis[ter]'	'your father'

In the kinship terms there is at least one peculiar example of this vowel lowering alternation applying incompletely, a phenomenon that might be explained as preservation of the root, as in (61).

(61) /i/ → [e] avoidance in kinship root

[ʔ]a:diké:kʰe (H ms.)
ʔa:dike:kʰe
||ʔa:-di-ki-:kʰe||
/ʔa:-di-ke-:kʰe/
1-older.sister-GS-POSS
'my o[lder] sis[ter's]'

This process of vowel lowering applied in the distant past to common nouns—compare Southern Pomo *behše* '(deer) meat' with Kashaya *bihše* 'deer'—and it is shared to an extent with the geographically distant Northeastern Pomo language (McLendon 1973: 43).[51] However, this specific change applied completely only to Southern Pomo (Oswalt 1976a: 17). As already mentioned, there is no synchronic allomorphy in common nouns to allow modern speakers to uncover the older vowel. As such, there is no evidence to support an analysis of this vowel harmony rule as a productive part of nominal phonology.

There are two additional types of productive vowel lowering alternations: an assimilatory one and another that is dissimilatory in nature. The first involves /u/ becoming [o] in an initial syllable when the vowel of the second syllable from the left is [o].

/u/ → [o] / #C_C(C)o(C)

The preceding rule can be combined with the previous vowel-lowering rule, but it can be established with some certainty that the two alternations arose at separate times in the language. The change of /u/ → [o] to assimilate to an /o/ in the following syllable is quite an old alternation and is shared with Southern Pomo by Kashaya Pomo, Northeastern Pomo, and Eastern Pomo, and is therefore reconstructed as part of Proto Pomo phonology; however, the change of /i/ → [e] to assimilate to an /e/ in the following syllable is not shared by Eastern Pomo and Kashaya Pomo, and was only applied consistently across the lexicon in Southern Pomo (Oswalt 1976a: 17).

The dissimilatory vowel lowering alternation applies when the vowel of the initial syllable in a verb is /u/ and the vowel of the second syllable from the left is /i/. When this occurs, the /u/ lowers to [o].

/u/ → [o] / #C_C(C)i(C)

This can only be analyzed as a productive alternation in verbs,[52] which have several prefixes with an underlying /u/ that surfaces as [o] according to the rules above. (There are no prefixes with rounded vowels in the kinship terms or pronouns.) Examples of both of these /u/ → [o] alternations are shown in (62a–63b) following.

(62a) Verbs with the prefixes *šu-* 'by pulling' and *du-* 'by finger' (H ms.)[53]
[čʰeʔ[:]et̯máywan] šuhkʰečí:le
čʰeʔ:et̯maywan šuhkʰeči:le

||čʰeʔ:eṱmay=wan šu-hkʰe-čič̓-le||
/čʰeʔ:eṱmay=wan šu-hkʰe-či:-le/
basket=DET by.pulling-move-REFL-PL.IMP
['Pull the basket closer to yourselves!']

(62b) duhkʰeʔč̓in (H ms.)
duhkʰeʔč̓in
||du-hkʰe-čič̓-Vn||
/du-hkʰe-ʔč̓-in/
by.finger-move-REFL-SG.IMP
'move it toward yourself'

(63a) *šu-* 'by pulling' and *du-* 'by finger' surfacing as *šo-* and *do-*
/$oʔdiw/ (O D: ED)
šoʔdiw
||šu-ʔdi-w||
/šo-ʔdi-w/
by.pulling-move.one-PFV
'to go bring s[ome]o[ne]'

(63b) dóṭ:ow (H V: 11)
doṭ:ow
||du-ṭ:o-w||
/do-ṭ:o-w/
by.finger-peel-PFV
'skinned'

The /u/-lowering rules do not apply synchronically outside the verbs of Southern Pomo; this type of vowel lowering is a distributional fact elsewhere in the lexicon, but it is one with no synchronic alternations to allow speakers to know which, if any, of the initial syllables of non-verbs with /o/ might originally have had /u/. One possible example of fossilized nominal evidence for this rule is provided by three reptile terms: *mus:a:la* 'snake' (general term), *muṱʰ:u:nu* 'lizard' (general term), and *mohṱʰi* 'rattlesnake'. Though there is no solid evidence at this time, it seems possible that the initial syllables in all three words might descend from a single morpheme (perhaps a compounding element meaning something like 'serpentine'). If this is true, the initial syllable of 'rattlesnake' would represent an allomorph with vowel lowering according to the pattern established in verbs.[54]

There is also one well-documented case of a borrowed word being affected by /u/ lowering in recent times. The Russian word for 'bottle' entered Kashaya Pomo as *puṱilka* and was perceived as a monomorphemic word in that language. Southern Pomo borrowed Kashaya *puṱilka* and changed it to *p^h^oṱ:ilka*, a word which Oswalt reports was interpreted as both a verb and a noun and which was parsed by native speakers as containing three morphemes: (1) the instrumental prefix *p^h^u-* 'by wind or blowing'; (2) a root *-ṱ:il-* 'the sound of glass breaking'; and (3) *-ka* the INFERENTIAL evidential suffix. Oswalt records that the word could thus be understood to mean 'it must have blown over and broken' (1971a: 189). What is most interesting, however, is the fact that the dissimilatory /u/-lowering rule resulted in the *p^h^o-* allomorph of the prefix ||p^h^u-||, a change that can be dated to within a few decades of the Russians' landing in Pomoan territory. Such a recent application of the vowel-lowering rule supports an analysis of this alternation as a productive one in the language (at least during the last generations of monolingual speakers).

2.6.1.1. *Vowel Harmony across Glottals*

There is another phonological phenomenon relating to vowel harmony in the language: monomorphemic stems with /ʔ/ as their second consonant (the pseudo-consonant /:/ may precede or follow the glottal stop in this position) must have the same vowel quality in the syllables preceding and following the glottal stop, as in example (64).

(64) Vowel harmony across /ʔ/ in monomorphemic stems

čiʔ:i-	'to do, to make'
heʔ:e	'(head) hair'
baʔ:ay	'woman'
hoʔ:o	'tooth'
ču:ʔu	'arrow'

This pattern is not true of polymorphemic stems like the kinship term in (65):

(65) Lack of vowel harmony across /ʔ/ in polymorphemic stem
máʔ[:]en
maʔ:en
||maH-ʔe-n||
/ma-ʔ:e-n/
3C-father-PAT
'his fa[ther]'

Compare example (65), which shows that cross-glottal vowel harmony does not operate across a morpheme boundary, with the form *meʔ:en* ||miH-ʔe-n|| 2-father-PAT 'your father', which shows the /i/→[e] lowering rule does apply across morpheme boundaries.

2.6.1.2. Assimilatory Variants of the Epenthetic/Default Vowel

The epenthetic/default vowel of Southern Pomo is not properly an example of vowel harmony, but one of its allomorphs might be analyzed as an instance of vowel harmony, and the other allomorphs have a distribution that hints at assimilatory origins. Southern Pomo shares with Kashaya Pomo a most unusual epenthetic vowel. Indeed, the predictable distributions of the peculiar variants of this vowel (nearly identical in both languages) have led to Buckley's terming it the "crazy rule" (Buckley 2004). This vowel is here labeled as epenthetic or default because it is not clear that all its occurrences are synchronic instances of epenthesis. Oswalt distinguishes between a vowel, which he symbolizes as *v̂*, that only surfaces after consonants according to the distributions laid out in (i–iv) following, and an epenthetic vowel that only follows patterns seen in (i) and (iv) (Oswalt 1976a: 20).

(i) ||V|| → [a] after /m/ and /ak/
[ʔ]ehkʰéman (H ms.)
ʔehkʰeman
||ʔehkʰe-m-Vn|| → [ʔeh.ˈkʰe.man]
/ʔehkʰe-m-an/

move.body-DIR-SG.IMP
'move across!'

[ʔ]ekʰ:ékan (H ms.)
ʔekʰ:ekan
||ʔekʰ:e-ak-Vn|| → [ʔek.ˈkʰe.kan]
/ʔekʰ:e-k-an/
move.body-DIR-SG.IMP
'move out! (sp[eaker] in[side])'

(ii) ||V|| → [u] after /d/
[ʔ]ekʰ:édun (H ms.)
ʔekʰ:edun
||ʔekʰ:e-ad-Vn|| → [ʔek.ˈkʰe.dun]
/ʔekʰ:e-d-un/
move-DIR-SG.IMP
'move along, toward me!'

(iii) ||V|| → [o] after /ok/
[ʔ]ekʰ:ékon (H ms.)
ʔekʰ:ekon
||ʔekʰ:e-ok-Vn|| → [ʔek.ˈkʰe.kon]
/ʔekʰ:e-k-on/
move-DIR-SG.IMP
'move out (sp[eaker] out[side])'

(iv) ||V|| → [i] elsewhere
[ʔ]ekʰ:elméc̆̓in (H ms.)
ʔekʰ:elmec̆̓in
||ʔekʰ:e-alamec̆̓-Vn|| → [ˌʔek.kʰel.ˈme.ʧʼin]
/ʔekʰ:e-lmec̆̓-in/
move.body-DIR-SG.IMP
'move down from above!'

Suffixes which have an underlying ||V|| that surfaces according to (i–iv) include ||-Vn|| SINGULAR.IMPERATIVE and ||-Vn|| SAME.SUBJECT.SIMULTA-

NEOUS (these suffixes are homophonous but distributionally distinct: the former is restricted to main verbs; the latter is restricted to dependent verbs). Oswalt states that the epenthetic vowel that developed to break certain consonant clusters in Western Pomoan (a branch which includes Southern Pomo) and other Pomoan languages only surfaces according to (i) and (iv) (Oswalt 1976a: 20). However, this assertion is perhaps a diachronic truth that is not synchronically true in Southern Pomo. There are no doubt instances of [i] and [a] in the language that can be traced back to an earlier epenthetic vowel (possible examples of which are discussed later in this section). But it is also possibly the case that all modern instances of an epenthetic vowel do follow (i–iv), and ||V|| would therefore be the epenthetic vowel in a synchronic description of Southern Pomo. Hence there are two possible analyses: (1) ||V|| is the retention of an older vowel that is now morpheme-specific and can only surface after consonants as one of four vowel qualities on the basis of preceding phonemes; or (2) ||V|| is really the default epenthetic vowel and is not morpheme-specific.

The CONDITIONAL is a good example of a morpheme that might be analyzed as either vowel-initial (and therefore as having ||V|| as its first underlying segment) or not vowel-initial, in which case the vowel which precedes it when it is suffixed to a consonant-final stem is purely epenthetic. In (a–e) following, all allomorphs of this morpheme in my database are listed with examples (others possibly await discovery):

(a) /-o:ba/ after an underlying ||-ok-|| (which surfaces as /-k-/)
[ʔ]ekʰ:ekó:baʔwaʔmáya (H ms.)
ʔekʰ:e-k-o:ba=ʔwa=ʔmaya
/ʔekʰ:e-k-o:ba=ʔwa=ʔmaya/
move.body-DIR-COND=COP.EVID=2PL.AGT
'ye ought to move out!'

(b) /-a:ba/ after /m/
duhsuma:ba (H EA: 46a)
duhsuma:ba
/duhsum-a:ba/
quit-COND
'he would stop'

čoh:omá:ba (H VI: 13)
čoh:oma:ba
/čoh:om-a:ba/
marry-COND
'ought to marry him'

(c) /-u:ba/ after /d/
[ʔ]á:šimʔdú:ba (H II: 4)
ʔa:šimʔdu:ba
/ʔa:ši-mʔd-u:ba/ or /ʔa:ši-mʔdu-:ba/[55]
name-?-COND name-?-COND
'he should name'

(d) /-i:ba/ after other consonants
[ʔ]ahnaṱí:baʔkáʔma (H ms.)
ʔahnaṱi:baʔkaʔma
/ʔa-hnaṱ-i:ba=ʔka=ʔma/
with.leg-try-COND=INTER=2SG.AGT
'are you going to try it w[ith] heel?'

(e) /-:ba/ after vowels
mi:ṭí:ba (H ms.)
mi:ṭi-:ba
/mi:ṭi-:ba/
lie-COND
'ought to lie [down]'

Oswalt lists the reconstructed morpheme from which the Southern Pomo conditional suffix descends as *-..ba... (the dots represent additional, unknown phonological material); he lists the Southern Pomo reflex as *-:ba* (i.e., not vowel-initial), but the reflex of the same morpheme in Kashaya is given with an initial *v̂-*, his symbol for what is herein written as ||V|| (Oswalt 1976a: 25). The allomorphs of the Southern Pomo conditional listed here need only add an instance of [-a:ba] after /ak/ in order to show the same distribution as the ||V|| (as seen in the singular imperative), and this missing form is surely an accidental gap in the database from which these examples were drawn. If Oswalt considers the Southern Pomo conditional to be without an initial vowel, ||-:ba|| instead of ||-V:ba||, then the epenthetic vowel of Southern Pomo would be identical to ||V|| if his segmenting of the morpheme is correct.

This grammar chooses a middle path: the likelihood that the ||V|| of several morphemes is really an epenthetic vowel and that other instances of otherwise unexpected vowels conforming to the peculiar surface variants of ||V|| (e.g., [a] after /m/ or /ak/ and [u] after /d/) might also be epenthetic is not denied; however, those suffixes which have consonantal segments that may be separated from the final consonant of a preceding morpheme by ||V|| are treated as though ||V|| is an inseparable initial segment, one that counts toward the total number of underlying syllables in a word.

The question of whether ||V|| is an epenthetic vowel or a peculiar vowel attached only to particular morphemes is less important than the recognition that several final-position morphemes (TAM suffixes on main verbs and switch-reference suffixes on dependent verbs) have a vowel the quality of which is entirely predictable on the basis of preceding underlying phonemes with little sound phonetic motivation for the variants.[56]

An understanding of the surface variants of ||V|| is critical in deciphering suffixes that might otherwise surface as homophones, like the previous examples with /-k-/ in ||ʔek^{h}:e-ok-Vn|| → *ʔek^{h}:ekon* 'move out! (speaker outside)' and ||ʔek^{h}:e-ak-Vn|| → *ʔek^{h}:ekan* 'move out! (speaker inside)'. This vowel interacts with other sound changes to produce otherwise inexplicable allomorphy, the most unusual of which involves the free variation between [l] and [m] in stem-final position before a vowel-initial suffix (covered later in the discussion on consonant allomorphy).

Outside final position suffixes like those already discussed, there are several affixes and roots which have vowels that might have arisen through epenthesis. Several irregular verbs, such as *ʔahṯi-* 'to put foot' and *ʔahp^{h}i-* 'to carry', seem to have developed their root vowel through epenthesis for it only surfaces before consonant-initial suffixes, such as *-mač-*'in from outside' and *-čič̓-* 'start'[57] (e.g., *ʔahṯi-may* 'put foot-in from outside' and *ʔahp^{h}i-čiy* 'carry-to start'), but does not surface before vowel-initial suffixes, such as *-ala-* and *-akač-* (e.g., *haṯ:-ala-w* 'put foot-down-PFV' and *ʔap^{h}:-akay*

Table 21. Sample of verb stem allomorphy of glottal-initial verb stems[58]

	Underlying forms	||ha-hpʰi-|| 'to carry'	||ha-hča-|| 'to fly'	||ha-ht̪i-|| 'to put foot'	||hi-hkʰe-|| 'to move body'
1	Before C-initial suffixes	/ʔa-hpʰi-/	/ʔa-hča-/	/ʔa-ht̪i-/	/ʔe-hkʰe-/
2	Before V-initial suffixes (e.g., *-aywač-* 'against' and those with /d/)	/ʔa-pʰ:e-/	/ha-č:a-/	/ha-t̪:-/	/ʔe-kʰ:e-/
3	Before other V-initial suffixes	/ʔa-pʰ:-/	/ha-č:a-/	/ha-t̪:-/	/ʔe-kʰ:e-/

'carry-up').[59] As is discussed in the section on vowel deletion (§2.6.2), if [i] were historically present in all forms of the roots of these stems, the expected allomorphs of the vowel-initial suffixes *-ala-* and *-akač-* would begin with [l] and [k] respectively.

Southern Pomo verb stems show a great deal of allomorphy, some of which is partially phonologically predictable, some of which is morphologically conditioned, and some of which cannot be predicted on any level. The verb stems for *ʔahpʰi-* 'to carry', *ʔehkʰe-* 'to move body', *ʔahča-* 'to fly', and *ʔaht̪i-* 'to put the foot', which have been used throughout this section, are good examples of this complex allomorphy. Each of these verbs begins with glottal-initial syllables, which are actually the instrumental prefixes ||ha-|| 'by leg, arm, wing' (in 'to carry', 'to fly', and 'to put the foot') and ||hi-|| 'with the body' (in 'to move body'). Table 21 gives all of the stem allomorphs for these verbs together with a simplified explanation of their distribution. Note that the forms in || || given thus far for these verbs have been a simplification (the prefixes have not been segmented off the verbs and the allomorphs in each example have been treated as underlying), but they are fully segmented in the table and in all examples hereafter.

Some verb roots have vowel-less allomorphs, as seen for 'to carry' and 'to put foot' in table 21. As has already been mentioned, the vowel [i] of the root allomorphs of 'to carry' and 'to put foot' found before consonant-initial suffixes almost surely originated as an epenthetic vowel. As seen in the distribution of ||V||, [i] is the default (or at least the surface variant with the widest distribution), and Buckley treats [i] as the default vowel for epenthesis in Kashaya (subject to similar alternations seen in Southern

Pomo ||V||) (1994: 32–34, 103–5). However, vowel epenthesis in roots is rejected as a synchronic analysis because speakers must learn unpredictable verb stem allomorphy (such as the variant with [e] as the root vowel in 'to carry') that cannot be explained with epenthesis whether or not a subset of otherwise irregular verbs can be explained through historic epenthesis, and there is no compelling reason to believe that Southern Pomo speakers learn the [i] as anything more than an integral part of the root, albeit an irregular one on par with the other irregularities found in verbs.

2.6.1.3. Vowel Assimilation after /ok/

The foregoing discussion of the default vowel only relates to vowel harmony in that one variant of ||V||, specifically [o], is conditioned by a preceding /ok/. The factual evidential suffix ||-a|| has three allomorphs,[60] one of which patterns like ||V|| in that its vowel also surfaces as [o] after /ok/:

i. ||-a|| → [-wa] /V__
ii. ||-a|| → [-o] / /ok/__
iii. ||-a|| → [-a] elsewhere

At first blush the [o] variants of the default vowel ||V|| and the factual evidential suffix ||-a|| appear to be examples of vowel assimilation across a consonant to a preceding vowel. The facts are more complex, however. This [o] allomorph has a wider distribution than has thus far been stated and actually occurs in at least three specific environments: (1) after verb stems ending in /-ok/ or /-ok̓/; (2) after directional suffixes which end in /-ok/; and (3) after the directional suffix ||-ok-|| 'out (speaker outside)', which has several allomorphs, all of which condition a following ||V|| or the factual evidential ||-a|| to surface as [o].

This last environment, that after the directional suffix for 'out (speaker outside)' is the most problematic. In Kashaya the cognates for the Southern Pomo suffixes ||-ok-|| 'out (speaker inside)' and ||-mok-|| 'in (speaker inside)' have /a/ rather than /o/ yet still condition a following default vowel to surface as [o]. Oswalt states that the Southern Pomo forms for these suffixes are *-ok-* and *-mok-* respectively, whereas he transcribes the Kashaya cognate forms as *-Xâoq-* and *-maoq-* (1976a: 23).[61] It is because these Kashaya forms cannot be analyzed as simply containing an underlying /ok/

within them that an analysis of the conditioning environment for [o] variants is more problematic than it is in Southern Pomo. Buckley handles this difficulty in Kashaya by positing an elegant analysis with an underlying [q^w] to which a following vowel assimilates in rounding, an analysis forcing the creation of an underlying phoneme that never surfaces anywhere in the language, which, though not an ideal solution, is necessitated by the fact that no other analysis works for Kashaya, and the [o] variants would otherwise therefore be unpredictable (1994: 105–13). The principal need for such an abstract analysis for this phenomenon in Kashaya is the lack of a rounded vowel in any surface realizations (and, in Buckley's analysis, any underlying representation) in the two directional suffixes that are cognate with Southern Pomo ||-ok-|| and ||-mok-||.

The situation in Southern Pomo is not quite as complex as in Kashaya, and there is therefore no need to posit an underlying rounded dorsal obstruent to deal with the rounded variants of ||V|| and ||-a||. However, the case of ||-ok-|| 'out (speaker outside)' is not quite as straightforward as that of ||-mok-|| 'in (speaker inside)'.[62] The vowel of this suffix is often deleted according to vowel deletion rules described later (§2.6.2). This suffix is therefore homophonous with the suffix ||-ak-|| 'out (speaker inside)' in many situations (both surfacing as /-k-/), and it is solely the quality of the vowel of the following morpheme (if that morpheme begins with ||V|| or is the factual evidential suffix ||-a||) that distinguishes between them. The opacity of the conditioning environment for ||V|| and ||-a|| variants leaves the entire functional load for the identification of the preceding morpheme on these vowels. Examples (66) and (67) provide two forms of the verb ||hi-hk^{h}e-|| 'to move the body' which differ in only one morpheme, ||-ak-|| 'out (speaker inside)' versus ||-ok-|| 'out (speaker outside)', but in which the differing morphemes are homophonous and can only be distinguished by the quality of ||V|| in the singular imperative suffix ||-Vn|| that follows these directionals in each word.

(66) ||-ak-|| 'out (speaker inside)' surfacing as /-k-/

[ʔ]ek^h:ékan (H ms.)

ʔek^h:ekan

||hi-hk^{h}e-ak-Vn||

/ʔe-k^{h}:e-k-an/
with.body-move-DIR-SG.IMP
'move out (sp[eaker] in[side])[!]'

(67) ||-ok-|| 'out (speaker outside)' surfacing as /-k-/
[ʔ]ek^{h}:ékon (H ms.)
ʔek^{h}:ekon
||hi-hk^{h}e-ok-Vn||
/ʔe-k^{h}:e-k-on/
with.body-move-DIR-SG.IMP
'move out (sp[eaker] out[side])[!]'

The process whereby the initial vowels of the directional suffixes in these examples are deleted is explained in the following section.

2.6.2. Vowel Deletion

When two underlying vowels come together, the second is deleted with no effect on the quality or quantity of the remaining vowel.[63] This is most clearly observed in a large number of directional suffixes which begin with a vowel. These suffixes can only surface with their initial vowel when affixed to a consonant-final stem, as shown in (68) and (69).

(68) V → Ø / V__ with vowel-initial directional suffixes
[ʔ]ek^{h}:élan (H ms.)
ʔek^{h}:elan
||hi-hk:e-ala-Vn|| → [ʔek.ˈk^{h}e.lan]
/ʔe-k^{h}:e-la-n/
with.body-move-DIR-SG.IMP
'1 move down!'

(69) V → Ø / V__ with vowel-initial directional suffixes
[ʔ]ap[^{h}]:éč:in (H ms.)
ʔap^{h}:eč:in
||ha-hp^{h}e-aduč-Vn|| → [ʔap.ˈp^{h}et̪.ʧin]
/ʔap^{h}:e-č:-in/

carry-DIR-SG.IMP
'carry it away!'

Compare the foregoing examples with the combinations of vowel-initial suffix and consonant-final verb stem in (70) following.

(70) Preservation of initial vowel after consonant-final verb stem
hwálaw (H I: 6)
hwalaw
||hu:w-ala-w|| → ['hwa.law]
/hw-ala-w/
go-DIR-PFV
'went down'

The process of vowel deletion after another vowel is not further considered in §2.6.2.1 on syncope: there is no difference between light syllables which descend from an earlier $V_1+V_2 \rightarrow V_1$ process and those which descend from an original short vowel. (However, to avoid this complication, all examples of light syllable avoidance in the following section make use of either consonant-initial directional suffixes or consonant-final verb stems.)

2.6.2.1. Vowel Syncope

Vowel syncope is one of the most characteristic features of Southern Pomo phonology. Polymorphemic grammatical words with four or more underlying syllables lose a syllable to syncope if two or three light syllables abut one another. In order to prevent two light syllables coming together, one is lost to syncope and has its onset resyllabified as the coda of the preceding light syllable. Both CVC and CVV syllables are heavy in the language. All Southern Pomo words (with the exception of a small number of grammatical morphemes like *yo-* ~ *=yo-*aux) must begin with a heavy syllable, and final syllables are extrametrical with regard to syncope, and such a deletion therefore is not necessary when two light syllables end a word. The two aforementioned facts drastically reduce the number of logically possible heavy and short syllable combinations in the language. Table 22 lists the attested patterns of heavy and light syllables found in verbs.[64] Only words of one to four syllables have been found (or not found) in sufficient numbers

Table 22. Attested surface patterns of heavy and light syllables in verbs *(H = CVC and CVV, L = CV)*

σ	σσ	σσσ	σσσσ	σσσσσ
N/A[65]	HH	HHH	HHHH	HHHHL
		HHL	HHHL	HHLHL
		HLL	HHLL	HLHHL
		HLH	HLHH	
			HLHL	
			HHLH	

to be confident of the patterns; however, the verbs of five syllables which have been analyzed are also suggestive of this pattern.[66]

Examples of verbs with two underlying non-final light syllables undergoing syncope are given below with the verbs *ʔehkʰe-* 'to move (body)', *ʔahča-* 'to fly', *ʔaht̯i-* 'to move the foot', and *ʔahpʰi-* 'to carry'.[67]

(71) $H_1L_2L_3H_4 \rightarrow H_1H_2H_4$
[ʔ]ehkʰémčin (H ms.)
ʔehkʰemčin
||hi-hkʰe-mač-Vn|| → [ʔeh.ˈkʰem.ʧin]
/ʔe-hkʰe-mč-in/
with.body-move-DIR-SG.IMP
'move in (speaker outside)!'

(72) $H_1L_2L_3L_4 \rightarrow H_1H_2L_4$
[ʔ]ahčámko (H ms.)
ʔahčamko
||ha-hča-mok-a|| → [ʔah.ˈʧam.ko]
/ʔahča-mk-o/
fly-DIR-EVID
'flew into'

(73) $H_1L_2L_3L_4H_5 \rightarrow H_1L_2H_3H_5$
<hat:alokč̓in> (O ms.)
hat̯:alokč̓in
||ha-ht̯-alokoč̓-Vn|| → [ˌhat̪.t̪a.ˈlok.ʧʼin][68]

/hat̪:-alokč̓-in/
move.foot-DIR-SG.IMP
'[move foot] up out of[!]'

(74) $H_1L_2L_3L_4H_5 \rightarrow H_1H_2L_4H_5$
<ʔahtimkocin> (O ms.)
ʔaht̪imkočin
||ha-ht̪i-mokoč-Vn|| → [ˌʔah.t̪im.ˈko.ʧin]
/ʔaht̪i-mkoč-in/
move.foot-DIR-SG.IMP
'[put foot] back[!]'

[ʔ]ap[ʰ]:alméč̓in (H ms.)
ʔapʰ:alameč̓in
||ha-hpʰ-alameč̓-Vn|| → [ˌʔap.pʰal.ˈme.ʧ'in]
/ʔapʰ:-almeč̓-in/
carry-DIR-SG.IMP
'[carry] down from above[!]'

As already stated, two light syllables may surface together only when one is final (and therefore extrametrical), as in (75).

(75) HHLL verb with extrametrical final light syllable (HHL<L>)
ha:čat̪̓bíča (H ms.)
ha:čat̪̓biča
||ha-hča-t̪-bič-a|| → [ˌha:.ʧat̪'.ˈbi.ʧa]
/ha:ča-t̪̓-bič-a/
fly-PL.ACT-raise-EVID
'took off (1 by 1)'

Southern Pomo primary stress is always on the penult, and the examples already given make clear that deletion of light syllables is not due to synchronic stress-assignment needs: both heavy and light penultimate syllables may bear stress. More important, in forms like those in (73) and (74), where HLLLH may be changed to HHLH or HLHH, it is clear that heavy syllables are neither necessary nor preferred for the assignment of pen-

Table 23. Examples of $H_1L_2L_3L_4H_5 \rightarrow H_1H_2L_4H_5$ and $H_1L_2L_3L_4H_5 \rightarrow H_1L_2H_3H_5$

Source	**Verb**	**$H_1L_2L_3L_4H_5 \rightarrow H_1H_2L_4H_5$**	**$H_1L_2L_3L_4H_5 \rightarrow H_1L_2H_3H_5$**
(O ms.)	*ʔahti̯-* 'to move foot'	2	1
(H ms.)	*ʔahpʰi-* 'to carry'	2[69]	0
(H ms.)	*ʔehkʰe-* 'to move body'	2	0
(H ms.)	*ʔahča-* 'to fly'	1	0
Total		**7**	**1**

ultimate stress. Stress, therefore, is not a factor in the choice of which light syllable's vowel to delete.

Though both $H_1L_2L_3L_4H_5 \rightarrow H_1H_2L_4H_5$ (as in ||ha-hti̯-mokoč-Vn|| → *ʔahti̯mkočin* '[put foot] back[!]') and $H_1L_2L_3L_4H_5 \rightarrow H_1L_2H_3H_5$ (as in ||ha-ht̯-alokoč̓-Vn|| → *hat̯:alokč̓in* '[move foot] up out of[!]') are attested, it is actually the former, the one that creates an antepenultimate (and therefore unstressed) heavy syllable, that is most frequent in the verb paradigms which were consulted for this analysis. Table 23 gives the number of such forms found in the four verb paradigms.

There are relatively few examples of either phenomenon in the large paradigms consulted for these data; however, it is clear that the creation of an antepenultimate heavy syllable instead of a penultimate heavy syllable is possible across the paradigms. If the distribution seen in table 23 is representative of all such forms in the language, then there appears to be a strong preference for the pre-antepenultimate light syllable to become the antepenultimate (and therefore unstressed) heavy syllable. Whatever the actual frequency of both types of syncope throughout the language, syllable weight is obviously not a factor in synchronic stress assignment, and the language not only allows light syllables to bear primary stress but possibly favors the creation of an unstressed heavy syllable when vowel deletion could instead have created a stressed heavy syllable.

This peculiar situation is possibly a fossilized pattern from an earlier time when Southern Pomo had a stress system more like that of Kashaya Pomo, its sister language, or other Pomoan languages. Kashaya stress can be predicted, but the complex processes behind stress assignment make it possible for any of the first five syllables of the stress domain to bear the primary stress. If the complexities of the Kashaya system are peeled away, it can be summarized as an iambic stress system in which stress falls on the nearest well-formed foot from the left edge of the domain: branching iambic feet include (CV CV), (CV CVV), and (CV CVC); non-branching feet include only heavy syllables (CVV) and (CVC); other processes, such as iambic lengthening, make the strong syllables of surface (CV CV) feet which bear stress do so on long vowels (Buckley 1994: 169–91).

The complexities of the Kashaya system are not necessarily those of an earlier stage of Southern Pomo, but the basic facts of the Kashaya system as a weight-sensitive stress system point to the strong possibility that an earlier stage of Southern Pomo (perhaps more recently than the shared common language of both Kashaya and Southern Pomo) might have assigned stress from the left edge of the stress domain on the basis of syllable weight rather than from the right on the basis of syllable count, as is the case now. The Kashaya system suggests the possibility of weight sensitivity as an earlier component of stress, but it does not provide clear evidence for why Southern Pomo might prefer to change the second syllable from the left to a heavy syllable.

Julius Moshinsky notes that stress in Proto Pomo was placed on the "first stem syllable," which is equivalent to the second syllable of most words, and notes that the seven daughter languages have diverged from this system in various ways: Northern, Eastern, and Central Pomo generally retain stress on the same syllables postulated to have been stressed in Proto Pomo, but various sound changes (including loss of initial syllables) render these daughter languages' stress systems unpredictable synchronically; only Southeastern Pomo and Southern Pomo have regularized their stress systems, and Moshinsky flatly states that the Southern Pomo stress system is "quite aberrant" and results in stress falling on syllables which historically never bore stress (Moshinsky 1976: 56–57). Two patterns, therefore, are to be observed in the other Pomoan languages: (1) weight-sensitive stress (in Kashaya); and (2) a preference for stress on the same syllable that bore it in Proto Pomo, namely, the root syllable, which in Proto Pomo was generally the second syllable from the left edge of the word.

Southern Pomo forms which fall into the $H_1L_2L_3L_4H_5 \rightarrow H_1H_2L_4H_5$ category, such as ||ha-hṯ̂i-mokoč-Vn|| → *ʔahṯ̂imkočin* '[put foot] back[!]', which show a preference for the creation of a heavy syllable on the second syllable from the left, might do so because, like Kashaya, an earlier stage of the language had a weight-sensitive stress system and, like Proto Pomo (and several daughter languages), the first syllable of the root (or second syllable from the left) was the one which bore stress. If this is the case, then the synchronic Southern Pomo phenomenon of vowel syncope is a conventionalized process that does nothing more than prevent adjacent light syllables from surfacing and is not otherwise completely predictable.

Thus far the examples of syncope have been restricted to verbs, but the process may also apply to kinship terms in order to avoid sequences of two light syllables (neither of which is final), as shown in example (76).

(76) $H_1L_2L_3H_4 \rightarrow H_1H_2H_4$ in kinship terms
miy:áṭʰkʰan (H VI: 1)
miy:aṭʰkʰan
||miy:a-dakʰad-Ø|| → [mij.ˈjatʰ.kʰan]
/miy:a-ṭʰkʰan-Ø/
3-spouse-AGT
'his wife'

However, the avoidance of non-final light syllables appears to be inactive on kinship terms with monosyllabic roots in order to protect the root syllable, as seen in example (77).

(77) $H_1L_2L_3L_4$ remaining $H_1L_2L_3L_4$ in kinship term with monosyllabic root
miy:aṭ̓íki (H VI: 1)
miy:aṭ̓iki
||miy:a-ṭ̓i-ki-Ø|| → [ˌmij.ja.ˈtʼi.ki]
/miy:a-ṭ̓i-ki-Ø/
3-younger.sibling-GS-AGT
'his y[ounger] bro[ther]'

Syncope is also prevalent in word classes other than verbs and kinship terms, though its application in them is not based on syllable weight. Nominal compounds and reduplicated adjectives and reduplicated verb stems (independent of the syllable-weight-based phenomena given earlier) lose the vowel of the first syllable of the second element to syncope, as shown in (78)–(80).

(78) $\sigma_1\sigma_2 + \sigma_3\sigma_4 \rightarrow \sigma_1\sigma_2\sigma_4$ in compound nouns
muhwayʔmi (O ms.)
muhwayʔmi
||muhway + ʔim:i|| → [muh.ˈwayʔ.mi]
/muhway-ʔmi/
fawn-black.berry
'strawberry'

ʔahk^{h}apṭaka (O ms.)
ʔahk^{h}apṭaka
||ʔahk^{h}a + bu:ṭaka|| → [ˌʔah.k^{h}ap.ˈta.ka]
/ʔahk^{h}a-pṭaka/
water-bear
'sea lion'

(79) $\sigma_1\sigma_2 + \sigma_3\sigma_4 \rightarrow \sigma_1\sigma_2\sigma_4$ in reduplicated adjectives
p[^{h}]al:áp[^{h}]la (H ms.)
p^{h}al:ap^{h}la
||p^{h}al:a + p^{h}al:a|| → [p^{h}al.ˈlap^h.la]
/p^{h}al:a-p^{h}la/
each-each
'[various]'[70]

bahṭ^{h}epṭ^{h}e (W: OF)
bahṭ^{h}epṭ^{h}e
||bahṭ^{h}e + bahṭ^{h}e|| → [bah.ˈt^{h}ep.t^{h}e]
/bahṭ^{h}e-pṭ^{h}e/
big.COLL-big.COLL
'huge'

(80) $\sigma_1\sigma_2 + \sigma_3\sigma_4 \rightarrow \sigma_1\sigma_2\sigma_4$ in reduplicated verb stems
p[ʰ]oht̪óp̪t̪ow (H VII: 2)
pʰuht̪opt̪ow
||pʰu-ht̪o-pʰu-ht̪o-w|| → [pʰuh.ˈt̪op.t̪ow]
/pʰuht̪o-pʰuht̪o-w/
boil ~ ITER-PFV
'boils'

These two types of word-internal vowel deletion are motivated by different considerations: verbs and kinship terms delete vowels to avoid two or more light syllables surfacing together word-medially, whereas two grammatical words (noun, adjective, verb stem) which come together through compounding or reduplication lose the vowel of the first syllable of the second grammatical word despite that vowel always being in an underlying heavy syllable. Though the two syncope processes operate in different ways, they both tend to produce the same result (though not absolutely so); namely, the second syllable from the left edge tends to become heavy after syncope has taken place. Again, this is not always the case and cannot be used as descriptive option for unifying the two processes. But it is possible that the syncope seen in compounding and reduplication is also a relic from a time when Southern Pomo stress was not penultimate and regular but weight-sensitive and root-borne.

2.6.3. Consonant Alternations

With the exception of some morpheme-specific allophony in the instrumental prefixes, consonant alternations are most commonly encountered in syllables other than the first and second syllables of a grammatical word.

2.6.3.1. Stops (Plosives and Affricates)

Ejective stops are the only voiceless stops which are allowed in final position on phonological words. With the exception of /č/ and /č̓/, which show some unique phonological alternations, voiceless stops must surface as ejectives in phonological-word-final position whether or not they are underlying ejectives. Example (81) gives two verb stems, *šuhnat̪-* 'to try by pulling' and *kahsak-* 'to desert', which have a non-ejective final voiceless stop surface as an ejective in word-final position.

(81) Non-ejective stop surfacing as an ejective word-finally

šuhnát̪in (H VIII: 4)	šúhnat̪̓ (H VIII: 4)
šuhnat̪in	*šuhnat̪̓*
||šu-hnat̪-Vn||	||šu-hnat̪-Ø ||
/šu-hnat̪-in/	/šu-hnat̪̓-Ø /
by.pulling-try-SG.IMP	by.pulling-try-PFV
'try (to pull)!'	'he tries to pull'
kahsaka (O I: 25D)	kahsak̓ (O I: 14)
kahsaka	*kahsak̓*
||kahsak-a||	||kahsak-Ø||
/kahsak-a/	/kahsak̓-Ø/
desert-EVID	desert-PFV
'deserted'	'deserting'

Compare the stems in example (81) with the verb stem *him:ok̓-* 'to fall' in (82), which has an underlying ejective stop as the stem-final segment.

(82) Ejective stop surfacing both medially and word-finally

<him*ok'o> (O D: EA)	<him*ok'> (O D: ED)
him:ok̓o	*him:ok̓*
||him:ok̓-a||	||him:ok̓-Ø||
/him:ok̓-o/	/him:ok̓-Ø/
fall-EVID	fall-PFV
'fell down'	'to fall over (of person)'

Alternations between word-medial plain stops and word-final ejective stops are attested for /t̪/, /ṭ/, and /k/; there are no /p/-final morphemes which can surface in final position within a phonological word.

This cross-linguistically unusual distribution in which only ejective plosives may surface word-finally has a plausible diachronic explanation. Neighboring Kashaya Pomo has a morpheme (the so-called 'assertive') which takes the form /-ʔ/ after vowels (e.g., *hayu-ʔ* 'it is a dog'). When this morpheme is added to a stem ending in a consonant, it combines with the final consonant to produce a glottalized consonant (thus ||mihyoq-ʔ|| 'woodrat-ASSERTIVE' → [mih.ˈjoq'] 'it is a woodrat'); however, when a word with a final plain plosive does not have the assertive added to it, its final consonant debuccalizes to [ʔ] (thus ||mihyoq|| 'woodrat' → [mih.ˈjoʔ]). Words with underlying ejective stops do not undergo debuccalization, and they are suspected of descending from earlier combinations of final consonants and the assertive (Buckley 1994: 99–103).

Compare the foregoing Kashaya forms for 'woodrat' and 'it is a woodrat' with the cognate Southern Pomo word *mihyok̓* [ˈmih.jok'] 'woodrat', which has no form corresponding to the assertive in Kashaya.[71] Southern Pomo might have gone through a stage during which a cognate to the Kashaya assertive was applied so often to final stops that speakers reanalyzed word-final glottalization as an obligatory feature of the language and glottalization was applied to new environments. Eventually the over-application of the glottal feature would have erased all semantic force for the assertive, and all words with final voiceless plosives would have surfaced as ejectives as the new default.

The phonemes /č/ and /č̓/ behave differently in word-final position than the voiceless plosives of Southern Pomo; they also behave differently than the other affricate that may occur word-finally, /ċ/, which undergoes no changes in any position. Both /č/ and /č̓/ become /y/ [j] in word final position, as shown in (83) and (84), where morphemes with /č/ and /č̓/ are shown in both final and non-final position.

(83) Examples of /č/ and /č̓/ → [j]/__#

mí:may (H I: 27)
mi:may
||mi-:mač-Ø|| → [ˈmi:.maj]
/mi:mač-Ø/
cry-PFV
'she cries'

čaʔṭemhuy (W: OF)
||ča-ʔṭe-mhuč̓-Ø|| → [ʧaʔ.ˈṭ'em.huj]
/čaʔṭe-mhuč̓-Ø/
fight-RECIP-PFV
'to fight'

(84) The same morphemes with /č/ and /č̓/ surfacing before a vowel

mi:mačen (O I: 9)

mi:mačen

||mi-:mač-en||[72] → [mi:.ˈma.ʧen]

/mi:mač-en/

cry-D.SIM

'crying'

dáʔţamč̓íʔya (H I:6)

daʔţamč̓iʔya

||da-ʔţa-mhuč̓-V=ʔya|| → [ˌdaʔ.ţ'am.ˈʧ'iʔ.ja]

/daʔţa-mč̓-i=ʔya/

encounter-RECIP-HORTATIVE=1PL.AGT

'let's meet together'

There are three words which inexplicably do not conform to the above statements and do surface with a final palato-alveolar affricate, albeit only an ejective one: *he:č̓* 'nail, claw'; *ʔahsič̓* 'hard, difficult'; and *kʰaʔbekʰač̓* 'raptor species'. These words are unlikely to be recent borrowings; *he:č̓* 'nail, claw', for example, can be reconstructed for Proto Pomo (McLendon 1973, 70). In the absence of a clear explanation for these anomalous forms, they must be set aside as aberrancies.

The voiced plosive /d/ behaves in a different way than the other stops in morpheme-final position. (The other voiced stop, /b/, does not appear in this position.) Oswalt states that Southern Pomo /d/ becomes [n] "syllable-finally" (1976a: 21). The data show that this is true of underlying syllable structure, as seen in the allomorphy for the root ||-kod-|| 'sister's husband' and the suffix ||-aded-|| 'hear and there' in (85) and (86) following.

(85) Alternation between [d] and [n] in the root ||-kod-|| 'sister's husband'

mak:odan (O I: 13)

mak:odan

||maH-kod-an|| → [mak.ˈko.dan]

/ma-k:od-an/

3-sister's.husband-PAT

'her own brother-in-law'

miy:akon (O I: 14)
miy:akon
||miy:a-kod-Ø|| → [mij.ˈja.kon]
/miy:a-kon-Ø/
3-sister's.husband-AGT
'the sister's husband'

(86) Alternation between [d] and [n] in the suffix ||-aded-|| 'here and there'
pʰey:ed:u (W: OF)
||pʰi-y:e-aded-u|| → [pʰej.ˈjed.du]
/pʰey:e-d:-u/
look.for-DIR-PFV
'looking for'

pʰey:edenṯi (W: OF)
||pʰi-y:e-aded-ṯi|| → [ˌpʰej.je.ˈden.ṯi]
/pʰey:e-den-ṯi/
look.for-DIR-INTENT
'[in order] to look for'

However, Oswalt's statement can be emended somewhat to account for both the underlying and surface syllable structure: /d/ becomes [n] in coda position before a morpheme boundary.

/d/ → [n] /__]$_{\text{MORPHEME}}${C, #}

This change is necessary because once /d/ becomes a non-word-final coda within a morpheme it assimilates in voicing to the following morpheme-internal consonant and does not necessarily become [n], as seen in the allomorphs for the word ||-dakʰad-|| 'spouse', which has two /d/ segments in the root: (1) a morpheme-final one that surfaces as [n] at a word boundary; and (2) a morpheme-initial one that assimilates in voicing to the following consonant once it has become a coda through syncope, as shown in (87):

(87) Alternation between [d] and [t] in morpheme-internal coda position

maʔdákʰden (H IV: 1)

maʔdakʰden

||maH-dakʰad-en|| → [maʔ.ˈdakʰ.den]

/ma-ʔdakʰd-en/

3C-spouse-PAT

'her husband'

miy:aṭkʰan (Oswalt 1978: 15)

miy:aṭkʰan

||miy:a-dakʰad-Ø|| → [mij.ˈjat.kʰan]

/miy:a-ṭkʰan-Ø/

3-spouse-AGT

['his spouse']

The morpheme-internal voicing assimilation seen in /d/ here is also found with /b/ (e.g., ||bahṭʰe + bahṭʰe|| → [bah.ˈtʰep.tʰe] 'huge'). There is an additional alternation involving /d/ and nasals discussed in the next section.

2.6.3.2. *Nasals and Liquids*

Southern Pomo underwent a sound change after splitting from its sister languages in which all nasals and liquids surface as [n] in word-final position. This change is in addition to the much older alternation between [d] and [n] in coda position before a morpheme boundary. Examples (88) and (89) show word-final alternation between [l] and [n] and between [m] and [n].

(88) Word-final alternation between [l] and [n] in ||du-hṭʰal-|| 'to feel pain'

duhṭʰála (H V: 6)

duhṭʰala

||duhṭʰal-a|| → [duh.ˈtʰa.la]

/duhṭʰal-a/

feel.pain-EVID

'it pains'

<duh7^han> (O D: ED)
duhṭʰan
||duhṭʰal-Ø|| → [ˈduh.tʰan]
/duhṭʰan-Ø/
feel.pain-PFV
'[feel] . . . ache'

(89) Word-final alternation between [m] and [n] in the suffix ||-m-|| ESSIVE
<?ahtiman> (O ms.)
ʔaht̪iman
||ha-ht̪i-m-Vn|| → [ʔah.ˈt̪i.man]
/ʔaht̪i-m-an/
put.foot-ESSIVE-SG.IMP
['hold the foot still!']

<?ahtin> (O ms.)
ʔaht̪in
||ha-ht̪i-m|| → [ˈʔah.t̪in]
/ʔaht̪i-n/
put.foot-ESSIVE
['holding the foot still']

Thus /n/, /d/, /l/, and /m/ all surface as [n] in word-final position. The stem ||duhṭʰal-|| 'to feel pain' and the suffix ||-m-|| ESSIVE given in (88) and (89) show the underlying lateral and bilabial sonorants surfacing before vowel-initial suffixes. The situation is not quite as simple as these examples might suggest.

A morpheme-final consonant that surfaces as [n] when it is also word-final, if it is not an underlying /d/, may freely surface as either [m] or [l] before a vowel-initial suffix unless it is an allomorph of one of three morphemes (all of which are homophonous): ||-m-|| ESSIVE, ||-m-|| PL.ACT, and ||-m-|| 'across'; these three suffixes, two of them quite rare, surface only as [m] before vowels (Oswalt 1976a: 21). Oswalt points out that even words with a word-final [n] that descends from Proto Pomo *n have this segment alternate with [l] and [m] before vowels; word-final [n] may never surface before a vowel (Oswalt 1976a: 21).

It is only in morpheme-final position that a consonant surfacing as [n] when it is also word-final may surface as [l] or [m] before a vowel-initial suffix. However, [l] and [m] in this environment vary freely, and the same speaker may choose either allophone.[73] This free variation has frustrating ramifications when it is combined with the baroque rules which dictate the choice of surface forms for ||V||. If the [l] allophone is chosen, ||V|| surfaces as [i]; if the [m] allophone is chosen, ||V|| surfaces as [a]. Thus Oswalt notes that ||hu:w-mul-Vn|| go-DIR-S.SEQ 'while going around' may surface as either *hu:-mum-an* [hu:.ˈmu.man] or *hu:-mul-in* [hu:.ˈmu.lin], and he states that these two forms "are freely used in the same contexts with the same meaning" (1976a: 21).[74]

The natural discourse recorded in the texts collected from Annie Burke by Halpern bear out Oswalt's observations. The following forms in (90a–c) all come from one text and show the stem ||mu-:kʰel-|| 'to throw and make several slide' surfacing as /mu:kʰen/ without a vowel-initial suffix and as both /mu:kʰel-/ and /mu:kʰem/ before the vowel-initial switch-reference suffix ||-Vn|| S.SEQ.[75]

(90a) Stem-final /n/ surfacing as [l] or [m] before vowel with the same stem not prevocalic with [l] and [n]
mú:kʰel( )háywan mú:kʰen (H V: 3)
mu:kʰelhaywan mu:kʰen
||mu-:kʰel+ʔah:ay=wan mu-:kʰel-Ø|| → [ˌmu:.kʰel.ˈhaj.wan ˈmu:.kʰen]
/mu:kʰel-hay=wan mu:kʰen-Ø/
throw.and.slide.sev.-stick=DET.OBJ throw.and.slide.sev.-PFV
'scaling their scaling-sticks'

(90b) prevocalic with [l]
mu:kʰélin (H V: 3)
mu:kʰelin
||mu-:kʰel-Vn|| → [mu:.ˈkʰe.lin]
/mu:kʰel-in/
throw.and.slide.sev.-S.SEQ
['while sliding scaling sticks']

(90c) prevocalic with [m]

mú:kʰel( )háywan mú:kʰéman (H V: 17)

mu:kʰelhaywan mu:kʰeman

||mu-:kʰel+ʔah:ay=wan mu-:kʰel-Vn|| → [ˌmu:.kʰel.ˈhaj.wan mu:.ˈkʰe.man]

/mu:kʰel-hay=wan mu:kʰem-an/

throw.and.slide.sev.-stick=DET.OBJ throw.and.slide.sev.-S.SEQ

'scaling (their) scaling-sticks'

Alternations like these provide the best evidence that Southern Pomo speakers did not distinguish between [n], [m], and [l] in morpheme-final position.[76] Hereafter all stems with such endings are transcribed as ||N|| (e.g., *mu:kʰelin* ~ *mu:kʰeman* would be ||mu:kʰeN-Vn||).

Though /d/ (with its morpheme-final allophones [d] and [n]) does not participate in the alternations just discussed, it does pattern with the nasals in an unusual alternation when immediately followed by a lateral-initial suffix.[77] When /d/ or a nasal is morpheme-final and is followed by an /l/-initial suffix, the first consonant is deleted and replaced by /:/ and the /l/ surfaces as [n]. In other words, the nasality of the nasals (including the [n] allophone of /d/) is transferred to the lateral and provides the only clue as to the nature of the consonant surfacing as /:/. Examples (91b) and (92b) show this nasal spreading process with suffix ||-le|| PLURAL.IMPERATIVE and its nasal-spreading-induced allomorph [-ne] after both /d/ and ||N||.[78]

(91a) /d/ allophony without nasal spreading

huw:ádun (H VI: 11)

huw:adun

||hu:w-ad-Vn|| → [huw.ˈwa.dun]

/huw:-ad-un/

go-DIR-SG.IMP

'come!'

(91b) /d/ allophony with nasal spreading (/d/ + /le/ → [:n])

huw:á:ne (H V: 19)

huw:a:ne

||hu:w-ad-le|| → [huw.ˈwa:.ne]

/huw:-a:-ne/
go-DIR-PL.IMP
'come ye[!]'

(92a) ||N|| allophony without nasal spreading
[ʔ]ehk^{h}éma (H ms.)
ʔehk^{h}ema
||hi-hk^{h}e-m-a|| → [ʔeh.ˈk^{h}e.ma]
/ʔe-hk^{h}e-m-a/
with.body-move-DIR-EVID
'1 is moving across'

(92b) ||N|| allophony with nasal spreading (||N|| + /le/ → [:n])
[ʔ]ehk^{h}é:ne (H ms.)
ʔehk^{h}e:ne
||hi-hk^{h}e-m-le|| → [ʔeh.ˈk^{h}e:.ne]
/ʔe-hk^{h}e-:-ne/
with.body-move-DIR-PL.IMP
'(in-law) move across!'

This rather unusual process whereby /d/ and ||N|| are replaced by length and spread nasality to the following consonant when they immediately precede a lateral might have originated via the following path:

… ||N|| ~ /d/-lV → … ||N|| ~ [n]-lV → … [n]-nV → … [:]-nV

There is evidence, however, that this alternation followed a slightly different path. Oswalt records at least one form in which ||N|| + ||-le|| → [ʔne], and this example comes from Elizabeth Dollar's Dry Creek dialect rather than the Cloverdale dialect of the preceding examples. Example (93) provides the glottal form of ||N|| and two nasal variants using the verb 'to sing'.

(93) Dry Creek dialect nasal spreading with *ʔihmin* ||ʔihmiN-|| 'to sing'
[without nasal spreading]
<ʔihmin> (O D: ED, OD: EA) <ʔihmiman> (O D: ED)
ʔihmin *ʔihmiman*

||ʔihmiN-Ø|| → ['ʔih.min]
/ʔihmin-Ø/
sing-PFV
'to sing'

||ʔihmiN-Vn|| → [ʔih.'mi.man]
/ʔihmim-an/
sing-SG.IMP
'Sing!'

[with nasal spreading and glottal variant]
<ʔihmiʔne> (O D: ED)
ʔihmiʔne
||ʔihmiN-le|| → [ʔih.'miʔ.ne]
/ʔihmiʔ-ne/
sing-PL.IMP
'Sing! (Pl.)'

What is most unusual about the [ʔne] variant in example (93) is that it is caused by a final ||N||, an underspecified sonorant with no evidence of glottalization in any other environment. The most likely explanation for this bears upon the diachronic path postulated earlier. Southern Pomo /d/ descends from a Proto Pomo *n̓, which is preserved in Kashaya Pomo as /n̓/ with [d] as its prevocalic allophone (Buckley 1994: 36–47). Though the form in (93) shows ||N|| alternating with [ʔ] with nasal spreading, it is likely that additional forms are to be uncovered showing that this Dry Creek variant occurs after both ||N|| and /d/ (like the ||N|| or /d/ + /l/ → [:ne] seen in the Cloverdale data earlier). If so, it is perhaps likely that nasal spreading developed via this path:

1. /l/ assimilated in nasality (but not place) to a preceding nasal
   ... [+nas]-lV → ... [+nas]-nV
2. the preceding nasals assimilated in place to the nasal allomorph of /l/, which would leave only two variants, one glottalized and one plain
   i. ... [n̓]-nV
   ii. ... [n]-nV
3. /n̓/ → [ʔ] / __[n]
   i. ... [ʔ]-nV
   ii. ... [n]-nV
4. Form (ii) → form (i) through analogy

The Cloverdale form [:n] might first have gone through the preceding developments postulated for Dry Creek and added a fifth step where the glottal stop was replaced by /:/, or it might have skipped steps 3 and 4 entirely and simply replaced all the nasals with /:/ after nasal spreading.

2.6.4. Consonant Assimilation and Dissimilation

Consonants show assimilation in place and voicing (sometimes both) within and across morpheme boundaries.

2.6.4.1. Assimilation in Place

After syncope, /d/ undergoes complete assimilation in voicing and place if it is followed by /č/ within the same morpheme, as in (94).

(94) Morpheme-internal assimilation of /d/ to /č/
[ʔ]ekʰ:éč:in (H ms.)
ʔekʰ:eč:in
||hi-hkʰe-aduč-Vn|| → [ʔek.ˈkʰet̪̥.ʧin]
/ʔe-kʰ:e-č:-in/
with.body-move-DIR-SG.IMP
'move over[!]'

Nasals (including ||N|| and nasals which derive from /d/) assimilate in place to a following consonant.

(95a) Examples of nasal place assimilation with the verb ||čoh:oN-|| 'to marry'
[without assimilation]
čoh:on (O I: 3)
čoh:on
||čoh:oN-Ø|| → [ˈʧoh.hon]
/čoh:on-Ø/
marry-PFV
'marry'

(95b) [with velar assimilation]
čoh:onhkʰe (O I: 4)
čoh:onhkʰe

||čoh:oN-kʰ:e|| → [ʧoh.ˈhoŋŋ̊͡.kʰe]

/čoh:onh-kʰe/

marry-FUT

'will let marry'

(95c) [with labial assimilation]

čoh:omba (O I: 9)

čoh:omba

||čoh:oN-ba|| → [ʧoh.ˈhom.ba]

/čoh:om-ba/

marry-S.SEQ

'having married'

When a nasal is followed by /w/ within a grammatical word, the nasal assimilates to the labial nature of /w/ and /w/ disappears, and the surfacing nasal may also assimilate in its phonation to the next surface segment, as in (96).[79]

(96) Nasal assimilation before /w/

hwadém?du (H VIII: 1)

hwadem?du

||hu:w-aded-wadu|| → [hwa.ˈdemm̰͡.du]

/hw-adem-?du/

go-DIR-HAB

'always goes around'

2.6.4.2. *Assimilation in Voicing*

In addition to the nasal spreading assimilatory process already described and the morpheme-internal voicing assimilation for /d/ discussed earlier (§2.6.3.1), there are other types of consonant assimilation both within and across morpheme boundaries.

Voiced stops assimilate in voicing to a following voiceless consonant when syncope brings them together within the same morpheme (the same alternation seen for morpheme-internal /d/ earlier). The actual phonetic realization of the devoiced allophones of /b/ and /d/ has not been consistently recorded. Oswalt states that the /b/ of the suffix *-bič-* '(part of whole) to raise up; begin', which he transcribes as *-X b c-*, becomes the ejective [p̓] after syncope (1976a: 24). The historic change of *b → [p̓] / __[+cons,-voice] is attested in Central Pomo, which has forms like *p̓še* [p̓ʃe] corresponding to Southern Pomo *behše* '(deer) meat' (McLendon 1973: 72). However, Halpern consistently transcribes a non-ejective voiceless stop in all such positions, and Oswalt does the same in some of his work. These voiceless allophones are also often recorded as aspirated, a feature which is not distinctive in coda position, and any such records should be read as indicating an audible release. The plain unaspirated non-ejective voiceless allophones are used throughout this grammar because they are the most frequent in the records and match up with what I have heard from living speakers.

(97a) Morpheme-internal voicing assimilation after syncope
[/b/→ /p/]
bahṭ^{h}epṭ^{h}e (W: OF)
||bahṭ^{h}e + bahṭ^{h}e|| → [bah.'t^{h}ep.t^{h}e]
/bahṭ^{h}e-pṭ^{h}e/
big.COLL-big.COLL
'huge'

(97b) [/b/→ /p/]
[ʔ]ek^{h}:épčin (H ms.)
ʔek^{h}:epčin
||hi-hk^{h}e-bič-Vn|| → [ʔek.'k^{h}:ep.ʧin]
/ʔe-k^{h}:e-pč-in
with.body-move-DIR-SG.IMP
'move up!'

(97c) [/d/→ /ṭ/]
miy:aṭk^{h}an (Oswalt 1978: 15)
miy:aṭk^{h}an
||miy:a-dak^{h}ad-Ø|| → [mij.'jat.k^{h}an]
/miy:a-ṭk^{h}an-Ø/
3-spouse-AGT
['his spouse']

Sonorants also show similar voicing assimilation, though this process appears to be more sporadic and, in some cases, might vary according to dialect. Nasals in particular often devoice partially before aspirated consonants, which may occur across morpheme boundaries, but they are also recorded as devoicing before unaspirated voiceless consonants, as shown in (98) and (99).

(98) Voicing assimilation in sonorants before aspirated C

[ʔ]ahčáŋhkʰay (H IV: 5)

ʔahčanhkʰay

||ʔahča=li=kʰač|| → [ʔah.ˈʧaŋ͡ŋ̊.kʰaj]

/ʔahča=nhkʰay/

house=ward

'[to] home'

čoh:onhkʰe (O I: 4)

čoh:onhkʰe

||čoh:oN-kʰ:e|| → [ʧoh.ˈhoŋ͡ŋ̊.kʰe]

/čoh:onh-kʰe/

marry-FUT

'will let marry'

(99) Voicing assimilation in sonorant before voiceless unaspirated C

mht̯o (H IV: 7)

mht̯o

||mi:t̯o|| → [m͡m̥t̪o][80]

2SG.PAT

'you'

2.6.4.3. *Glottal Dissimilation*

Halpern notes that the glottals /ʔ/ and /h/ are in partial complementary distribution as initials (1984: 7–8). Stems which have /ʔ/, a voiced stop, or an ejective as their second consonant may not begin with /ʔ/; stems which have /h/, aspirated obstruents, or fricatives as their second consonant may not begin with /h/; stems with sonorants or voiceless unaspirated supra-

Table 24. Distribution of glottal-initial syllables[81]

Second (non-increment) consonant of the stem →	C	C^h	C'
Laryngeal increment ↓			
/h/	ʔV-	ʔV-	
/ʔ/			hV-
/:/	ʔV- & hV-	ʔV-	hV-

laryngeal consonants as their second consonant may begin with either /ʔ/ or /h/.[82]

The preceding description is an oversimplification: the conditioning environment is affected by both the second consonant of the stem (which is equivalent to the root consonant of verbs and most kinship forms) and the laryngeal increment that precedes or follows the second consonant of the stem (i.e., the second consonant is understood to be exclusive of the laryngeal increment, which may appear before or after it). Table 24 summarizes the distribution of glottal-initial syllables with the following abbreviations for the phonetic properties of the second consonant of the stem:

C = /p m w t̪ ṭ n l c č y k/ (sonorants and voiceless unaspirated stops)
C^h = /pʰ t̪ʰ ṭʰ s čʰ š kʰ h/ (fricatives and aspirated stops)
C' = /p̓ b t̪̓ ṭ̓ d c̓ č̓ k̓ ʔ/ (glottalized and voiced stops)

Following are examples of attested patterns from table 24 (only a sample of each consonant type has been included).

(100) Examples of ʔVhCV . . .

[with sonorants]	[with voiceless unaspirated stops]
ʔahlok̓ 'to fall off'	*ʔahka* 'game'
ʔiyha 'bone'	*ʔahča* 'house'

(101) Examples of ʔV:CV . . .

[with sonorants]	[with voiceless unaspirated stops]
ʔa:ma 'thou'	*ʔo:koṭin* 'pass several!'
ʔam:a 'earth; thing'	*ʔat̪:o* 'me'

(102) Examples of hV:CV . . .

[with sonorants]	[with voiceless unaspirated stops]
hi:no 'ash'	*ha:čat̯lawa* 'many fly down'
ham:an 'she'	*hač:alwa* 'one flies down'

(103) Examples of ʔVhC^h . . .

[with fricatives]	[with aspirated stops]
ʔahša 'fish'	*ʔahk^{h}a* 'water'
ʔohso 'clover'	*ʔehp^{h}et̯* 'fart'

(104) Examples of ʔV:C^h . . .

[with fricatives]	[with aspirated stops]
ʔa:suw 'to scratch'	*ʔa:p^{h}at̯kačin* 'carry up several!'
ʔah:a 'mouth'	*ʔap^h:akčin* 'carry it up!'

(105) Examples of hVʔC' . . .

[with voiced stops]	[with ejectives]
hiʔbu 'potato'	*haʔćat̯* 'to whip'
hudʔakay 'to want'	*hoʔk̓oy* 'to drink'

(106) Examples of hV:C' . . .

[with glottal stop]	[with ejectives]
he:ʔey 'where'	*hi:t̯ad:edu:šu* 'touchy'
heʔ:e 'hair (of head)'	*hak̓:an* 'my friend'

The preceding distributional facts account for the variants of the glottal-initial instrumental prefixes ||ha-|| 'long object through air, by limb or wing', ||hi-|| 'with body', and ||hu-|| 'with/by sound, speech or hearing', each of which has an /ʔ/-initial allomorph. For a subset of verb stems with glottal initial prefixes there is a productive alternation between /ʔ/ and /h/ as the initial consonant of the prefix within individual verb paradigms. These productive alternations are caused by morphologically conditioned changes to the laryngeal increment (see §2.6.6 for a discussion of laryngeal increment behavior and distribution). For some glottal-initial verb stems with an /h/ increment on a voiceless unaspirated root consonant, the allomorphs of the glottal-initial instrumental prefix vary between /hV-/ and

/ʔV-/ on the basis of the presence or absence of the /h/ increment. Example (107) gives two allomorphs of the verb stem ||ha-hča-|| 'to fly', one with the /ha-/ allomorph of the instrumental prefix ||ha-|| 'long object through air, by limb or wing', and one with the /ʔa-/ allomorph of the same prefix.

(107) Glottal dissimilation in the verb ||ha-hča-|| 'to fly'

[with /ʔa-/ allomorph]	[with /ha-/ allomorph]
[ʔ]ahčamók^{h}t̯^{h}u (H ms.)	ha:čat̯́mók^{h}t̯^{h}u (H ms.)
ʔahčamokt̯^{h}u	*ha:čat̯́mokt̯^{h}u*
||ha-hča-mok-ka-t̯^{h}u||	||ha-hča-t̯-mok-ka-t̯^{h}u||
/ʔa-hča-mo-k-t̯^{h}u/	/ha-:ča-t̯́-mo-k-t̯^{h}u/
w.wing-fly-DIR-CAUS-PROH	w.wing-fly-PL.ACT-DIR-CAUS-PROH
'[don't let] it [fly in]!'	'don't let them fly in!'

The preceding examples show that glottal-initial instrumental prefixes may surface with either glottal phoneme once morphologically conditioned changes have altered the laryngeal increment and removed the environment that would otherwise prohibit one or the other glottal from surfacing (*ʔahčamokt̯^{h}u* fits the pattern ʔVhC . . . , and *ha:čat̯́mokt̯^{h}u* fits the pattern hV:C . . .). However, it is not possible to predict whether a verb stem with an initial glottal and a voiceless unaspirated root consonant (as in example 107) will show productive alternations in the initial consonant due to glottal dissimilation. Example (108) gives the verb ||ʔihči-|| 'to carry (one) by handle, drag', which shows the same laryngeal increment variations seen with 'to fly' in (107) without the same alternations in the initial glottal consonant.

(108) Lack of alternation in the glottal-initial verb stem ||ʔihči-||

[with /h/ increment]	[with /:/ increment]
<?ihciw > (O D: EA)	<?ec*eduy> (O D: EA)
ʔihčiw	*ʔeč:eduy*
||ʔihči-w||	||ʔihči-aduč-Ø||
/ʔihčiw/	/ʔeč:eduy/
'wear [from neck?]'	'to carry on back or with handle'

There appears to be no sure way to predict whether a given glottal-initial verb stem will show productive alternations between an initial /h/ and /ʔ/. The underlying form ||ʔihči-|| has been chosen on the basis of Oswalt's decision not to segment the initial syllable as the instrumental prefix ||hi-|| 'with the body' in his entry in (O D), and it is possible that productive alternations in the glottals of glottal-initial stems might be restricted to instrumental prefix allomorphy (i.e., monomorphemic glottal-initial stems might show no alternations). However, the initial syllable in ||ʔihči-|| might well be ||hi-|| 'with the body'; the semantic range of most instrumental prefixes is sufficiently broad to allow such an analysis.[83] The question of why some verb stems do not participate in the variation is unknown at this time and, perhaps, is not susceptible to being answered with the extant data (if there is an answer to be found).

In addition to the verb stems, there is very restricted allomorphy in the glottal-initial first-person possessed prefix of kinship terms due to glottal dissimilation (discussed in detail in §2.8.1.3), and there is some evidence of the effects of glottal dissimilation in nominal compounding (discussed in §2.8.1).

2.6.5. Consonant Deletion

Within verbs, the first of two underlying consonants is replaced with /:/ unless it is a liquid or nasal.

[+cons,-son] → [:] / __[+cons]

This rule takes effect before vowel syncope, and consonants which form clusters after syncope are therefore immune to deletion and replacement with /:/.

(109) Word-internal consonant deletion and replacement with /:/
[final consonant of ||-aduč-|| 'away' surfacing]
<dadʔeduy> (O D: EA)
dadʔeduy
||da-ʔde-aduč-Ø|| → [dad.ˈʔe.duj][84]
/da-dʔe-duy-Ø/
with.palm-move.one-DIR-PFV
'to push s[ome] o[ne] sitting over or away'

[final consonant of ||-aduč-|| 'away' being replaced by /:/]
dadʔedú:t̪[ʰ]u (H ms.)
dadʔedu:t̪ʰu
||da-ʔde-aduč-t̪ʰu|| → [ˌdad.ʔe.ˈdu:.t̪ʰu]
/da-dʔe-du:-t̪ʰu/
with.palm-move.one-DIR-PROH
'don't [push it away!]'

2.6.6. Laryngeal Increments

The second consonant of every Southern Pomo stem (save for monosyllabic function words) must be immediately preceded or followed by one of the segments /h/, /ʔ/, or /:/ (notated as H in CVHCV- ~ CVCHV-). Following Oswalt (1976a: 20), these three segments are termed 'laryngeal increments' when they are combined with the second consonant of the stem.[85] The laryngeal increments have been discussed in some detail already (§2.2.1). This section introduces specific terminology and summarizes the partial complementary distribution of the increments.

The laryngeal increments /h/, /ʔ/, and /:/ may be pre-consonantally incremented or post-consonantally incremented to the second consonant of the stem (which is generally equal to the root consonant of verbs).[86] When a pre-consonantally incremented laryngeal increment is moved to become a post-consonantal increment (CVHCV- → CVCHV-), it is said to be transcremented. In addition to changing the location of the laryngeal increment from the left of the incremented consonant to the right, the transcremented increment surfaces as /:/ (regardless of its pre-transcremental character) when the incremented consonant is voiceless (C_1VHC_2V- → C_1VC_2:V- when C_2 is [-voice]). Transcrementing is morphologically conditioned; several vowel-initial directional suffixes cause transcrementing and are therefore termed transcremental suffixes. These suffixes are discussed individually in section §2.8.3. Example (110) shows the verb stem ||hi-hkʰe-|| 'to move the body' and its transcremented allomorph /ʔekʰ:e-/ with the transcremental suffix ||-alameč̓-|| 'down from above'. (This verb stem also undergoes vowel lowering and glottal dissimilation in the prefix.)

(110) Laryngeal increment movement with transcremental suffix

[ʔ]ekʰ:elméč̓in (H ms.)

ʔekʰ:elmeč̓in

||hi-hkʰe-alameč̓-Vn|| → [ʔek.kʰel.me.tʃ'in]

/ʔe-kʰ:e-lmeč̓-in/

with.body-move-DIR-SG.IMP

'move down from above!'

Oswalt's terminology for laryngeal increments as used in the entries in (O D) is adopted throughout this work; however, there is a mismatch between this terminology as it applies to Southern Pomo and its application by Oswalt and Buckley to neighboring Kashaya. The suffixes herein termed transcrements for Southern Pomo are cognate with Kashaya suffixes which Oswalt and Buckley label as decrements (Oswalt 1961; Oswalt 1976a; Buckley 1994). The decrements of Kashaya completely delete the laryngeal augment (they therefore de-increment it). This is never the case in Southern Pomo. Following Oswalt's usage in (O D), only the plural act affix is labeled as a decrement, as it does not move the increment and replaces all laryngeal increments (whether /h/, /ʔ/, or /:/) with /:/. This decremental affix blocks a following transcremental suffix from transcrementing the laryngeal increment. Example (111) shows the verb stem ||hi-hkʰe-|| 'to move the body' and its decremented allomorph /ʔe:kʰe-/ with the decremental plural act affix ||-t̯-|| preceding the transcremental affix ||-alameč̓-|| 'down from above'.[87]

(111) Laryngeal increment change with the decremental plural act affix

[ʔ]e:kʰet̯lamé:le (H ms.)

ʔe:kʰet̯lame:le

||hi-hkʰe-t̯-alameč̓-le|| → [ʔe:.ˌkʰet̪.la.ˈme:.le]

/ʔe-:kʰe-t̯-lame:-le/

with.body-move-PL.ACT-DIR-PL.IMP

'2 [move down from above]!'

The laryngeal increments are in partial complementary distribution. The increment /:/ has little restriction on which consonants it can precede

Table 25. Possible combinations of increment and second consonant of stem

	Pre-consonantal increment			**Post-consonantal increment**		
	/ʔ/	/h/	/:/	/ʔ/	/h/	/:/
Sonorants	✓	✓	✓	✓	✓	✓
Voiced stops	✓	No	✓	✓	No	No
Ejectives	✓	No	✓	No	No	✓
Glottals	No	No	✓	No	No	✓
Other voiceless consonants	No	✓	✓	No	No	✓

or follow. The increments /h/ and /ʔ/, however, can be partially predicted depending upon the phonetic quality of the consonant around which they are incremented. Halpern summarizes the basics of laryngeal increment distribution:

> ... length occurs before or after all C, except that length does not occur after b, d. Glottal stop occurs before but not after glottalized consonants. The h-[increment] occurs before all voiceless and intermediate [=voiceless unaspirated] stops, affricates and spirants but not after.... [The voiced stops are] post-[incremented] only by glottal stop; glottal stop and h, however, are pre-and post-[incremented] only by length. (Halpern 1984: 16)

Halpern also notes that sonorants may be both "pre-and post-augmented by all three" laryngeal increments (1984: 17). Table 25 summarizes the possible combinations of consonants and laryngeal increments.[88]

2.7. RELAXED SPEECH RULES AND CONTRACTIONS

Oswalt states that "the forms of words in Southern Pomo are more variable, more in flux, than in any other language I have heard of—almost all independent words have two or more forms" (1978, 15). However, the majority of the examples Oswalt lists are properly the domain of predictable phonological stem alternations and not relaxed speech rules. It is not the

Table 26. Contracted variants of words with pre-vocalic /h/

Full form in careful speech	**Contracted forms**	**Gloss**
ha:mini-	hni- ~ ni	'and then' (pro-verb)
huw:adu-	hwadu- ~ wadu-	'to go along'
nih:i-	hnihi- ~ hni- ~ nihi- ~ ni-	'to say'

case that every phonological word of Southern Pomo has one or more variants. In rapid speech, however, it is true that several of the most common words have reduced variants. Words with a pre-vocalic /h/ are most likely to have a reduced variant, examples of which are given in table 26.

In addition to these examples, there are words without pre-vocalic /h/ which have contracted forms, such as *kʰaṭ:ič̓aw* 'bad' and *ṭʰač̓:aw* ~ *t̪eč̓:aw* ~ *čeč̓:aw* 'much', which have the respective contracted variants *kʰač̓:aw* and *ṭʰač̓aw* ~ *t̪eč̓aw* ~ *čeč̓aw* (the choice of the initial syllable for 'much' seems to be based on idiolectal differences).

2.8. WORD CLASSES

Southern Pomo word classes and subclasses can be established on the basis of phonological, morphological, and syntactic criteria. Of these, morphological criteria are the most useful. The two largest word classes are verbs and nouns, and the vast majority of words in the lexicon fall into these two classes. Nouns can be further divided into four subclasses: common nouns (the largest), proper names, kinship terms, and pronouns. Of these, the kinship terms are the most morphologically divergent from other nouns. Adverbs and adjectives form much smaller word classes, as do more grammatical words (such as auxiliaries and postpositions), which are generally bound morphemes. There are also onomatopoeic words and interjections.[89]

2.8.1. Nouns

Southern Pomo nouns can be defined on the basis of morphological, phonological, and syntactic criteria. As has already been stated, Southern Pomo nouns can be divided into additional subclasses. Common nouns are the most numerous and morphologically simplest of these nominal subclasses.

2.8.1.1. *Common Nouns*

Common nouns, like verb stems, are overwhelmingly disyllabic. Unlike verbs, common noun stems are monomorphemic and can surface without any additional morphology: a common noun root may also be a stem, a grammatical word, and a phonological word. Examples (112)–(114) show monomorphemic common nouns in connected speech in a variety of grammatical roles without any bound morphemes affixed or cliticized to them (each noun under consideration is in bold and underlined).

(112) The common noun *nup^{h}:e* 'striped skunk' as a phonological word
núp[^{h}]:e nóp[^{h}]:ow ka:wíya bahṭ^{h}éǩo (H V: 1)
<u>nup^{h}:e</u> *nop^{h}:ow ka:wiya bahṭ^{h}eǩo*
/nup^{h}:e nop^{h}:o-w ka:wi-ya bahṭ^{h}e=ǩo/
striped.skunk dwell.PL-PFV child-PL big.COLL=COM
'Skunk Woman lived, with many children'

(113) The common noun *ʔač:ay* 'man' as a phonological word
[ʔ]iš:aw [ʔ]áč:ay (H III: 1)
ʔiš:aw ***<u>ʔač:ay</u>***
/ʔiš:aw ʔač:ay/
take.as.spouse-PFV man
'He abducted her, a man.'[90]

(114) The common noun *hi:mo* 'hole' as a phonological word
hí:mo č̓íʔ[:]iw (H I: 1)
<u>hi:mo</u> *č̓iʔ:iw*
/hi:mo č̓iʔ:i-w/
hole make-PFV
'(she) made a hole'

There are very few nominal affixes; most bound morphemes which attach to nouns are actually phrasal enclitics, which are listed in the discussion on noun phrases (§2.9). The nominal affixes, all of which are suffixes, are listed in the following section.

2.8.1.1.1. Common Noun Suffixes

The most clearly attested nominal suffix is ||-ya|| -ya PLURAL, an affix which is also found in the kinship terms and the pronouns. In common nouns, this suffix has a very restricted distribution. It only occurs on animate nouns, and it is possible that some of these forms are more appropriately treated as synchronically monomorphemic, as in 'twins' in example (115).[91]

(115) Examples of common nouns with the plural suffix ||-ya|| *-ya*

ka:wíya	(H V: 1)	ʔu*ya	(O ms.)	
ka:wiya		*ʔu:ya*		
/ka:wi-ya/		/ʔu:ya/	or	/ʔu:-ya/
child-PL		twins	or	twin-PL?
'children'		'twins'		

There is an additional plural suffix, ||-čʰma|| *-čʰma,* one which is not shared with pronouns and kinship terms. This morpheme is so rare and combines with so few stems that those words with this ancient affix might be alternatively analyzed as monomorphemic irregular plurals.[92]

(116) Common noun with the suffix ||-čʰma|| *-čʰma* PLURAL

še:bačʰma (O I: 1)
še:bačʰma
||še:wey+baʔ:ay-čʰma|| → [ʃe:.ˈbatʃʰ.ma]
/še:+ba-čʰma/
young+woman-PL
'young women'

Another bound morpheme which attaches to common nouns and appears to be an affix is the locative suffix ||-:na||, which roughly translates as 'at' and appears to have a highly restricted distribution.[93] This morpheme appears to be cognate with Eastern Pomo *-n̥a* 'indicating contact' (McLendon 1975: 123–24).[94] This suffix is transcremental, as seen in (117) following.

(117) Common noun with the suffix ||-:na|| *-:na* LOCATIVE
[ʔ]akʰ:á:na (H I: 3)
ʔakʰ:a:na
||ʔahkʰa-:na||
/ʔakʰ:a-:na/
water-LOC
'at water'

There is another transcremental suffix that combines with common nouns, though it has no surface form beyond transcrementation (see §2.6.6). Halpern notes that variation in the laryngeal increments of noun stems may be altered to indicate the "contrast ... between point and area" (1984: 18).[95] Nouns with this suffix undergo transcrementation; there is no other surface evidence of the affix.

||CVHCV-Ø|| → CVC:V-Ø

Halpern also notes that this pattern is optionally seen when *=wi* INSTRUMENTAL is attached to certain nouns (e.g., *kʰa:ma* 'foot' vs. *kʰam:a=wi* 'with foot'), and that some verbs show the same alternation to indicate a stative meaning (e.g., *mi:ṭi-w* lie-PFV 'to lie' vs. *miṭ:i-w* 'lying') (1984: 18). This morpheme is herein represented as ||-Ø|| *-Ø* DIFFUSE, and as Halpern correctly observes, its addition to a nominal stem derives a meaning (in English translation) such as 'at ...' or 'in (the area of) ...', as seen in (118).

(118) The common noun transcremental oblique suffix ||-Ø||

[ʔ]ač:a (H I: 1)	kal:i (Halpern 1984: 18)
ʔač:a	*kal:i*
||ʔahča-Ø||	||ka:li-Ø||
/ʔač:a-Ø/	/kal:i-Ø/
house-DIFFUSE	up-DIFFUSE
'inside [house]'	'up above (as an area)'

It would also be possible to treat this as a form of derivational ablaut rather than an affix; however, there is comparative evidence suggesting that the post-consonantal increment /:/ of Southern Pomo stems was historically stem-final rather than combined with the second consonant of the stem (i.e., *CVHCV: became CVC:V). Southern Pomo common nouns with the shape CVC:V regularly correspond to Kashaya Pomo forms with the shape CVCV: (e.g., Southern Pomo *nup^h:e* 'striped skunk' and its Kashaya cognate *nup^{h}e:*), and Southern Pomo forms with the an /h/-post-consonantally incremented sonorant correspond to Kashaya forms which preserve the /h/-increment and show /:/ on the second vowel of the stem (e.g., Southern Pomo *kawhe* 'gum, pitch' and its Kashaya cognate *qahwe:*) (Halpern 1984: 19–21). The ||-Ø|| DIFFUSE suffix mostly likely surfaced as final /-:/ in an earlier stage of the language, and this /:/ might have originated through compensatory lengthening after the loss of a consonant.

*CVHCV-C > *CVHCV-: > CVC:V

It is therefore historically plausible that this morpheme was once a suffix represented by a final segment, and it is convenient to represent it as such now. If the morpheme ||-Ø|| DIFFUSE is treated as a suffix, it is possible to assign it to the long list of Southern Pomo transcremental suffixes.

There are two additional morphemes that show suffix-like properties when applied to common nouns. Both appear to be enclitics in certain situations, but it is possible they are actually suffixes when applied to common nouns.

The first one is the problematic morpheme *-n* GOAL, which Halpern glosses as "object destination" (1984: 18). This morpheme is especially common in combination with ||=k^{h}ač|| 'ward'.[96] Example (119) shows this morpheme alone and in combination with ||=k^{h}ač|| 'ward' (*-n* is in bold and underlined).

(119) Examples of *-n* GOAL

ka:wíʔwan [ʔ]ám[:]an bá:neba (H I: 8)

*ka:wiʔwan ʔam:a**<u>n</u>** ba:neba . . .*

/ka:wi=ʔwan ʔam:a-n ba:ne-ba/

child=DET.OBJ earth-GOAL lay-S.SEQ

'. . . (he) put the child on the ground . . .'

ham[:]íṭow [ʔ]am[:]áŋhk^{h}ay hwálaw (H I: 11)

ham:iṭow ʔam:anhk^{h}ay hwalaw

/ham:i=t̪ow ʔam:a-nh=kʰay hw-ala-w/
there=ABL earth-GOAL-ward go-DIR-PFV
'thence (he) went downhill'

Halpern analyzes *-n* as a "final position variant" of the "suffix *-li*" (1984: 18). The evidence, however, does not point to clear allomorphy between *-n* GOAL and a [li] allomorph. There is a well-attested enclitic *=li* 'at' that surfaces as [li] in final position, though it is unclear whether it attaches to nouns, other word classes, or phrasal constituents. Example (120) gives *=li* 'at' on the stem *nopʰ:o-*, which can be both a noun ('village ~ rancheria') and a verb ('to dwell, many sit').

(120) Example of *=li* 'at'
niba ʔyodo ham:i ʔat̪:iyey nopʰ:o:=li (O I: 11)
nibaʔyodo ham:i ʔat̪:iyey nopʰ:o:li
/ni-ba=ʔyo-do ham:i ʔat̪:i-yey nopʰ:o-:=li/
and.then-S.SEQ=be-QUOT there 3C-PL.AGT live-PFV?=at
'Then, it is said, there where they were living,'

The preceding example is puzzling: if *=li* and *-n* are allomorphs of one morpheme (with *-n* the expected form in word-final position), why does *=li* surface unchanged in 120? However, this example is not a clear refutation of Halpern's analysis. Until further research proves otherwise, the *-n* GOAL morpheme, though it might be a true suffix separate from *=li* 'at' (at least on common nouns), is treated as an allomorph of ||=li||. It will remain unparsed when in combination with ||-kʰač-|| 'ward', as the two appear to be a fused unit.

The second problematic suffix-like morpheme is the patient case marker *=(y)čon*, which attaches to NPs and is therefore treated as a clitic. However, it has some suffix-like properties. In the pronouns and kinship terms this morpheme is almost surely a suffix and is one of three allomorphs of the patient case in those word classes. However, its distribution is not quite so random in these word classes.

In the kinship terms it appears to be restricted to plural forms. In the pronouns it is also restricted to plural forms; however, it is not the only patient case allomorph allowed to attach to plurals. The plural of at least one common noun, *ka:wi-ya* child-PL 'children', which is not part of the nominal subclass of kinship terms in the language, has an irregular form when the patient case morpheme is attached, as in (121).

(121) Irregular patient form of *ka:wi* 'child'

ká:čon (H V: 29)

ka:čon

||ka:wi-ya-yčon|| or ||ka:wi-ya=yčon||

/ka:čon/	*or*	/ka:-čon/	*or*	/ka:=čon/
children.PAT		child-PL.PAT		child.PL=PAT

Though the word *ka:wi* 'child' is not a member of the kinship term subclass, it has obvious semantic similarities to kinship terms, and it is possible that speakers applied the plural patient suffix from the kinship system to this word. (The patient enclitic on common nouns, though it is homophonous with the plural patient suffix of kinship terms, is used on singular common nouns.)

The denominalizer ||-t̯-|| -t̯̓- ~ -t̯-

Body part nouns maybe turned into verbs by addition of the suffix ||-t̯-||, as shown in example (122) (the surface form of ||-t̯-|| is in bold).

(122) Example of denominalizer ||-t̯-||

ká[:]li huʔ[:]út̯̓bi[:]( )ba šó:čiw (H I: 5)

ka:li huʔ:ut̯̓bi:ba šo:čiw

||ka:li huʔ:uč-t̯-bič-ba šo:či-w||

/ka:li	huʔ:u-t̯̓-bi:-ba	šo:či-w/
up	face-DENOM-DIR-S.SEQ	listen-PFV

'raised his head and listened'

2.8.1.1.2. Common Noun Compounding

As previously mentioned (§2.6.2.1), there is a robust compounding process in which two disyllabic stems are reduced to three syllables once compounded. It is the first syllable of the second noun in the compound that is lost to syncope, as in (123).

(123) $\sigma_1\sigma_2 + \sigma_3\sigma_4 \rightarrow \sigma_1\sigma_2\sigma_4$ in compound nouns
ʔahkʰapṭaka (O ms.)
ʔahkʰapṭaka
||ʔahkʰa + bu:ṭaka|| → [ˌʔah.kʰap.ˈta.ka]
/ʔahkʰa-pṭaka/
water-bear
'sea lion'

muhwayʔmi (O ms.)
muhwayʔmi
||muhway + ʔim:i|| → [muh.ˈwayʔ.mi]
/muhway-ʔmi/
fawn-black.berry
'strawberry'

The final consonant of the initial member of the compound can be lost to avoid impermissible consonant clusters, as in (124) following.

(124) Consonant deletion in compound $C_1VC_2{:}VC_3 + C_1V?C_2V \rightarrow C_1VC_2{:}VC_1C_2V$
huʔ[:]úkʰbe (H VI: 3)
huʔ:ukʰbe
||huʔ:uy + kʰaʔbe|| → [huʔ.ˈʔukʰ.be]
/huʔ:u-kʰbe/
'face-rock'
'eyes'

The final syllable of the first member of the compound may be lost when the first word is trisyllabic, as in (125), which also shows the complete loss of the onset and nucleus of the initial syllable in the second member.

(125) Syllable deletion in trisyllabic + disyllabic compounds
mih[:]ílhkʰa (H VII: 4)
mih:ilhkʰa
||mih:ila + ʔahkʰa||
/mih:il-hkʰa/

west-water
'ocean'

However, when the first member of a compound is trisyllabic and the second element has more than two syllables, the only sure phonological change is the loss of the vowel of the initial syllable of the second element. Example (126) illustrates the variation in the forms for 'Dry Creek' (Southern Pomo: 'west water location', the name for the village and tribal unit from which the modern members of the Dry Creek Rancheria descend), as used in the Dry Creek dialect and the Cloverdale dialect (note the /l/ → [n] change in the Cloverdale variant).

(126) Dialectal differences in compound 'Dry Creek' (from Oswalt 1981: 49)[97]

[Dry Creek dialect form]	[Cloverdale dialect form]
mih:ilaʔk^hawna	mih[:]ink^hawna
mih:ilaʔk^hawna	*mih:ink^hawna*
||mih:ila + ʔahk^ha=win:a||	||mih:ila + ʔahk^ha=win:a||
/mih:ila-ʔk^ha-wna/	/mih:in-k^ha-wna/
west-water-LOC	west-water-LOC
'Dry Creek'	'Dry Creek'

Example (126) highlights the great variability in the changes which may occur in the first syllable of the second member of the compound when it is glottal-initial. Compare the two compound-internal variants of ||ʔahk^ha|| 'water' (*-ʔk^ha-* and *-k^ha-*) with that seen earlier in (125) with the compound *mih:ilhk^ha* 'ocean', which has ||ʔahk^ha|| 'water' surfacing as *-hk^ha*.

In addition to being unstable as the second member of a compound, glottal-initial words may optionally undergo aphesis when they are the first member of a compound, as seen in the variants for 'Skaggs Springs' (a hot spring) in (127).

(127) Optional aphesis in glottal-initial compound
ʔahk^haho( )ʔwa:ni ~ k^haho( )ʔwa:ni (Oswalt 1981: 30)
ʔahk^hahoʔwa:ni ~ k^hahoʔwa:ni
||ʔahk^ha + ʔoh:o=ʔwa:ni||
/(ʔah)k^ha-ho=ʔwa:ni/

Table 27. Inflectional case-marking on proper names in Northern Pomo

Agent	**Patient**	**Oblique**
-Ø	-t̪uh	-wiʔ

water-hot=LOC

'Skaggs Springs'

2.8.1.2. Proper Names

There is evidence from other Pomoan languages suggesting that proper names should form a robust noun subclass with its own morphology in Southern Pomo. One of the hallmark features of this nominal subclass in other Pomoan languages is the ability to take inflectional case suffixes. Kashaya Pomo, for example, allows for inflectional case-marking suffixes on proper names and includes a vocative form (Oswalt 1961: 112). Northern Pomo makes use of a set of inflectional case-marking morphemes that are restricted to proper names (pronouns and kinship terms have different inflectional case-marking suffixes), as shown in table 27, which reproduces the Northern Pomo forms given by O'Connor (1987: 159).[98]

Sadly, insufficient data exist in Southern Pomo to establish the case-marking system (if there was one) for proper names.

Very few Southern Pomo proper names have been recorded, a fact that might relate to cultural conventions regarding the sparing use of such names.[99] O'Connor notes that proper names were seldom used for reference or direct address in Northern Pomo (1987: 158–59). And this avoidance of proper names appears to be shared by Southern Pomo. Oswalt states that "proper names of individuals cannot be used in ordinary secular situations; instead, a kinship term is almost invariably employed as a term of address" (2002: 314). It is not clear, however, whether there was a strict prohibition on all use of personal names in so-called secular situations. The recorded Southern Pomo proper names appear to fall into at least two categories:

1. names based on everyday things (e.g., animals or other parts of the physical world)

Table 28. Southern Pomo proper names

Christian name	Elizabeth Dollar	Christian name unknown	Olive Fulwider	Nellie Cordova
Relationship to Elizabeth Dollar	Self	Elizabeth Dollar's mother's father's father	Elizabeth Dollar's sister's daughter	Elizabeth Dollar's sister's daughter; Olive Fulwider's younger sister
Southern Pomo	*mukʰ:aṭ̓kʰa:nimen* /mukʰ:aṭ̓=kʰa:ni-men/ dry=LOC-FEM	*mok:oli:yey* /mok:oli:=yey/ curly.haired=AGT	*na:hoʔmen* /na:ho-ʔmen/ ?-FEM or /na:hoʔ-men/ ?-FEM	*ṭʰak̓men* /ṭʰak̓-men/ ?-FEM
English translation (if any)	'brazen, bold-woman' (lit: 'dry inside') [Oswalt specifically notes this is a 'nickname']	['curly haired man/one']	No known meaning[100]	No known meaning[101]
Type	(1)	(1)	(2)	(2)
Source	(O D: ED)	(O D: ED)	(W: OF)	(W: OF)

2. names that carry no synchronic meaning beyond their being attached to specific humans (similar to English names like Byron or Harry)

It is unclear whether the first type of name is really in the same class as the second, and it might be the case that individuals had more than one name: type (1) names might therefore be nicknames, and type (2) names might be given names. Table 28 lists the four Southern Pomo names given by fluent speakers before 1930.[102]

The name of Elizabeth Dollar is specifically mentioned by Oswalt as being her nickname, and it seems likely that type (1) names are all nicknames.[103] The female names in the table reveal slightly more about this word class and the cultural norms which surround it. The names for all of the women in table 28 end in a feminine suffix, which might be restricted to this word class. It is unclear whether this suffix is ||-men|| or ||-ʔmen||. Olive Fulwider remembers that her mother dropped the feminine suffix for direct address, and this vocative form was *na:ho* [ˈnaː.ho] with no final glottal stop. If the /ʔ/ of *na:hoʔmen* were part of the proper name stem, its disappearance in the vocative might be an isolated irregularity or a glimpse into a more widespread phenomenon in the proper names for which we have no evidence. Because the majority of the scant records of this suffix show no hint of a preceding glottal stop when the feminine suffix follows a vowel, the form ||-men|| is treated as basic hereafter.

The name of Nellie Cordova, *ṭʰak̓men,* has been passed down through her oldest daughter's line as the name for the oldest daughter in each generation. And the modern bearers of the name apparently know it only with the feminine ending. Whether Nellie's name also took an unsuffixed vocative form is not known at this time. However, both of these type (2) proper names, *na:hoʔmen* and *ṭʰak̓men,* do not appear to have been used sparingly in the home environment. It is difficult to determine how remembered usage of proper names in the home environment meshes with previous scholars' statements about proper name prohibitions.[104]

There is evidence that the feminine suffix ||-men|| might have functioned as a productive derivational suffix which created proper names from any word class, including borrowed words. The name <Panumen> with the translation "Handkerchief Lady" is listed in the kinship lists for Dry Creek, which were created as part of a project by the Army Corps of Engineers (Theodoratus et al. 1975: 283). On the basis of the translation, the first two syllables of the name <Panumen> appear to have been adapted to Southern Pomo phonology from the original Spanish word *pañuelo* [pa.ˈɲũe.lo] 'handkerchief', and the final syllable <-men> is clearly the feminine suffix ||-men||.

It does not appear that this morpheme is restricted to proper names in Southern Pomo. Kashaya Pomo makes use of the cognate morpheme *-meń* on several feminine kinship terms, such as forms for 'wife', 'granddaughter', and 'spouse's sister' (Buckley 1994: 375–80). And there is evidence for the use of ||-men|| on kinship terms in Southern Pomo. One possible example is the sequence *-med-* in the word *mahṯikmeden* 'his/her/their own daughter', but if the *-med-* of this word is an allomorph of the ||-men|| morpheme seen in female proper names, it behaves quite differently than its Kashaya cognate. Buckley states that the Kashaya feminine suffix *-meṅ* is underlyingly a feminine suffix ||-me-|| and the agent case suffix ||-eṅ|| (1994: 380).[105] However, the word for 'daughter' given earlier has *-med-* before what is presumably the patient case suffix *-en* (i.e., *mahṭ̪ik-med-en*).[106]

An additional possible allomorph of the feminine suffix, *-md-*, appears in Gifford's record of "kademde or kad'emen" for "g[rand]d[aughter]" (1922: 113).[107] The first variant listed by Gifford might be parsed as *kade-md-e*, though the component parts cannot be glossed with confidence at this time if, indeed, this is an example of a kinship term with the feminine suffix. If Gifford's forms do have the feminine suffix, this morpheme must have the three allomorphs *-md-*, *-med-*, *-men*, and only one of two possibilities would hold true: (1) these are all allomorphs of a single feminine suffix ||-med-|| and are therefore evidence that the feminine suffix in Southern Pomo is not synchronically a combination with the agent case marker as its second member, as in Kashaya; or (2) these allomorphs might descend from the same morpheme as the feminine suffix in proper names but are now inseparable parts of the kinship stems to which they were once suffixed and are not synchronic allomorphs of the feminine suffix seen on proper names. Without additional data, neither of these possibilities can be ruled out, and no further attempt to do so is made hereafter.

The final morpheme *-yey* of *mok:oli:-yey* '[curly haired one/man]', the name of Elizabeth Dollar's mother's father's father and the sole male name in table 28, appears to serve a different role in this context than is otherwise observed in the use of this morpheme with the pronouns, kinship terms, and common nouns. It seems that this '*-yey*' is the masculine counterpart of ||-men|| on proper names.

O'Connor notes that the Northern Pomo case enclitics *=yaʔ* AGENT, *=yačul* PATIENT, and *=yačuʔ* OBLIQUE might once have been "inflected noun stems" and that the first part of these clitics might be cognate with the Kashaya morpheme *yaʔ* 'person'; however, she observes that her Northern Pomo consultant does not view the Northern Pomo form "as a meaningful nominal element" (O'Connor 1987: 155). This *yaʔ* of Kashaya is actually ||-yač-||, which has a final allomorph *yaʔ* after debuccalization of the final consonant; it is a morpheme that "is common[ly applied] to Kashaya names" in addition to the kinship terms of that language; however, it may be used without regard to the gender of the referent (Buckley 1994: 379–80).

The Southern Pomo morpheme -yey is an enclitic ||=yey|| on common nouns and indicates agentive case (AGENT); on kinship terms and pronouns, this morpheme is actually the suffix ||-yey|| and indicates plurality and agentive case (PLURAL.AGENT). In each of these nominal subclasses—common nouns, pronouns, kinship terms—this morpheme can only be used on agentive arguments and is affixed or encliticized to such subclasses without respect to gender. The cognate Kashaya morpheme ||-yač-|| is not reported to have any inherent plurality on kinship terms in that language, but it does mark the agentive case (Buckley 1994: 383).[108] If proper names in Southern Pomo make use of *-yey* as a masculine suffix, this gender associaton would be unique to this subclass, both within Southern Pomo and to Southern Pomo within Pomoan. It is hoped that further research uncovers additional names which might shed light on the difficulties and possibilities discussed in this section.

2.8.1.3. *Kinship Terms*

Kinship terms are the most morphologically complex subclass of nouns. Unlike common nouns, kinship terms must be inflected and take both prefixes and suffixes. A basic template is given in table 29.

Only the root and at least one marker of case must be present in all kinship forms. The morpheme types listed in the preceding template are discussed in templatic order with each individual morpheme listed in its own subsection.

2.8.1.3.1. Possessive Prefixes

With the exception of two types of vocative (formal direct and informal direct), every kinship term in Southern Pomo must begin with a possessive prefix. These prefixes are not exclusive of possessive pronouns: a speaker may say *ʔay:a-:kʰe ʔa:-me-n* 1PL-POSS 1-father-AGT 'our father', which is literally 'our my/our father'. Each possessive prefix is discussed separately in this section. Forms are given between pipes only when useful. The gloss-

Table 29. Kinship term template

Possessive prefix	Root	Generation suffix/ informal vocative	Number	Case_1	Case_2

ing convention of this work is included in parentheses at the right of each subheading.

ʔa:- ~ ʔaw:i- ~ wi- ~ ha- 'my/our' (1-)

This prefix is used for both singular and plural first-person possession 'my' and 'our'; however, the free pronouns *ʔaw:i:k^{h}e* 'my' and *ʔay:a:k^{h}e* 'our' may be combined with kinship terms inflected with this prefix to clarify number. This suffix shows a large number of allomorphs, and these appear to have a non-random distribution. The allomorph *ʔa:-* is overwhelmingly the commonest of them and the one seen on consanguineal kin terms, as shown in (128).

(128) The *ʔa:-* allomorph of (1-) on consanguineal kinship terms

[ʔ]a:káčen (H ms.)
ʔa:kačen
/ʔa:-ka-č-en/
1-mother's.mother-GS-AGT
'my mo[ther's] mo[ther]'

[ʔ]a:káto̪ (H ms.)
ʔa:kato̪
/ʔa:-ka-to̪/
1-mother's.mother-PAT
'my gr[and]mo[ther]'

[ʔ]ay[:]á:k^{h}e [ʔ]á:men (H ms.)
ʔay:a:k^{h}e ʔa:men
/ʔay:a-:k^{h}e *ʔa:-me-n*
1PL-POSS 1-father-AGT
'our fa[ther]'

[ʔ]a:méto̪ (H ms.)
ʔa:meto̪
/ʔa:-me-to̪/
1-father-PAT
'my father'

The allomorphs *ʔaw:i-* and *wi-* are prefixed to affinal kin terms, as illustrated in (129).

(129) The *ʔaw:i-* and *wi-* allomorphs of (1-) on affinal kinship terms

<awitgan> (Gifford 1922: 115)
ʔaw:iṭk^{h}an

<witkade> (Gifford 1922: 115)
wiṭk^{h}ade(ʔ)[109]

/ʔaw:i-ṭkʰan-Ø/	/wi-ṭkʰad-e(ʔ)/
1-spouse-AGT	1-spouse-AGT
'[spouse]'[110]	'[spouse!]'

The choice between *ʔaw:i-* and *wi-* appears to be lexically determined and therefore irregular.

The allomorph *ha-* appears to be entirely restricted to one kinship term, 'friend', a word which was used for distant in-law relations and with strangers whom speakers did not consider enemies (hence the English approximation). This form is perhaps one of the most interesting relics within Southern Pomo kinship morphology. Together with the other allomorphs of the first-person possessive prefix, the allomorph *ha-* lends support to McLendon's reconstruction of the first-person pronoun of Proto Pomo as *haʔáw for the "Subject" (=agent) first-person pronoun and *haʔáwí for the first-person possessive pronoun (McLendon 1973: 56). The Southern Pomo word for 'friend' is the only corner of the language which preserves an /h/-initial morpheme with first-person semantics. It likely survived in this special context due to glottal dissimilation (though see the suppletive form for 'my mother' in the section on kinship roots). Example (130) shows the allomorph *ha-* on a variety of forms for 'friend'.

(130) The *ha-* allomorph of (1-) on the kinship term 'friend'
<hag'kan> (Gifford 1922: 115)
hak̓:an
/ha-k̓:a-n/
1-friend-AGT
'C[ousin's] w[ife ~] friend'

hak̓:áičon (H ms.)
hak̓:ayčon
/ha-k̓:a-yčon/
1-friend-PL.PAT
'friends'

There are also affinal kinship terms which do take the more common *ʔa:-* allomorph, such as *ʔa:mac̓en* 'father's mother, father's mother's sister, father's father's sister, father's brother's wife', though only one of the relations expressed by this word is affinal, and that affinal relation is clearly not perceived in the same way within the culture. Therefore the apparently non-random distribution of the allomorphs of the first-person possessive kinship prefix do fit a pattern and are herafter treated as discrete morphemes within || ||, though they are all glossed as 1- (the translation of the root is sufficient to determine consanguineal vs. affinal status).

||miH-|| mi- ~ me-'thy/your' (2-)

The second-person possessive prefix has much simpler allomorphy than the first-person prefix. It is represented with ||-H|| because it must surface with a laryngeal increment on the following kinship term root. The choice of increment is determined by the factors covered earlier (§2.6.6). The *me-* allomorph is the result of vowel lowering when the kinship term root has /e/ (see §2.6.1). This prefix is used to indicate both second-person singular possession ('thy') and second-person plural possession ('your'). Examples of each allomorph are given in (131) and (132).

(131) The *mi-* allomorph of ||miH-|| (2-) 'thy/your'
mík:aċ (H ms.)
mik:aċ
/mi-k:a-ċ-Ø/
2-mother's.mother-GS-AGT
'[thy] mo[ther's] mo[ther]'

(132) The *me-* allomorph of ||miH-|| (2-) 'thy/your'
méʔ[:]en (H ms.)
meʔ:en
/me-ʔ:e-n/
2-father-PAT
'[thy] father'

||miy:a-|| miy:a-'his/her/their' (3-)

This prefix contrasts with the coreferential prefix ||maH-|| of the following section. In connected speech, it is used when the possessor of the kinship term is not the subject of the main verb. This prefix satisfies the need for an initial heavy syllable in Southern Pomo, and as a disyllabic morpheme, it does so without affecting the kinship term root, which does not take a laryngeal increment when prefixed with *miy:a-*. This prefix is therefore a true decrement (of the type seen in Kashaya) in its ability to remove any trace of a laryngeal increment from the root. As this is the only kinship prefix to have any effect on laryngeal increments, it is not necessary to create an additional term or to restrict decrement to this prefix and thereby be forced to create a new term for the plural act affix ||-t̪-|| (see §2.6.6). Following are examples of the third-person possessive prefix with incrementless kinship roots.

(133) Examples of ||miy:a-|| *miy:a-* 'his/her/their' (3-)

miy:áṭʰe (H ms.)	miy:aṭíki (H ms.)
miy:aṭʰe	*miy:aṭiki*
/miy:a-ṭʰe-Ø/	/miy:a-ṭi-ki-Ø/
3-mother-AGT	3-younger.sibling-GS-AGT
'his mother'	'his y[ounger] bro[ther or] sis[ter]'

There is a single kinship root which does not lose its laryngeal increment after taking the ||miy:a-|| prefix. This kinship term ||-k̓:a-|| ~ ||-k̓:ad-|| 'friend' has an underlying geminate consonant which descends from a historic change of *-CVCV ... > -CCV ..., as evidenced by comparing the modern Southern Pomo form with the Kashaya cognate *k̓aṭʰíń* 'my friend (agentive case)', which has preserved two distinct consonants and an intervening vowel. Example (134) gives ||miy:a-|| with the root for 'friend'.

(134) Example of ||miy:a-|| *miy:a-* 'his/her/their' (3-) with 'friend'
miy[:]ak̓:an( )wám:u (H ms.)
miy:ak̓:anwam:u
/miy:a-k̓:an-Ø=wa=m:u/
3-friend-AGT=COP.EVID=3SG
'it's his friend'

There is one additional kinship root that surfaces with an increment after prefixation, though this record is somewhat suspect. The root for 'mother's mother' has been recorded as *-k:a-* after being prefixed with *miy:a-*, which is most unexpected because this root can otherwise surface with a singleton consonant after other prefixes (e.g., *ʔa:kaċen* 'my mother's mother'). This unexpected form has one of three explanations: (1) it is an error made by Halpern; (2) it reflects a lost second consonant within the root, much as seen for 'friend', but leaving no evidence elsewhere in the paradigm of the root and that has no corroborating evidence in Kashaya; or (3) it an analogical change made more recently by speakers on the basis of 'friend' (they might have decided that /:/ must always be applied to velar plosives after *miy:a-* prefixation). The first explanation seems most probable. Example (135) provides an instance of the unexpected augment on ||-ka-|| 'mother's mother' after *miy:a*-prefixation (note the double indication of possession with both the free pronoun *ham:uba:kʰe* 'his' and the use of the prefix *miy:a-*).

(135) Unexpected occurrence of /:/ after *miy:a-* prefixation
hám:ubá:kʰe miy:ak:aċwám:u (H ms.)
ham:uba:kʰe miy:ak:aċwam:u
/ham:uba-:kʰe miy:a-k:a-ċ=wa=m:u/
3SG.MASC-POSS 3-mother's.mother-GS=COP.EVID=3SG
'it's his mo[ther's] mo[ther]'

||maH-|| ma-'his/her/their own' (3C-)

This morpheme is represented with ||-H|| because the following root must surface with a laryngeal increment, and as is the case with ||miH-|| 'thy/your', the choice of increment is conditioned by the factors discussed earlier (§2.6.6).

This prefix has clear cognates in Kashaya, Central Pomo, and Northern Pomo (Buckley 1994: 378; Mithun 1990: 366; O'Connor 1987: 237, 266–97).[111] Oswalt describes this prefix as one which "means the agent of the verb is the possessor" of the kinship term, a concept he labels "co-reference" (1978: 12). There is a great deal of variety in terminology used over several decades in the description of the cognates for this prefix in the sister languages of Southern Pomo, but for convenience, the terminology used by Oswalt (1978) for Southern Pomo is maintained in this work (without hyphenation), and this prefix is hereafter termed third-person coreferential possessive prefix (3C-).

Oswalt's statement, however, needs clarification: it is not the agent of the verb that is coreferential with the possessor of kinship terms prefixed with ||maH-||; rather, it is the least patient-like argument, which, for convenience, may be termed the subject, a term which is also useful in order to distinguish this phenomenon from the actual agent/patient case-marking system seen elsewhere in the grammar.

The following sentence in (136) includes both third-person possessive prefixes. In the example, ||miy:a-|| *miy:a-* is prefixed to *-ki-* 'older brother' because it is the older brother—both brothers are the same species of raptor—who sits beside *his own* younger brother and combs *his own* younger brother's hair.[112] The older brother is the subject of *bak^{h}:ay*, the main verb of the sentence, and it is therefore he who is the third-person possessor of the younger brother, and ||maH-|| *ma-* is therefore prefixed to *-:ṭ̓iki-* 'younger brother'. The prefixed kinship terms are in bold in (136).

(136) ||miy:a-|| (3-) and ||maH-|| (3C-) in the same sentence (H VI: 3)

miy:aki k^{h}aʔbék^{h}ač^{h}yey ma:ṭikí( )sa:ma čahčíba,

miy:aki *k^{h}aʔbek^{h}ač^{h}yey* ***ma:ṭ̓ikisa:ma*** *čahčiba*

/miy:a-ki-Ø	k^{h}aʔbek^{h}ač^{h}=yey	ma-:ṭi-ki=sa:ma	čahči-ba/
3-older.bro.-AGT	raptor.species=AGT	3C-y.bro.=beside	sit-S.SEQ

[ʔ]ahčipk^{h}aywi heʔ[:]éʔwan bák^{h}:ay.

ʔahčipk^{h}aywi heʔ:eʔwan bak^{h}:ay

/ʔahči-pk^{h}ay=wi	heʔ:e=ʔwan	bak^{h}:ay-Ø/
louse-comb=INSTR	head.hair=DET.OBJ	comb-PFV

'His older bro., the Fish Hawk, having sat down near his y. bro., combed (his) hair with a louse-comb.'

The prefix ||maH-|| *ma-* works in concert with the switch-reference suffixes (one of which can be seen on 'sit' in the preceding example) and the third-person coreferential pronouns to track subject across multi-clause sentences. Other Pomoan languages which have cognate morphemes for Southern Pomo ||maH-||, its switch-reference suffixes, and its third-person coreferential pronouns show them to behave in a more nuanced manner in certain genres of natural discourse in which the third-person morphemes indicate speaker empathy with a third-person argument and not coreferentiality (Mithun 1990; Mithun 1993). However, the data for Southern Pomo, which come from elicitations and monologic narratives, consistently show a simple coreferential function, which might indicate a difference between Southern Pomo and some Pomoan languages; it also might be the result of an incomplete database, one which was not able to make use of a living community of speakers who interact with one another during data collection.

The third-person coreferential suffix ||maH-|| *ma-* does have one clear non-third-person use in Southern Pomo: kinship terms with this prefix are apparently the citation form and are used in constructions that translate with 'have' in English, as shown in (137a and 137b).

(137a) Non-third-person use of ||maH-|| *ma-* in a 'have' construction
ma?[:]éko?ká?ma (H ms.)
ma?:eko?ka?ma
/ma-?:e=ko=?ka=?ma/
3c-father=COM=INTER=2SG.AGT
'have you a father[?]'

(137b) Non-third-person use of ||maH-|| *ma-* in a 'have' construction
ma?[:]éko?wá?a (H ms.)
ma?:eko?wa?a
/ma-?:e=ko=?wa=?a/
3c-father=COM=COP.EVID=1SG.AGT
'I have a father'

The glossing 3C- in these constructions does not in any way line up with the semantics; however, for the sake of consistency, this morpheme is glossed in the same way throughout this grammar whether it appears in its canonical role or the specialized construction in (137).

2.8.1.3.2. Kinship Term Roots

The kinship term roots show a split between monosyllabic and disyllabic roots. The monosyllabic roots of the shape -CV- are overwhelmingly those which stand for consanguineal kinship terms. Disyllabic roots and monosyllabic roots with a consonant cluster in general stand for affinal terms. The most glaring exception to these generalizations is ||-k̓:a|| ~ ||-k̓:ad-|| 'friend', which is an irregular root, one variant of which does have a second consonant, and is cognate with a Kashaya form that suggests this root descends from a root with two consonants, as discussed in the previous section (§2.8.1.3.1). The following are taken from appendix I of Walker (2013), which lists incomplete paradigms for each of these roots. Gifford (1922) lists many more terms, but his inability to hear and record the sounds correctly renders them too inaccurate to be included here.[113] Each of the following roots includes a translation that should not be considered exhaustive; they are listed together with the generational suffix (described in the next section) with which each combines in some forms.

||-ba-ċ-||	*-ba- ~ -ba:- ~ -bʔa-* 'father's father, father's father's brother'
||-ča-ċ-||	*-ča- ~ -č:a-* 'mother's father, mother's father's brother, mother's older brother'
||-či-ki-||	*-či- ~ -č:i-* 'father's younger brother, stepfather, mother's younger sister's husband, father's sister's son'
||-ču-ċ-||	*-ču- ~ -č:u-* 'mother's younger brother'
||-dak^{h}ad-||	*-ʔdakd- ~ -ʔdakan ~ -ṭk^{h}ad- ~ -ṭk^{h}an* 'spouse'
||-di-ki-||	*-di- ~ -dʔi-* 'older sister'
||-ka-ċ-|| ~ ||k:a-ċ-||	*-ka- ~ -k:a-* 'mother's mother, mother's mother's sister'
||-k̓:a-|| ~ ||-k̓:ad-||	*-k̓:a- ~ -k̓:ad- ~ -k̓:an* 'friend, cousin's wife?'
||-kod-||	*-k:od- ~ -kon* 'sister's husband'

||-ma-c̓-||	*-ma- ~ -m:a-*
	‘father’s mother, father’s mother’s sister, father’s father’s sister, father’s brother’s wife’
||-me-|| ~ ||-ʔe-||	*-me- ~ -ʔ:e-*
	‘father’
||-mi-ki-|| ~ ||-ki-||	*-mi- ~ -:ki- ~ -ki-*
	‘older brother’
||-mu-c̓-||	*-mu- ~ -m:u-*
	‘father’s younger brother’s wife, father’s sister, father’s younger brother’s wife’
||-pʰak-ki-||	*-pʰak-*
	‘son’
||-ši-ki-||	*-ši-*
	‘mother’s younger sister’
||-šu-c̓-||	*-šu- ~ -š:u-*
	‘mother’s older sister’
||-ṭ̓i-ki-||	*-ṭ̓i- ~ -:ṭ̓i-*
	‘younger sister, younger brother’
||-ṭʰe-|| ~ ||-č̓e-||	*-ṭʰe- ~ -hṭʰe- ~ -č̓e-*
	‘mother’

As can be seen in the preceding list, there are some irregular roots, such as ‘friend’ and ‘older brother’, and both forms for ‘father’ and ‘mother’ have suppletive forms. McLendon notes that Eastern Pomo uses suppletion together with prefixation to distinguish between ego’s parent versus a second or third person’s parent (1975: 115). The suppletive forms of Southern Pomo, however, do not seem to serve the same function. The two roots for ‘mother’ are distributed as follows: the root ||-č̓e-|| is restricted to first-person-possessed forms and the formal vocative; ||-ṭʰe-|| is found in all other situations. The suppletive forms for father, however, are not distributed along the same lines: ||-ʔe-|| is restricted to second-person-possessed forms and third-person-coreferential-possessed forms; ||-me-|| is restricted to first-person-possessed forms and third-person-possessed forms.

2.8.1.3.3. The Generational Suffixes ||-ċ-|| -ċ- and ||-ki-|| -ki- ~ -ke- ~ -k- (GS)

There are two generational suffixes which attach directly to the kinship root. The suffix ||-ċ-|| *-ċ-* is attached to roots which stand for consanguineal relations who are of ego's parents' generation or earlier. This should not be taken to mean that only blood relations were referenced with kinship terms bearing the ||-ċ-|| *-ċ-* suffix; Southern Pomo kin terms are more inclusive than the glosses indicate. For example, the attested translations for the root ||-ma-|| 'father's mother', which takes the *-ċ-* suffix, actually applies to several female kin, including one affinal relation, and a more complete translation would be: 'father's mother, father's mother's sister, father's father's sister, father's brother's wife'. However, it is clear that the core meaning of this suffix includes consanguineal kin, and any affinal relations referenced by kinship terms with the ||-ċ-|| *-ċ-* suffix are those which Southern Pomo culture included within a broader consanguineal category.

The ||-ċ-|| suffix is very ancient within Pomoan; it is reconstructed for Proto Pomo as *-:ċi- 'one's own kinsman in generations above ego' (McLendon 1973: 56). Those kinship terms which take the ||-ċ-|| generational suffix do so in all forms within their respective paradigms with two exceptions: (1) first-person-possessed kin terms in the patient case lose ||-ċ-|| before the *-t̪o* allomorph of the patient case suffix (an allomorph that is only found on first-person-possessed forms within this subclass), though the patient case suffix may surface with /:/ as evidence of the otherwise missing generational suffix; (2) it is absent from the reduplicated informal (or child speech) vocative. Thus *ʔa:-ču-ċ-en* 1-mother's.younger.brother-GS-AGT 'my uncle' and *ču-ċ-eʔ* mother's.brother-GS-VOC 'uncle!' both show this generational suffix surfacing, but it only surfaces as length on the patient suffix in *ʔa:-ču-t̪:o* 1-mother's.brother-GS-AGT 'my uncle' and is entirely omitted in *t̪u:-t̪u* mother's.younger.brother ~ INFORMAL.VOC 'uncle!'.

The second generational suffix, ||-ki-|| *-ki-* ~ *-ke-* ~ *-k-*, is applied to consanguineal kin terms which stand for relations who are younger than ego's parents (e.g., father's younger brother, older brother, older sister, younger sibling, etc.). This suffix has three allomorphs, each of which can be predicted on the basis of the following morpheme. The three allomorphs of ||-ki-|| are discussed next.

The -ke- allomorph of ||-ki-||

This form is found before suffixes with an underlying /e/ and is the result of the regular vowel lowering alternation already discussed (§2.6.1). The following suffixes create the environment for the allomorph *-ke-*: the first-person-possessed agentive suffix ||-en||, the vocative suffix ||-eʔ|| (or any allomorph of the vocative with an /e/);[114] and the possessive suffix ||-:kʰe||. The vowel initial suffixes which trigger this allomorph subsequently lose their initial vowel (and therefore the visible evidence of the trigger) due to the V→Ø/__V rule discussed earlier (§2.6.2). Examples are given in (138)–(140) of ||-ki-|| surfacing as *-ke-* before each of these suffixes.

(138) *-ke-* allomorph of ||-ki-|| before the suffix ||-en|| AGENTIVE
[ʔ]a:díken (H ms.)
ʔa:diken
||ʔa:-di-ki-en||
/ʔa:-di-ke-n/
1-older.sister-GS-AGT
'my o[lder] sis[ter]'

(139) *-ke-* allomorph of ||-ki-|| before the suffix ||-eʔ|| VOCATIVE
díkeʔ (H ms.)
dikeʔ
||di-ki-eʔ||
/di-ke-ʔ/
older.sister-GS-VOC
'o[lder] sis[ter !]'

(140) *-ke-* allomorph of ||-ki-|| before the suffix ||-:kʰe|| possessive
[ʔ]a:diké:kʰe čʰeʔ[:]eṭmay( )wám:u (H ms.)
ʔa:dike:kʰe čʰeʔ:eṭmaywam:u
||ʔa:-di-ki-:kʰe čʰeʔ:eṭmay=wa=m:u||
/ʔa:-di-ke-:kʰe čʰeʔ:eṭmay=wa=m:u/
1-older.sister-GS-POSS basket=COP.EVID=3SG
'this is my o[lder] sis[ter's] basket'

The -k- allomorph of ||-ki-||

This allomorph is in free variation with *-ki-* before certain /y/-initial suffixes, though the *-k-* form is by far the most commonly recorded allomorph in this context. Example (141) displays an instance of recorded free variation before the plural suffix *-ya* (the *-k-* allomorph is in bold).

(141) Free variation between *-ki-* and *-k-* allomorphs of ||-ki-|| before ||-ya|| PL
[ʔ]ák^{h}:o má:ṭ̓ikiyačó:k̓oʔwáʔa ~ má:ṭ̓ikyačó:k̓oʔwáʔa (H ms.)
ʔak^{h}:o ma:ṭ̓ikyačo:k̓oʔwaʔa
||ʔak^{h}:o maH-ṭ̓i-ki-ya-čo:=k̓o=ʔwa=ʔa||
/ʔak^{h}:o ma-:ṭ̓i-k-ya-čo:=k̓o=ʔwa=ʔa/
two 3C-younger.sibling-GS-PL-OBL=COM=COP.EVID=1SG.AGT
'I have 2 y[ounger] siblings'

The ||-ki-|| generational suffix surfaces as *-ki-* in all other contexts. Like the ||-ċ-|| generational suffix, ||-ki-|| is ancient and has been reconstructed for Proto Pomo as *-qi 'ego's own older siblings or the younger siblings of one's parents' (McLendon 1973: 56). It has been reported that the Kashaya cognate of this morpheme in combination with a case suffix marks kin terms (and proper names) as specifically masculine and does not indicate relative age within generations (Buckley 1994: 379–80). There is no indication that this suffix has any masculine semantics in Southern Pomo. The Kashaya cognate must have changed the semantics of this suffix since its split from its shared ancestor with Southern Pomo or the masculine-only semantics have been incorrectly analyzed.

2.8.1.3.4. The Informal Vocative (Child Speech Vocative)

Kinship terms have a special informal vocative (child speech vocative) which is formed with the reduplicative affix ||-:ř-||. Forms in the informal vocative may optionally take the vocative suffixes ||-eʔ|| or ||-deʔ||. These forms are associated with child speech and are roughly comparable to English forms like 'dad ~ daddy', 'mom ~ mama ~ mommy', 'sis ~ sissy', 'bubba', etc. Examples of reduplicated informal vocatives are given in (142).[115]

(142) Informal vocatives with reduplicative affix ||-:ř-||

ma:maʔ

||ma-:ř-eʔ||

/ma-:ma-ʔ/

father's.mother ~ INFORMAL.VOC-VOC

'[grandma!]'

ṭʰe:ṭʰe

||ṭʰe-:r||

/ṭʰe-:ṭʰe/

Mother ~ INFORMAL.VOC

'[mommy!]'

In addition to reduplication of the root, the informal vocative replaces /č/ with /ṭ/, as seen in (143).[116]

(143) Examples of /č/ → /ṭ/ with informal vocative

ṭa:ṭaʔ

||ča-:ř-eʔ||

/ṭa-:ṭa-ʔ/

mother's.father ~ INFORMAL.VOC-VOC

'mo[ther's] fa[ther] baby talk'

ṭu:ṭu ~ ṭu:ṭudeʔ

||ču-:r|| ~ ||ču-:ř-deʔ||

/ṭu-:ṭu-deʔ/

mother's.brother ~ INFORMAL.VOC-VOC

'[uncle!]'

The reduplicative informal vocative does not apply to kinship roots which take the generational suffix ||-ki-||; however, the informal vocative may be kept distinct from the formal vocative with such roots by not combining the ||-ki-|| with the vocative suffix ||-eʔ|| and thereby preserving the vowel of ||-ki-||; compare (144) and (145) (the generational suffix on the informal vocative is uniquely marked as GS.INFORMAL.VOC).

(144) Informal vocative with ||-ki-|| GS
diki
||di-ki||
/di-ki/
older.sister-GS.INFORMAL.VOC
'[sister!]'

(145) Formal vocative with ||-ki-|| GS
dikeʔ
||di-ki-eʔ||
/di-ke-ʔ/
older.sister-GS-VOC
'[sister!]'

The one exception to the prohibition on reduplication with kinship terms which take the generational suffix ||-ki-|| is the irregular root ||-mi-|| ~ ||-ki-|| 'older brother', which is *mikeʔ* in the formal vocative but *ki:ki* in the informal vocative. (The informal version is clearly reduplicated, as evidence by the /:/ of the first syllable; *ki:ki* is not simply the irregular root ||-ki-|| plus the generational suffix ||-ki-||.)

2.8.1.3.5. Plural Marking and Case on Kinship Terms

Plural marking and case cannot be disentangled on the kinship terms, and both are therefore covered in this section. Plural marking is discussed first, and all the morphemes which may fit into the CASE1 slot of the template in (§2.8.1.3) are then discussed before the thorny question of why number and case are combined in some morphemes is addressed. The suffixes and enclitics which may fill the CASE2 slot of the kinship template are discussed last.

Plural suffixes on kinship terms

Number marking is obligatory on kinship terms; however, the distinct plural suffix ||-ya-|| only appears as a clearly segmentable morpheme when combined with certain non-agentive cases. Example (146) gives kinship terms with the plural suffix ||-ya-|| coming after a generational suffix and before a non-agentive case suffix (the plural suffix is in bold and underlined).

(146) Plural suffix ||-ya-|| on kinship terms
[ʔ]a:díkyačó:kʰe čaw:ánwa (H ms.)
*ʔa:dik**yа**čo:kʰe čaw:anwa*
||ʔa:-di-ki-ya-čo-:kʰe čaw:an=wa||
/ʔa:-di-k-ya-čo-:kʰe čaw:an=wa/
1-older.sister-GS-PL-OBL-POSS stuff=COP.EVID
'these are my older sisters' [things]'

mídʔikyáčon [ʔ]uhṱéhṱen (H ms.)
*midʔik**ya**čon ʔuhṱehṱen*
||miH-di-ki-ya-čon ʔuhṱehṱe-Vn||
/mi-dʔi-k-ya-čon ʔuhṱehṱe-n/
2-older.sister-GS-PL-PAT tell-SG.IMP
'tell your o[lder] sisters'

The *-ya-* allomorph of ||-ya-|| PLURAL only occurs after the generational suffixes ||-ċ-|| and ||-ki-||. The allomorph *-y-* is seen elsewhere, as shown in (147).[117]

(147) The *-y-* allomorph of ||-ya-|| PLURAL
hak̓:áičon (H ms.)
hak̓:ayčon
||ha-k̓:a-ya-čon||
/ha-k̓:a-y-čon/
1-friend-PL-PAT
'my friends'

The final morpheme combination seen in (147), namely /-y-čon/ PL-PAT is phonetically identical with *=yčon*, a post-vocalic allomorph of the patient case enclitic of common nouns, which is encliticized to NPs without regard to number.

When a plural kinship term is in the agentive case, it is marked with the suffix ||-yey|| *-yey* PLURAL.AGT, as shown in (148) (*-yey* is in bold).

(148) Kinship term with the suffix ||-yey|| PLURAL.AGENT

mibʔáčyey (H ms.)

*mibʔač***yey**

/mi-bʔa-č-yey/

2-father's.father-GS-PL.AGT

'your gr[and]fa[ther]s. (i.e. your fa[ther's]fa[ther] & his bro[ther])'

híy:o [ʔ]á:mačyey( )wám:u (H ms.)

hiy:o ʔa:mač**yey**wam:u

/hiy:o ʔa:-ma-č-yey=wa=m:u/

yes 1-father's.mother-GS-PL.AGT=COP.EVID=3SG

'yes these are my gr[and]mo[ther]s'

Kinship term case suffixes

All kinship terms must be marked for case. There are two core cases, agentive and patient, and a number of oblique cases, most of which are indicated by adding a suffix or enclitic to the oblique suffix used for the formal vocative.[118] The case-marking morphemes of the kinship system show morphologically conditioned allomorphy, and there is a division between first-person-possessed kinship terms and all others in terms of case marking allomorphy. Each case is discussed individually.

The agentive case on kinship terms

The agentive case on kinship terms is split two ways: singular and plural are marked with completely unrelated suffixes, and singular kinship terms that are prefixed with the first-person possessive prefix take a different agentive case suffix than all other singular kinship terms. These divisions are summarized in table 30.

Examples of each of these agentive case suffixes are given in (149)–(151) (the overtly expressed agentive case suffixes are in bold).

(149) The agentive case suffix ||-en|| *-en* ~ *-n* on first-person-possessed terms

[ʔ]a:čáċen (H ms.) [ʔ]a:díken (H ms.)

*ʔa:čać***en** *ʔa:dik***en**

||ʔa:-ča-ċ-en|| ||ʔa:-di-ki-en||

Table 30. Suffixes which mark the agentive case on kinship terms

	Prefixed with first-person possessive	**Not prefixed with first-person possessive**
Singular	*-(e)n*	*-∅*
Plural	*-yey*	*-yey*

/ʔa:-ča-ċ-en/ /ʔa:-di-ke-n/
1-mother's.father-GS-AGT 1-older.sister-GS-AGT
'my mo[ther's] fa[ther]' 'my o[lder] sis[ter]'

(150) The agentive case suffix ||-∅|| on non-first-person-possessed terms

míy:ačaċ (H ms.)	midʔíki (H ms.)
miy:ačaċ	*midʔiki*
||miy:a-ča-ċ-∅||	||miH-di-ki-∅||
/miy:a-ča-ċ-∅/	/mi-dʔi-ki-∅/
3-mother's.father-GS-AGT	2-older.sister-GS-AGT
'his mo[ther's] fa[ther]'	'your o[lder] sis[ter]'

(151) The agentive case suffix ||-yey|| on plural kinship terms

[ʔ]á:čaċyey (H ms.)	míy:ačáċyey (H ms.)
*ʔa:čaċ**yey***	*miy:ačaċ**yey***
||ʔa:-ča-ċ-yey||	||miy:a-ča-ċ-yey||
/ʔa:-ča-ċ-yey/	/miy:a-ča-ċ-yey/
1-mother's.father-GS-PL.AGT	3-mother's.father-GS-PL.AGT
'my mo[ther's] fa[ther]s'	'his mo[ther's] fa[ther]s'

The patient case on kinship terms

Like the agentive case, the patient case on kinship terms is split two ways: singular and plural are marked with completely unrelated suffixes, and singular kinship terms which are prefixed with the first-person possessive prefix take a different agentive case suffix than all other singular kinship terms. These divisions are summarized in table 31 (the allomorphs of the plural suffix ||-ya-|| are included for the plural patient case forms).

Examples of each of these patient case suffixes are given in (152)–(154) (the patient case suffixes are in bold).

Table 31. Suffixes which mark the patient case on kinship terms

	Prefixed with first-person possessive	**Not prefixed with first-person possessive**
Singular	*-t̪o*	*-(e)n*
Plural	*-y(a)-čon*	*-y(a)-čon*

(152) The patient case suffix ||-t̪o|| *-t̪o* on first-person-possessed terms

[ʔ]á:bat̪o (H ms.)	[ʔ]a:mét̪o (H ms.)
*ʔa:ba**t̪o***	*ʔa:me**t̪o***
||ʔa:-ba-t̪o||[119]	||ʔa:-me-t̪o||
/ʔa:-ba-t̪o /	/ʔa:-me-t̪o /
1-father's.father-PAT	1-father-PAT
'our fa[ther's] fa[ther]'	'my father'

(153) Patient case suffix ||-en|| *-en* ~ *-n* on non-first-person-possessed terms

mábʔac̓en (H ms.)	míy:amen (H ms.)
*mabʔac̓**en***	*miy:ame**n***
||maH-ba-ċ-en||	||miy:a-me-en||
/ma-bʔa-ċ-en /	/miy:a-me-n/
3C-father's.father-GS-PAT	3-father-PAT
'his gr[and]fa[ther]'	'his fa[ther]'

(154) The plural + patient case suffixes ||ya-čon|| on plural kinship terms

[ʔ]á:kac̓yáčon (H ms.)	hak̓:áičon (H ms.)
*ʔa:kac̓**yačon***	*hak̓:a**yčon***
||ʔa:-ka-ċ-ya-čon||	||ha-k̓:a-ya-čon||
/ʔa:-ka-ċ-ya-čon/	/ha-k̓:a-y-čon/
1-mother's.mother-GS-PL-PAT	1-friend-PL-PAT
'my gr[and]mo[ther]s'	'my friends'

There is also the rare patient case allomorph *-an* found on at least one singular kinship term; this patient case allomorph is also found on the third-person singular non-coreferential pronouns (see §2.8.2.1). An example of the *-an* patient case allomorph is given in (155).

(155) The *-an* allomorph of the patient case suffix on singular kinship terms

mak:odan (O I: 13)

mak:odan

||maH-kod-an||

/ma-k:od-an/

3-sister's.husband-PAT

'her own brother-in-law'

The vocative case on kinship terms

In addition to the reduplicative informal vocative ||-:ř-|| described earlier (§2.8.1.3.4), there are other vocative suffixes, all of which can be used to form formal vocatives. The vocative case in Southern Pomo is unique in three ways:

1. The formal vocative is the only corner of the language in which disyllabic (or larger) words take no laryngeal increment.
2. Vocative kinship terms (both formal and informal) are the only forms that do not require a possessive prefix.
3. Word-final glottal stops are only reported from some formal vocative forms within the kinship terms.

There is a division between singular formal vocative kinship terms and plural ones. The singular formal vocative is formed with an unprefixed root, a generational suffix (if one is needed), and one of the vocative suffixes. There are at least two phonologically unrelated vocative suffixes: ||-eʔ|| *-eʔ* ~ *-ʔ* ~ *-e* and ||-deʔ|| *-deʔ* ~ *-de*.[120] These suffixes might have been in free variation on some kinship terms.[121] There is no evidence that the choice of one suffix over another carried any semantic weight. There is an observable tendency for the ||-deʔ|| variant to attach to kinship terms without a generational suffix, but the data are not complete enough to confirm this pattern. Unlike the diversity seen in singular vocative suffixes, the plural vocative is simply formed by the combination ||-ya-|| PLURAL + ||-čo-|| OBLIQUE. The singular and plural vocative suffixes are summarized in table 32 (the allomorphs of the plural suffix ||-ya-|| are included for the plural vocative forms).[122]

Table 32. Suffixes which mark the patient case on kinship terms

	Vocative case suffixes
Singular	||-eʔ|| *-eʔ ~ -ʔ ~ -e*
	||-deʔ|| *-deʔ ~ -de*
Plural	||ya-čo-|| *-yačo ~ -yčo*

Examples of each of these vocative case suffixes are given in (156)–(158) (the vocative case suffixes are in bold).

(156) The vocative suffix ||-eʔ|| *-eʔ ~ -ʔ ~ -e* on formal vocative kinship terms

báče̓ʔ (H ms.)	kače (W: OF)
*bač**eʔ***	*kač**e***
||ba-č̓-eʔ||	||ka-č̓-eʔ||
/ba-č̓-eʔ/	/ka-č̓-e/
father's.father-GS-VOC	mother's.mother-GS-PAT
'fa[ther's] fa[ther!]'	'[grandmother!]'[123]

(157) The vocative suffix ||-deʔ|| *-deʔ ~ -de* on formal vocative kinship terms

médeʔ ~ méde (H ms.)	čéde (H ms.)
*me**deʔ***	*če**de***
||me-deʔ||	||če-deʔ||
/me-deʔ/	/če-de/
father-VOC	mother-VOC
'father!'	'mo[ther]!'

(158) The plural + oblique vocative ||-ya-čo|| on plural kinship terms

bačyáčo (H ms.)	dikyáčo (H ms.)
*bač**yačo***	*dik**yačo***
||ba-č̓-ya-čo||	||di-ki-ya-čo||
/ba-č̓-ya-čo/	/di-k-ya-čo/
father's.father-GS-PL-VOC[124]	older.sister-GS-PL-VOC
'fa[ther's] fa[ther]s!'	'o[lder] sis[ter]s[!]'

Thus far the vocative forms (both informal and formal) have not borne possessive prefixes. There are, however, two types of vocatives which do take possessive prefixes. The first appears to be an emphatic variant of the prefixless formal forms already discussed; it takes the first-person-possessed prefix and is otherwise formed in the exactly the same way as the formal vocative. Example (159) gives a recorded instance of the prefixed and unprefixed formal vocative in free variation (though the prefixed form, as already stated, is suspected to be an emphatic form).

(159) Variation between prefixed and unprefixed formal vocatives
[ʔ]a:mikyáčo ~ mikyáčo (H ms.)
ʔa:mikyačo ~ mikyačo
||ʔa:-mi-ki-ya-čo|| ~ ||mi-ki-ya-čo||
/ʔa:-mi-k-ya-čo/ ~ /mi-k-ya-čo/
1-older.brother-GS-PL-VOC ~ older.brother-GS-PL-VOC
'o[lder] bro[ther]s!'

In the plural, a first-person possessed vocative sometimes appears with the sequence ||-ya-čol-e||, where the surfacing [l] before the vocative ||-e|| appears to be the underlying form of what otherwise always surfaces as [n].

(160) First-person-possessed vocative with |ya-čol|-e|| PL.IMP
hak̓:aičóle (H ms.)
hak̓:ayčole
||ha-k̓:a-ya-čol-e||
/ha-k̓:a-y-čo-le/
1-friend-PL-OBL-VOC
'friends!'

The other type of vocative with a possessive prefix is formed by adding the third-person-possessed prefix ||miy:a-|| to the formal vocative and suffixing ||-deʔ|| to the vocative of the unprefixed form. In this form, the only attested allomorph of ||-deʔ|| is *-:de,* though this might be a function of the small number of attested examples of this formation. Third-person-possessed vocatives are used to address a kinsman by his or her relationship to another person; they are tecnonyms and formed part of the apparatus with which Southern Pomo speakers could avoid addressing someone

Table 33. Oblique case-marking morphemes on kinship terms

	Suffix	**Enclitic**
Allative	*-šan*	
Comitative		*=k̓o*[125]
Locative ('beside')		*=sa:ma*
Possessive	*-:kʰe*	
Singular.oblique	*-e(:)-*	

with an incorrect or impolite term (Oswalt 2002: 315). Example (161) gives a tecnonymic vocative and includes both Halpern's free translation and another free translation published later by Oswalt.

(161) Tecnonymic vocative with third-person-possessed prefix ||miy:a-||
ká:wiʔyóka míy:ač:aćé:de (H VI: 5)
ka:wiʔyoka miy:ač:aće:de
/ka:wi=ʔyo-ka miy:a-č:a-ć-e-:de/
child=AUX-INFERENTIAL 3-mother's.father-GS-VOC-VOC
'It's our child, his mo[ther's] fa[ther]'
"It must be our child . . . O Father of his Mother!" (Oswalt 2002: 318)

Additional oblique cases on kinship terms

In addition to the vocative affixes, kinship terms may take other oblique case markers. Table 33 lists these additional case markers.

These case markers attach in different ways to different bases, with a major division between singular and plural kinship terms. Singular kinship terms with the generational suffix ||-ć-|| or a consonant-final root must have the singular oblique suffix *-e:-* (which is probably a variant of the singular informal vocative suffix ||-eʔ||) between the final consonant of the base (whether that base be a root+||-ć-|| or a consonant-final root) and a following oblique case marker. Singular kinship terms with the generational suffix ||-ki-|| may have /:/ between the generational suffix and the oblique case marker, but the details of this phenomenon are unclear at present. Singular kinship terms with no generational suffix may have the oblique case markers attach directly to the root. Examples of each of these types of singular kinship term combined with the oblique case marker

||-:kʰe|| POSSESSIVE are provided in (162)–(164) (||-:kʰe|| POSSESSIVE is in bold and underlined).

(162) Oblique case marker ||-:kʰe|| POSS on kinship term with ||-c̓-|| GS
míbʔac̓é:kʰe [ʔ]ahčaʔwá:ni hwákan (H ms.)
*mibʔac̓e***:kʰe** *ʔahčaʔwa:ni hwakan*
||miH-ba-c̓-e:-:kʰe ʔahča=ʔwa:ni hu:w-ak-Vn||
/mi-bʔa-c̓-e-:kʰe ʔahča=ʔwa:ni hw-ak-an/
2-father's.father-GS-OBL-POSS house=LOC go-DIR-SG.IMP
'go down to your gr[and]fa[ther]'s house[!]'

(163) Oblique case marker ||-:kʰe|| POSS on kinship term with ||-ki-|| GS
midʔikí:kʰeʔka[ ]má:mu (H ms.)
*midʔiki***:kʰe***ʔka ma:mu*
||miH-di-ki-:kʰe=ʔka ma:mu||
/mi-dʔi-ki-:kʰe=ʔka ma:mu/
2-older.sister-GS-POSS=INTER DEM
'is this your sister's'

(164) Oblique case marker ||-:kʰe|| POSS attached to vowel-final kinship root
má:muʔwa [ʔ]a:č̓é:kʰe čʰeʔ[:]ét̯̓may (H ms.)
*ma:muʔwa ʔa:č̓e***:kʰe** *čʰeʔ:et̯̓may*
||ma:mu=ʔwa ʔa:-č̓e-:kʰe čʰeʔ:et̯̓may||
/ma:mu=ʔwa ʔa:-č̓e-:kʰe čʰeʔ:et̯̓may/
DEM=COP.EVID 1-mother-POSS basket
'this is my mo[ther]'s basket'

When these oblique case markers are attached to plural kinship terms, they must be attached to the plural+oblique combination ||ya-čo:-|| regardless of the component morphemes of the kinship term to which the oblique case marker is to be attached.[126] Examples of oblique case markers on plural kinship terms follow (the oblique case markers are in bold).

(165) Plural kinship term with oblique case marker ||-šan|| ALLATIVE
mač:ác̓yačó:šan hač̓:ow (H V: 4)
*mač:ac̓yačo:***šan** *hač̓:ow*

||maH-ča-ċ-ya-čo:-šan hač̓:o-w||
/ma-č:a-ċ-ya-čo:-šan hač̓:o-w/
3c-mother's.father-GS-PL-OBL-ALL arrive-PFV
'They arrived at their mother's fathers' place.'

(166) Plural kinship term with oblique case marker ||-k̓o|| COMITATIVE
má:ṭikiyačó:k̓oʔwáʔa (H ms.)
*ma:ṭikiyačo:**k̓o**ʔwaʔa*
||maH-ṭi-ki-ya-čo:=k̓o=ʔwa=ʔa||
/ma-:ṭi-ki-ya-čo:=k̓o=ʔwa=ʔa/
3c-younger.sibling-GS-PL-OBL=COM=COP.EVID=1SG.AGT
'I have 2 y[ounger] siblings'

(167) Plural kinship term with oblique case marker ||=sa:ma|| LOCATIVE
mik̓:áičosá:ma čí(:)y[:]on (H ms.)
*mik̓:ayčo**sa:ma** či:y:on*
||miH-k̓:a-y-čo=sa:ma či:y:o-Vn||
/mi-k̓:a-y-čo=sa:ma či:y:o-n/
2-friend-PL-OBL=LOC sit-SG.IMP
'sit next to your friends!'

(168) Plural kinship term with oblique case marker ||-:kʰe|| POSSESSIVE
[ʔ]a:díkyačó:kʰe čaw:ánwa (H ms.)
*ʔa:dik**ya**čo:kʰe čaw:anwa*
||ʔa:-di-ki-ya-čo-:kʰe čaw:an=wa||
/ʔa:-di-k-ya-čo-:kʰe čaw:an=wa/
1-older.sister-GS-PL-OBL-POSS stuff=COP.EVID
'these are my older sisters' [things]'

Summary of number and case in kinship terms

Southern Pomo uses suffixes and enclitics to indicate number and case on kinship terms. The core cases are the agentive and patient cases. Oblique cases include different types of vocative (informal, formal, formal emphatic, and tecnonymic), oblique suffixes based on the vocative affixes, the allative, the comitative, the possessive, and a locative ('beside'). All kinship terms are obligatorily marked for number, and singular and plural kinship terms may also differ in the allomorphs of the case-marking morphemes with which they combine. Number and case-marking morphemes show a great deal of allomorphic variation, some of which is morphologically conditioned, some of which is phonologically conditioned, and some of which appears to have no synchronic conditioning factors. Table 34 summarizes the number and case-marking patterns discussed in this section. The ALLATIVE, COMITATIVE, LOCATIVE, and POSSESSIVE cases are omitted from the table; they are completely regular across number and prefix category, and all that is shown is the oblique suffix used to connect them (optionally in the case of vowel-final singular bases).

As can be seen in table 34, the agentive case suffix of first-person-possessed kinship terms is homophonous with the patient case of non-first-person-possessed kinship terms. This rather unfortunate situation arose through word-final sonorant neutralizations which are unique to Southern Pomo within Pomoan. In Kashaya Pomo, the agentive case of kinship terms with the first-person possessive prefix is indicated with the suffix *-(e)n̓*, and the patient case of kinship terms without the first-person possessive prefix is *-el* (Buckley 1994: 10, 380–83). Both *n̓ and *l merged with [n] in word-final position at some point after Southern Pomo split from Kashaya, which gave rise to homophonous agentive and patient case suffixes distinguished only by their privileges of co-occurrence with certain possessive prefixes.

The preceding table only covers case marking on kinship terms; however, there is a peculiarity relating to homophonous case-marking morphemes between the kinship terms and common nouns that must be covered here. The plural agentive suffix ||-yey|| of the kinship terms is homophonous with the agentive case enclitic ||=yey|| that attaches to non-kinship NPs regardless of number, a fact which parallels the homophony between one allomorph of ||ya-čon|| PL-PAT and the patient case enclitic ||=yčon|| that attaches to NPs regardless of number. Example (169) provides a sentence in which two common nouns are each singular and marked with case-marking enclitics which are identical to allomorphs of the plural case-marking suffixes of the kinship terms (the case-marking morphemes are in bold).

Table 34. Summary of number and case marking on kinship terms

Case → Prefix ↓		AGT	PAT	INFORMAL VOC	FORMAL VOC	EMPH FORMAL VOC	TECNONYMIC VOC	OBLIQUE
||ʔa:-|| ~ ||ʔaw:i-|| ~ ||wi-|| ~ ||ha-|| (First-person possessive prefix)	SG	*-(e)n*	*-t̯o*			*-e(ʔ) ~* *-de(ʔ)*		*none ~* *-e(:)-*
	PL	*-yey*	*y(a)-čon*			*y(a)-čo ~* *y(a)-čol-e*		*-čo(:)-*
||miH-||, ||miy:a-||, ||maH-|| (Non-first-person possessive prefixes)	SG	*-Ø*	*-(e)n ~* *-an*				*-e:-de(ʔ)*[127]	*none ~* *-e(:)-*
	PL	*-yey*	*y(a)-čon*				*???*	*-čo(:)-*
No possessive prefix	SG			||-:ř-|| ~ ||-:ř-||+*-e(ʔ)* ~ ||-:ř-||+*-de(ʔ)*	*-e(ʔ) ~ -de(ʔ)*			
	PL			*???*	*y(a)-čo*			

(169) Agentive and patient case markers on common nouns

kʰaʔbéyey čú:maṭčon [ʔ]óh:ow [ʔ]aṭ:í:kʰe ċú:ʔu (H V: 3)

*kʰaʔbe**yey** ču:maṭ**čon** ʔoh:ow ʔaṭ:i:kʰe ċu:ʔu*

||kʰaʔbe=yey ču:maṭ=yčon ʔoh:o-w ʔaṭ:i-:kʰe ċu:ʔu||

/kʰaʔbe=yey	ču:maṭ=čon	ʔoh:o-w	ʔaṭ:i-:kʰe	ċu:ʔu/
rock=AGT	gray.squirrel=PAT	give-PFV	3C.SG-POSS	arrow

'Rock handed his arrow to Squirrel'

Thus Rock and Squirrel, two individuals represented by common nouns in (H V), are marked with case-marking morphemes that would indicate they were plural were they kinship terms.

What explains this unusual split between plural-only semantics on kinship terms and number-neutral semantics on common nouns with these morphemes? Other Pomoan languages have similar morphemes which offer clues. In Kashaya the morphemes *-yač* and *-yačol* indicate agentive and patient case, respectively (Buckley 1994: 383).[128] Northern Pomo has the morphemes *=yaʔ*, *=yačul*, and *=yačuʔ*, which mark agentive, patient, and oblique cases, respectively (O'Connor 1987: 155).[129] And Central Pomo has the morpheme *ya*, glossed as TOPIC by Mithun (1990: 373), which appears to be cognate with the agentive case markers of the other languages. Recall that Southern Pomo marks the plural on highly animate nouns, specifically pronouns, kinship terms, and a few common nouns. In most cases plurality is marked with the suffix *-ya*, which is the Southern Pomo reflex of the Proto Pomo plural suffix *-aya (McLendon 1973: 55). On the basis of the cognates listed, the following diachronic process can be postulated in order to explain how ||-yey|| PL.AGT and ||=yey|| AGT split:

Diachronic path for ||-yey|| PL.AGT
*-aya=yač > *-ya=yač > *-ya=yay > *-y:ay > *-yay >-yey

Diachronic path for ||=yey|| AGT
*=yač > *=yay > =yey

In short, the kinship term suffix ||-yey|| is in actuality a portmanteau morpheme made up of the agentive enclitic and the plural suffix. This explains its semantics and its status as a suffix rather than an enclitic. The sound changes needed for this hypothesis to be acceptable are known to have happened (or are still happening) in Southern Pomo. Pre-palatal vowel raising is a well-attested process in the language and has been applied haphazardly in the dialects. The Cloverdale dialect has *ʔahčahčey* 'human; Indian' corresponding to Dry Creek dialect *ʔahčahčay*, both of which forms' final syllable is a contraction of *ʔač:ay* 'man', a word for which both dialects preserve /a/ before /y/. And the change of /č/ → /y/ in word-final position is also a well-established synchronic and diachronic fact of Southern Pomo phonology (see §2.6.3.1). The other changes (vowel deletion and degemination) are so common cross-linguistically that they need no explanation.

The same argumentation could be applied to the combination ||ya-čon||, which I have heretofore treated as two morphemes. On the basis of Pomoan cognates, this morpheme likely traveled a similar diachronic path:

> *Diachronic path for ||-ya-čon||* PL-PAT
> *-aya=yačol > *-ya=yačol > *-y:ačol > *-yačol > *yačon > ya-čon

This path postulates the splitting of the portmanteau by speakers after its creation. In other words, speakers reanalyzed the initial syllable of the case-marking enclitic as the plural through analogy to other plurals (e.g., *ʔa:ma* 2SG versus *ʔa:ma-ya* 2-PL). This is the analysis adopted herein, but the alternate analysis, namely that ||-ya-čon|| PLURAL-PATIENT is actually the portmanteau ||-yačon|| PLURAL.PATIENT, is also valid.

2.8.2. Pronouns

Southern Pomo does not mark person on the verb, and any reference to arguments which are not represented by a full noun phrase may be represented by pronouns or inferred from context. The pronouns also show a third-person coreferential form that parallels the third-person coreferential prefix already seen in the kinship terms (§2.6.3.1). Personal pronouns are marked for number, and both they and the interrogative pronoun are obligatorily marked for case. The demonstrative pronouns are poorly understood at this time.

2.8.2.1 Personal Pronouns

Southern Pomo personal pronouns have at least two forms: full forms which conform to the expected disyllabic shape of word stems in the language, and encliticized forms which tend to attach as second-position clitics (see §2.5 for a detailed description of the test for clitic-hood). Though there is no person marking on the verb in Southern Pomo, pronouns are not obligatory. Categories frequently seen in North America, such as dual number or a first-person inclusive versus exclusive distinction, are not found in Southern Pomo or its pronouns.

The pronouns show diverse number and case-marking affixes, including some irregularities which have not yet been introduced. In all pronouns except the plural third-person coreferential, the agentive case is unmarked.[130] There are three unrelated morphemes which mark the patient case: *-(a)n*, *-t̪o*, and *-:čon* (which is restricted to the third-person plural coreferential pronoun). In the first- and second-person pronouns, the ancient Pomoan plural is retained as *-ya*. The third-person plural appears to be a recent innovation: it is composed of the gender-neutral third-person singular pronoun *ham:u* and the collective enclitic *=hča*.

The second person distinguishes between singular and plural in all cases; the third-person singular (non-coreferential) distinguishes between masculine and feminine, though the third-person pronoun used for agentive masculine reference is not exclusively masculine and is more of a neuter pronoun. In the patient and oblique cases, however, the third-person singular masculine pronouns are exclusively masculine.

Each pronoun has one or more truncated forms, most of which are generally enclitics. The most reduced forms are found as enclitics attached to consonant-final hosts. Table 35 gives all the pronouns of Southern Pomo. The encliticized variants are written below the full forms; post-vocalic clitics are written above post-consonantal clitics. The oblique stems are those used with oblique case markers such as *-šan* ALLATIVE, *=k̓o* COMITATIVE, =sa:ma LOCATIVE ('beside'), =:kʰe POSSESSIVE, morphemes already discussed in the section on kinship terms (§2.8.1.3.5); the oblique pronominal stems may also take =t̪on LOCATIVE 'on', which translates as 'over' or 'because of' when applied to pronouns (e.g., *mi:ma:-t̪ʰu ʔaw:i=t̪on* cry-PROH 1SG.OBL=LOC 'don't cry over me!').

In addition to the morphemes already discussed, the oblique stems of pronouns may be suffixed with a special emphatic reflexive morpheme *-mhya* '-self'.[131]

Table 35 does not include all morphemes which serve as pronouns. There is the morpheme *wi(:)-*, which is in free variation with the third-person singular (non-coreferential) stems seen in table 35. Outside the agentive case, this morpheme differs according to gender, and any additional syllables are shared with the regular third-person singular pronouns. Examples of this *wi(:)-* (and different forms in different cases) are given in (170)–(172).

(170) Alternate 3SG.M pronoun *wi(:)-* 'he'
wíʔwáʔt̪o kʰáʔbe ba:nét̪way (H ms.)
wiʔwaʔt̪o kʰaʔbe ba:net̪way
/wi=ʔwa=ʔt̪o kʰaʔbe ba:ne-t̪-way-Ø/
3SG.M=COP.EVID=1SG.PAT rock throw-PL.ACT-DIR-PFV
'it's he who threw rocks at me'

(171a) Alternate 3SG.F pronoun *wi:man* 'she'
wáʔ[:]an mi:máča wí:man (H ms.)
waʔ:an mi:mača wi:man
/waʔ:an mi:mač-a wi:man/
now cry-EVID 3SG.F
'she's starting to cry'

(171b) mi:ma:t̪[ʰ]í:baʔwa wí:man (H ms.)
mi:ma:t̪ʰi:baʔwa wi:man
/mi:ma:-t̪ʰ-i:ba=ʔwa wi:man/
cry-NEG-COND=COP.EVID 3SG.F
'she won't cry'

(172) Free variation with *wi:ba:kʰe ~ ham:uba:kʰe* 'his'
wí:ba:kʰe ~ hám:ubá:kʰe miy:ak:aćwám:u (H ms.)
wi:ba:kʰe ~ ham:uba:kʰe miy:ak:aćwam:u
/wi:ba-:kʰe ~ ham:uba-:kʰe miy:a-k:a-ć=wa=m:u/
3SG.M-POSS ~ 3SG.M-POSS 3-mother's.mother-GS=COP.EVID=3SG
'it's his mo[ther's] mo[ther]'

Table 35. Southern Pomo pronouns[132]

	Number →	Singular			Plural		
Person ↓	**Case →**	AGENTIVE	PATIENT	OBLIQUE	AGENTIVE	PATIENT	OBLIQUE
1		*ʔa:ʔa*	*ʔat̪:o*	*ʔaw:i-*	*ʔa:ya*	*ʔa:yan*	*ʔay:a-*
		ʔa:	*=ʔt̪o*	*ʔaw-*	*ya*	*=ʔyan*	*ʔya-*
		=ʔa	*=t̪o*	*=ʔk^he*	*=ʔya*	*=yan*	*ya-*
				=k^he	*=ya*		
2		*ʔa:ma*	*mi:t̪o*	*mi-*	*ʔa:maya*	*ʔa:mayan*	*ʔa:maya-*
		=ʔma	*=mt̪o*	*(me-)*	*=ʔmaya*	*=ʔmayan*	*=ʔmaya-*
		=ma	*(=mt̪a)*	*=m-*	*=maya*	*=mayan*	*=maya-*
3	MASC	*ham:u*[133]	*ham:uban*	*ham:uba-*	*ham:uhča*	*ham:uhčan*	*ham:uhča-*
		=m:u	*=m:uban*	*=m:uba-*	*=m:uhča*	*=m:uhčan*	*=m:uhča-*
		=mu	*=muban*	*=muba-*	*=muhča*	*=muhčan*	*=muhča-*
	FEM	*ham:an*	*ham:adan*	*ham:ada-*			
		=m:an	*=m:adan*	*=m:ada-*			
		=man	*=madan*	*=mada-*			
3COREFERENTIAL		*ʔat̪:i*	*ʔat̪:it̪o*	*ʔat̪:i-*	*ʔat̪:iyey*	*ʔat̪:i:čon*	*ʔat̪:i:čo-*
		=ʔt̪i	*=ʔt̪it̪o*	*ʔt̪i-*	*=ʔt̪iyey*	*=ʔt̪i:čon*	*=ʔt̪i:čo-*
		=t̪i	*=t̪it̪o*	*=t̪i-*	*=t̪iyey*	*=t̪i:čon*	*=t̪i:čo-*

There are also three enigmatic morphemes which are in free variation with *ham:uhča-* 3PL-:

ʔahčuk̓un-	'they' ~ 'people (suppletive plural of *ʔahčahčay* 'human; Indian'); they'
mahčuk̓un-	'they'
wihčuk̓un-	'they'

Oswalt reports that these enigmatic third-person plurals "perhaps differ in some deictic fashion, though both E[lizabeth] D[ollar] and E[lsie] A[llen] denied a difference among the three" (O D). They are most unusual for a number of reasons: (1) they are trisyllabic but not synchronically segmentable; (2) they only differ in their initial syllables, each of which is homophonous with a kinship prefix, yet they show no signs of shared semantics with prefixed kinship terms; and (3) they are in free variation with *ham:uhča-*, and it is particularly unexpected that there would be no fewer than four trisyllabic words in free variation.

These unexpected third-person plurals and the alternate third-person singular stem *wi(:)-* hint at a corner of the grammar that might have passed from active usage among speakers in the near past. The fact that *wi-* is shared as the initial syllable by the alternate third-person singular and one of the alternate third-person plurals seems to indicate that they might both have been part of shared system, one which distinguished distance from the speaker in space or time (compare *ma:li* 'here' with *wi:li* 'yonder'). Whatever their former meanings, there is no modern evidence for any semantic difference between the alternate third-person pronouns and those in table 35.

2.8.2.1.1. Encliticized Pronouns

AOV (SV and OV) is the expected ordering when two NPs are present in a clause, as seen in (173):

(173) Canonical word order with two full NPs in a clause
k^{h}áʔbek^{h}áč$^{\check{h}}$yey dó:lon čóh:on (H VI: 1)
k^{h}aʔbek^{h}ač̓yey do:lon čoh:on
/k^{h}aʔbek^{h}ač̓=yey do:lon čoh:on-Ø/

raptor.species=AGT bobcat marry-PFV
'Fish Hawk[134] married Wildcat'

The ordering of encliticized pronouns is the reverse; two pronominal enclitics come together with the order OA (VOA when they are attached to a verb), as in (174):

(174) OA ordering of pronominal enclitics when combined
mihyanákʰ:eʔwamt̪áʔa (H VIII: 6)
mihyanakʰ:eʔwamt̪aʔa
/mihyana-kʰ:e=ʔwa=mt̪a=ʔa/
kill-FUT=COP.EVID=2SG.PAT=1SG.AGT
'I'm going to kill you'

2.8.2.1.2. Third-Person Coreferential Pronouns

The third-person coreferential pronouns (glossed as 3C) function in the same manner as kinship terms prefixed with the third-person coreferential possessive prefix ||maH-||: these pronouns are coreferential with the subject of the main verb. These pronouns translated into English as 'his/her own' for the singular or 'their own' for the plural. The examples of *ʔat̪:i* 3C.SG.AGT and *ʔat̪:i*-3C.SG.OBL- in complete clauses are given together with brief explanations (see §3.4.2 for additional discussion of the coreferential pronouns).

In the following example, the protagonist (a raptor not named in this clause) is the subject of the verb *muʔt̪ʼakaw* 'cooked', and he is also the subject of the verb 'brought' within the nominalized clause. The sentence literally means 'cooked some of what he brought'. It is the coreferential pronoun that allows for the correct interpretation of the unexpressed subject of 'cooked'. If a non-coreferential third-person pronoun were used within the nominalized clause, there would still be no need for an overt subject of 'cooked', but the meaning would change to one of his cooking what another person had brought. (In this example, the relevant pronoun is in bold in Southern Pomo and the English translation, and phrasal constituents of which the pronoun is a part are marked with [ ] in both the Southern Pomo and the English.)

(175) *ʔaṯ:i* 3C.SG.AGT within a nominalized clause in a sentence
[ʔ]aṯ[:]i ćíhṯa mí:hak̓( )wanṯóŋhkʰle muʔṯ̓ákaw (H I: 4)
[***ʔaṯ:i*** *ćihṯa mi:hak̓wanṯonhkʰle*]$_{NP}$ *muʔṯ̓akaw*
/ʔaṯ:i ćihṯa mi:hak̓=wan=ṯonhkʰle muʔṯ̓a-ka-w/
3C.SG.AGT bird bring=DET.OBJ=some heat-CAUS-PFV
'(he) cooked [some of the game that **he** had brought in]$_{NP}$'

2.8.2.1.3. Interrogative Pronoun 'Who'

The interrogative pronoun is *čaʔ:a*, which is inflected with the *-ṯo* suffix to form the patient case. It must be combined with the interrogative clitic *=ka*. Examples of the interrogative pronoun in both the agentive and patient case are given in (176) and (177).

(176) Interrogative pronoun 'who' in agentive case
čaʔ[:]áʔkam:u [ʔ]áṭʰ:a [ʔ]ahsóduy (H ms.)
čaʔ:aʔkam:u ʔaṭʰ:a ʔahsoduy
/čaʔ:a=ʔka=m:u ʔaṭʰ:a ʔahso-duy-Ø/
who=INTER=3SG gravel throw.many.small-DIR-PFV
'who threw the gravel[?]'

(177) Interrogative pronoun 'whom' in patient case
čaʔ:aṯoʔkaʔma dihkaw (Halpern 1984: 7)
čaʔ:aṯoʔkaʔma dihkaw
/čaʔ:a-ṯo=ʔka=ʔma dihka-w/
who-PAT=INTER=2SG.AGT give.one-PFV
'to whom did you give it?'

2.8.2.2. Demonstrative Pronouns

The demonstrative pronoun subclass is poorly understood. The demonstrative pronoun *ham:u* is used as both the third-person masculine singular pronoun and a demonstrative; Oswalt records that it may be used for 'that', 'it', 'he', and even 'she' (1978: 12). It is inflected for patient case with the suffix *-n* (*ham:un*). Thus *ham:an* 'she' and the patient case form *ham:adan* 'she; her' can only refer to a feminine argument, but *ham:u* and *ham:un* may refer to any third-person singular argument.

Table 36. Kashaya demonstrative pronouns

Case → **Gloss ↓**	**Subjective**	**Objective**
‘that, this, it, those, these, they (vague demonstrative or anaphoric reference)’	mu:	mul
‘this, these (the closer object)’	maʔu	maʔal
‘that, those (the further object)’	haʔu	haʔal

Additional demonstrative pronouns have been recorded, but there are apparent gaps in the record. Kashaya Pomo has three demonstratives, which inflect for case. Table 36 gives the Kashaya demonstrative pronouns as presented by Oswalt (1961: 112).[135]

The attested Southern Pomo forms appear to show a similar three-way distinction with case marking; however, there are gaps in the record and the glosses upon which semantic judgments must now be made are not sure guides to the nuanced glosses Oswalt provides for Kashaya.

In addition to the demonstrative *ham:u,* the forms *ma:* and *ma:mu* are frequently encountered. These are perhaps cognate with the first syllable of Kashaya *maʔu* of table 36. At this time it is unclear what semantic differences, if any, distinguish *ma:* and *ma:mu* from each other and from *ham:u.* Example (178) gives an instance of *ma:* as the agent of the verb *ʔiš:aw* ‘to take a wife (without consent?)’; the direct object of the verb (translated as ‘her’) is not overtly present in the clause.

(178) The demonstrative *ma:* as the agent of a clause

ma: ʔíš:aw (H ms.)

ma: ʔiš:aw

/ma: ʔiš:a-w/

DEM.AGT take.spouse-PFV

‘he takes her, reclaims her’

The following clause in (179) is an equational clause which begins with the demonstrative *ma:mu.*

(179) The demonstrative *ma:mu* in an equational clause

ma:muʔwaʔk^{h}e [ʔ]a:diken (H ms.)

ma:muʔwaʔk^{h}e ʔa:diken

/ma:mu=ʔwa=ʔk^{h}e	ʔa:-di-ke-n/
DEM.AGT=COP.EVID=1SG.POSS	1-older.sister-GS-AGT

'this is my o[lder] sis[ter]'

There is also a demonstrative, *ma:ʔan,* which is clearly cognate with Kashaya *maʔu* and *maʔal,* though how it differs from *ham:u/ham:un, ma:,* and *ma:mu* in terms of semantics is unclear. The final [n] of *ma:ʔan* is probably *-(a)n,* the patient case suffix that is cognate with Kashaya *-al*. Example (180) gives an instance of *ma:ʔan* as the patient of a clause.

(180) The demonstrative *ma:ʔan* as the patient of a clause

má:ʔan yá:laʔwa hodʔómʔdu (H ms.)

ma:ʔan ya:laʔwa hodʔomʔdu

/ma:ʔa-n	ya:laʔwa	hodʔo-mʔdu/
DEM-PAT	always=COP.EVID	handle-?[136]

'he always handles this'

Example (181) provides another instance of *ma:ʔan* in which it is nonagentive.

(181) The demonstrative *ma:ʔan*

čá:dun má[:]ʔan [ʔ]át̪:o héʔ[:]e (H IV: 7)

ča:dun ma:ʔan ʔat̪:o heʔ:e

/ča:dun	ma:ʔan	ʔat̪:o	heʔ:e/
look-SG.IMP	DEM-PAT	1SG.PAT	head.hair

'Look at this hair of mine'

[perhaps: 'Look at this, my hair!']

There is also an additional demonstrative *hi:ʔin,* which is similar to Kashaya *haʔu/haʔal* (though the vowel differences suggest separate origins). The [n] of this demonstrative appears to be the patient case suffix *-(a)n*. Examples (182) and (183) give instances of the demonstrative *hi:ʔin.*

(182) The demonstrative *hi:ʔin*

hí:ʔinnat̪i dan:át̪[ʰ]u (H ms.)

hi:ʔinnat̪i dan:at̪ʰu

/hi:ʔin=nat̪i dan:a-t̪ʰu/

DEM=but cover-PROH

'don't cover any of them[!]'

(183) The demonstrative *hi:ʔin*

hi:ʔin:át̪i duk:elhé:t̪ʰot̪̓ kʰaʔbéyey (H VIII: 6)

hi:ʔin:at̪i duk:elhe:t̪ʰot̪̓ kʰaʔbeyey

/hi:ʔi-n=nat̪i duk:elhe:=t̪ʰot̪̓ kʰaʔbe=yey/

DEM-PAT=but hard.to.do=NEG rock=AGT

'He had no difficulty with any of them whatever, the Rock.'

['None of them was difficult (for) rock (man)']

At this point the most useful assumption is that the Southern Pomo demonstratives functioned in ways which were similar to the system reported for Kashaya, its nearest congener. If the attested Southern Pomo demonstratives are converted into a table that resembles the layout of table 36 of the Kashaya demonstratives, the distribution of Southern Pomo demonstratives might be separated as in table 37.

The form hi:ʔi is postulated on the basis of *hi:ʔin*; I have no evidence for it. What semantic differences, if any, these demonstratives have in Southern Pomo cannot be determined at this time.

2.8.3. Verbs

Verbs are the largest word class within Southern Pomo. This section details the shape of the verb and lists the affixes which may attach to the verb. Derivational affixes are separated from inflectional affixes, and within each broad category of affix, the individual affixes are discussed in left-to-right templatic order.

2.8.3.1. Verb Structure

Verb stems are built around roots; most roots are monosyllabic, but some are disyllabic. Monosyllabic roots must combine with an instrumental pre-

Table 37. Hypothetical organization of Southern Pomo demonstratives

Agent	**Patient**	**Kashaya cognates**
ham:u	*ham:un*	*mu: / mul*
ma: ~ ma:mu	*ma:ʔan*	*maʔu / maʔal*
[hi:ʔi]	*hi:ʔin*	*haʔu / haʔal*

Table 38. Southern Pomo verb template

Instrumental prefix	Plural act prefix	Root	Reduplicative affixes	Plural act infix/suffix	Directional suffixes	Valence-changing suffixes	TAM

fix in order to form a verb stem. Verbs are the most morphologically complex word class within Southern Pomo, and all may take several affixes; no verb may surface without at least one affix. The template in table 38 provides a simplified summary of the relative ordering of affixes with respect to a monosyllabic verb root.

Each of these slots is discussed in the following sections. The verb root is covered within the remainder of this section. The instrumental prefixes, plural act affixes, reduplicative affixes, directional suffixes, and valence-changing suffixes are covered in the next section (§2.8.3.2.), and the TAM suffixes (which, for the purposes of the template, include the evidentials) are discussed thereafter (§2.8.3.3.).

The final consonants of some verb stems are or were separate morphemes, and the decision to separate these consonants from the stem is a difficult one. In some cases it is clear that an affix is present (e.g., *mehše-y* smell-SEM 'to smell something' versus *mehše-w* smell-PFV '(something) smells'); however, in other cases, an affix can be identified in one member of the pair with some certainty but not in the other (e.g., *čoh:o-y* lie.with.someone-SEM 'to lie with (someone) once' versus *čoh:on* 'to marry'). And in cases where there are no examples of the verb stem without the final consonant, it is impossible to know with any surety the morphemic status of the stem-final consonant (e.g., *šuhnaṭ-Ø* by.pulling.try-PFV 'test by pulling'). In most cases the final consonants of stems do not have any clear effect on the semantics of the stem.

2.8.3.1.1. Verb Roots

Verb roots may have the following shapes:[137]

i. -HCV-
ii. -HCVC-
iii. -CVHCV-
iv. -CVHCVC-

Some root-final sonorant consonants may also have an additional glottal consonant as part of the root (e.g., /-lh/, /-lʔ/; see §2.2.1 for a discussion). There are also some roots (most of them irregular allomorphs) which take the shape -HC-; and at least one root, ||hu:w-|| 'go', takes the shape CVHC-. Disyllabic verb roots can be further subdivided into those which are both a root and a stem (e.g., *č̓iʔ:i-* 'to do or make') and those which are only a root (e.g., *-k:elhe-* 'to be difficult to do').

The semantic content of verb roots varies according to the shape of the root. Disyllabic verb roots tend to have narrower meanings; monosyllabic roots may have obvious meanings, but many are vague or cover such a broad range of concepts that it is not useful to gloss them independently of the instrumental prefix with which they must combine to form a verb stem.[138]

(184) Disyllabic root that is only a root
root: ||-k:elhe-|| 'to be hard/painful to do; give up trying to do'
sample prefix + root combination:
dek:el:aw (O D: EA)
dek:el:aw
||di-k:elhe-ala-w||
/de-k:el-la-w/
by.gravity-hard.to.do-DIR-PFV
'to hurt going down throat'

(185) Disyllabic root that is also a stem
root: ||dihka-|| 'to give one thing'
dihkaw (O D: ED)
dihkaw

||dihka-w||
/dihka-w/
give.one-PFV
'to give'

(186) Monosyllabic roots with narrow meaning
root: ||-c̓:a-|| 'to break'
sample prefix + root combinations:

čac̓:aw (O D: ED)	šuc̓:aw (O D: ED)
čac̓:aw	*šuc̓:aw*
||ča-c̓:a-w||	||šu-c̓:a-w||
/ča-c̓:a-w/	/šu-c̓:a-w/
with.butt-break-PFV	by.pulling-break-PFV
'to sit on and break (a spring)'	'break in two by pulling'

(187) Monosyllabic roots with broader meaning
root: ||-s:uN-|| 'to remove small pieces; liquid to flow; to bother'
sample prefix + root combinations:

mus:un (O D: ED)	ʔus:un (O D: ED)
mus:un	*ʔus:un*
||mu-s:uN-Ø||	||hu-s:uN-Ø||
/mu-s:un-Ø/	/ʔu-s:un-Ø/
with.non.long.obj.-ROOT-PFV	with.sound-ROOT-PFV
'[for] fruit to drop'	'to make noise for no reason'

Throughout the next section, monosyllabic roots with narrower meanings are chosen in order to highlight the semantic content of the instrumental prefixes.

Southern Pomo verbs may inherently distinguish number: some verbs may only be used to describe actions done by more than one agent; some verbs may only be used to describe an action done by one agent. This dichotomy is an oversimplification, however, as the precise semantics are affected by the addition of plural act affixes (which add unpredictable semantics when applied to each verb stem). And some verbs differ on the basis of the number of non-agential arguments. The two broad types of verb are hereafter referred to as singular and plural verbs when there is a pair of verbs to warrant the division; verbs for which there is no separate plural are not called singular.

Plural verbs are not derived, inflected, or suppletive versions of singular verbs. In some pairs, a root might be shared between them, but the initial syllables are not morphemes with singular or plural meaning (e.g., *mi:ṭi-* 'one to lie (down)' vs. *ba:ṭi-* 'many to lie (down)', which have initial syllables which would usually mean 'with the nose/by counting' and 'with the beak/by poking' respectively). In other cases there is no relationship between the singular and plural forms (e.g., *čahnu-* 'one to talk' versus *ʔalhok̓oy-* 'many to talk'). Other Pomoan languages share this feature. For some concepts, neighboring Central Pomo has different verb stems depending on number of agents or patients of intransitive verbs and the number of patients of transitive verbs (Mithun 1988: 522–23). However, plural verb stems in Central Pomo may have singular cognates in Southern Pomo: compare Central Pomo *hli-* '(several) went' with its Southern Pomo cognate *ho:li-* '(any number) leave', and Central Pomo *hʔo-w* 'give (several)' with its Southern Pomo cognate *ʔoh:o-w* 'give contained mass; give a long object'. Plural verbs are indicated in the gloss with the 'many' for a verb indicating plural agents or 'several' to a verb indicating plural patients.

2.8.3.2. Derivational Affixes

The following derivational affixes are covered in this section: instrumental prefixes, plural act affixes, reduplicative affixes, directional suffixes, and valence-changing suffixes.

2.8.3.2.1. Instrumental Prefixes

Every monosyllabic root (with the exception of a few irregular roots like ||hu:w-|| 'go') must take one of the instrumental prefixes. These prefixes are ancient and can be reconstructed for Proto Pomo (McLendon 1973; Oswalt 1976a). In many Pomoan languages, several instrumental prefixes have merged, and Southern Pomo is reported to retain the largest number of these prefixes within Pomoan (Oswalt 1978: 16). Because of their great age, the prefixes have had millennia in which to undergo various semantic shifts, and the meanings of most are quite broad. It seems likely that the twenty-one attested instrumental prefixes of Southern Pomo, though no other Pomoan languages distinguishes more, might descend from a larger number in the past. Such a possibility is pure conjecture and cannot be proved with Pomoan-internal reconstructions because Southern Pomo is the most conservative surviving language with regard to these prefixes.[139]

Each Southern Pomo prefix is listed independently; the expanded definitions all come from Oswalt's definitions for Kashaya and his notes on Southern Pomo differences therefrom (1976a, 15–19).[140] Wherever possible, at least one of the following roots is used in examples in order to highlight the instrumental prefixes: ||-č̓:a-|| 'to break', ||-hnat̯-|| 'try, investigate', and ||-ʔt̯̓a-|| 'seem, perceive, feel'.[141] Following each prefix and definition, the examples are numbered, but there is no additional commentary unless needed to clarify an unexpected root or unusual gloss. In the glosses of each example, the prefix under discussion is given a simplified gloss due to spacing constraints; the same is true of example roots. The allomorphs of each prefix are listed after the morphophonemic form. See §2.6.1 and §2.6.1.2 for an explanation of vowel lowering and glottal dissimilation, the processes that account for all instrumental prefix allomorphy.

||ba-|| ba-'mouth, snout, beak, face striking or pushing against something'

(188) ||ba-|| prefixed to the root ||-hnat̯-|| 'try, investigate'
<bahnat'> (O D: EA)
bahnat̯̓
||ba-hnat̯-Ø||
/ba-hnat̯̓-Ø/
by.poking-try-PFV
'to test (path) with cane by poking (as in going through swamp)'

(189) ||ba-|| prefixed to the root ||-ʔt̯̓a-|| 'seem, perceive, feel'
<baʔt'aw> (O D: ED)
baʔt̯̓aw
||ba-ʔt̯̓a-w||
/ba-ʔt̯̓a-w/
by.poking-feel-PFV
'to poke with a stick'

||bi-|| bi- ~ be- ‘soft opposed forces, both arms, lips, encircle, sew’

(190) ||bi-|| prefixed to the root ||-hnat̯-|| ‘try, investigate’
<bihnat’> (O D: EA)
bihnat̯̓
||bi-hnat̯-Ø||
/bi-hnat̯̓-Ø/
with.lips-try-PFV
‘to taste (grapes)’

(191) ||bi-|| prefixed to the root ||-ʔt̯̓a-|| ‘seem, perceive, feel’
<bi?t’aw> (W: OF; O D: ED)
biʔt̯̓aw
||bi-ʔt̯̓a-w||
/bi-ʔt̯̓a-w/
with.lips-perceive-PFV
‘to taste (good)’

||da-|| da- ‘palm of hand, push, waves, fog; many projecting objects’[142]

This prefix has taken on the meaning of ‘by sight’ in some verbs; see *daʔt̯̓aw* ‘to find’ (194).

(192) ||da-|| prefixed to the root ||-c̓:a-|| ‘to break’
<das’*ayaw> (O D)
dac̓:ayaw
||da-c̓:a-ya-w||
/da-c̓:a-ya-w/
with.palm-break-DEFOC-PFV
‘broken’

(193) ||da-|| prefixed to the root ||-hnat̯-|| ‘try, investigate’
<dahnat’> (O D: EA)
dahnat̯̓
||da-hnat̯-Ø||
/da-hnat̯̓-Ø/

with.palm-try-PFV
'to push s[ome]t[thing] (to see how heavy it is)'

(194) ||da-|| prefixed to the root ||-ʔṭ̓a-|| 'seem, perceive, feel'
<daʔt'aw> (O D: EA)
daʔṭ̓aw
||da-ʔṭ̓a-w ||
/da-ʔṭ̓a-w/
by.sight?-perceive-PFV
'to find, see, discover'

||di-|| di- ~ de- 'gravity, fall; genetics, race; many long objects'

(195) ||di-|| prefixed to the root ||-ċ:a-|| 'to break'
díċ:aw (H VIII: 6)
diċ:aw
||di-ċ:a-w||
/di-ċ:a-w/
by.fall-break-PFV
'he breaks w[ith] body'

(196) ||di-|| prefixed to the root ||-hnaṭ-|| 'try, investigate'
<ʔahay dihna*ka*li> (O D: EA)
ʔah:ay dihna:ka:li
||ʔah:ay di-hnaṭ-ka:li||
/ʔah:ay di-hna:-ka-:li/
stick by.gravity-try-CAUS-D.SEQ
'He dropped the stick (testing it) . . . "

||du-|| du- ~ do- 'finger, work, action'

(197) ||du-|| prefixed to the root ||-hnaṭ-|| 'try, investigate'
<duhnat'> (O D: EA)
duhnaṭ̓
||du-hnaṭ-Ø||
/du-hnaṭ̓-Ø/

by.finger-try-PFV
'to feel (peaches) to see if ripe'

(198) ||du-|| prefixed to the root ||-ʔt̪̓a-|| 'seem, perceive, feel'
<duʔt'aw> (O D: ED)
duʔt̪̓aw
||du-ʔt̪̓a-w ||
/du-ʔt̪̓a-w/
by.finger-perceive-PFV
'to touch'

||ma-|| ma- 'sole of foot, hoof, claw of bird; twist of wrist'

(199) ||ma-|| prefixed to the root ||-c̓:a-|| 'to break'
<mas'*an> (O D: ED)
mac̓:an
||ma-c̓:a-Vn||
/ma-c̓:a-n/
by.wrist.twist-break-SG.IMP
'Break in two with a twist of wrist!'

(200) ||ma-|| prefixed to the root ||-hnat̪-|| 'try, investigate'
<mahnat'du> (O D: EA)
mahnat̪̓du
||ma-hnat̪-ad-u||
/ma-hnat̪̓-d-u/
with.foot-try-DIR-PFV
'to feel around with foot (testing path)'

(201) ||ma-|| prefixed to the root ||-ʔt̪̓a-|| 'seem, perceive, feel'
<maʔt'aw> (O D: ED)
maʔt̪̓aw
||ma-ʔt̪̓a-w||
/ma-ʔt̪̓a-w/
with.foot-perceive-PFV
'to feel with the bottom of the foot'

||mi-|| mi- ~ me- 'protuberance near end of long object, toe, nose, horn; reckon, read'

(202) ||mi-|| prefixed to the root ||-hnat̪-|| 'try, investigate'
<miʔdi$ wan ton(h)k^hle mihnatin> (O D: EA)
miʔdišwant̪onhk^{h}le mihnat̪in
||miʔdiš=wan=t̪onhk^{h}le mi-hnat̪-Vn||
/miʔdiš=wan=t̪onhk^{h}le mi-hnat̪-in/
nut=DET.OBJ=some by.reckoning-try-SG.IMP
'Test some of the nuts by cracking (to see if good inside)! (no smell meaning)'

(203) ||ča-|| prefixed to the root ||-ʔt̪̓a-|| 'seem, perceive, feel'
<k'oʔdi miʔt'aw> (O D: ED)
k̓oʔdi miʔt̪̓aw
||k̓oʔdi miʔt̪̓aw||
/k̓oʔdi miʔt̪̓aw/
good with.toe-perceive-PFV
'to feel good to the toe (no smell meaning)'

||mu-|| mu- ~ mo- 'non-long object through air; fire, heat, cold, light, emotions, mind'

(204) ||mu-|| prefixed to the root ||-hnat̪-|| 'try, investigate'
<ʔahk^ha muhnat'> (O D)
muhnat̪̓
||ʔahk^{h}a mu-hnat̪-∅||
/ʔahk^{h}a mu-hnat̪̓-∅/
water with.mind?-try-PFV
'to try out (a swift river to see if it is safe)'

(205) ||mu-|| prefixed to the root ||-ʔt̪̓a-|| 'seem, perceive, feel'
<muʔt'aw> (O D: ED)
muʔt̪̓aw
||mu-ʔt̪̓a-w||
/mu-ʔt̪̓a-w/
with.heat-perceive-PFV
'to be cooked'[143]

||p^{h}a-|| p^{h}a- 'long object move lengthwise into contact with; with hand'[144]

This prefix has not been found in combination with any of the three roots used throughout this section, and the following stem has been chosen because it is quite common (it is used in the compound *paʔċiwčay* 'policeman').

(206) ||p^{h}a-|| prefixed to the root ||-ʔċi-|| 'catch hold'
<p∧haʔs'iw> (O D: ED)
p^{h}aʔċiw
||p^{h}a-ʔċi-w||
/p^{h}a-ʔċi-w/
with.hand-catch.hold-PFV
'to grab'

||p^{h}i-|| p^{h}i- ~ p^{h}e- 'long object act sidewise, chop, bat, see, eyes, face, neck

(207) ||p^{h}i-|| prefixed to the root ||-hnat̯-|| 'try, investigate'
<p∧hihnac*iy> (O D: ED)
p^{h}ihnač:iy
||p^{h}i-hnat̯-čič̓-Ø||
/p^{h}i-hnač-čiy-Ø/
by.sight-try-REFL-PFV
'to give a quick investigatory look back'

(208) ||p^{h}i-|| prefixed to the root ||-ʔt̯a-|| 'seem, perceive, feel'
<k'oʔdi p∧hiʔt'aw> (O D: ED)
k̓oʔdi p^{h}iʔt̯aw
||k̓oʔdi p^{h}i-ʔt̯a-w||
/k̓oʔdi p^{h}i-ʔt̯a-w/
good by.sight-perceive-PFV
'to look good'

||p^{h}u-|| p^{h}u- ~ p^{h}o- 'blow, burn transitive'

(209) ||p^{h}u-|| prefixed to the root ||-ċ:a-|| 'to break'
<p∧hus'*aw> (O D: ED)

p^{h}uc̓:aw
||p^{h}u-c̓:a-w||
/p^{h}u-c̓:a-w/
by.blowing-break-PFV
'wind to break off one (or branch just fall off)'

(210) ||p^{h}a-|| prefixed to the root ||-ʔt̪̓a-|| 'seem, perceive, feel'
<p∧hu?t'aw> (O D: ED)
maʔt̪̓aw
||p^{h}u-ʔt̪̓a-w||
/p^{h}u-ʔt̪̓a-w/
with.blowing-perceive-PFV
'to feel wind on self, feel draft'[145]

||ka-|| ka- 'hard opposed forces, teeth, jaw, pliers, chew, eat, pry'

(211) ||ka-|| prefixed to the root ||-hnat̪-|| 'try, investigate'
<kahnat'> (O D: EA)
kahnat̪̓
||ka-hnat̪-Ø||
/ka-hnat̪̓-Ø/
with.teeth-try-PFV
'to taste'[146]

(212) ||ka-|| prefixed to the root ||-ʔt̪̓a-|| 'seem, perceive, feel'
<ka?t'aw> (O D: ED)
kaʔt̪̓aw
||ka-ʔt̪̓a-w||
/ka-ʔt̪̓a-w/
with.jaws-perceive-PFV
'to talk to s[ome]o[ne] in no mood to talk'

||si-|| si- ~ se- 'water, rain, tongue, slip, float, drink, whistle, whisper; cut'

(213) ||si-|| prefixed to the root ||-hnat̪-|| 'try, investigate'
<sihnat'> (O D: ED)
sihnat̪̓

||si-hnat̯-Ø||
/si-hnat̯̓-Ø/
by.drinking-try-PFV
'sip'

(214) ||si-|| prefixed to the root ||-ʔt̯̓a-|| 'seem, perceive, feel'
<si?t'aw> (O D: ED)
maʔt̯̓aw
||si-ʔt̯̓a-w||
/si-ʔt̯̓a-w/
involving.liquid-perceive-PFV
'to taste liquid'

||ša-|| ša- 'long object move lengthwise into; through a membrane, skin, net, sieve'

(215) ||ša-|| prefixed to the root ||-c̓:a-|| 'to break'
<$as'*aw> (O D: ED)
šac̓:aw
||ša-c̓:a-w||
/ša-c̓:a-w/
long.obj.move.lengthwise.into-break-PFV
'to break gig, knife, etc. while striking s[ome]t[hing] with it'

||šu-|| šu- ~ šo- 'pull, breathe, long flexible object, rope, stockings'

(216) ||šu-|| prefixed to the root ||-c̓:a-|| 'to break'
<$us'*aw> (O D: ED)
šuc̓:aw
||šu-c̓:a-w||
/šu-c̓:a-w/
by.pulling-break-PFV
'to break in two by pulling'

(217) ||šu-|| prefixed to the root ||-hnat̯-|| 'try, investigate'
<$uhnat'> (O D: EA)
šuhnat̯̓

||šu-hnat̯-Ø||
/šu-hnat̯̓-Ø/
by.pulling-try-PFV
‘to test by pulling’

(218) ||šu-|| prefixed to the root ||-ʔt̯̓a-|| ‘seem, perceive, feel’
<$u?t’aw> (O D: ED)
šuʔt̯̓aw
||šu-ʔt̯̓a-w||
/šu-ʔt̯̓a-w/
by.pulling-perceive-PFV
‘to feel s[ome]t[hing] pulling’

||č^{h}i-|| č^{h}i- ~ č^{h}e- ‘small part of larger object, handle, hook, pendant object’

(219) ||č^{h}i-|| prefixed to the root ||-hnat̯-|| ‘try, investigate’
<c∧hihnat’> (O D: EA)
č^{h}ihnat̯̓
||č^{h}i-hnat̯-Ø||
/č^{h}i-hnat̯̓-Ø/
by.handle-try-PFV
‘to test a backpack; try out pack’

||ča-|| ča- ‘rear end, massive object, knife, sit, back up’

(220) ||ča-|| prefixed to the root ||-ċ:a-|| ‘to break’
<cas’*aw> (O D: ED)
čaċ:aw
||ča-ċ:a-w||
/ča-ċ:a-w/
with.butt-break-PFV
‘to sit on and break (a spring)’

(221) ||ča-|| prefixed to the root ||-hnat̯-|| ‘try, investigate’
<cahnat’> (O D: EA)
čahnat̯̓
||ča-hnat̯-Ø||

/č̣a-hnaṯ̓-Ø/

with.massive.obj.-try-PFV

'to test weight of large object by putting shoulder to it and pushing'

(222) ||ča-|| prefixed to the root ||-ʔṯ̓a-|| 'seem, perceive, feel'

<caʔt'aw> (O D: ED)

čaʔṯ̓aw

||ča-ʔṯ̓a-w||

/ča-ʔṯ̓a-w/

with.butt-perceive-PFV

'to feel s[ome]t[hing] with butt'

||ču-|| ču- ~ čo- 'non-long object, rock, head; flow; shoot, gamble; vegetative growth'

(223) ||ču-|| prefixed to the root ||-hnaṯ-|| 'try, investigate'

<cuhnat'> (O D: EA)

čuhnaṯ̓

||ču-hnaṯ-Ø||

/ču-hnaṯ̓-Ø/

by.shooting-try-PFV

'to try out a gun on a target'

||ha-|| ha- ~ ʔa- 'long object through air, leg, arm, wing'

This prefix has not been found in combination with any of the three roots used throughout this section.

(224) ||ha-|| prefixed to the root ||-l:iṯ-|| 'fan'

<hal*it> (O D: EA)

hal:iṯ̓

||ha-l:iṯ-Ø||

/ha-l:iṯ̓-Ø/

with.long.obj.through.air-fan-PFV

'to wave (branch) to chase flies'

||hi-|| hi- ~ he- ~ ʔi- ~ ʔe- 'with unspecific part of body; without agent'[147]

(225) ||hi-|| prefixed to the root ||-c̓:a-|| 'to break'

<ma*kina his'*aw> (O D: ED)

ma:kina hic̓:aw

||ma:kina hi-c̓:a-w||

/ma:kina hi-c̓:a-w/

machine without.agent-break-PFV

'The car broke down.'

(226) ||hi-|| prefixed to the root ||-hnat̯-|| 'try, investigate'

<?ihnat'> (O D: ED)

ʔihnat̯̓

||hi-hnat̯-Ø||

/ʔi-hnat̯̓-Ø/

without.agent-try-PFV

'to weigh'

||hu-|| hu- ~ ho- ~ ʔu- ~ ʔo- 'sound, speak, hear'

(227) ||hu-|| prefixed to the root ||-hnat̯-|| 'try, investigate'

<?uhnat'> (O D)

ʔuhnat̯̓

||hu-hnat̯-Ø||

/ʔu-hnat̯̓-Ø/

with.speech-try-PFV

'to ask a question'

(228) ||hu-|| prefixed to the root ||-ʔt̯a-|| 'seem, perceive, feel'

<hu?t'aw> (O D: ED)

huʔt̯̓aw

||hu-ʔt̯a-w||

/hu-ʔt̯̓a-w/

by.sound-perceive-PFV

'to hear'

2.8.3.2.2. Plural Act Affixes

In addition to verb stems which differ according to number, Southern Pomo has a robust (and very ancient) system of derivational affixes indicating a plurality of things. Kashaya and Central Pomo, the two Pomoan languages with which Southern Pomo shared a common border, share this feature, and fine shades of meaning have been reported in those languages (Oswalt 1961; Mithun 1988). In Southern Pomo the data are unclear. The semantics imparted by the following plural act affixes appear lexically determined to a certain extent. And the rarer affixes are largely fossilized in a handful of verbs. Because it is not clear that they have different meanings, all these affixes are glossed as PLURAL.ACT.

These affixes are a diverse group: one is a prefix (the sole prefix that is not an instrumental prefix); one may be either an infix or a suffix; and the other two are only suffixes, are extremely rare, and are homophonous with other affixes. Discussion of each plural act affix follows.

||-:lv-|| -:la-, -:le-, -:li-, -:lo-, -:lu- plural act prefix

This is the only verbal prefix which is not an instrumental prefix. It must come between an instrumental prefix and the root. It has two phonological properties which are unique within the language: (1) its vowel is copied completely from the vowel of the following root; and (2) it is the only true decremental verbal affix: roots to which this prefix is affixed completely lose their laryngeal increment. This prefix has a very limited distribution and is only to be found in combination with a small number of roots. One of the clearest examples of this prefix comes from (H VIII), a text in which a massive rock man attempts to kill a cunning gray squirrel in a gambling dispute. Example (229) comes from this text, and the effect of the plural act prefix ||-:lv-|| in this passage is one of multiple patients (the trees); without this affix, there is no indication of number. This example also illustrates the phonological characteristics of this prefix: its allomorph has copied the vowel of the root, and the laryngeal increment (in this case /:/) of the root ||-ċ:a-|| is gone. (The plural act prefix is in bold and underlined.)

(229) The plural act prefix ||-:lv-|| on the verb root ||-ċ:a-|| 'break'

kʰa:léʔwan kúʔmu di:láċaw, kʰaʔbéyey (H VIII: 6)

*kʰa:leʔwan kuʔmu di:**la**c̓aw, kʰaʔbeyey*
||kʰa:le=ʔwan kuʔmu di-:lv-c̓:a-w kʰaʔbe=yey||
/kʰa:le=ʔwan   kuʔmu   di-:la-c̓a-w   kʰaʔbe=yey/
tree=DET.OBJ   whole   by.fall-PL.ACT-break-PFV   rock=AGT
'He broke them all (with his body), the Rock'

Because this prefix copies the vowel of the following root, it is possible for a root to which ||-:lv-|| is prefixed to lose its vowel after syncope, the vowel of the prefix thereafter providing the only clue to the lost vowel. Example (230) gives the same stem as in (229), but in this case the vowel of the root ||-c̓:a-|| 'break' has been completely lost (in addition to the loss of its laryngeal increment). (The affected root is in bold and underlined.)

(230) Surface form of ||-:lv-|| as only clue to root vowel
kʰá:le di:lác̓kaw   (H VIII: 6)
*kʰa:le di:la**c̓**kaw*
||kʰa:le di-:lv-c̓:a-ka-w||
/kʰa:le   di-:la-c̓-ka-w/
tree   by.fall-PL.ACT-break-CAUS-PFV
'He broke all the trees'

||-ṱ-|| ~ ||-ṱa-|| <ṱ> ~ <ṱa> ~ <ṱ̓> ~ -ṱ- ~ -ṱa- ~ -ṱ̓- ~ -:- ~ -Ø- plural act affix (infix ~ suffix)

This affix is one of the commonest morphemes in the language; it is also one of the most irregular. This affix has a number of allomorphs, which are not completely predictable. In general, it surfaces as /-ṱ̓-/ in coda position, whether pre-consonantally within a word or in word-final position. Elsewhere it may surface as /-ṱ-/ or /-ṱa-/. The most distinctive phonological feature of this affix is its status as a decrement: the laryngeal increment of the verb root is lost and replaced by /:/ to the left of the root consonant regardless of the original increment (unless the root consonant is a sonorant).

CVHCV … ~ CVCHV … + ||-ṱ-|| ~ ||-ṱa-|| → CV:CV- ||-ṱ-|| ~ ||-ṱa-|| …

This morpheme implies multiple events, but the extant translations of verbs with this affix are not clear enough to be sure of its full semantic range. Multiple actions (or agents/undergoers performing/undergoing actions) are implied when this plural act morpheme is affixed to an intransitive verb. The following examples of intransitive verbs with and without the plural act affix come from Halpern (1984: 17). (The plural act is in bold.)

(231) Intransitive verbs with and without the plural act affix ||-t̪-|| ~ ||-t̪a-||

[ʔ]ahk^{h}a čahčawa		[ʔ]ahk^{h}a ča:čat̪a	
ʔahk^{h}a čahčawa		*ʔahk^{h}a ča:ča**t̪a***	
/ʔahk^{h}a	čahča-wa/	/ʔahk^{h}a	ča:ča-t̪-a/
water	rise-EVID	water	rise-PL.ACT-EVID
'creek is rising'		'creeks are rising'	

(232) Intransitive verbs with and without the plural act affix ||-t̪-|| ~ ||-t̪a-||

[ʔ]ahč^{h}aw	[ʔ]a:č^{h}at̪
ʔahč^{h}aw	*ʔa:č^{h}a**t̪***
/ʔahč^{h}a-w/	/ʔa:č^{h}a-t̪-Ø/
fall-PFV	fall-PL.ACT-PFV
'fall over'	'sev[eral] fall over'

When applied to a transitive verb, this plural act affix indicates a distributive sense with many events affecting multiple parties. Example (233) has the verb stem *dihka-* 'to give one object' with and without ||-t̪-|| ~ ||-t̪a-||. The form with the plural act affix means to give one thing to several recipients individually; it does not mean to give one thing to a group. This example comes from Halpern (1984: 17). (The plural act affix is in bold.)

(233) The plural act affix ||-t̪-|| ~ ||-t̪a-|| on the verb *dihka-* 'to give one object'

dihkan	dihkat̪in
dihkan	*di:ka**t̪**in*
/dihka-n/	/di:ka-t̪-in/
give.one.obj.-SG.IMP	give.one.obj.-PL.ACT-SG.IMP
'give (one obj. to one person)!	'give (one to each)!'

When the ||-t̪-|| variant of the plural act affix comes directly before another consonant, it surfaces as /:/, as seen in (234).

(234) /-:-/ allomorph of ||-t̪-||
ha:čá:čiw (H ms.)
ha:ča:čiw
||ha-hča-t̪-či-w||
/ha:ča-:-či-w/
fly-PL.ACT-SEM-PFV
'birds (flying around) land'

When the ||-t̪-|| variant of the plural act affix comes directly before a consonant cluster, it may disappear entirely. In such cases, the only surface evidence of the plural act is the decremental process of removing the laryngeal increment and replacing it with /:/ to the left of the root consonant. Compare example (235) with (234).

(235) The /-Ø-/ allomorph of ||-t̪-||
ċíht̪a ha:čáčwa (H ms.)
ċiht̪a ha:čačwa
||ċiht̪a hahča-t̪-či-a||[148]
/ċiht̪a ha:ča-Ø-č-wa/
bird fly-PL.ACT-SEM-EVID
'the birds have landed'

When it is attached to a consonant-final verb root, this affix is an infix and separates the final consonant of the root from the root vowel (i.e., -HCVC- → -HCV<PL.ACT>C-). An example of the plural act affix variant ||-t̪a-|| surfacing as an infix is presented in example (236) in the verb stem *ʔahlok̓-* 'one (piece) to fall off' (plural act in bold).

(236) Example verb with and without ||-t̪-|| PL.ACT

[without plural act]	[with plural act]
[ʔ]ahlok̓o (Halpern 1984, 17)	[ʔ]a:lhot̪ak̓ (Halpern 1984: 17)
ʔahlok̓o	*ʔa:lho**t̪ak̓***
/ʔahlok̓-o/	/ʔa:lho<t̪a>k̓-Ø/
piece.to.fall-EVID	piece.to.fall<PL.ACT>-PFV
'one (piece) falls off'	'(pieces) drop off'

Note that the laryngeal increment is actually transcremented after the addition of the plural act morpheme in this example because the root consonant is a sonorant.[149]

This plural act affix may combine with the plural imperative suffix ||-le||. Examples (237) and (238) give four instances of the verb stem ||ʔohko-|| 'to pass' in four imperative conjugations, two of which include the plural act affix.

(237) Singular imperative with and without ||-t̪-|| ~ ||-t̪a-||

[without plural act]		[with plural act]	
[ʔ]óhkon	(H ms.)	[ʔ]o:kót̪in	(H ms.)
ʔohkon		*ʔo:kot̪in*	
||ʔohko-Vn||		||ʔohko-t̪-Vn||	
/ʔohko-n/		/ʔo:ko-t̪-in/	
pass-SG.IMP		pass-PL.ACT-SG.IMP	
'1 pass 1!'		'1 pass sev[eral]'	

(238) Singular imperative with and without ||-t̪-|| ~ ||-t̪a-||

[without plural act]		[with plural act]	
[ʔ]ohkóle	(H ms.)	[ʔ]o:kó:le	(H ms.)
ʔohkole		*ʔo:ko:le*	
||ʔohko-le||		||ʔohko-t̪-le||	
/ʔohko-le/		/ʔo:ko-:-le/	
pass-PL.IMP		pass-PL.ACT-SG.IMP	
'2 pass 1!'		'2 pass sev[eral]!'	

In these examples the combination of the plural act affix and the plural imperative suffix results in a distributive meaning. However, this is not the automatic interpretation of such a combination. The Southern Pomo plural imperative suffix descends from an earlier conditional, which Oswalt reconstructs for Proto Pomo as * . . . le (1976a: 25). This suffix has two modern uses in the language: (1) as a true plural imperative used for commands to more than one person; and (2) as a politeness suffix for use in commands given to in-laws and other people who warrant respect, a usage which might descend from its earlier use as a conditional.[150] In this latter function, the plural imperative must be combined with the plural act affix in order to be interpreted as a command to more than one person.

It is unclear whether the meanings of such combinations are pragmatically conditioned. Can any verb with the combination PLURAL.ACT+PLURAL.IMPERATIVE have a distributive meaning unless addressed to an in-law? Are these interpretations restricted to certain verbs? The data are insufficient to answer these questions with complete confidence. However, it seems most likely that the special semantics involved in addressing in-laws are understood in context, and that the following examples might have a plural (collective) versus plural distributive meaning if addressed to someone not deserving of in-law levels of respect in the culture. Examples (239) and (240) give two instances of the verb 'to move the body' with the plural imperative; only the form with both the plural imperative and the plural act affix has a true plural meaning. (The plural imperative and the plural act affixes are in bold.)

(239) Example of plural imperative ||-le|| as singular command to in-law
[ʔ]ek^{h}:elmé:le (H ms.)
*ʔek^{h}:elme:**le***
||hi-hk^{h}e-alameč̓-le||
/ʔe-k^{h}:e-lme:-le/
with.body-move-DIR-PL.IMP
'(in-law) move down from above!'

(240) ||-t̯-|| PL.ACT + ||-le|| PL.IMP as plural command to in-law
[ʔ]e:k^{h}et̯lamé:le (H ms.)
*ʔe:k^{h}e**t̯**lame:**le***
||hi-hk^{h}e-t̯-alameč̓-le||
/ʔe-:k^{h}e-t̯-lame:-le/
with.body-move-PL.ACT-DIR-PL.IMP
'2 move down from above!'

||-m-|| -m- ~ (other?) and ||-ak-|| -a:- ~ -k- ~ (other?) plural act suffixes

The first of these two suffixes is very poorly understood and is quite rare in the records. In Central Pomo, Mithun reports that the suffix *-ma-*, which is the cognate of the *-m-* suffix in Southern Pomo, specifically indicates "joint or collective effort" (1988: 524–25). There is no evidence of such a clear meaning in Southern Pomo, and whereas the Central Pomo cognate is reported to be quite productive, this suffix is found only sporadically in the records.[151] Part of the problem in the identification of this suffix (if, indeed, many examples await identification) lies in its being homophonous with the essive *-m-* and the directional suffix 'across' *-m-* (and in its being part of the general phonological confusion that surrounds sonorants in word-final position in the language). It is, however, more clearly a separate morpheme than the possible plural act suffix ||-ak-||.

The suffix ||-ak-|| has clear cognates in Central Pomo and Kashaya (||-aq-|| in both); however, it has not been reported from Southern Pomo, and Oswalt lists no Southern Pomo cognate for this suffix in his list of Pomoan affixes (1976a: 22). At least one Southern Pomo form appears to have a plural meaning derived from both ||-m-|| and ||-ak-|| combined as plural act suffixes. The two forms in example (241) make no sense unless the sequences *-mk-* and *-ma:-* include ||-m-|| as a plural act suffix; and though it is possible that the *-k-* ~ *-a:-* is the directional ||-ak-|| 'out', the semantics of the translation leave little room for such an analysis. It therefore seems likely that this form contains both ||-m-|| and ||-ak-||. (The possible plural act suffixes are in bold and underlined.)

(241) Possible instance of ||-m-ak-|| PLURAL.ACT+PLURAL.ACT
sú:le šu:némkan (H ms.)
*su:le šu:ne**mk**an*
||su:le šu-:ne-m-ak-Vn||
/su:le šu-:ne-m-k-an/
rope by.pulling-grasp-PL.ACT-PL.ACT-SG.IMP
'tie several ropes onto it!'

(242) Possible instance of ||-m-ak-|| PLURAL.ACT+PLURAL.ACT
sú:le šu:nemá:le (H ms.)
*su:le šu:ne**ma:**le*
||su:le šu-:ne-m-ak-le||
/su:le šu-:ne-m-a:-le/

rope by.pulling-grasp-PL.ACT-PL.ACT-PL.IMP
'2 tie several ropes onto it!'

2.8.3.2.3. Reduplicative Suffixes

There are two reduplicative suffixes in Southern Pomo: (1) ||-R-||, which reduplicates the entire verb stem; and (2) ||-ř-||, which reduplicates only the verb root. In the case of ||-R-||, subsequent vowel syncope and assimilatory processes may obscure the sounds of the suffixed portion. Translations of verbs with ||-R-|| generally have an iterative meaning, as in examples (243)–(245).

(243) Verb with ||-R-|| and iterative meaning
<mahk∧hemk∧hed*u> (O D: ED)
mahk^{h}emk^{h}ed:u
||ma-hk^{h}e-R-ded-u||
/ma-hk^{h}e-mk^{h}e-d:-u/
by.foot-move.body ~ ITER-DIR-PFV
'to shuffle along'

(244) Verb with ||-R-|| and iterative meaning
p[^{h}]oht̪ópt̪ow (H VII: 2)
p^{h}uht̪opt̪ow
||p^{h}u-ht̪o-p^{h}u-ht̪o-w|| → [p^{h}uh.ˈt̪op.t̪ow]
/p^{h}uht̪o-p^{h}uht̪o-w/
boil ~ ITER-PFV
'boils'

(245) Verb with ||-R-|| and iterative meaning
<bahk∧hopk∧how> (O D: ED)
bahk^{h}opk^{h}ow
||ba-hk^{h}o-R-w||
/ba-hk^{h}o-pk^{h}o-w /
by.poking-contact[152] ~ ITER-PFV
'to give many quick little pokes'

Verbs with ||-ř-|| may also have iterative meaning, as in (246) and (247).

(246) Verb with ||-ř-|| and iterative meaning
<du?ba?baw> (O D: ED)
duʔbaʔbaw
||du-ʔba-ř-w||
/du-ʔba-ʔba-w/
by.finger-bother ~ ITER-PFV
'to bother s[ome]o[ne] with the fingers'

(247) Verb with ||-ř-|| and iterative meaning
<dohohow> (O D: EA)
dohšohšow
||du-hšo-ř-w||
/do-hšo-hšo-w/
by.finger-strip.off ~ ITER-PFV
'to be removing corn kernels w[ith] finger'

However, some verbs with ||-ř-|| show no obvious iterative meaning, such as the verb for 'to tell', which is given in (248).

(248) Verb with ||-ř-|| and no iterative meaning
[ʔ]uhṱehṱew (H ms.)
ʔuhṱehṱew
||hu-hṱe-ř-w||
/ʔu-hṱe-hṱe-w/
by.sound-tell ~ ?-PFV
'tells'

It is unclear how freely either reduplicative suffix may be used with various roots and stems. In the case of ||-R-||, most stems which take this affix do not appear in the extant records without it. The same situation holds true for ||-ř-||, and most stems which take this affix do not appear without it. In the case of verbs like 'to tell' (248), no discernable semantic content is imparted by ||-ř-||, and its presence in such words is simply lexicalized.

Another question is whether these two reduplicative affixes might carry slightly different semantics. Data from neighboring congeners point to two possibilities: (1) the two reduplicative morphemes might have different semantics, as in Kashaya Pomo; or (2) both reduplicative morphemes are simple iteratives, as might be the case for Central Pomo. The Kashaya cognate for ||-R-|| is a frequentative morpheme, whereas the Kashaya cognate for ||-ř-|| is an iterative morpheme; the semantic difference is one of an "action . . . repeated in quick succession" (the frequentative) and one of an "action . . . repeated a few times" (the iterative) (Oswalt 1961: 155–56; Buckley 1994: 354–68). It is therefore possible that Southern Pomo maintains a similar distinction, which it would have inherited from the parent language of both it and Kashaya.

Mithun reports that Central Pomo, Southern Pomo's sister language to the north, has a similar reduplicative process; reduplication in Central Pomo indicates "single events with repetitive internal structure," and no mention is made of a distinction between reduplication of the stem versus reduplication of the root (Mithun 1988: 527). The reduplicative morphemes of Southern Pomo might have collapsed into a single iterative morpheme, as appears to be the case in Central Pomo.

There is no reason to assume that Southern Pomo reduplication is identical to either of its nearest congeners; the language can, of course, chart its own course with regard to the semantics of its reduplicative morphemes. At this time it is not possible to say with certainty that both ||-R-|| and ||-ř-|| are distinct in semantics or both iteratives. Both are glossed hereafter as ~ ITERATIVE when the semantics warrant such a glossing; when a reduplicative morpheme appears fossilized with no synchronic iterative meaning (as in *ʔuhṭ̂ehṭ̂ew* 'to tell'), it is indicated as ~ ? in the glossing.

2.8.3.2.4. Directional Suffixes

Most verbs of motion in Southern Pomo must take one of the directional suffixes.[153] These suffixes indicate very fine shades of meaning, and many of them appear to be compositional in origin, though they cannot be productively parsed in synchronic analysis (Oswalt 1976a: 23). Unless they begin with /m/, all directional suffixes are transcremental.

Thus far all directionals have been simply glossed as DIR because there are so many of them and because precise English translations are too long to fit within the glossing; however, the free translations have been adequate for identification of semantic difference between various directional affixes. This practice continues throughout the remainder of this work. Each directional suffix is listed individually below. Where possible, the verb stems *ʔahča-* 'to fly', *dak̓:aṭ-* 'to lead several', *ʔehkʰe-* 'to move the body', and *ʔahpʰi-* 'to carry' are used in the examples.

||-m-|| -m- ~ -:- ~ -n(?) 'across'

This suffix is homophonous with the essive suffix ||-m-|| and the rare plural act suffix ||-m-||. Examples of this suffix are given in (249) and (250) (the surface form of ||-m-|| is in bold).

(249) Example of ||-m-|| 'across' on the verb *ʔehkʰe-* 'to move the body'
[ʔ]ehkʰéman (H ms.)
*ʔehkʰ***eman**
||hi-hkʰe-m-Vn||
/ʔe-hkʰe-ma-n/
with.body-move-DIR-SG.IMP
'move across!'

(250) Example of ||-m-|| 'across' on the verb *ʔehkʰe-* 'to move the body'
[ʔ]ehkʰé:ne (H ms.)
ʔehkʰe:ne
||hi-hkʰe-m-le
/ʔe-hkʰe-:-ne/
with.body-move-DIR-PL.IMP
'(in-law) move across!'

||-muN-|| -mul- ~-mum- ~ -ml- ~ -mu:- ~ -mun ~ -mil-(?) 'around'

Oswalt identifies cognates of this suffix in every Pomoan language except Northeastern Pomo and he glosses it as "Around, to the other side" (1976a: 23). In Southern Pomo this suffix carries only the meaning of physically going around something; it does not carry the other English sense of verbs modified with 'around' (i.e., it does not mean to 'go around' as in 'going about'). Examples (251)–(254) provide instances of this suffix surfacing with various allomorphs (the surface forms of the suffix ||-muN-|| are in bold).

(251) The *-mul-* and *-mum-* allomorphs of ||-muN-||[154]

hu:mulin (Oswalt 1976a: 21)	hu:muman (Oswalt 1976a: 21)
*hu:**mul**in*	*hu:**mum**an*
||hu:w-muN-Vn||	||hu:w-muN-Vn||
/hu:-mul-in/	/hu:-mum-an/
go-DIR-S.SIM	go-DIR-S.SIM
'while going around'	'while going around'

(252) The *-mun-* allomorph of ||-muN-||
kʰá:le hú:mun (H ms.)
*kʰa:le hu:**mun***
||kʰa:le hu:w-muN-Ø||
/kʰa:le hu:-mun-Ø/
tree go-DIR-PFV
'walk around tree'

(253) The *-mu:-* allomorph of ||-muN-||
[ʔ]akʰ:óhča kʰá:le hu:mú:ne (H ms.)
*ʔakʰ:ohča kʰa:le hu:**mu:**ne*
||ʔakʰ:o=hča kʰa:le hu:w-muN-le||
/ʔakʰ:o=hča kʰa:le hu:-mu:-ne/
two=COLL tree go-DRI-PL.IMP
'2 [walk around tree]!'

(254) The *-ml-* allomorph of ||-muN-||
ká:wiʔwan [ʔ]áhča [ʔ]ahp[ʰ]ímlin (H ms.)
*ka:wiʔwan ʔahča ʔahpʰ**iml**in*
||ka:wi=ʔwan ʔahča ʔahpʰi-muN-Vn||
/ka:wi=ʔwan ʔahča ʔahpʰi-ml-in/
child=DET.OBJ house carry-DIR-SG.IMP
'carry baby around house!'

The allomorphy of this suffix is somewhat problematic. Its expected allomorphs are *-mul-* ~ *-mum-* ~ *-mu:-* ~ *-mun* ~ *-ml-*; however, there appears to have been confusion between these forms, which conform to patterns seen elsewhere in the language, and inexplicable variants. Annie Burke, Halpern's first Cloverdale dialect consultant, shows two unexpected variants of this affix. When ||-muN-|| is followed by the plural imperative suffix ||-le||, Halpern records that Burke produced both the expected allomorph *-mu:-* (with nasal spreading to the /l/) and an unexpected form with an epenthetic [i] separating ||-muN-|| from ||-le||, as seen in examples (255) and (256) (the surface forms of ||-muN-|| are in bold).

(255) Expected use of allomorph of ||-muN-|| before ||-le|| by Annie Burke

[ʔ]ak^{h}:óhča k^{h}á:le hu:mú:ne (H ms.)

*ʔak^{h}:ohča k^{h}a:le hu:**mu:**ne*

||ʔak^{h}:o=hča k^{h}a:le hu:w-muN-le||

/ʔak^{h}:o=hča k^{h}a:le hu:-mu:-ne/

two=COLL tree go-DRI-PL.IMP

'2 [walk around tree]!'

(256) Unexpected use of [i] between ||-muN-|| and ||-le|| by Annie Burke

šóʔdimlíle (H ms.)

*šoʔdi**ml**ile*

||šu-ʔdi-muN-le||

/šo-ʔdi-ml-i-le/

by.pulling-move-DIR-EPENTHETIC.VOWEL-PL.IMP

'2 [lead him around]!'

An even more peculiar allomorph is *-mil-* for the expected *-mul-* in Annie Burke's speech, as seen in (257) (the surface form of||-muN-|| is in bold).

(257) The unexpected allomorph *-mil-*

dák̓:aṭmílin (H ms.)

*dak̓:aṭ**mil**in*

||dak̓:aṭ-muN-Vn||[155]

/dak̓:aṭ-mil-in/

lead.several-DIR-SG.IMP
'1 lead them around!'

Compare the preceding example with (258) following, which shows the expected vowel /u/, a form spoken by the same speaker and differing from (257) only in that the final imperative suffix is plural rather than singular (the surface form of ||-muN-|| is in bold).

(258) The allomorph *-mu:-* with the expected vowel /u/
dak̓:aṭmú:ne (H ms.)
*dak̓:aṭ**mu:**ne*
||dak̓:aṭ-muN-le||
/dak̓:aṭ-mu:-ne/
lead.several-DIR-PL.IMP
'2 lead them around!'

These unusual allomorphs cannot be explained at this time; however, one possible analysis would treat all instances of [i] within or following ||-muN-|| as epenthetic vowels. The directional suffix ||-muN-|| is unique among directionals in being monosyllabic with two sonorants, and the allophony of sonorants in coda position in the language is such that speakers might have introduced the epenthetic [i] between the final sonorant of ||-muN-|| and a following sonorant-initial affix to avoid confusion. The [i] of the *-mil-* allomorph would therefore also be an example of an epenthetic vowel, though such an analysis would require the speakers to lose the underlying vowel to syncope and then decide to break up the cluster with [i] rather than the underlying vowel (i.e., ||-muN-|| → *-mul-* → *-ml-* → *-mil-*). Whatever the conditioning factors, if any, the identification of this suffix is not controversial.

||-maduč-|| -madu:- ~ -mač:- (~ -maduč- ~ -maduy ~ -mʔduy) 'as far as, up to (here)'

The preceding allomorphs in parentheses are not in my database but are to be expected on the basis of phonological patterns seen elsewhere in the language. The two allomorphs for which there are examples in my database are given in (259) and (260) (the surface forms of ||-maduč-|| are in bold).

(259) The *-madu:-* allomorph of ||-maduč-||
má:li dak̓:áṭmadú:le (H ms.)
*ma:li dak̓:aṭ**madu:**le*
||ma:li dak̓:aṭ-maduč-le||
/ma:li dak̓:aṭ-madu:-le/
here lead.several-DIR-PL.IMP
'2 bring sev[eral] here!'

(260) The *-mač:-* allomorph of ||-maduč-||
dak̓:aṭmáč:in (H ms.)
*dak̓:aṭ**mač:**in*
||dak̓:aṭ-maduč-Vn||
/dak̓:aṭ-mač:-in/
lead.several-DIR-SG.IMP
'bring sev. here!'

||-mač-|| -mač- ~ -mč- ~ -ma:- ~ -may 'in from outside'

The suffix is used for movement into something from outside. Oswalt notes that it may also carry the meaning of 'northward' (1976a: 23). Examples of this suffix are given in (261)–(264) (the surface forms of ||-mač-|| are in bold).

(261) The *-mač-* allomorph of ||-mač-||
dak̓:aṭmáčin (H ms.)
*dak̓:aṭ**mač**in*
||dak̓:aṭ-mač-Vn||
/dak̓:aṭ-mač-in/
lead.several-DIR-SG.IMP
'take sev. inside'

(262) The *-mč-* allomorph of ||-mač-||
[ʔ]ahp[ʰ]ímčin (H ms.)
*ʔahpʰi**mč**in*
||ʔahpʰi-mač-Vn||
/ʔahpʰi-mč-in/

carry-DIR-SG.IMP
'carry it in (speaker outside)'

(263) The *-ma:-* allomorph of ||-mač-||
[ʔ]ahp[^{h}]imá:le (H ms.)
*ʔahp^h**ima:**le*
||ʔahp^{h}i-mač-le||
/ʔahp^{h}i-ma:-le/
carry-DIR-PL.IMP
'2 [carry it in (speaker outside)]'

(264) The *-may* allomorph of ||-mač-||
k^{h}aʔ[:]át̪̓may (H I: 6)
*k^{h}aʔ:at̪̓**may***
||k^{h}aʔ:at̪̓-mač-Ø||
/k^{h}aʔ:at̪̓-may-Ø/
run-DIR-PFV
'ran inside'

||-mok-|| -mok- ~ -mk- ~ -mo:- ~ -mok̓ 'in from inside'

This suffix is used for movement into something relative to the speaker's being inside. Thus a speaker inside a house would use this suffix instead of ||-mač-|| to command someone to enter the same structure. Examples of this suffix are given in (265)–(267) (surface forms of ||-mok-|| are in bold).

(265) Example of ||-mok-||
dak̓:aṭmókon (H ms.)
*dak̓:aṭ̓**mok**on*
||dak̓:aṭ-mok-Vn||
/dak̓:aṭ̓-mok-on/
lead.several-DIR-SG.IMP
'1 bring them in!'

(266) Example of ||-mok-||
[ʔ]ehk^{h}émkon (H ms.)
*ʔehk^h**emk**on*

||hi-hk^{h}e-mok-Vn||
/ʔe-hk^{h}e-mk-on/
with.body-move-DIR-SG.IMP
'move in (speaker inside)!'

(267) Example of ||-mok-||
[ʔ]e:k^{h}et̪̓mó:le (H ms.)
*ʔe:k^{h}et̪̓**mo:**le*
||hi-hk^{h}e-t̪̓-mok-le||
/ʔe-:k^{h}e-t̪̓-mo:-le/
with.body-move-PL.ACT-DIR-PL.IMP
'2 move in (Sp[eaker]. in)'

||-ak-|| -ak- ~ -ak̓ ~ -a:- ~ -k- ~ -k̓ ~ -:- 'out from inside'

This is a transcremental suffix. Oswalt glosses this morpheme as 'out hence, away, off' (1976a: 23). His use of 'out hence' is shorthand for 'out (speaker outside)', which is at odds with the glossing used herein. This suffix is one of four suffixes which indicate either direction into or direction out of something relative to the speaker's being inside or outside. Table 39 gives all four suffixes.

Oswalt (1976a) flips the definitions for ||-ak-|| and ||-ok-|| so that they line up with the directionals for motion into forms which share the same vowels. Thus ||-mok-|| and ||-ok-|| are for use by a speaker inside and ||-mač-|| and ||-ak-|| are for use by a speaker outside in Oswalt's glossing.

I follow Halpern's glossing of ||-ok-|| and ||-mač-|| as being reserved for use by a speaker who is outside, and ||-ak-|| and ||-mok-|| as being used by a speaker who is inside. Oswalt's glossing might be true for Kashaya or etymologically correct; however, it is at odds with all of Halpern's handwritten glosses as he worked with Annie Burke (Oswalt 1976a: 23). Examples of ||-ak-|| are given in (268)–(270) (the surface forms of ||-ak-|| are in bold).

(268) Example of ||-ak-||
hídʔa [ʔ]ap[^{h}]:ákan (H ms.)
*hidʔa ʔap^{h}:**ak**an*
||hidʔa ʔap^{h}:a-k-Vn||

Table 39. Directional suffixes indicating motion into or out of something

	Motion into	**Motion out of**
Speaker inside	||-mok-||	||-ak-||
Speaker outside	||-mač-||	||-ok-||

/hidʔa ʔap^{h}:-ak-an/
outside carry-DIR-SG.IMP
'carry it outside (speaker inside)'

(269) Example of ||-ak-||
háč:ak̓ (H ms.)
*hač:**ak̓***
||ha-hča-ak-Ø||
/ha-č:a-k̓-Ø/
by.wing-fly-DIR-PFV
'flying through'

(270) Example of ||-ak-||
hídʔa ha:čat̪á:le (H ms.)
*hidʔa ha:čat̪**a:**le*
||hidʔa ha-hča-t̪-ak-le||
/hidʔa ha-:ča-t̪-a:-le/
outside by.wing-fly-PL.ACT-DIR-PL.IMP
'2 fly out (from here)!'

||-ok-|| -ok- ~ -ok̓ ~ -o:- ~ -k- ~ -k̓- ~ -:- 'out from outside'

This directional suffix is transcremental. It is used when the speaker is outside. Examples of this suffix are given in (271)–(273) (the surface forms of ||-ok-|| are in bold).

(271) Example of ||-ok-||
hídʔa [ʔ]ap[^{h}]:ákon (H ms.)
*hidʔa ʔap^{h}:**ak**on*
||hidʔa ʔap^{h}:a-ok-Vn||

/hidʔa ʔapʰ:a-k-on/
outside carry-DIR-SG.IMP
'carry it outside (speaker outside)[!]'

(272) Example of ||-ok-||
má:li dak̓:aṭó:le (H ms.)
*ma:li dak̓:aṭ**o:**le*
||ma:li dak̓:aṭ-ok-le||
/ma:li dak̓:aṭ-o:-le/
here lead.several-DIR-PL.IMP
'2 bring out sev.[!]'

(273) Example of ||-ok-||
má:li dak̓:aṭʰkon (H ms.)
*ma:li dak̓:aṭʰ**k**on*
||ma:li dak̓:aṭ-ok-Vn||
/ma:li dak̓:aṭʰ-k-on/
here lead.several-DIR-SG.IMP
'1 bring out sev.[!]'

||-ala-|| -ala- ~ -al- ~ -la- ~ -l- ~ -alʔ- ~ -lʔ- 'down'

This is a transcremental suffix. The allomorphs with the excrescent glottal stop only occur before voiced stops. Examples of ||-ala-|| are given in (274) and (275) (the morpheme is in bold).

(274) Example of ||-ala-||
[ʔ]ekʰ:élan (H ms.)
*ʔekʰ:**ela**n*
||hi-hkʰe-ala-Vn||
/ʔe-kʰ:e-la-n/
with.body-move-DIR-SG.IMP
'1 move down !'

(275) Example of ||-ala-||
[ʔ]ap[ʰ]:ál:e (H ms.)
*ʔapʰ:**al**:e*

||ʔapʰ:-ala-le||
/ʔapʰ:-al-:e/
carry-DIR-PL.IMP
'2 carry it down 1 each!'

||-akač-|| -akač- ~ -aka:- ~ -akay ~ -ak(ʰ)č- ~ -k(ʰ)č- ~ -kač- -ka:- ~ -kay 'up from here'

This is a transcremental suffix. Oswalt glosses this morpheme as 'up hence' (1976a: 23). On the basis of his use of 'hence' in his glossing elsewhere and the examples of this suffix to be found in connected narrative, it appears that this suffix means 'up from here' and is used for upward movement away from the speaker. Examples of the directional suffix ||-akač-|| are given in (276)–(279) (surface forms of ||-akač-|| are in bold).

(276) Example of ||-akač-||
[ʔ]ap[ʰ]:ákʰčin (H ms.)
*ʔapʰ:**akʰčin***
||ʔapʰ:-akač-Vn||
/ʔapʰ:-akʰč-in/
carry-DIR-SG.IMP
'1 carry it up[!]'

(277) Example of ||-akač-||
[ʔ]ap[ʰ]:aká:le (H ms.)
*ʔapʰ:**aka:**le*
||ʔapʰ:-akač-le||
/ʔapʰ:-aka:-le/
carry-DIR-PL.IMP
'2 carry it up[!]'

(278) Example of ||-akač-||
[ʔ]a:p[ʰ]at̯káčin (H ms.)
*ʔa:pʰat̯**kač**in*
||ʔa:pʰa-t̯-akač-Vn||[156]
/ʔa:pʰa-t̯-kač-in/

carry-PL.ACT-DIR-SG.IMP
'I carry up sev.!'

(279) Example of ||-akač-||
[ʔ]ekʰ:ékʰčin (H ms.)
*ʔekʰ:**ekʰč**in*
||hi-hkʰe-akač-Vn||
/ʔe-kʰ:e-kʰč-in/
with.body-move-DIR-SG.IMP
'move up onto!'

||-alok-|| -alok- ~ -alok̓ ~ -lok- ~ -lok̓ ~ -alo:- ~ -lo:- ~ -alk- ~ -lk- 'up to here'

This is a transcremental suffix. Oswalt glosses this morpheme as 'up hither' (1976a: 23). On the basis of his use of 'hither' in his glossing elsewhere and the examples of this suffix to be found in connected narrative, it appears that this suffix means 'up to here' and is used for upward movement toward the speaker. Examples of the directional suffix ||-alok-|| are given in (280)–(283) (surface forms of ||-alok-|| are in bold).

(280) Example of ||-alok-||
[ʔ]ihčálok̓ (H I: 7)
*ʔihč**alok̓***
||ʔihč-alok-Ø||[157]
/ʔihč-alok̓-Ø/
drag-DIR-PFV
'drags up'

(281) Example of ||-alok-||
má:li šudʔálkon (H ms.)
*ma:li šudʔ**alk**on*
||ma:li šu-ʔd-alok-Vn||[158]
/ma:li šu-dʔ-alk-on/
here by.pulling-move-DIR-SG.IMP
'I bring it up h[ere!]'

(282) Example of ||-alok-||
má:li dáḱ:al:ókon (H ms.)
*ma:li daḱ:al:**ok**on*
||ma:li daḱ:aṭ-alok-Vn||
/ma:li daḱ:al-lok-on/
here lead.several-DIR-SG.IMP
'1 bring them up here!'

(283) Example of ||-alok-||
má:li daḱ:al[:]ó:le (H ms.)
*ma:li daḱ:al:**o:**le*
||ma:li daḱ:aṭ-alok-le||
/ma:li daḱ:al-lo:-le/
here lead.several-DIR-PL.IMP
'2 bring them up here!'

||-alokč̓-|| -alokč̓- ~ -aloko:- ~ -alokoy ~ -lokoč̓- ~ -loko:- ~ -lokoy ~ -lkoč̓- ~ -lko:- ~ -lkoy ~ -alok(ʰ)č̓- ~ -lok(ʰ)č̓- ~ -alkoč̓- ~ -alko:- ~ -alkoy 'up out of'

This is a transcremental suffix. It is omitted from the list of Pomoan directionals in Oswalt (1976a), but it is listed as a separate suffix in a verb paradigm in Oswalt's unpublished notes and is recorded by Halpern. Examples of ||-alokoč̓-|| are given in (284)–(289) (the surface forms of ||-alokoč̓-|| are in bold).

(284) Example of ||-alokoč̓-||
haṭ̯:alokč̓in (O ms.)
*haṭ̯:**alokč̓**in*
||haṭ̯:-alokoč̓-Vn||
/haṭ̯:-alokč̓-in/
put.foot-DIR-SG.IMP
['put the foot up out of']

(285) Example of ||-alokoč̓-||
[ʔ]akʰ:a:náṭ̯ow [ʔ]ekʰ:elkó:le (H ms.)
*ʔakʰ:a:naṭ̯ow ʔekʰ:**elko:**le*

||ʔahkʰ:a-:na=t̯ow hi-hkʰe-alokoč̓-le||
/ʔakʰ:a-:na=t̯ow ʔe-kʰ:e-lko:-le/
water-LOC=ABL with.body-move-DIR-PL.IMP
'in-law (move out of water)[!]'

(286) Example of ||-alokoč̓-||
hač:alkóč̓in (H ms.)
*hač:a**lkoč̓**in*
||ha-hča-alakoč̓-Vn||
/ha-č:a-lkoč̓-in/
by.wing-fly-DIR-SG.IMP
'flyout! (speaker outside)'

(287) Example of ||-alokoč̓-||
ha:čat̯̓lokó:le (H ms.)
*ha:čat̯̓**loko:**le*
||ha-hča-t̯-alokoč̓-le||
/ha-:ča-t̯̓-loko:-le/
by.wing-fly-PL.ACT-DIR-PL.IMP
'2 fly out!'

(288) Example of ||-alokoč̓-||
hídʔa ha:čat̯lókoy (H ms.)
*hidʔa ha:čat̯**lokoy***
||hidʔa ha-hča-t̯-alokoč̓-Ø||
/hidʔa ha-:ča-t̯-lokoy-Ø/
outside by.wing-fly-PL.ACT-DIR-PFV
'birds fly out of [something]'

(289) Example of ||-alokoč̓-||
ha:čat̯lókʰč̓a (H ms.)
*ha:čat̯**lokʰč̓**a*
||ha-hča-t̯-alokoč̓-a||
/ha-:ča-t̯-lokʰč̓-a/
by.wing-fly-PL.ACT-DIR-EVID
'they're flying out'

||-alameč̓-|| -alameč̓- ~ -alame:- ~ -alamey ~ -lameč̓- ~ -lame:- ~ -lamey ~ -lmeč̓- ~ -lme:- ~ -lmey ~ -alamč̓- (?) ~ -lamč̓- (?) 'down off of'

This is a transcremental suffix. It is not listed in Oswalt (1976a); however, it is found in a verb paradigm in Oswalt's unpublished notes and in Halpern's records. The allomorphs followed by (?) are yet to be found, but they are expected on the basis of phonological patterns in the language. This suffix means 'down off of ~ down from above'. Examples of ||-alameč̓-|| are given in (290)–(294) (the surface forms of ||-alameč̓-|| are in bold).

(290) Example of ||-alameč̓-||
hat̪:almey (O ms.)
*hat̪:**almey***
||hat̪:-alameč̓-Ø||
/hat̪:-almey-Ø/
put.foot-DIR-PFV
['put foot down off of']

(291) Example of ||-alameč̓-||
[ʔ]ap[ʰ]:alméč̓in (H ms.)
*ʔapʰ:**almeč̓**in*
||ʔapʰ:-alameč̓-Vn||
/ʔapʰ:-almeč̓-in/
carry-DIR-SG.IMP
'climb down from above'

(292) Example of ||-alameč̓-||
[ʔ]ap[ʰ]:almé:le (H ms.)
*ʔapʰ:**alme:**le*
||ʔapʰ:-alameč̓-le||
/ʔapʰ:-alme:-le/
carry-DIR-PL.IMP
'2 carry 1 down!'

(293) Example of ||-alameč̓-||
[ʔ]a:p[ʰ]at̪lamé:le (H ms.)
*ʔa:pʰat̪**lame:**le*

||ʔa:pʰa-t̯-alameč̓-le||
/ʔa:pʰa-t̯-lame:-le/
carry-PL.ACT-DIR-PL.IMP
'2 carry 1 down 1 each!'

(294) Example of ||-alameč̓-||
[ʔ]ekʰ:elméč̓in (H ms.)
*ʔekʰ:e**lmeč̓**in*
||hi-hkʰe-alameč̓-Vn||
/ʔe-kʰ:e-lmeč̓-in/
with.body-move-DIR-SG.IMP
'move down from above!'

||-mokoč-|| -mokoč- ~ -moko:- ~ -mokoy ~ -mkoč- ~ -mko:- ~ -mkoy ~ -mok(ʰ)č- (?) 'back'

This directional suffix is not transcremental, as is the case for all /m/-initial suffixes. It is absent from the list of Pomoan directional suffixes in Oswalt (1976a). I have not yet found examples of this suffix in Halpern's notes; however, it is present in a verb paradigm in Oswalt's unpublished notes. Oswalt glosses it as 'back', and in the absence of additional examples, it is impossible to give more information on the semantics of this suffix. Examples of ||-mokoč-|| are given in (295)–(298) (surface forms of the suffix are in bold). The preceding allomorph followed by (?) is not in the current record but is to be expected on the basis of phonological patterns in the language. Because the extant examples of this suffix come from an unfinished paradigm table, one that did not directly gloss each entry, the glosses are my own and are based on Oswalt's definition of the verb stem as written across the top of the page (glossed as 'to put the foot') and the directional definition written to the left of the row from which these forms come (glossed as 'back').

(295) Example of ||-mokoč-||
<ʔahtimkoy> (O ms.)
*ʔaht̯i**mkoy***
||ʔaht̯i-mokoč-Ø||

/ʔaht̯i-mkoy-Ø/
put.foot-DIR-PFV
['to put the foot back']

(296) Example of ||-mokoč-||
<ʔahtimkocin> (O ms.)
*ʔaht̯i**mkočin***
||ʔaht̯i-mokoč-Vn||
/ʔaht̯i-mkoč-in/
put.foot-DIR-SG.IMP
['put the foot back!']

(297) Example of ||-mokoč-||
<ʔahtimko:le> (O ms.)
*ʔaht̯i**mko:**le*
||ʔaht̯i-mokoč-le||
/ʔaht̯i-mko:-le/
put.foot-DIR-PL.IMP
['put foot back (in-law ~ y'all)!']

(298) Example of ||-mokoč-||
<ʔa:tit'moko:le> (O ms.)
*ʔa:t̯it̯̓**moko:**le*
||ʔaht̯i-t̯-mokoč-le||
/ʔa:t̯i-t̯̓-moko:-le/
put.foot-PL.ACT-DIR-PL.IMP
['put foot, y'all! (to in-law) ~ put foot several times, y'all!]

||-akoč̓-|| -akoč̓- ~ -ako:- ~ -akoy ~ -koč̓- ~ -ko:- ~ -koy ~ -k(ʰ)č̓- 'out from within'

This is a transcremental suffix. It is not in the list of Pomoan directional suffixes in Oswalt (1976a), but it is present in verbs elicited by Halpern (H ms.). The extant examples suggest that this morpheme specifically means movement of an object (inanimate or body part) out of a container or hole. Examples are provided in (299)–(302) (the surface forms of ||-akoč̓-|| are in bold).

(299) Example of ||-akoč̓-||
čʰidʔákoy (H ms.)
*čʰidʔ**akoy***
||čʰi-dʔ-akoč̓-Ø||
/čʰi-dʔ-akoy-Ø/
by.small.part-move-DIR-PFV
'to take out 1 rock'

(300) Example of ||-akoč̓-||
ho:dóṯkoy (H ms.)
*ho:doṯ**koy***
||hoʔdo-ṯ-akoč̓-Ø||
/ho:do-ṯ-koy-Ø/
put.hand-PL.ACT-DIR-PFV
'to put hand in hole and take it out, pull'

(301) Example of ||-akoč̓-||
hodʔókʰč̓in (H ms.)
*hodʔo**kʰč̓**in*
||hoʔdo-akoč̓-Vn||
/hodʔo-kʰč̓-in/
put.hand-DIR-SG.IMP
'pull it out[!]'

(302) Example of ||-akoč̓-||
hó:doṯkó:le (H ms.)
*ho:doṯ**ko:**le*
||hoʔdo-ṯ-akoč̓-le||
/ho:do-ṯ-ko:-le/
put.hand-DIR-PL.IMP
'2 pull arms out!'

||-ad-|| -ad- ~ -a:- ~ -an- ~ -am- ~ -d- ~ -n- ~ -m- ~ -:- 'along'

This is a transcremental suffix. It is homophonous with the suffix ||-ad-|| IMPERFECTIVE; however, only the directional suffix ||-ad-|| is transcremental, and this is the only phonological distinction between them. The two suffixes are probably related historically, and the directional suffix ||-ad-|| has an imperfective-like meaning of moving about or along (i.e., continuous movement in no particular direction). When followed by an imperative suffix, this directional carries the meaning of motion toward the speaker. The allomorphs with [m] only occur before labial consonants. Examples of the directional suffix ||-ad-|| are given in (303)–(306) (surface forms of ||-ad-|| are in bold).

(303) Example of directional ||-ad-||
dó:noŋhk^{h}ay hwadu (H I: 6)
*do:nonhk^{h}ay hw**adu***
||do:no=li=k^{h}ač hu:w-ad-u||
/do:no=nhk^{h}ay hw-ad-u/
hill=ward go-DIR-PFV
'went uphill'

(304) Example of directional ||-ad-||
kúṭ:u hač:áŋkan (H ms.)
*kuṭ:u hač:**ankan***
||kuṭ:u ha-hča-ad-ka-Vn||
/kuṭ:u ha-č:a-n-ka-n/
just by.wing-fly-DIR-CAUS-SG.IMP
'let it fly toward here'

(305) Example of directional ||-ad-||
[ʔ]ek^h:édu (H ms.) [ʔ]ek^h:édun (H ms.)
*ʔek^h:**edu*** *ʔek^h:**edun***
||hi-hk^{h}e-ad-u|| ||hi-hk^{h}e-ad-Vn||
/ʔe-k^h:e-d-u/ /ʔe-k^h:e-d-un/
with.body-DIR-PFV with.body-DIR-SG.IMP
'to move along' 'move along, toward me'

(306) Example of directional ||-ad-||
[ʔ]e:k^{h}eṭ̯á:ne (H ms.)
*ʔe:k^{h}eṭ̯**a:ne***

||hi-hkʰe-t̯-ad-le||
/ʔe-:kʰe-t̯-a:-ne/
with.body-move-PL.ACT-DIR-PL.IMP
'2 move along, towards me!'

||-aduč-|| -aduč- ~ -adu:- ~ -aduy ~ -duč- ~ -du:- ~ -duy ~ -du- ~ -č:- 'away'

This is a transcremental suffix. When combined with an imperative suffix, it means motion away from the speaker. The form *-du-* occurs only before a geminate consonant or consonant cluster. Examples of the directional suffix ||-aduč-|| are given in (307)–(311) (surface forms of ||-aduč-|| are in bold).

(307) Example of ||-aduč-||
dak̓:ad:účin (H ms.)
*dak̓:ad:**učin***
||dak̓:aṭ-aduč-Vn||
/dak̓:ad-duč-in/
lead.several-DIR-SG.IMP
'1 take sev. away!'

(308) Example of ||-aduč-||
[ʔ]ekʰ:edú:le (H ms.)
*ʔekʰ:**edu:**le*
||hi-hkʰe-aduč-le||
/ʔe-kʰ:e-du:-le/
with.body-move-DIR-PL.IMP
'2 move away! (sitting or lying)'

(309) Example of ||-aduč-||
hač:áduy (H ms.)
*hač:**aduy***
||ha-hča-aduč-Ø||
/ha-č:a-duy-Ø/
by.wing-fly-DIR-PFV
'1 flies away'

(310) Example of ||-aduč-||
*ʔa:ʔa kʰaṭ:**aduk**ʰ:e̯tʰoṭ̓* (W: OF)
||ʔa:ʔa kʰaṭ:-aduč-kʰ:e=ṯʰoṭ̓||[159]
/ʔa:ʔa kʰaṭ:-adu-kʰ:e=ṯʰoṭ̓/
1SG.AGT run-DIR-FUT=NEG
'I didn't run away'

(311) Example of ||-aduč-||
[ʔ]ekʰ:éč:in (H ms.)
*ʔekʰ:**eč:**in*
||hi-hkʰe-aduč-Vn||
/ʔe-kʰ:e-č:-in/
with.body-move-DIR-SG.IMP
'move over! away!'

||-aded-|| -aded- ~ -ade:- ~ -aden- ~ -adem- -ad:- ~ -ded- ~ -de:- ~ -den- ~ -dem- ~ -d:- 'here and there'

This is a transcremental suffix. It is absent from the list of Pomoan directional suffixes in Oswalt (1976a), but Oswalt glosses it in his notes as 'here & there'. The allomorphs with [m] are only found before labial consonants. Examples of ||-aded-|| are given in (312)–(314) (the surface forms of ||-aded-|| are in bold).

(312) Example of ||-aded-||
hwademba (H EA: 14a)
*hw**adem**ba*
||hu:w-aded-ba||
/hw-adem-ba/
go-DIR-S.SEQ
['having gone']

(313) Example of ||-aded-||
kuṭ:u hač:adéŋkan (H ms.)
*kuṭ:u hač:**aden**kan*
||kuṭ:u ha-hča-aded-ka-Vn||

/kuṭ:u ha-č:a-den-ka-n/
just by.wing-fly-DIR-CAUS-SG.IMP
'let it fly away'

(314) Example of ||-aded-||
hač:ád:u (H ms.)
*hač:a**d:**u*
||ha-hča-aded-u||
/ha-č:a-d:-u/
by.wing-fly-DIR-PFV
'flying around'

This affix is also found on some verbs that are not verbs of motion. It is unclear what semantic content, if any, is added in such cases. The most common combination of this sort is with the verb stem ||čahnu-|| 'to speak', which has an unpredictable vowel change in combination with ||-aded-|| (||čahnu-aded-|| → /čanhoded-/). An example is given in (315) (the surface form of ||-aded-|| is in bold).

(315) Example of ||-aded-|| on ||čahnu-|| 'speak'
čáhnu ḱóʔdi čánhodenṯ[ʰ]í:baʔwáʔa (H ms.)
*čahnu ḱoʔdi čanho**denṯʰ**i:baʔwaʔa*
||čahnu ḱoʔdi čahnu-aded-ṯʰ-V:ba=ʔwa=ʔa||
/čahnu ḱoʔdi čanho-den-ṯʰ-i:ba=ʔwa=ʔa/
speech good speak-DIR-NEG-COND=COP.EVID=1SG.AGT
'I can't talk well'

||-aywač-|| -aywač- ~ -aywa:- ~ -ayway ~ -ywač- ~ -ywa:- ~ -yway- ~ -wač- ~ -wa:- ~ -way 'right up to'

This is a transcremental suffix. Oswalt glosses this directional as 'against, into contact with, onto' (1976a: 24). When used with an imperative suffix, this directional may mean motion away from the speaker or toward the speaker. Examples of the directional suffix ||-aywač-|| are given in (316)–(319) (the surface forms of the suffix are in bold).

(316) Example of ||-aywač-||
mi:má:k̓oʔyá:laʔwáʔt̪o hwaywáyʔdu (H ms.)
*mi:ma:k̓oʔya:laʔwaʔt̪o hw**ayway**ʔdu*
||mi:mač=k̓o=ʔya:la=ʔwa=ʔt̪o hu:w-aywač-wadu||
/mi:ma:=k̓o=ʔya:la=ʔwa=ʔt̪o hw-ayway-ʔdu/
cry=COM=only=COP.EVID=1SG.PAT go-DIR-HAB
'he always comes to me crying'

(317) Example of ||-aywač-||
ka:wíʔwan [ʔ]ap[h]:eywáčin (H ms.)
ka:wiʔwan ʔap^{h}*:e**ywačin***
||ka:wi=ʔwan ʔap^{h}:e=aywač-Vn||
/ka:wi=ʔwan ʔap^{h}:e-ywač-in/
child=DET.OBJ carry-DIR-SG.IMP
'carry it right up to him'

(318) Example of ||-aywač-||
ka:wíʔwan [ʔ]ap[h]:eywá:le (H ms.)
ka:wiʔwan ʔap^{h}*:e**ywa:**le*
||ka:wi=ʔwan ʔap^{h}:e-aywač-le||
/ka:wi=ʔwan ʔap^{h}:e-ywa:-le/
child=DET.OBJ carry-DIR-PL.IMP
'2 carry it right up to him!'

(319) Example of ||-aywač-||
ka:wíyaʔwan [ʔ]á:p[h]et̪̓wá:le (H ms.)
ka:wiyaʔwan ʔa:p^{h}*et̪̓**wa:**le*
||ka:wi-ya=ʔwan ʔap^{h}:e-t̪-aywač-le
/ka:wi-ya=ʔwan ʔa:p^{h}e-t̪̓-wa:-le/
child-PL=DET.OBJ carry-PL.ACT-DIR-PL.IMP
'2 carry babies right up to him 1 each'

||-bič-|| -bič- ~ -biy ~ -bi:- ~ -pč- 'up; begin'

This is a transcremental suffix. Oswalt (1976a: 24) believes the voiceless bilabial stop of the syncopated allomorph *-pč-* is actually the ejective [p'];

however, I have not heard this, and Halpern also consistently records a plain [p] for this allomorph. Oswalt later treats this *-pč-* allomorph as [ptʃ] rather than [p'tʃ] in an unpublished verb paradigm that appears to have been written out in 1995; his analysis, it would seem, changed over time with regard to the allomorphy of this morpheme. Oswalt notes that this suffix is reserved for short upward distance or the raising of "one part of the body relative to the rest" (1976a: 24). This suffix may also carry an inceptive meaning. Examples of ||-bič-|| are given in (320)–(323) (surface forms of ||-bič-|| are in bold).

(320) Example of ||-bič-||
dúw:ehkónt̪o há:čat̪̓bíča (H ms.)
*duw:ehkont̪o ha:čat̪̓**biča***
||duw:e=ʔahkon=ʔat̪:o ha-hča-t̪-bič-a||[160]
/duw:e=hkon=t̪o ha-:ča-t̪̓-bič-a/
night=long=1SG.PAT by.wing-fly-PL.ACT-DIR-EVID
'I kept getting up all night'

(321) Example of ||-bič-||
<hat:abiy> (O ms.)
*hat̪:a**biy***
||hat̪:a-bič-Ø||
/hat̪:a-biy-Ø/
put.foot-DIR-PFV
['raise foot']

(322) Example of ||-bič-||
[ʔ]e:k^{h}et̪̓bí:le (H ms.)
*ʔe:k^{h}et̪̓**bi:**le*
||hi-hk^{h}e-t̪-bič-le||
/ʔe-:k^{h}e-t̪̓-bi:-le/
with.body-move-PL.ACT-DIR-PL.IMP
'2 move up!'

(323) Example of ||-bič-||
<hat:apcin> (O ms.)
*hat̯:a**pč**in*
||hat̯:a-bič-Vn||
/hat̯:a-pč-in/
put.foot-DIR-SG.IMP
[‘raise foot!’]

2.8.3.2.5. Valence-Changing Suffixes

There are four valence-changing suffixes: ||-ka-|| CAUSATIVE, ||-ya-|| DEFOCUS, ||-č̓-|| REFLEXIVE, and ||-mhuč̓-|| RECIPROCAL. Each of these is discussed in the following subsections together with examples.

||-ka-|| -ka- ~ -ki- ~ -k- ~ -k^{h}- CAUSATIVE

The causative suffix ||-ka-|| adds an argument to the verb to which it is affixed. This additional argument need not be overtly expressed. This morpheme has two meanings (at least in English translation): forcing and allowing. The *-ki-* allomorph only occurs before the suffix ||-ya-|| DEFOCUS and is in free variation with the allomorph *-k-* in that position. Examples of the other allomorphs follow. (The causative suffix ||-ka-|| is in bold.)

(324) Example of ||-ka-|| CAUSATIVE
má:ṭ̓ikin [ʔ]uht̯eht̯ékan (H ms.)
*ma:ṭ̓ikin ʔuht̯eht̯e**ka**n*
||maH-ṭ̓i-ki-n ʔuht̯e-ht̯e-ka-Vn||
/ma-:ṭ̓i-ki-n ʔuht̯e-ht̯e-ka-n/
3C-younger.sibling-GS-PAT tell~tell-CAUS-SG.IMP
‘let him tell his y. sibling’

(325) Example of ||-ka-|| CAUSATIVE
mi:mák^{h}t̯[^{h}]u mádan (H ms.)
*mi:ma**k^{h}**t̯^{h}u madan*
||mi:mač-ka-t̯^{h}u ham:ad-an||
/mi:ma-k^{h}-t̯^{h}u mad-an/

cry-CAUS-PROH 3SG.F-PAT
'don't make her cry'

||-ya-|| -ya- DEFOCUS

The defocus suffix ||-ya-|| removes the most agentive argument of a verb. Though it may be translated with a passive construction in English, it shares little in common with the English passive. Unlike the English passive, the argument removed by ||-ya-|| may not reappear in an oblique, and the remaining non-agentive argument does not take on a new syntactic role; rather, this suffix removes the most agentive argument completely without affecting the remaining arguments. Because there is no argument marking on the verb and overt arguments (full NPs and pronouns) are not obligatory in Southern Pomo, this suffix may be applied to a verb with no overt arguments present. Halpern often translates verbs with this suffix by means of an impersonal 'they' in the English, which might lead to a mistaken impression that this suffix carries some number-marking function, which it does not. This suffix may be combined with the perfective suffix ||-w|| to derive nouns from verbs—for example, ||čuh:u-|| 'eat' vs. ||čuh:u-ya-w|| 'food', which is literally '(it) is eaten'—though this combination does not derive nouns by default. Examples of this suffix follow (with the suffix in bold).

(326) Example of ||-ya-|| DEFOCUS
míp[ʰ]:ak:i[:]kʰe yúh[:]u [ʔ]ohčóyaw (H III: 1)
*mipʰ:ak:i:kʰe yuh:u ʔohčo**ya**w*
||miH-pʰak-ki-:kʰe yuh:u ʔohčo-ya-w||
/mi-pʰ:ak-ki-:kʰe yuh:u ʔohčo-ya-w/
2-son-GS-POSS pinole put.shapeless.mass-DEFOC-PFV
'They have put up pinole for your son.'
[lit: 'Pinole has been put up for your son']

As mentioned in the earlier section on the causative suffix ||-ka-||, the defocus suffix follows the causative when both are present in the valence-changing slot of the verb. In this position the causative may surface as the allomorph *-ki-*, as shown in (327) (the defocus suffix ||-ya-|| is in bold).

(327) Example of ||-ya-|| DEFOCUS following ||-ka-|| CAUSATIVE
[ʔ]iš:i [ʔ]aṭʰ:éba hám:i čahčíkiyaw (H III: 6)
*ʔiš:i ʔaṭʰ:eba ham:i čahčiki**ya**w*
||ʔiš:i ʔaṭʰ:e-ba ham:i čahči-ka-ya-w||
/ʔiš:i ʔaṭʰ:e-ba ham:i čahči-ki-ya-w/
blanket spread-S.SEQ there sit-CAUS-DEFOC-PFV
'Having spread a blanket, they let her sit down there'
[lit: 'After spreading a blanket, [she] was allowed to sit there']

||-č̓-|| ~ ||-čič̓-|| -č̓- ~ -:- ~ -y ~ -čič̓- ~ -či:- ~ -čiy ~ -ʔč̓- REFLEXIVE

There are two unpredictable underlying forms of the reflexive, ||-č̓-|| and ||-čič̓-||, the second of which might be a fossilized combination with the semelfactive ||-č-||. This ||-čič̓-|| form may also carry an inceptive meaning, and the assignment of reflexive or inceptive meaning appears to be lexically conditioned. This suffix occurs after the causative when both occur together on a verb (as in the common form *hudʔa-ka-y* want-CAUS-REFL 'like' (literally: 'cause(s) self to want'). Examples of the reflexive suffix follow (the suffix is in bold).

(328) Example of ||-č̓-|| REFLEXIVE
čʰeʔ[:]eṱmáywan šuhkʰέč̓in (H ms.)
*čʰeʔ:eṱmaywan šuhkʰe**č̓**in*
||čʰeʔ:eṱmay=ʔwan šu-hkʰe-č̓-Vn||
/čʰeʔ:eṱmay=wan šu-hkʰe-č̓-in/
basket=DET.OBJ by.pulling-move-REFL-SG.IMP
'move basket closer to self[!]'

The form ||-čič̓-|| is often found before a consonant, as in (329), which is the plural imperative version of the clause from (328) (the surface form of ||-čič̓-|| is in bold).

(329) Example of ||-čič̓-|| REFLEXIVE
čʰeʔ[:]eṱmáywan šuhkʰečí:le (H ms.)
*čʰeʔ:eṱmaywan šuhkʰe**či:**le*
||čʰeʔ:eṱmay=ʔwan šu-hkʰe-čič̓-le||

/čʰeʔ:eṭmay=wan šu-hkʰe-či:-le/
basket=DET.OBJ by.pulling-move-REFL-PL.IMP
'2 move basket closer to self!'

The form ||-čič̓-|| carries an inceptive meaning on some verbs, as in (330) (where the surface form of the suffix is in bold).

(330) Example of ||-čič̓-|| REFLEXIVE with an inceptive meaning
[ʔ]ahp[ʰ]íči[y] (H ms.)
*ʔahpʰ**iči̇y***
||ʔahpʰi-čič̓-Ø||
/ʔahpʰi-čiy-Ø/
carry-REFL-PFV
'to start carrying on back'

When ||-čič̓-|| REFLEXIVE is preceded by a coronal stop, that stop may optionally assimilate to the first consonant of the suffix, as in (331) (with the surface forms of ||-čič̓-|| in bold).

(331) Optional assimilation of coronal before ||-čič̓-||
[ʔ]ihnaṭčíč̓in ~ [ʔ]ihnač:íč̓in (H ms.)
*ʔihnaṭ**čič̓**in ~ ʔihnač:**ič̓**in*
||hi-hnaṭ-čič̓-Vn||
/ʔi-hnaṭ-čič̓-in/
with.body-try-REFL-SG.IMP
'try on clothes[!]'

The choice between the two underlying forms of the reflex, ||-č̓-|| and ||-čič̓-||, is apparently arbitrary in most cases, and some verbs show free variation between the two, as in (332) (where the surface forms of ||-č̓-|| and ||-čič̓-|| are in bold).

(332) Free variation between ||-č̓-|| and ||-čič̓-||
duhkʰéč̓in [~] duhkʰeʔč̓in (H ms.)
*duhkʰe**č̓**in ~ duhkʰe**ʔč̓**in*
||du-hkʰe-č̓-Vn|| ~ ||du-hkʰe-čič̓-Vn||

/du-hkʰe-č̓-in/ ~ /du-hkʰe-ʔč̓-in/
with.fingers-move-REFL-SG.IMP with.fingers-move-REFL-SG.IMP
'bring it toward self[!]' [~] 'move it towards yourself[!]'

||-mhuč̓-|| -mhuč̓- ~ -mhu:- ~ -mhuy ~ -m(ʔ)č̓- RECIPROCAL

Verbs with the reciprocal suffix ||-mhuč̓-|| have two arguments. These arguments need not be overtly expressed. The final segment of this morpheme likely descends from the reflexive ||-č̓-||, but there is no reason to parse it off from the rest of ||-mhuč̓-|| as the sequence [-mhu-] has no meaning of its own. Examples of ||-mhuč̓-|| RECIPROCAL follow (with the surface forms of the suffix in bold).

(333) Example of ||-mhuč̓-|| RECIPROCAL
há:miní(:)ba baʔ[:]áywan hódʔómhuy (H I: 2)
*ha:miniba baʔ:aywan hodʔo**mhuy***
||ha:mini-ba baʔ:ay=ʔwan hodʔo-mhuč̓-Ø||
/ha:mini-ba baʔ:ay=wan hodʔo-mhuy-Ø/
and.then-S.SEQ woman=DET.OBJ handle-RECIP-PFV
'Then (he) made love to the woman'

Additional examples of this suffix are given in the following examples (the surface forms are of the reciprocal are in bold in each example).

(334) Example of ||-mhuč̓-|| RECIPROCAL
méhṭʰen čanhodémʔč̓in (H ms.)
*mehṭʰen čanhode**mʔč̓in***
||miH=ṭʰe-n čahnu-aded-mhuč̓-Vn||
/me-hṭʰe-n čanho-de-mʔč̓-in/
2-mother-PAT speak-DIR-RECIP-SG.IMP
'speak to your mother!'

(335) Example of ||-mhuč̓-|| RECIPROCAL
čáhnu [ʔ]á:lhok̓omhú:le (H ms.)
*čahnu ʔa:lhok̓o**mhu:**le*
||čahnu ʔa:lhok̓oč̓-mhuč̓-le||

/čahnu ʔa:lhok̓o-mhu:-le/
speech several.talk-RECIP-PL.IMP
'2 speak to e[ach] o[ther!]'

(336) Example of ||-mhuč̓-|| RECIPROCAL

be:némhuy (H ms.)	bé:nemhú:le (H ms.)
*be:ne**mhuy***	*be:ne**mhu:**le*
||bi-:ne-mhuč̓-Ø||	||bi-:ne-mhuč̓-le||
/be-:ne-mhuy-Ø/	/be-:ne-mhu:-le/
with.arms-grasp-RECIP-PFV	with.arms-grasp-RECIP-PL.IMP
'they hug e[ach] o[ther]'	'2 hug e[ach] o[ther]!'

(337) Example of ||-mhuč̓-|| RECIPROCAL
bé:nemhúṱ[h]le (H ms)
*be:ne**mhuṱ**ʰle*
||bi-:ne-mhuč̓-ṱʰu-le||
/be-:ne-mhu-ṱʰ-le/
with.arms-grasp-RECIP-PROH-PL.IMP
'2 don't hug e[ach] o[ther]!'

2.8.3.2.6. Other Derivational Suffixes

||-č-|| -č- ~ -:- ~ -y SEMELFACTIVE

The semelfactive is an aspectual suffix that indicates punctuated action, whether in realis or irrealis conjugations. As such, it is quite unlike the inflectional aspectual suffixes which do not combine with other TAM suffixes. The semelfactive may also affect the valence of some words by deriving transitive verbs from intransitive verbs, though it is unclear whether this phenomenon extends beyond a few attested words. Because the effects of the affix on the semantics of a verb stem are not completely predictable and may result in transitivity changes, it is treated as a derivational suffix herein. The identification of this affix can be challenging. Two of its allophones are completely homophonous with the reflexive suffix ||-č̓-||, and though it shares little with the reflexive in terms of semantic contribution, it is quite possible that the variant form of the reflexive ||-čič̓-|| once began with the semelfactive. Examples of ||-č-|| are given in (338) (with the surface forms of ||-č-|| in bold).

(338) Example of ||-č-|| SEMELFACTIVE

čahnúčin (H ms.)	čahnú:le (H ms.)
*čahnu**č**in*	*čahnu**:**le*
||čahnu-č-Vn||	||čahnu-č-le||
/čahnu-č-in/	/čahnu-:-le/
speak-SEM-SG.IMP	speak-SEM-PL.IMP
'speak up!'	'2 [speak up]!'

On some verbs the addition of the semelfactive appears to derive a transitive verb. Example (339) gives two verbs for 'to smell', one without the semelfactive is intransitive, and one with the semelfactive is transitive (though not syntactically transitive in the example because overt arguments are not necessary in Southern Pomo clauses). (The surface forms of ||-č-|| SEMELFACTIVE are in bold.)

(339) Example of ||-č-|| SEMELFACTIVE deriving a the transitive verb 'to smell'

méhšey (H ms.)	mehšéčin (H ms.)
*mehše**y***	*mehše**č**in*
||mi-hše-č||[161]	||mi-hše-č-Vn||
/me-hše-y/	/me-hše-č-in/
with.nose-smell-SEM	with.nose-smell-SEM-SG.IMP
'to smell something'	'smell it!'

Compare the foregoing example with the verb for 'smell' without the semelfactive, as given in (340).

(340) Example of the intransitive verb 'to smell' without the semelfactive

ḱoʔdi méhšew (H ms.)
ḱoʔdi mehšew
||ḱoʔdi mi-hše-w||
/ḱoʔdi me-hše-w/
good with.nose-smell-PFV
'it smells good'

||-m-|| -m- ~ -:- ~ -n ESSIVE

The essive is homophonous with the directional suffix ||-m-|| 'across' and the plural act suffix ||-m-||. Oswalt (1976a: 22) describes this suffix as follows:

> [The e]ssive indicat[es] a steady condition or state, action in a delimited area, or, when the verb root already denotes an unmoving position (verbs for 'lie', 'sit', 'stand'), then that position is on something up off the ground.

I have not found evidence for all of the meanings given by Oswalt. The examples which follow show the essive used to indicate an action in a delimited area (as mentioned by Oswalt) and to indicate an unmoving position off the ground. (Surface forms of the essive are in bold.)

(341) Example of ||-m-|| ESSIVE indicating action in delimited area

kʰáʔbe č̓á:ʔa( )wín:a ba:néman (H ms.)

*kʰaʔbe č̓a:ʔawin:a ba:ne**m**an*

||kʰaʔbe č̓a:ʔa=win:a ba:ne-m-an||

/kʰaʔbe č̓a:ʔa=win:a ba:neman/

rock one=atop put.one.nonlong.object-ESSIVE-SG.IMP

'put a rock on it'

(342) ||-m-|| ESSIVE indicating an unmoving position off the ground

<ʔahtin> (O ms.)	<ʔahtiman> (O ms.)
*ʔaht̪i**n***	*ʔaht̪i**m**an*
||ʔaht̪i-m-Ø||	||ʔaht̪i-m-Vn||
/ʔaht̪i-n-Ø/	/ʔaht̪i-m-an/
put.foot-ESSIVE-PF	put.foot-ESSIVE-PFV
['hold the foot still above ground']	['hold the foot still above ground!']

2.8.3.3. *Inflectional Suffixes*

The inflectional affixes include suffixes for tense, aspect, mood, evidentiality, negation, and, possibly, person marking.[162] Every finite verb in Southern Pomo must have at least one of these suffixes. Other inflectional affixes include the dependent clause suffixes, most of which are clearly switch-reference markers. These dependent clause suffixes may not be combined with the TAM suffixes; the TAM-bearing main verb supplies tense/aspect/mood to the dependent verbs. (At least some of the evidential suffixes may follow the dependent clause suffixes in special situations, such as on the pro-verb *ha:mini-*; see the section on evidentials, §2.8.3.3.4, for an example of this.) Each of these categories of inflectional suffixes is covered in the following subsections. A few enclitics have been included in these sections when they share semantic similarities with a group of affixes (e.g., the negative enclitic ||=t̪ʰoṭ̓|| NEGATIVE.PERFECTIVE has been included with the negative suffixes to which it is historically related and with which it shares negative semantics; it only differs in not being an affix).

2.8.3.3.1. Tense

There are only two tense suffixes in Southern Pomo, both of which are futures. Thus the only tense markers in the language are irrealis suffixes, and the only aspectual suffixes are realis. Indeed, it might be more productive to divide all TAM suffixes not by the categories tense/aspect/mood, as I have done here, but between realis (aspectual suffixes) and irrealis (tense and mood suffixes), a division that is clearly made in the dependent clause suffixes. The two futures are discussed here together with examples.

||-kʰ:e-|| -kʰ:e- ~ -kʰe FUTURE

This is a simple future. Its cognate in neighboring Central Pomo is an enclitic rather than affix and may be used as part of a purposive complementation strategy, as shown in (343) (the Central Pomo verb marked with the future enclitic is in bold in the text, glossing, and the translation).

(343) Central Pomo ||=ʔkʰe|| cognate of S. Pomo ||-kʰ:e-|| as a purposive

qʰá=:l	*yó-hi*	*maʔá*	***qʰa:díway=ʔkʰe***
water=to	go-same	food	**buy=FUTURE**

'He'**ll** go down and **buy** groceries' (adpated from Mithun 1993:124)[163]

The Southern Pomo morpheme does not appear to be used as a purposive; that function is handled by the future intentive discussed in the next section.[164] Examples of the future suffix ||-kʰ:e-|| are given below (verbs marked with the future are in bold in the text, glossing, and translation).

(344) Example of ||-kʰ:e-|| FUTURE
[ʔ]á:bat̪o haččʼ̓okʰ[:]eʔwáʔya (H ms.)
*ʔa:bat̪o hač̓:o**kʰ:e**ʔwaʔya*
||ʔa:-ba-t̪o hač̓:o-kʰ:e=ʔwa=ʔa:ya||
/ʔa:-ba-t̪o hač̓:o-kʰ:e=ʔwa=ʔya/
1-father's.father-PAT **arrive-FUT**=COP.EVID=1PL.AGT
'we'**re going to visit** our fa[ther's].fa[ther].'

(345) Example of ||-kʰ:e-|| FUTURE
*but̪:e kaʔma čoh:onh**kʰe*** (W: OF)
||but̪:e ka=ʔa:ma čoh:oN-kʰ:e||
/but̪:e ka=ʔma čoh:onh-kʰe/
when INTER=2SG.AGT **marry-FUT**
'when **will** you **get married**?'

(346) Example of ||-kʰ:e-|| FUTURE
[ʔ]á:č̓et̪o [ʔ]uht̪éht̪ekʰ[:]eʔwáʔa (H ms.)
*ʔa:č̓et̪o ʔuht̪eht̪e**kʰ:e**ʔwaʔa*
||ʔa:-č̓e-t̪o ʔuht̪e-ht̪e-kʰ:e=ʔwa=ʔa:ʔa||
/ʔa:-č̓e-t̪o ʔuht̪e-ht̪e-kʰ:e=ʔwa=ʔa/
1-mother-PAT **tell ~ tell-FUT**=COP.EVID=1SG.AGT
'I **will tell** my mother'

(347) Example of ||-kʰ:e-|| FUTURE
[ʔ]a:mayá:k̓o mí:ṭikʰ:ét̪ʰot̪̓wáʔa (H ms.)
*ʔa:maya:k̓o mi:ṭi**kʰ:e**t̪ʰot̪̓waʔa*
||ʔa:maya=:k̓o mi:ṭi-kʰ:e=t̪ʰot̪̓=ʔwa=ʔa:ʔa||
/ʔa:maya=:k̓o mi:ṭi-kʰ:e=t̪ʰot̪̓=wa=ʔa/
2PL.AGT=COM **lie-FUT**=NEG=COP.EVID=1SG.AGT
'I **won't lie** w[ith] ye'

||-t̪i-|| ~ ||-t̪iʔdu-|| -t̪i- ~ -t̪iʔdu- ~ -t̪iʔd- FUTURE INTENTIVE (NEAR FUTURE)

In Oswalt's list of Pomoan suffixes, he lists a distinction in Southern Pomo between ||-t̪i-||, which he glosses as an intentive that expresses "purpose, in order to, near future", and ||-t̪iʔdu||,[165] which he glosses as a near future that means "about to" (1976a: 25). Though he gives both a near future meaning, only ||-t̪i-|| is ascribed a purposive meaning. The examples that follow support such an interpretation of the data; however, it is quite possible that more data might reveal these two forms, ||-t̪i|| and ||-t̪iʔdu||, to be in free variation or lexically conditioned. Minimal pairs showing the contrast between a purposive (intentive) meaning and near future meaning have not been found. I have therefore chosen to treat them as variants of a single morpheme for the present work. Examples of the variants of the future intentive follow (verbs with the suffix are in bold in the text, the glossing, and the translation).

(348) Example of ||-t̪i-|| with purposive meaning

*ka:wi ʔa: čuh:uka**t̪i** ho:li:na* (W: OF)

/ka:wi	ʔa:	čuh:u-ka-t̪i	ho:li-:na/
child	1SG.AGT	**eat-CAUS-FUT.INTENT**	leave-FIRST.PERSON

'I'm going **to feed** my baby'

The future intentive is homophonous with the inchoative morpheme ||t̪i-|| ~ ||=t̪i-||, which is applied to verbs and adjectives. The future intentive may be suffixed to the inchoative morpheme, though other affixes generally separate them, as shown in (349) (where only the predicate marked with the future intentive is in bold in the text, glossing, and translation).

(349) Example of ||-t̪i-|| FUTURE.INTENTIVE combined with ||t̪i-|| INCHOATIVE

kʰáʔbe [ʔ]oh:óʔwan mi:t̪álaw, (H VI: 6)

kʰaʔbe ʔoh:oʔwan mi:t̪alaw,

/kʰaʔbe	ʔoh:o=ʔwan	mi:t̪a-la-w/
rock	fire=DET.OBJ	put.several-DIR-PFV

[ʔ]ahkʰá [ʔ]oh:o t̪ikʰt̪i.

*ʔahkʰa **ʔoh:o t̪ikʰt̪i**.*

/ʔahkʰa	ʔoh:o	t̪i-kʰ-t̪i/
water	**fire**	**INCH-CAUS-FUTURE.INTENTIVE**

'. . . they dropped the rocks, the hot rocks . . . **in order to have** the water **become hot**.'

As shown in the previous two examples, the future intentive is often part of a sentence with more than one clause when it carries a purposive meaning. Mono-clausal sentences are more likely to take the ||-t̪iʔdu-|| form in my database, and in these sentences the English translations line up with a near future meaning rather than a purposive one. Examples of this follow (||-t̪iʔdu-|| in bold in the text, the glossing, and the translation).

(350) ||-t̪iʔdu-|| with near future meaning in mono-clausal sentence
sí:maʔt̪o mí:ṭit̪íʔda (H ms.)
*si:maʔt̪o mi:ṭi**t̪iʔd**a*
/si:ma=ʔt̪o mi:ṭi-t̪iʔd-a/
sleep=1SG.PAT lie-**FUT.**INTENT-EVID[166]
'I'm **going to** go to sleep'

(351) ||-t̪iʔdu-|| with near future meaning in mono-clausal sentence
ha:čat̪du:t̪íʔda ~ hi:biʔdu:t̪íʔda (H ms.)
*ha:čat̪du:**t̪iʔd**a ~ hi:biʔdu:**t̪iʔd**a*
/ha:ča-t̪-du:-t̪iʔd-a/ ~ /hi:biʔ-du:-t̪iʔd-a/
fly-PL.ACT-DIR-**FUT.INTENT**-EVID sev.fly-DIR-**FUT.INTENT**-EVID
'birds are **going to** fly away'

(352) ||-t̪iʔdu-|| with near future meaning in mono-clausal sentence
[ʔ]á:baċe:kʰe [ʔ]ahčat̪óŋhkʰay hó:lit̪iʔdú:na (H ms.)
*ʔa:baċe:kʰe ʔahčat̪onhkʰay ho:li**t̪iʔdu**:na*
/ʔa:-ba-ċ-e-:kʰe ʔahča=t̪onhkʰay ho:li-t̪iʔdu-:na/
1-fa's.fa-GS-OBL-POSS house=toward leave-FUT.INTENT-FIRST.PERSON
'I am going to my fa[ther's] fa[ther]'s house after a while'

2.8.3.3.2. Aspectual Suffixes

There are three inflectional aspectual suffixes in Southern Pomo: an imperfective, a perfective, and a habitual. Following Bernard Comrie, aspect is herein defined as a way "of viewing the internal temporal constituency of a situation" (Comrie 1976, 3). Each of these inflectional aspectual affixes is amenable to being fit within such a definition; however, the commonest of these suffixes, the perfective, has many more uses and cannot be analyzed as a strictly aspectual affix. Each of these suffixes is described individually in the following sections.

Table 40. Distinguishing between ||-ad|| IPFV and ||-ad-|| DIR

Suffix→ **Properties↓**	||-ad-|| IMPERFECTIVE	||-ad-|| DIRECTIONAL 'along'
Transcrements the laryngeal increment	No	Yes

||-ad-|| ~ ||-adu-|| -ad- ~ -an- ~ -n ~ -:- (?) ~ -adu ~ -du IMPERFECTIVE

The imperfective is used to indicate an ongoing realis event. In Oswalt's terminology, this is the "durative" (1976a: 24). The allomorphs of this affix are homophonous with the directional suffix ||-ad-|| 'along'. Though the imperfective shares much in its semantics with this suffix (and might be historically related to it), it can be distinguished from it, though identification of isolated instances can be challenging if the phonological context is insufficient for correct diagnosis. Table 40 sets out the differences between these two suffixes.

As can be seen in table 40, it is not the case that there are clear semantic differences between these affixes. The directional ||-ad-|| does not have any real directional meaning to it; rather, it translates well as 'along,' as in 'going along', which carries an imperfective meaning. Indeed, Halpern specifically identifies this directional suffix as the "durative" (1984: 18). Thus both Oswalt and Halpern identify an imperfective morpheme, which they term *durative*, but Oswalt assigns this to the morpheme herein termed the imperfective, and Halpern assigns this to the morpheme herein termed the directional 'along'.

Though Oswalt (1976a and 1978) consistently lists this suffix as having no final vowel, the examples below clearly show ||-ad-|| suffixed to a verb that is not a verb of motion (and therefore should not be expected to take a directional suffix) without transcrementing the laryngeal increment. In these examples, the allomorph of ||-ad-|| is *-adu* in word final position. It is worth returning to Halpern's identification of his so-called durative suffix: it is not the case that he assigned an imperfective meaning to the transcrementing directional ||-ad-||; rather, he conflates imperfective ||-ad-|| with the directional ||-ad-||, both of which he internally reconstructs as *-de, a reconstruction he uses to explain their word-final form of *-du* as the product of an earlier combination with the perfective suffix ||-w|| (i.e., *-de + *-w > *-du*). Though Oswalt's distinction between a transcremental directional ||-ad-|| and an non-transcremental imperfective ||-ad-|| is maintained in this work, I agree with Halpern's historical analysis and his synchronic identification of *-du* as the word-final variant; however, I also keep the initial vowel from Oswalt's analysis. I therefore treat *-(a)du* as the word-final allomorph of both ||-ad-|| suffixes. Thus the word-final allomorph of the imperfective was once a combination of the earlier imperfective suffix *-ade- and a perfective suffix *-w in word-final position. A similar process of combining several aspectual suffixes can be reconstructed for the word-final habitual suffix ||-wadu-||, which probably descends from a combination of the the perfective *-w + imperfective *-ade + the perfective *-w. Of course, these historical data do not affect the synchronic semantics of these suffixes. Examples of the imperfective suffix follow (with the imperfective suffix in bold in the text).

(353) Example of *-du* allomorph ||-ad-|| ~ ||-adu|| IPFV
šú:kʰay [ʔ]uhnáṭ̓du (H ms.)
*šu:kʰay ʔuhnaṭ̓**du***
||šu:kʰač-Ø hu-hnaṭ-adu||[167]
/šu:kʰay-Ø ʔu-hnaṭ̓-du/
breathe-PFV by.speech-try-IPFV
'to tease s[ome]o[ne]'[168]

(354) Example of *-an-* allomorph ||-ad-|| ~ ||-adu|| IPFV
šú:kʰay [ʔ]uhnaṭánṭ[ʰ]u (H ms.)
*šu:kʰay ʔuhnaṭ**an**ṭʰu*
||šu:kʰač-Ø hu-hnaṭ-ad-ṭʰu||
/šu:kʰay-Ø ʔu-hnaṭ-an-ṭʰu/
breathe-PFV by.speech-try-IPFV-PROH
'don't tease him (w[ith] words)[!]'

||-w|| ~ ||-u|| ~ ||-Ø|| -w ~ -u ~ -Ø PERFECTIVE

The perfective is by far the commonest suffix in Southern Pomo. This suffix, which Oswalt (1976a and 1978) glosses as an "absolutive," has several functions. Oswalt states that in Kashaya, Central Pomo, and Southern Pomo, this suffix "is the citation form of verbs, forms verbal nouns and adjectives, and is the main verb of sentences in stories" (1976a: 24). In reference to Southern Pomo alone, Oswalt writes that this suffix is "roughly comparable to the English infinitive or -ing form" (1978: 13). All these uses of this suffix are confirmed by the extant data.

The use of the term *perfective* for this suffix within this work is more of a convenience than a statement of fact about its only value. There are three choices with regard to glossing this morpheme: (1) follow Pomoan scholarly tradition as set forth by Oswalt (1976a and throughout his work on Kashaya, Central Pomo, and Southern Pomo) and gloss this suffix with the problematic term *absolutive*; (2) follow Pomoan scholarly tradition as set forth by Mithun (1993 and throughout her work on Central Pomo) and gloss it as *perfective*; or (3) create a new term. Because this suffix has several functions, one of which is perfective aspect, the decision has been made to pick the most accurate gloss that stays within Pomoan scholarly tradition, one which avoids the unwanted baggage of Oswalt's use of the term *absolutive*, rather than introduce something new.

The perfective suffix is the citation form of verbs and it may be used to derive nouns from verbs (especially in combination with the defocus suffix ||-ya-||). However, it does have a clear perfective aspectual meaning in most instances, and Oswalt's characterization of its being analogous to an English infinitive is rather misleading. Comrie states that the perfective aspect does not give "direct expression to the internal structure of a situation" and "denote[s] a complete situation, with beginning, middle, and end" (1976a: 17–18). This definition fits the most common usage of the perfective in Southern Pomo discourse. It is the default suffix on verbs and does not refer to time (i.e., is not past tense), nor does it provide any information about the internal structure of the event.

When applied to verbs of motion which do not have a directional suffix preceding the perfective, there is a completive meaning, which Oswalt glosses in his notes as "terminate." Even this completive meaning, however, is not outside the bounds of what perfective aspect might do (even if it is not expected function). Comrie states that the use of the perfective to indicate "the end of a situation [i.e., as a completive] is at best only one of the possible meanings" to be ascribed to this aspect (Comrie 1976: 19). Though this is hardly enthusiastic support for a perfective that functions as a completive in some corners of the grammar, the fact that this completive meaning is restricted to verbs of motion with no directional suffixes (an uncommon phenomenon) confirms it as "only one of the possible meanings," as allowed by Comrie's definition of perfective aspect.

Every finite verb in Southern Pomo that does not have another TAM suffix must bear the perfective suffix. The perfective has three forms: ||-w|| *-w* after all five vowel qualities (though it is exceedingly uncommon after /e/ and is inconsisently recorded after /u/ by Halpern); ||-u|| *-u* after /d/; and ||-Ø|| after all other consonants. Examples of each of the variants follow.

(355) Example of ||-w|| PERFECTIVE after /i/
ho:liw (W: OF)
||ho:li-w||
/ho:li-w/
leave-PFV
'went'

(356) Example of ||-w|| PERFECTIVE after /e/
[ʔ]uhṱéhṱew (H III: 1)
ʔuhṱehṱew
||ʔuhṱe-hṱe-w||
/ʔuhṱe-hṱe-w/
tell ~ tell-PFV
'tells it'

(357) Example of ||-w|| PERFECTIVE after /a/
di:láċaw (H VIII: 6)
di:laċaw
||di-:lv-ċa-w||
/di-:la-ċa-w/
by.falling-PL.ACT-break-PFV
'He broke'

(358) Example of ||-w|| PERFECTIVE after /o/
kʰáʔbe [ʔ]áčʰ:ow (H VIII: 8)
kʰaʔbe ʔačʰ:ow
||kʰaʔbe ʔačʰ:o-w||
/kʰaʔbe ʔačʰ:o-w/
rock NEG.EXISTENTIAL-PFV
'there [was] no rock'

(359) Example of ||-w|| PERFECTIVE after /u/
diʔbuw (O I: 24)
diʔbuw
||diʔbu-w||
/diʔbu-w/
bury-PFV
'buried'

(360) Example of ||-u|| PERFECTIVE after /d/
huw:adu (H I: 12)
huw:adu
||hu:w-ad-u||
/huw:-ad-u/
go-DIR-PFV
'came'

(361) Example of ||-Ø|| PERFECTIVE after consonant other than /d/
šúhnaṭ̯ (H VIII: 4)
šuhnaṭ̯
||šu-hnaṭ̯-Ø||
/šu-hnaṭ̯-Ø/
by.pulling-try-PF
'he tried pulling it'

||-wad-|| ~ ||-wadu-|| -wadu- ~ -wad- ~ -wʔdu- ~ -ʔdu HABITUAL

The habitual is used for actions which happen often, and this suffix may be used on verbs which are preceded by the adverb *č̓a:šba* 'always'. Comrie states that habitual aspect (in the world's languages) is used to "describe a situation which is characteristic of an extended period of time, so extended in fact that the situation referred to is viewed not as an incidental property of the moment but, precisely, as a characteristic feature of a whole period" (Comrie 1976: 28). The Southern Pomo habitual fits this definition. In the narrative texts it is often used to set the stage when characters are introduced (e.g., *ho:li-wʔdu-n* leave-HAB-S.SIM 'always went' from the beginning of (H I): "Sparrowhawk, it is said, always went to the outside to trap birds"). Examples of the habitual follow (the surface forms of the suffix are in bold; the verbs affected by it are in bold in the translations).

(362) Example of ||-wad-|| ~ ||-wadu-|| HABITUAL
lík̓lisyey yódo kú:luŋhkʰay ho:líwʔdun, (H I: 1)
*lik̓lisyey yodo ku:lunhkʰay ho:li**wʔdu**n*
||lik̓lis=yey yo-do ku:lu=li=kʰač ho:li-wadu-Vn||
/lik̓lis=yey yo-do ku:lu=nhkʰay ho:li-wʔdu-n/
raptor.species=AGT AUX=QUOT outside=ward leave-HAB-S.SIM
'Sparrowhawk, it is said, **always went** to the outside to trap birds'

(363) Example of ||-wad-|| ~ ||-wadu-|| HABITUAL
há:meṭ yá:laʔyowám:an ča:máwʔdu (H ms.)
*ha:meṭ ya:laʔyowam:an ča:ma**wʔdu***
||ha:meṭ ya:la=ʔyo-wa=ham:ad ča:ma-wadu||
/ha:meṭ ya:la=ʔyo-wa=m:an ča:ma-wʔdu/
thus only=AUX-EVID=3 F.SG.AGT twine-HAB
'she's **always twining** this kind of basket'

As already stated, the habitual may be suffixed to verbs which are also modified by the adverb *č̓a:šba* 'always', as shown in the following example (where both the adverb *č̓a:šba* 'always' and the habitual suffix are in bold; the translations for the verb with the habitual and the adverb 'always' are also in bold).

(364) Example of HABITUAL together with adverb č̓a:šba 'always'
č̓á:šbaʔwám:u mábʔaċen hačč̓ówʔdu (H ms.)
č̓a:šba**ʔwam:u mabʔaċen hač̓:o**wʔdu

||č̓a:šba=ʔwa=ham:u maH-ba-ć-en hač̓:o-wadu||
/č̓a:šba=ʔwa=m:u ma-bʔa-ć-en hač̓:o-wʔdu/
always=COP.EVID=3SG 3C-fa's.fa-GS-AGT arrive-HAB
'he **always visits** his gr[and]fa[ther]s.'

2.8.3.3.3. Mood and Modality

R. M. Dixon states that the term mood is properly applied only to the declarative, interrogative, and imperative moods; modality must be kept separate (2010a: 95–97). If this division is to be followed, the imperative suffixes discussed in this section are the only true mood markers. There is no declarative mood morpheme, and the interrogative morpheme ||ka|| ~ ||=ʔka|| is not an affix, nor does it pattern with the the other mood/modality morphemes. Modal suffixes include a conditional and a hortative. There is also an optative enclitic. Whatever usefulness might be had by distinguishing between mood and modality in cross-linguistic work, it is the case that the mood and modality suffixes of Southern Pomo pattern together, and it is useful to discuss them in the same section. All these mood/modality suffixes are irrealis. They are mutually exclusive with one another on a verb and cannot co-occur on the same verb; when they are the final inflection on a main verb with a dependent verb, that dependent verb must take an irrealis dependent clause suffix (this is also true of the future ||-kʰ:e||). One of the mood suffixes, the plural imperative, descends from an earlier conditional. Each of the mood/modal suffixes is discussed in this section.

||-V:ba|| -i:ba ~ -a:ba ~ -o:ba ~ -u:ba ~ -:ba CONDITIONAL

The conditional can be used to indicate obligation or ability. It can also be used to form a polite command (separate from the plural imperative, which is used as a sign of respect in commands to in-laws). Examples follow with the conditional in bold (the words corresponding to the conditional verb in the translations are also in bold).

(365) Example of ||-V:ba|| CONDITIONAL used for obligation/request
[ʔ]ay:áḱoʔwéṇṭoʔma mi:ṭí:ba (H ms.)
*ʔay:aḱoʔweṇṭoʔma mi:ṭi:**ba***

||ʔay:a=k̓o=ʔwen=ṭo-ʔa:ma mi:ṭi-V:ba||
/ʔay:a=k̓o=ʔwen=ṭo=ʔma mi:ṭi-:ba/
1PL=COM=?=CONTRAST=2SG.AGT lie-COND[169]
'you **ought to lie** w[ith] us'

(366) Example of ||-V:ba|| CONDITIONAL used for obligation/request
[ʔ]ek^{h}:ekó:baʔwaʔmáya (H ms.)
*ʔek^{h}:ek**o:ba**ʔwaʔmaya*
||hi-hk^{h}e-ok-V:ba=ʔwa=ʔa:maya||
/ʔe-k^{h}:e-k-o:ba=ʔwa=ʔmaya/
with.body-move-DIR-COND=COP.EVID=2PL.AGT
'(in-law) **move out** (Sp[eaker]. out)! = ye **ought to move out**[!]'

(367) Example of ||-V:ba|| CONDITIONAL used for ability
čáhnu k̓óʔdi čánhodenṱ[^{h}]í:baʔwáʔa (H ms.)
*čahnu k̓oʔdi čanhodenṱ^{h}**i:ba**ʔwaʔa*
||čahnu k̓oʔdi čahnu-aded-ṱ^{h}-V:ba=ʔwa=ʔa:ʔa||
/čahnu k̓oʔdi čanho-den-ṱ^{h}-i:ba=ʔwa=ʔa/
speech good speak-DIR-NEG-COND=COP.EVID=1SG.AGT
'I **can**'t talk well'

||-V-|| -i ~ -a ~ -o ~ -u ~ -Ø HORTATIVE

When applied to a vowel-final verb, the hortative surfaces as zero, and it appears that the bare stem is being used for the hortative (e.g., *ho:li=ʔya* ||ho:li-V=ʔa:ya|| leave-HORT=1PL.AGT 'let's go!'). An example of the hortative after a consonant is given in (368) (with the hortative suffix in bold and underlined).

(368) Example of ||-V-|| hortative after a consonant
dáʔṱamč̓íʔya (H I: 6)
*daʔṱamč̓**i**ʔ*ya
||daʔṱa-mhuč̓-V=ʔa:ya||
/daʔṱa-mč̓-i=ʔya/
find-recip-hort=1pl.agt
'Let's meet'

||-Vn|| -in ~ -an ~ -on ~ -un ~ -n SINGULAR IMPERATIVE

The singular imperative is used for commands to one individual. The plural imperative ||-le|| may replace it as a sign of respect when commands are given to in-laws. Examples of the singular imperative follow with the suffix in bold in the text.

(369) Example of ||-Vn|| SINGULAR.IMPERATIVE
[ʔ]ek^h:ékan (H ms.)
*ʔek^h:ek**an***
||hi-hk^{h}e-ak-Vn||
/ʔe-k^h:e-k-an/
with.body-move-DIR-SG.IMP
'move out (sp[eaker] in[side])[!]'

(370) Example of ||-Vn|| SINGULAR.IMPERATIVE
[ʔ]ek^h:ékon (H ms.)
*ʔek^h:ek**on***
||hi-hk^{h}e-ok-Vn||
/ʔe-k^h:e-k-on/
with.body-move-DIR-SG.IMP
'move out (sp[eaker] out[side])[!]'

(371) Example of ||-Vn|| SINGULAR.IMPERATIVE
<hat:apcin> (O ms.)
*haṱ:apč**in***
||haṱ:a-bič-Vn||
/haṱ:a-pč-in/
put.foot-DIR-SG.IMP
['raise foot!']

(372) Example of ||-Vn|| SINGULAR.IMPERATIVE
huw:ádun (H VI:11)
*huw:ad**un***
||hu:w-ad-Vn||
/huw:-ad-un/

go-DIR-SG.IMP
'come!'

(373) Example of ||-Vn|| SINGULAR.IMPERATIVE
*čuh:u**n**mkʰe čaw:an* (W: OF)
||čuh:u-Vn=mkʰe čaw:an||
/čuh:u-n=mkʰe čaw:an/
eat-SG.IMP=2SG.POSS stuff
'eat your food!'

||-le|| -le ~ -ne PLURAL IMPERATIVE (respect suffix for addressing in-laws)

The plural imperative is used for commands to two or more people. It is also used as a sign of respect in giving commands to one in-law. When more than one in-law is being addressed, it is combined with the plural act affix ||-t̪-||. Examples of ||-le|| follow (the plural imperative suffix is in bold).

(374) Example of ||-le|| PLURAL.IMPERATIVE
[ʔ]e:kʰet̪ʼbí:le (H ms.)
*ʔe:kʰet̪ʼbi:**le***
||hi-hkʰe-t̪-bič-le||
/ʔe-:kʰe-t̪ʼ-bi:-le/
with.body-move-PL.ACT-DIR-PL.IMP
'2 move up!'

[ʔ]ehkʰé:ne (H ms.)
*ʔehkʰe:**ne***
||hi-hkʰe-m-le||
/ʔe-hkʰe-:-ne/
with.body-move-DIR-PL.IMP
'(in-law) move across!'

||=ʔšen|| =ʔšen ~ =šen OPTATIVE

The optative is not a suffix in Southern Pomo, though it descends from a Proto Pomo suffix, *-Vš, and is cognate with optative suffixes in Kashaya, Central Pomo, and Eastern Pomo (Oswalt 1976a: 25). This morpheme is an enclitic, and it is like the pronominal enclitics, the auxiliary enclitic ||=ʔyo-||, and the interrogative enclitic ||=ʔka|| in behaving like a second-position (i.e., Wackernagel) clitic in most examples; it may attach to any word class. An example of the optative morpheme is given in (375) (with the optative in bold).

(375) Example of ||=ʔšen|| OPTATIVE
ham:uban( )šen ma:liʔyokan[170] (H ms.)
*ham:uban***šen** *ma:liʔyokan*
/ham:uban=šen ma:li=ʔyo-ka-n/
3M.SG.PAT=OPTATIVE here=AUX-CAUS-?[171]
'I wish he were here'

2.8.3.3.4. Evidentials

Southern Pomo has a rich set of evidential suffixes. Unfortunately, the spontaneous conversations (daily gossip, arguments, etc.) in which these suffixes might have been common are not part of the extant records. In the narrative texts, the evidential suffixes are not particularly frequent. Oswalt (1976a: 25) lists the Southern Pomo cognates for the reconstructed evidentials of Proto Pomo, and each of the evidentials from his list follows. However, I have no examples for his reported aural evidential.

||-a|| -a ~ -o ~ -wa FACTUAL

This evidential fills the roles of the both factual and visual evidentials of neighboring Pomoan languages (there is no separate visual evidential in Southern Pomo) (Oswalt 1976a: 25). The factual evidential suffix is used with events that have been or are being witnessed or experienced (in a non-auditory way). This suffix is part of the copula evidential clitic ||=ʔwa||, which is frequently encountered (examples are strewn throughout this grammar); however, I treat the copula evidential as an independent morpheme, and the examples that follow are solely those with the factual evidential suffixed to verb stems. This suffix has the allomorph *-wa* after vowels. This variant is likely the result of an earlier distribution in which this evidential was *-a and applied after the perfective suffix on verbs, and the current allomorphy probably developed along the following paths:

[V-final verb stem] +*-w PERFECTIVE + *-a FACTUAL.EVIDENTIAL > *-wa*
[C-final verb stem] + *-Ø PERFECTIVE + *-a FACTUAL.EVIDENTIAL > *-a*

The factual evidential is in bold in the following examples.

(376) Example of ||-a|| FACTUAL.EVIDENTIAL after a vowel
sí:maʔt̪o p[^{h}]iʔt̪̓áwa (H ms.)
*si:maʔt̪o p^{h}iʔt̪̓a**wa***
||si:ma=ʔat̪:o p^{h}i-ʔt̪̓a-wa||
/si:ma=ʔt̪o p^{h}i-ʔt̪̓a-wa/
sleep=1SG.PAT by.sight-discover-EVID
'I feel sleepy, getting sleepy'

(377) Example of ||-a|| FACTUAL.EVIDENTIAL after a consonant
ha:čat̪lók^{h}č̓a (H ms.)
*ha:čat̪lok^{h}č̓**a***
||ha-hča-t̪-alokoč̓-a||
/ha-:ča-t̪-lok^{h}č̓-a/
by.wing-fly-PL.ACT-DIR-EVID
'they're flying out'

When this morpheme is suffixed to a morpheme ending in an underlying ||...ok|| (regardless of the morpheme), it surfaces as the allomorph *-o*, as seen in (378) and (379).

(378) Example of ||-a|| FACTUAL.EVIDENTIAL after ||ok||
[ʔ]ahčámko (H ms.)
*ʔahčamk**o***
||ha-hča-mok-a||
/ʔahča-mk-o/
fly-DIR-EVID
'flew into'

(379) Example of ||-a|| FACTUAL.EVIDENTIAL after ||ok||
<him*ok'o> (O D: EA)
*him:ok̓**o***

||him:oḱ-a||
/him:oḱ-o/
fall-EVID
'fell down'

||-Vnʔda|| AURAL

Oswalt reconstructs *-v̂n. . .- as the Proto Pomo form from which the Southern Pomo suffix ||-Vnʔda|| descends; he lists the meaning of this evidential for Pomoan as "Aural, the speaker is telling of what he just heard happen but did not see" (Oswalt 1976a, 25). I have not yet uncovered examples of this suffix.

||-do|| -do QUOTATIVE

The quotative is used for hearsay information. It is frequently suffixed to the auxiliary ||yo|| ~ ||=ʔyo|| at the beginning of a story to indicate that the tale that follows was transmitted by word of mouth. An example of ||-do|| is given in (380) (the suffix and its translation are in bold).

(380) Example of ||-do|| QUOTATIVE.EVIDENTIAL
líḱlisyey yódo kú:luŋhkʰay ho:líwʔdun, (H I: 1)
*liḱlisyey yo**do** ku:lunhkʰay ho:liwʔdun*
||liḱlis=yey yo-do ku:lu=li=kʰač ho:li-wadu-Vn||

/liḱlis=yey	yo-do	ku:lu=nhkʰay	ho:li-wʔdu-n/
raptor.species=AGT	AUX=QUOT	outside=ward	leave-HAB-S.SIM

'Sparrowhawk, **it is said**, always went to the outside to trap birds'

||-ka|| -ka INFERENTIAL

Oswalt states that the inferential suffix in Pomoan is used when "the speaker is telling what he deduces has happened" (1976a, 25). An example of the inferential evidential suffix ||-ka-|| is given in (381) (the suffix is in bold).

(381) Example of ||-ka-|| INFERENTIAL.EVIDENTIAL
[ʔ]ám:awi din:áka (H ms.)
*ʔam:awi din:a**ka***

/ʔam:a=wi din:a-ka/
earth=INSTR cover-EVID
'it's [apparently] covered w[ith] dirt'

||-l:a|| -l:a ~ -na PERFORMATIVE

Oswalt states that the performative suffix in Pomoan is used when "the speaker is telling what he himself is doing" (1976a: 25). An example of the performative evidential suffix ||-l:a-|| is given in (382) (the suffix is in bold).

(382) Example of ||-l:a|| PERFORMATIVE.EVIDENTIAL

sí:ma mi:ṭíl:a	(H ms.)	*ho:li:na*	(W: OF)
*si:ma mi:ṭi**l:a***		||ho:li-ad-l:a||	
/si:ma mi:ṭi-l:a/		/ho:li-:-na/	
sleep lie-EVID		leave-IPFV-EVID	
'I'm going to sleep'		'I'm going . . .'	

2.8.3.3.5. Negative Suffixes

All the negative suffixes begin with the consonant /t̪ʰ/, which is roughly equivalent to the role /n/ plays in English. I have included the negative enclitic ||=t̪ʰoṭ̓|| ~ ||=t̪ʰot̪̓|| and the negative response particle ||t̪ʰe:|| in this section because of their obvious relationship to the negative suffixes. The negative existential morpheme ||ʔačʰ:o-|| is a verb in its own right (e.g., *kʰaʔbe=ʔkʰe ʔačʰ:o-w* rock=1SG.POSS NEG.EXISTENTIAL-PFV 'I have no money' [W: OF]), and it is therefore left out of this section.

||-t̪ʰ-|| -t̪ʰ- NEGATIVE

This suffix has not been encountered much in the data. In (383) it negates a conditional clause. It is unclear whether this negative is restricted to irrealis clauses or whether it has a wider distribution (the surface form of ||-t̪ʰ-|| is in bold in the following example).

(383) Example of ||-t̪ʰ-|| -t̪ʰ- NEGATIVE
čáhnu k̓óʔdi čánhodent̪[ʰ]í:baʔwáʔa (H ms.)
*čahnu k̓oʔdi čanhoden**t̪ʰ**i:baʔwaʔa*

||čahnu k̓oʔdi čahnu-aded-t̪ʰ-V:ba=ʔwa=ʔa:ʔa||
/čahnu k̓oʔdi čanho-den-t̪ʰ-i:ba=ʔwa=ʔa/
speech good speak-DIR-NEG-COND=COP.EVID=1SG.AGT
'I can't talk well'

||-t̪ʰe-|| -t̪ʰe- NEGATIVE

This suffix is also fairly rare. It is unclear how it differs from the preceding one, ||-t̪ʰ-||. Perhaps ||-t̪ʰe-|| is reserved for realis ongoing actions, and ||-t̪ʰ-|| is used with irrealis suffixes like the conditional (though the semantics of the preceding example of its use to indicate lack of ability make this a messy theory). An example of ||-t̪ʰe-|| is given in (384) (suffix in bold).

(384) Example of ||-t̪ʰe-|| NEGATIVE
hudʔat̪ʰé( )[ʔ]t̪o mí:t̪o. (H I: 25)
*hudʔa**t̪ʰe**ʔt̪o mi:t̪o*
/hudʔa-t̪ʰe=ʔt̪o mi:t̪o/
want-NEG=1SG.PAT 2SG.PAT
'I don't want you.'

||-t̪ʰu-|| -t̪ʰu ~ -t̪ʰ- PROHIBITIVE

The prohibitive is a negative imperative. It is used to give negative commands to one person. When negative commands are given to two or more people, the prohibitive is followed by the plural imperative suffix ||-le||. When it is combined with ||-le||, the prohibitive is homophonous with the general negative ||-t̪ʰ-||. I have chosen to treat it as an allomorph of the prohibitive in this situation for two reasons: (1) it has a prohibitive meaning; and (2) on the basis of syncope patterns seen elsewhere in the language it is expected that the /u/ of the prohibitive would disappear in this context. Examples of the prohibitive are given in (385) and (386) (with the suffix in bold in the text).

(385) Example of ||-t̪ʰu-|| PROHIBITIVE in command to one person
mi:mákʰt̪[ʰ]u mádan (H ms.)
*mi:makʰ**t̪ʰu** madan*
||mi:mač-ka-t̪ʰu ham:ad-an||

/mi:ma-kʰ-t̪ʰu mad-an/
cry-CAUS-PROH 3SG.F-PAT
'don't make her cry'

(386) Example of ||-t̪ʰu-|| PROHIBITIVE in command to more than one person
bé:nemhút̪[ʰ]le (H ms)
be:nemhut̪ʰle
||bi-:ne-mhuč̓-t̪ʰu-le||
/be-:ne-mhu-t̪ʰ-le/
with.arms-grasp-RECIP-PROH-PL.IMP
'2 don't hug e[ach] o[ther]!'

||-t̪ʰen-|| -t̪ʰen- NEGATIVE.IMPERFECTIVE

I have found few examples of this negative. It appears to negate events with a continuous meaning (as in the following example, where the subject of the verb could not sleep all throughout the night). The negative imperfective is in bold in (387).

(387) Example of ||-t̪ʰen-|| NEGATIVE.IMPERFECTIVE
sí:ma mí:ṭit̪ʰenṭ̓óʔt̪o dúw:e (H VIII: 2)
*si:ma mi:ṭi**t̪ʰen**ṭ̓oʔt̪o duw:e*
/si:ma mi:ṭi-t̪ʰen=ṭ̓o=ʔt̪o duw:e/
sleep lie-NEG.IPFV=CONTRAST=1SG.PAT night
'I can't sleep (at) night.'

||=t̪ʰoṭ̓|| ~ ||=t̪ʰot̪̓|| =t̪ʰoṭ̓ ~ =t̪ʰot̪̓ NEGATIVE.PERFECTIVE

This enclitic negates perfective actions. It also negates predicate nominals and predicate adjectives. It is by far the commonest negative morpheme in the extant records, though this might be an artifact of the types of elicited forms and narrative discourse which make up the bulk of the data. It is frequently found negating clauses with the future suffix ||-kʰ:e||. The variant with a final alveolar is used by Dry Creek speakers; the variant with a final dental is used by Cloverdale speakers. Examples of this morpheme are given in (388) and (389) (with the enclitic in bold).

(388) Example of ||=t̪ʰoṭ̓|| ~ ||=t̪ʰot̪̓|| NEGATIVE.PERFECTIVE
*ʔa:ʔa kʰat̪:adukʰ:e**t̪ʰoṭ̓*** (W: OF)
||ʔa:ʔa kʰat̪:-aduč-kʰ:e=t̪ʰoṭ̓||
/ʔa:ʔa kʰat̪:-adu-kʰ:e=t̪ʰoṭ̓/
1SG.AGT run-DIR-FUT=NEG
‘I didn't run away’

(389) Example of ||=t̪ʰoṭ̓|| ~ ||=t̪ʰot̪̓|| NEGATIVE.PERFECTIVE
[ʔ]a:mayá:k̓o mí:ṭikʰ:ét̪ʰot̪̓wáʔa (H ms.)
*ʔa:maya:k̓o mi:ṭikʰ:e**t̪ʰot̪̓**waʔa*
||ʔa:maya=:k̓o mi:ṭi-kʰ:e=t̪ʰot̪̓=ʔwa=ʔa:ʔa||
/ʔa:maya=:k̓o mi:ṭi-kʰ:e=t̪ʰot̪̓=wa=ʔa/
2PL.AGT=COM lie-FUT=NEG=COP.EVID=1SG.AGT
‘I won't lie w[ith] ye’

(390) Example of ||=t̪ʰoṭ̓|| ~ ||=t̪ʰot̪̓|| NEGATIVE.PERFECTIVE
[ʔ]á:čac̓yey( )t̪[ʰ]ot̪̓wa (H ms.)
*ʔa:čac̓yey**t̪ʰot̪̓**wa*
||ʔa:-ča-c̓-yey=t̪ʰot̪̓=ʔwa||
/ʔa:-ča-c̓-yey=t̪ʰot̪̓=wa/
1-mother's.father-GS-PL.AGT=NEG=COP.EVID
‘they are not my mo[ther's] fa[ther]s.’

||t̪ʰe:|| t̪ʰe: NEGATIVE RESPONSE PARTICLE

This morpheme is used as a negative response to a yes/no question, as shown in (391), which is an exchange between Olive Fulwider and Elsie Allen as remembered by Olive Fulwider.

(391) Example of ||t̪ʰe|| negative response particle (W: OF)
Elsie Allen: *pʰal:aʔčaykaʔma*
/pʰal:aʔčay=ka=ʔma/
white.person=INTER=2SG.AGT
‘Are you a white person?’

Olive Fulwider: *t̪ʰe: ʔahčahčaywaʔa*
/t̪ʰe: ʔahčahčay=wa=ʔa/
no Indian=COP.EVID=1SG.AGT
'No, I'm Indian.'

2.8.3.3.6. Person-Marking Suffixes

Thus far, the claim has been made that Southern Pomo lacks person-marking suffixes. This claim must, however, be qualified. There are two potentially enigmatic suffixes: (1) ||-V:na||, which consistently translates into English with a first-person argument; and (2) ||-:mu||, which consistently translates into English with a second-person argument.

These are actually the first two verbal suffixes I learned when I began studying the language with Olive Fulwider, and it is a point of continuing frustration that I do not feel comfortable with their actual meaning after more than a decade. When I first encountered these suffixes, I learned question and response pairs like the following (the possible person-marking suffixes are in bold):

(392) Sample of question and answer exchange with person-marking suffixes
Q: *he:ʔeykaʔma ho:li:**mu***
/he:ʔey=ka=ʔma ho:li-:mu/
where=INTER=2SG.AGT leave-SECOND.PERSON
'Where are you going?'

A: ʔa: ʔahčanhkʰay ho:li:na ~ ʔahčanhkʰay ho:li:na
/ʔa: ʔahča=nhkʰay ho:li-:na/ ~ /ʔahča=nhkʰay ho:li-:na/
1SG.AGT house=ward leave-? house=ward leave-?
'I'm going home.'

When these morphemes were first encountered, I naturally assumed that Southern Pomo, like Spanish, conjugated its verbs according to person and number. It is clear, however, that the language is not concerned about person and number in ways that are familiar to students of Indo-European languages. The question remains, however, whether Southern Pomo allows two person-marking suffixes to exist in one corner of the grammar. In Walker (2013), I left the door open for the possibility that these two affixes grammaticized as (non-obligatory) person markers. In the case of /-:na/, a new analysis is proposed here.

These two suffixes consistently translate with first- or second-person arguments, but they are not concerned with number, and most important, they are not obligatory (first-person and second-person arguments may be overtly present on a verb without these suffixes). Neither of these suffixes is mentioned in Oswalt's publications, though there is passing reference to a "1st person" morpheme (in O D). However, Oswalt's translations of verbs with these suffixes conforms to those given by Halpern and those I learned before accessing Halpern's or Oswalt's work. In fact, both of these morphemes often translate well with a present progressive meaning, though by no means do all of the glosses and translations appear in the progressive.

In the case of /-:na/, I now believe the /:/ segment is compensatory lengthening from the imperfective suffix ||-ad||, and nasal spreading from the /d/ has caused the lateral of the performative evidential ||-l:a|| to change to /n/; the /:/ of the performative has been lost because the cluster /dl:/ is impossible.

||-ad-l:a|| → /-:-na/

Examples are given in (393) through (396) with the IMPERFECTIVE-PERFORMATIVE in bold and glossed as FIRST.PERSON.

(393) Example of ||-ad-l:a|| IPFV-PERFORMATIVE as 'I' without additional pronoun

ṭ^{h}óʔ[:]o p[^{h}]oht̯ópt̯ow šo:čí:na (H VII: 2)

*ṭ^{h}oʔ:o p^{h}oht̯opt̯ow šo:či***:na**

/ṭ^{h}oʔ:o	p^{h}oht̯o-pt̯o-w	šo:či-:na/
acorn.mush	boil ~ ITER-PFV	hear-FIRST.PERSON

'I hear acorn soup boiling'

(394) Example of ||-V:na|| IPFV-PERFORMATIVE as 'I' without additional pronoun

<waʔ*an p^hi*li*na> (O D: EA)

*waʔ:an p^{h}i:li***:na**

/waʔ:an	p^{h}i:li-:na/
now	go-FIRST.PERSON

'I just moved in (to a house).'[172]

(395) Example of ||-V:na|| IPFV-PERFORMATIVE 'I' with pronoun

*ka:wi **ʔa:** čuh:ukat̪i ho:li**:na*** (W: OF)

/ka:wi	ʔa:	čuh:u-ka-t̪i	ho:li-:na/
child	1SG.AGT	eat-CAUS-FUT.INTENT	leave-FIRST.PERSON

'I'm going to feed my baby'

(396) Example of ||-V:na|| IPFV-PERFORMATIVE 'we' with pronoun

<ya waʔ*an p^hi*li*na> (O D: EA)

ya** waʔ:an pʰi:li**:na

/ya	waʔ:an	pʰi:li-:na/
1PL.AGT	now	go-FIRST.PERSON

'We just moved in.'

||-:mu|| -:mu SECOND-PERSON suffix

This suffix translates into English with a second-person argument. Unlike the preceding ||-V:na|| FIRST PERSON, which may be used without an overt pronominal element elsewhere in the clause, this suffix often co-occurs with a second-person pronoun. Examples follow (with ||-:mu|| and the second-person pronoun in bold).

(397) Example of ||-:mu|| SECOND PERSON

[ʔ]á:ma t̪ʰóʔ[:]o p[ʰ]oht̪ópt̪ow šo:čí:mu (H VII: 2)

ʔa:ma** t̪ʰoʔ:o pʰoht̪opt̪ow šo:či**:mu

/ʔa:ma	t̪ʰoʔ:o	pʰoht̪o-pt̪o-w	šo:či-:mu/
2SG.AGT	acorn.mush	boil ~ ITER-PFV	hear-SECOND.PERSON

'you hear acorn soup boiling'

(398) Example of ||-:mu|| SECOND PERSON

*he:ʔeyka**ʔma** ho:li**:mu*** (W: OF)

/he:ʔey=ka=ʔma	ho:li-:mu/
where=INTER=2SG.AGT	leave-SECOND.PERSON

'Where are you going?'

Without evidence to the contrary for /-:mu/, it is hereafter treated as an optional person-marking morpheme that is unconcerned with number,

Table 41. Switch-reference suffixes

	Same subject	**Different subject**
Sequential	||-ba|| *-ba*	||-:li|| *-li* ~ *-ni*
Simultaneous	||-Vn|| *-in* ~ *-an* ~ *-on* ~ *-un* ~ *-n*	||-en|| *-en* ~ *-wen*
Irrealis	||-p^{h}i|| *-p^{h}i*	||-p^{h}la|| *-p^{h}la*

Table 42. Additional switch-reference morphemes from Oswalt (1978)

	Same subject	**Different subject**
Oppositive	||-nat̪i|| *-nat̪i*	||-et̪i|| *-et̪i* ~ *-wet̪i*
Inferential	||-mna|| *-mna*	||-ben|| *-ben*

takes no other inflection, and is especially common in active conversation, and that might carry some sort of continuous aspectual meaning.

2.8.3.3.7. Dependent Clause Suffixes

Southern Pomo has a rich set of dependent clause suffixes. These suffixes serve both to combine clauses and to indicate whether the subject of a dependent verb is the same as or different from that of the main verb of a sentence. The complexities of the switch-reference system are discussed in a later section (§3.10.2). Each of these morphemes is provided in table 41, which is adapted from Oswalt (1978: 11).

In addition to the switch-reference dependent clause markers in table 41, all of which are well-attested in the extant records, Oswalt sets forth four additional morphemes which he analyzes as participating in the switch-reference system, as shown in table 42 following, which is adapted from from Oswalt (1978: 11).

The morphemes in table 42 above are more problematic. I have not been able to find any examples of either of the different subject suffixes ||-et̪i|| and ||-ben||; the same subject oppositive suffix is almost always encountered as the enclitic *=ʔnat̪i* and does not appear to have any actual switch-reference function; the same subject inferential is extremely rare in the records, and though the example of it presented later does fit a same subject inferential meaning, one example hardly constitutes sufficient evidence to accept the morphemes from table 42 above as true switch-reference morphemes. Each of the morphemes from tables 41 and 42 is discussed individually in the subsections that follow.

||-ba|| -ba SAME SUBJECT SEQUENTIAL

This suffix marks a dependent verb as having been completed prior to the action of the main verb on which it is dependent for TAM; it also marks the dependent verb as having the same subject as the main verb. An example is given in (399) (with ||-ba|| in bold).

(399) Example of ||-ba|| SAME SUBJECT SEQUENTIAL
čaːdúba dáʔt̯aw (H ms.)
*čaːdu**ba** daʔt̯aw*
/čaːdu-ba daʔt̯a-w/
look-S.SEQ find-PFV
'he looked and saw'

||-ːli|| -ːli ~ -ːni DIFFERENT SUBJECT SEQUENTIAL

This suffix marks a dependent verb as having been completed prior to the action of the main verb on which it is dependent for TAM; it also marks the dependent verb as having a different subject from the main verb. An example is given in (400) (with ||-ːli|| in bold).

(400) Example of ||-ːli|| DIFFERENT SUBJECT SEQUENTIAL
[ʔ]áːʔa [ʔ]áčːa čáːdukaːli dáʔt̯aw (H ms.)
*ʔaːʔa ʔačːa čaːduka**ːli** daʔt̯aw*
/ʔaːʔa ʔačːa-Ø čaːdu-ka-ːli daʔt̯a-w/
1SG.AGT house-DIFFUSE look-CAUS-D.SEQ find-PFV
'I let him look inside and he found it'

This suffix participates in nasal spreading (see §2.6.3.2 for a discussion of this phenomenon), as shown in (401) (with the surface form of ||-ːli|| in bold; the translation of the dependent verb to which it is affixed is also in bold).

(401) Example of *-:ni* allomorph of ||-:li|| DIFFERENT SUBJECT SEQUENTIAL

kʰaʔbekʰáčʰyey [ʔ]ahkʰalá:nṭi [k̓]aṭ:ak̓ dap̓:ó:ni (H VII: 11)

*kʰaʔbekʰačʰyey ʔahkʰala:nṭi k̓aṭ:ak̓ dap̓:o:**ni***

||kʰaʔbekʰač=yey ʔahkʰa=la:nṭi k̓aṭ:ak̓ dap̓:oN-:li||

/kʰaʔbekʰačʰ=yey	ʔahkʰa=la:nṭi	k̓aṭ:ak̓	dap̓:o-:ni/
raptor.species=AGT	water=LOC	acorn.woodpecker	steal-D.SEQ

ma: waʔ[:]an má:li bíʔdu híʔbay

ma: waʔ:an ma:li biʔdu hiʔbay

||ma: waʔ:an ma:li biʔdu hiʔbač-Ø||

/ma:	waʔ:an	ma:li	biʔdu	hiʔbay-Ø/
DEM	now	here	acorn	grow-PFV

'now, acorns grew in this place, **when** Fish Hawk **stole** the woodpeckers across the water'

||-Vn|| -in ~ -an ~ -on ~ -un ~ -n SAME SUBJECT SIMULTANEOUS

This suffix marks a dependent verb as ongoing during the action of the main verb on which it is dependent for TAM; it also marks the dependent verb as having the same subject as the main verb, as shown in (402) (with the surface form of the suffix in bold; the translation of the dependent verb to which it is affixed is also in bold).

(402) Example of ||-Vn|| SAME SUBJECT SIMULTANEOUS

ká:liŋhkʰay ha:čat̠káčin [ʔ]ám:aŋhkʰay ha:čat̠láwa (H ms.)

*ka:linhkʰay ha:čat̠kač**in** ʔam:anhkʰay ha:čat̠lawa*

/ka:li=nhkʰay	ha:ča-t̠-kač-in	ʔam:a=nhkʰay	ha:ča-t̠-la-wa/
up=ward	fly-PL.ACT-DIR-S.SEQ	earth=ward	fly-PL.ACT-DIR-EVID

'bird keeps **flying** up and [flying] down'

||-en|| -en ~ -wen DIFFERENT SUBJECT SIMULTANEOUS

This suffix marks a dependent verb as ongoing during the action of the main verb on which it is dependent for TAM; it also marks the dependent verb as having a different subject from the main verb, as shown in (403) (with the surface form of the suffix in bold; the translation of the dependent verb to which it is affixed is also in bold).

(403) Example of ||-en|| DIFFERENT SUBJECT SIMULTANEOUS

má:mu kʰaʔbéyey wí:miŋhkʰáyʔden (H VIII: 4)

*ma:mu kʰaʔbeyey wi:minhkʰayʔd***en**

||ma:mu kʰaʔbe=yey wi:mi=li=kʰač-wad-en||

/ma:mu	kʰaʔbe=yey	wi:mi-nhkʰay-ʔd-en/
DEM	rock=AGT	there-ward-HAB-D.SIM[173]

čú:maṭwám:u hoʔ[:]ówi biʔk̓ik̓:iw šiʔmiʔwan

ču:maṭwam:u hoʔ:owi biʔk̓ik̓:iw šiʔmiʔwan

||ču:maṭ=ʔwam:u hoʔ:o=wi biʔk̓i-R-w šiʔmi=ʔwan||

/ču:maṭ=wam:u	hoʔ:o=wi	biʔk̓i-k̓:i-w	šiʔmi=ʔwan/
gray.squirrel=DET.SUBJ	teeth=INSTR	gnaw ~ ITER-PFV	bow=DET.OBJ

'**While** this Rock **was facing towards there**, the Squirrel gnawed it with his teeth, the bow.'

This suffix has an epenthetic initial [w] when it follows vowels,[174] as shown in (404), which is a multi-clause sentence with four dependent verbs, two of which have this suffix, one with the post-consonantal allomorph *-en*, and one with the post-vocalic allomorph *-wen* (both these allomorphs are in bold; the translations of the dependent verbs to which the different subject simultaneous suffixes are affixed are also in bold).

(404) The *-wen* allomorph of ||-en|| DIFFERENT SUBJECT SIMULTANEOUS

ʔaṭ:i=ṭon mi:mačen, či:yowen, (O I: 9)

*ʔaṭ:iṭon mi:mač***en***, či:yo***wen***,*

||ʔaṭ:i=ṭon mi:mač-en či:yo-en||

/ʔaṭ:i=ṭon	mi:mač-en	či:yo-wen/
3C.SG=LOC	cry-D.SIM	sit-D.SIM

daʔṭ̓aba, čoh:omba, šudʔeduy.

daʔṭ̓aba, čoh:omba, šudʔeduy.

||daʔṭ̓a-ba čoh:oN-ba šu-ʔde-aduč-Ø||

/daʔṭ̓a-ba	čoh:om-ba	šu-dʔe-duy-Ø/
find-S.SEQ	marry-S.SEQ	by.pulling-move-DIR-PFV

'Having found her **sitting**, **crying** for him, he married her and led her away.'

||-p^{h}i|| -p^{h}i SAME SUBJECT IRREALIS

This suffix marks a dependent verb as irrealis, often as being expected to be completed prior to the action of the irrealis main verb; it also marks the dependent verb as having the same subject as the main verb. The translations of bi-clausal sentences with the suffix marking the dependent verb may be translated into English as 'if ... then', though this is not an exact translation (as sentences like 'if you go, you will wash it' and 'you go and wash it' are different in English, but 'go' would be marked the same in both sentences in Southern Pomo, with ||-p^{h}i||).

This suffix is used when the main verb is inflected with the future ||-k^h:e|| (though not with the future intentive ||-t̪i||), the singular imperative ||-Vn||, the plural imperative ||-le||, and the conditional ||-V:ba||, and the prohibitive ||-t̪^{h}u||. I have no data for its participation with the hortative ||-V-||. An example follows (with the surface form of the suffix in bold; the translation of the dependent verb to which it is affixed is also in bold).

(405) Example of ||-p^{h}i|| SAME SUBJECT IRREALIS
k^{h}aʔ[:]á:le[ʔ]waʔ( )máya kú:lun hó:lip[^{h}]i (H II: 1)
*k^{h}aʔ:a:leʔwaʔmaya ku:lun ho:li**p^{h}i***
||k^{h}aʔ:a:le=ʔwa=ʔa:maya ku:lu-n ho:li-p^{h}i||
/k^{h}aʔ:a:le=ʔwa=ʔmaya ku:lu-n ho:li-p^{h}i/
tomorrow=COP.EVID=2PL.AGT outside-GOAL leave-S.IRR

baʔ[:]á:yey híʔbu [ʔ]ehč^{h}ék^h[:]e
baʔ:a:yey hiʔbu ʔehč^{h}ek^h:e
||baʔ:ay=yey hiʔbu ʔehč^{h}e-k^h:e||
/baʔ:a:=yey hiʔbu ʔehč^{h}e-k^h:e
woman=AGT potato dig-FUT
'Tomorrow, you women will **go** to the outside and dig wild potatoes'

||-p^{h}la|| -p^{h}la DIFFERENT SUBJECT IRREALIS

This suffix marks a dependent verb as irrealis, often as being expected to be completed prior to the action of the irrealis main verb; it also marks the dependent verb as having a different subject from the main verb. As with

||-p^{h}i||, translations of bi-clausal sentences with this suffix marking the dependent verb may be translated into English as 'if . . . then'. This suffix is used when the main verb is inflected with the future ||-k^{h}:e|| (though not with the future intentive ||-t̯i||), the singular imperative ||-Vn||, the plural imperative ||-le||, and the conditional ||-V:ba||, and the prohibitive ||-t̯^{h}u||. I have no data for its participation with the hortative ||-V-||. Examples are given in (406) and (407) (with the surface form of the suffix in bold; the translations of the dependent verbs to which it is affixed are also in bold).

(406) Example of ||-p^{h}la|| DIFFERENT SUBJECT IRREALIS

[ʔ]a: ho:líp[^{h}]la [ʔ]aw[:]ít̯on mi:má:t̯[^{h}]u (H ms.)

*ʔa: ho:li**p^{h}la** ʔaw:it̯on mi:ma:t̯^{h}u*

/ʔa:	ho:li-p^{h}la	ʔaw:i=t̯on	mi:ma:-t̯^{h}u/
1SG.AGT	leave-D.IRR	1SG.OBL=LOC	cry-PROH

'**when** I'**m gone** don't cry for me[!]'

(407) Example of ||-p^{h}la|| DIFFERENT SUBJECT IRREALIS

mič:áċyey mehšek^{h}[:]éʔwa (H V: 26)

mič:aċyey mehšek^{h}:eʔwa

/mi-č:a-ċ-yey	me-hše-k^{h}:e=ʔwa/
2-mother's.father-GS-PL.AGT	with.nose-smell-FUT=COP.EVID

[ʔ]á:maya híʔṫ̯a das:ép[^{h}]la.

*ʔa:maya hiʔṫ̯a das:e**p^{h}la***

/ʔa:maya	hiʔṫ̯a	da-s:e-p^{h}la/
2PL.AGT	nearby	with.palm-wash-D.IRR

'Your grandfathers will smell (it) if you wash them nearby.'

||=nat̯i|| =ʔnat̯i ~ =nat̯i ~ nat̯i 'but' (SAME SUBJECT OPPOSITIVE?)

As stated earlier, this morpheme is analyzed by Oswalt as a same subject oppositive switch-reference marker. I have no evidence that would suggest that this morpheme is either a suffix or a switch-reference marker. It is most commonly encountered as an enclitic and may attach to more than one word class. It is generally translated as 'but' or 'however', and this oppositive meaning is all that can be isolated for this morpheme. However, even this meaning is not always clear, and it is sometimes translated as 'any' or 'whatsoever'. An example of this morpheme as an enclitic attached to a demonstrative is given in (408) (with the oppositive morpheme and its translation in bold).

(408) Example of ||=ʔnaṯi|| oppositive
hí:ʔinnaṯi dan:áṯ[h]u (H ms.)
*hi:ʔin:**aṯi** dan:aṯʰu*
/hi:ʔin=naṯi dan:a-ṯʰu/
dem=but cover-proh
'don't cover **any** of them[!]'

||-eṯi|| -eṯi ~ -weṯi 'but' (DIFFERENT SUBJECT OPPOSITIVE)

Oswalt (1978) lists this as the different subject equivalent of ||=ʔnaṯi||. I have no evidence of this morpheme, and it is therefore impossible to offer a critique of Oswalt's analysis. Oswalt transcribes this morpheme with a special symbol indicating that a [w] precedes it when it follows a vowel-final morpheme. I have chose to omit the [w] from the underlying form because this same alternation is seen elsewhere in the factual evidential suffix ||-a|| and the different subject simultaneous suffix ||-en||, both of which appear to have developed the epenthetic post-vocalic [w] from an earlier perfective *-w, and this seems like the most probable origin for the [w] of this oppositive morpheme. Of course, without examples of this oppositive, it is not possible to be sure of the actual distribution of [w].

||-mna|| -mna SAME SUBJECT INFERENTIAL

This suffix is supposed to mark a dependent verb as having the same subject as the main verb on which it is dependent. The action of the dependent verb is also indicated as having been inferred. I have found one example of this suffix, and it is only optional (according to Halpern's notes) and may be replaced with ||-ba|| SAME SUBJECT SEQUENTIAL, at least in the sole example, which follows (with ||-mna|| and the translation of the verb to which it is suffixed in bold).

(409) Example of ||-mna|| same subject inferential

hidʔáwi či:yóba ~ čahčímna hiʔda čan:áwa (H ms.)

*hidʔawi či:yoba hiʔda čan:awa ~ hidʔawi čahči**mna** hiʔda čan:awa*

/hidʔa= wi	či:yo-ba hiʔda	čan:a-wa/	~	/hidʔawi	čahči-mna	hiʔda	čan:a-wa/
road= instr	sit-s.seq road	block-evid	~	road=instr	sit-s. infer	road	block-evid

'1 **sat** in road and blocked road'

||-ben|| -ben DIFFERENT SUBJECT INFERENTIAL

According to Oswalt (1978), this is the different subject of the above inferential switch-reference suffix. I have found no evidence of this morpheme, and it is therefore not possible to confirm or deny Oswalt's analysis at this time.

2.8.3.3.8. Unidentified Suffixes

In addition to the verbal suffixes already discussed, there are a few suffixes which have not yet been identified. Each is discussed individually.

-ʔč̓edu- ~ -ʔč̓ed- ~ -ʔč̓en ???

This suffix (these suffixes?) may attach to the verb 'to know' and, perhaps, other verbs; an example is given in (410) (with the mystery suffix in bold).

(410) Example of possible suffix *-ʔč̓edu-*

čáhnu čanhódu híʔduʔč̓eduʔwám:u (H ms.)

*čahnu čanhodu hiʔdu**ʔč̓edu**ʔwam:u*

/čahnu	čanho-du	hiʔdu-ʔč̓edu=ʔwa=m:u
speech	speack-IPFV	know-?=COP.EVID=3SG

'he knows how to talk'

-(a)ṭway ???

This suffix probably derives a verb with plural agents from one unmarked for the number of agents, but the record is not clear. Halpern records instances of this ending with both the verb stem ||hu:w-|| 'go' and ||biʔde-|| 'handle'; he records this sequence on one or both of these stems during both his first fieldwork in the 1930s and later in the 1980s. An example of this mystery morpheme is given in (411) (in bold).

(411) Example of *-(a)ṭway*

hwaṭway (H EA)

*hw**aṭway***

||hu:w-aṭwač-Ø||

/hw-aṭway-Ø/

go-PL?-PFV

'Sev[eral] walking'

-yi:- ???

This suffix might be a lexically conditioned allomorph of the reflexive ||-č̓-||; perhaps it is ||-yič̓-||. There is not enough data to make a determination at this time. An example is given in (412) (with *-yi:-* in bold).

(412) Example of unidentified morpheme *-yi-*

sí:ma ba:ṭiyí:le (H ms.)

*si:ma ba:ṭi**yi:**le*

/si:ma ba:ṭi-yi:-le/

sleep sev.lie-?-PL.IMP

'2 go to sleep!'

2.8.4. Modifiers

This section covers the following small word classes: descriptive adjectives, non-numeral quantifiers, and numerals.

2.8.4.1. Descriptive Adjectives

Only a small number of words can be confidently assigned to the adjective word class. These words include the words for size, age, temperature, and color terms. Descriptive adjectives differ from verbs in their being monomorphemic. They need no additional morphology and take no inflectional suffixes. At least some adjectives may be reduplicated to indicate greater intensity (e.g., *bahṭʰepṭʰe* ||bahṭʰe-R|| 'huge' from *bahṭʰe* 'big.COLL'); however, this does not appear to be a productive synchronic process. Descrip-

Table 43. Collective vs. distributive adjectives for size

	'big'	'small'
Collective	*bahṭʰe*	*kic:idu*
Distributive	*ʔahṭʰiy*	*piʔni*

tive adjectives differ from nouns in their inability to take case-marking suffixes, and they may only take case-marking enclitics when they are modifying a noun as part of a noun phrase. They also differ from all nouns in that some of the adjectives for size are inherently collective or distributive (singular versus plural in Oswalt's notes). Table 43 lists the size words which show this distinction.

Within NPs, a descriptive adjective generally follows the noun that it modifies, as in (413).

(413) Example of descriptive adjective following the noun it modifies

nóp[ʰ]:o nop[ʰ]:óyaw nóp[ʰ]:o báhṭʰe (H VI: 1)

nopʰ:o nopʰ:oyaw, [nopʰ:o bahṭʰe]$_{NP}$

/nopʰ:o	nopʰ:o-ya-w	nopʰ:o	bahṭʰe/
village	sev.dwell-DEFOC-PFV	village	big.COLL

'They lived in a Rancheria, a big Rancheria.'

Table 44 lists some of the commonest adjectives; however, it is not an exhaustive list.

2.8.4.2. Non-Numeral Quantifiers

Thomas Payne states that non-numeral quantifiers include such concepts as "*much, many, few, some, a lot of, a great deal of, tons of*" (1997: 65). Only two words clearly fit within this category, and it is perhaps not useful to set up an entire subclass for two lexical items. The word *ṭʰeč̓:aw ~ t̪ʰeč̓:aw ~ t̪ʰač̓:aw ~čeč̓:aw ~ ṭʰeč̓aw ~ t̪ʰeč̓aw ~ t̪ʰač̓aw ~ čeč̓aw* 'many, much, a lot' is the most frequently encountered non-numeral quantifier. The various pronunciations are used by different speakers or reflect the rate of speech of an individual speaker. This word takes no morphology. In general, Halpern (working only with Cloverdale speakers) transcribes this word with an initial dental,

Table 44. Common adjectives

Category	Southern Pomo	Gloss
Size and age	*bahṭʰe*	'big.COLLECTIVE'
	ʔahṭʰiy	'big.DISTRIBUTIVE'
	kic:idu	'small.COLLECTIVE'
	piʔni	'small.DISTRIBUTIVE'
	ʔahkon	'long'
	še:wey	'new; young'
	bahṭʰepṭʰe	'huge'
Temperature	*kac:i*	'cold'
	ʔoh:o	'hot' (also the noun for 'fire')
Quality	*k̓oʔdi*	'good'
	kʰaṭ:ic̓̌aw[175]	'bad; hateful'
Color	*kahle*	'white'
	šaʔk̓a	'black'
	haṭ̓:a	'red'
	c̓ahkil	'blue'[176]
	čaʔča	'green'
	wa:yu	'yellow'[177]

an /e/ in the initial syllable and no length on the second consonant; Oswalt transcribes it with an initial alveolar, an /a/ in the initial syllable and, generally, no length on the second consonant; Tony Pete, in my hearing of his speech, generally (though not always) uses a palato-alveolar affricate as the initial. The initial vowel is generally a schwa in rapid speech, and this explains the disagreement over which non-high, unrounded vowel to use for this vowel in Halpern's and Oswalt's transcriptions.

Unlike the descriptive adjectives, this non-numeral quantifier precedes nouns which it modifies. An example is given in (414).

(414) Example of *ṭʰac̓̌aw* 'much' (O I: 17b)

ham:u( )ʔnaṭ̯i( )ʔma maʔben ṭʰac̓̌aw ma hodʔodenkʰe.

ham:uʔnaṭ̯iʔma maʔben ṭʰac̓̌aw ma hodʔodenkʰe

/ham:u=ʔnaṭ̯i=ʔma	maʔben	ṭʰac̓̌aw	ma	hodʔo-den-kʰe/
3SG=but=2SG.AGT	there?	much	thing	get-DIR-FUT

'But because of this you will get lots of [bad] things.'

The other non-numeral quantifier is *beṭ̓bu* 'some', which is used for an indeterminate quantity that is not part of a larger whole. There is a nominal enclitic *=ṭonhk^{h}le* 'some', which is used in a partitive sense (e.g., 'some of . . .'). An example of *beṭ̓bu* 'some' is given in (415).

(415) Example of non-numeral quantifier *beṭ̓bu* 'some'

beṭ̓bu ʔal:a:ša beṭ̓bu sema:nu (O I: 6)

beṭ̓bu ʔal:a:ša beṭ̓bu sema:nu

/beṭ̓bu	ʔal:a:ša	beṭ̓bu	sema:nu/
some	moon	some	week

'some months [and] some weeks'

2.8.4.3. *Numerals*

The numerals show some unique morphological characteristics. They may be suffixed with ||-hma|| 'place' (e.g., *mis:ibohma* 'three places'); this morpheme has not yet been identified with any full noun; it may also apply to adverbs (e.g., *na:piyo-hma ka:ne-w* all-place bite-PFV 'bite all over'). Numerals may also be made into adverbs with the adverbializing suffix ||-y:i-|| (e.g., *č̓ay:i* 'once'), and this suffix may take an additional suffix ||-kan|| to form the adverb *č̓ay:ikan* 'sometimes; once in a while'. A numeral may precede a noun it modifies, as in (416) (each of the three NPs is marked off with brackets; the numeral is in bold).

(416) Numeral preceding modified noun (H V: 1)

núp[^{h}]:e nóp[^{h}]:ow ka:wíya bahṭ^{h}ék̓o, lá:ṭ^{h}k^{h}o ka:wíya.

*[nup^{h}:e]$_{NP}$ nop^{h}:ow [ka:wiya bahṭ^{h}e]$_{NP}$k̓o, [**la:ṭ^{h}k^{h}o** ka:wiya]$_{NP}$*

/nup^{h}:e	nop^{h}:o-w	ka:wi-ya	bahṭ^{h}e=k̓o	la:ṭ^{h}k^{h}o	ka:wi-ya/
striped.skunk	sev.dwell-PFV	child-PL	big.COLL=COM	seven	child-PL

'Skunk Woman lived, with many children, seven children.'

The Southern Pomo numeral system shows traces of an earlier base four (e.g., *k^{h}omhča* 'eight' comes from ʔak^{h}:o 'two' + *mihča* 'four'), but there is no synchronic evidence that the system is built around four. In the past, before European and American expansion into Pomo lands, Southern Pomo people must have counted to very high numbers as part of their production and trade in shell money. Though this might have been the case, there is no record of higher numbers. All known numbers, as recorded by Halpern from Annie Burke, are given in the following list (I have provided a regularized transcription for 1–8; the numbers above eight are unfamiliar to me, and Halpern's transcription is therefore allowed to stand alone).

Southern Pomo numerals 1–20, 25, 30, 40, 100

(1) čá:ʔa	*č̓a:ʔa*	(11) ná:nč̓a
(2) [ʔ]ák^{h}:o	*ʔak^{h}:o*	(12) ná:nk^{h}o
(3) mis:íbo	*mis:ibo*	(13) ná:n síbo
(4) míhčá	*mihča*	(14) sím hmá šon
(5) ṭú:šo	*ṭu:šo*	(15) símhma [or] símhma ṭék̓
(6) lá:Ṇč̓a	*la:nhč̓a*	(16) símhma ná:nč̓a
(7) lá:ṭ^{h}k^{h}o	*la:ṭ^{h}k^{h}o*	(17) símhma ná:nk^{h}o
(8) k^{h}óMča	*k^{h}omhča*	(18) símhma ná:n síbo
(9) č̓áʔč^{h}o		(19) čámhmá šon
(10) č̓ášóṭ̓o		(20) čámhma [or] čámhma ṭek̓

(25) ṭu:šóhma [or] čámhma wína ṭú:šo

(30) la:Ṇč̓áhma

(40) č̓á: hay

(100) č̓a: sént̯u

Several of the numbers in this list are clearly compositional. The number *č̓áʔč̌^{h}o* 'nine' probably comes from *č̓a:ʔa* 'one' + *ʔač^{h}:o-* 'there is none' (literally 'one is absent'). The numbers above nine and below nineteen are a mystery. Ten has 'one' as its first syllable, but the following element is unknown. Similarly, the numbers for eleven through thirteen clearly have 'one', 'two', and 'three' added to the element *na:n*, but what this element might mean (or have meant in the past) is not clear. Fourteen through eighteen begin with the element *sim-*, and it is possible that this is an ancient variant of *mis:ibo* 'three'. If this analysis is correct, then *simhma*, one of the variants for 'fifteen', might literally mean 'three places' (*-hma* is the suffix for 'place' which may be attached to numerals), which might indicate that something was set down (in piles perhaps) in several places by fives during counting.

I believe this analysis is correct for 'fifteen', and it lines up well with a possible analysis for the numbers for 'twenty', 'twenty-five', and 'thirty', which might be 'four places', 'five places', and 'six places' respectively. These numbers seem to show evidence of counting by fives. However, note that the form for 'forty' is literally 'one stick'. Though I have no oral or written evidence, I believe the stick was literally—at some point, anyway—laid on the ground as part of counting, perhaps in trade, and that this is the origin of the term for 'forty'. If smaller items (shells, stones, etc.) were laid out for numbers below forty (perhaps by fives), the reservation of the stick for the unit 'forty' suggests that remnants of a base four system were part of the numeral system in the higher numbers. The number *č̓a: senṯu* 'hundred' is a combination of *č̓a:(ʔa)* 'one' and an obvious borrowing of Spanish *ciento* 'hundred'.

2.8.5. Adverbs

Adverbs in Southern Pomo are a small word class. Like the descriptive adjectives, they are not morphologically complex, and are not inflected. They are free words (i.e., both grammatical and phonological words), and can be divided according to semantic criteria into two broad groups: (1) locative adverbs, which include words for 'here', 'there', and 'yonder'; and (2) all other adverbs, which include temporal adverbs, manner adverbs (most of which relate how quickly or when the action takes place), and other adverbs, such concepts as 'only', 'just', and 'wholly. These types of adverb are discussed in the following sections.

2.8.5.1. Locative Adverbs

The locative adverbs include words for 'here', 'there', and 'yonder', which are poorly understood at this time. Table 45 gives the three locative adverbs for which there is good evidence.

The system of locative adverbs is not as simple as the table suggests. There is a patient case version of *ham:i* ~ *ha:mi* 'there', which is variously recorded as *ha:min* and *ham:il*. There are other words which appear to be part of the system, including the word *we:y* 'far off'; the base *wi:min-*, which is only recorded as a derived verb meaning 'this way'; the base *be-* ~ *ben-*, which also translates as 'here'; and the especially enigmatic form *maʔben*

Table 45. Three-way division of locative adverbs[178]

'here'	'there'	'yonder'
ma:li	*ham:i ~ ha:mi*	*wi:li*

(glossed as 'on this' by Oswalt), which seems to be a combination of the demonstrative *ma:* 'this' with *be- ~ ben-*.

Both *wi:min-* 'here'(?) and *ha:min-* 'there' may be made into verbs with the suffix *-(h)kʰe-*, as in *ha:min-hkʰe-w* there-verbalizer-PFV 'moved that way'. These two bases, *wi:min-* 'here'(?) and *ha:min-* 'there', together with *be- ~ ben-*, may have locative enclitics attached to them (e.g., *=nhkʰay* '-ward', *=sa:ma* 'near'); however, there is no evidence that *ma:li* 'here' and *wi:li* 'yonder' may take the same additional morphology. The examples are too few and the overall picture too incomplete to hazard an analysis of the locative adverbs beyond that given in table 45.

Locative adverbs are generally clause-initial, as in (417), which shows two of the three locative adverbs of table 45 in a single utterance (I have provided a more literal translation following Halpern's free translation).

(417) Example of locative adverb preceding clause

wí:li hwákʰčin hám:i hwa:káʔya (H ms.)

wi:li hwakʰčin ham:i hwa:kaʔya

/wi:li	hw-akʰč-in	ham:i	hw-a:-ka=ʔya/
yonder	go-DIR-SG.IMP	there	go-DIR-CAUS=1PL.AGT

'walk to one side, we'll let him go through here'

['Go up yonder! We shall allow (him) to pass through there.']

2.8.5.2. Other Adverbs

The remaining adverbs are generally morphologically simple. With rare exception, they do not take any inflectional or derivational morphology. These adverbs include words such as *ʔit̪ʰ:in* 'early', *kʰaʔ:aške̓aden* 'morning' (which is also a noun), and *duw:e* 'night' (also a noun; its derived verb is *duw:ey* 'night falls'). Of these, only *ʔit̪ʰ:in* 'early' is only an adverb; it is also unique in that takes unidentified suffixes in the form *ʔit̪ʰ:inmawi* 'once upon a time' (sometimes pronounced *ʔit̪ʰ:enmawi*). This latter form, much like the English ‘once upon a time’, only appears at the beginning of tales. The adverb *ʔit̪ʰ:in* ‘early’ may combine with *kʰaʔ:ašk̓aden* ‘morning’ to mean ‘early in the morning’ with no overt morphology connecting the two, as seen in (418), where they come clause-finally.

(418) The temporal adverbs *ʔit̪ʰ:in* ‘early’ and *kʰaʔ:ašk̓aden* ‘morning’ (H I:1)

miy[:]a[ṭʰ]kʰan bíʔdu čóhšin, kʰaʔ[:]ášk̓aden [ʔ]ít̪[ʰ]:in

miy:aṭʰkʰan biʔdu čohšin, kʰaʔ:ašk̓aden ʔit̪ʰ:in

/miy:a-ṭʰkʰan-Ø	biʔdu	čohšin-Ø	kʰaʔ:ašk̓aden	ʔit̪ʰ:in/
3-spouse-AGT	acorn	pound-PFV	morning	early

‘his wife was pounding acorns, early in the morning’

Additional adverbs include *ʔe:wen* ‘fast, quickly’, *mat̪:i* ‘long time’, *si:ṭ̓o* ‘immediately’, *waʔ:an* ‘now’, *ha:meṭ̓* ‘thus’ (which also appears as *ha:meṭ̓na*), and *pʰa:la* ‘too also, again’[179]. There are also numerals (and other words?) which can be converted into adverbs by *=mčin* ‘days’ worth’ (e.g., *ʔakʰ:omčin* ‘for two days’), which is an adverbializing enclitic related to the noun *ma:či* ‘day’. These adverbs are most frequently placed before the verb in a clause, as in (419), which has both ‘now’ and ‘immediately’ in the same clause.

(419) Example of manner adverb preceding verb

ṭʰoʔ:o hi:mayaw waʔ:a si:ṭ̓o čanhodenhkʰe (H ms.)

/ṭʰoʔ:o	hi:ma-y-aw	waʔ:a	si:ṭ̓o	čanhodenhkʰe/
acorn.mush	leach-DEFOC-PFV	now	immediately	speak-DIR-FUT

‘Now I’m going to talk about leaching acorns.’

Other adverbs which are frequently encountered include *kuṭ:u* ‘just’, *ya:la* ‘only’, and *kuʔmu* ‘all, wholly’. The word *na:pʰiyo-* ‘all’ is also quite common; however, its status as an adverb is not as clear. This word is derived from *na:pʰi* ‘all’, which is a pronoun that is morphologically a common noun. In (420) *na:pʰiyo-* ‘all’ is suffixed with *-hma* ‘place’ (a suffix already encountered in the numerals) and behaves like an adverb.

(420) Example of *na:pʰiyo-* as an adverb

ná:p[ʰ]iyohma ká:new (H ms.)

na:pʰiyohma ka:new

/na:pʰiyo-hma ka-:ne-w/
all-place with.jaws-grasp-PFV
'bite all over'

At least one word may function as both an adjective and an adverb: *ʔahsič* 'hard, strong, difficult'. As an adverb modifying a verb of motion, it means 'hard; with great effort' (as in colloquial English 'he ran real hard'). This peculiar word, which is alone in the Southern Pomo lexicon as a disyllabic word with a word-final palato-alveolar affricate that does not surface as /y/, may also be used as a verb imperative construction (e.g., 'be strong!').

2.8.6. The Auxiliary ||yo|| ~ ||=ʔyo||

Only one morpheme is analyzed as an auxiliary in the language: ||yo|| ~ ||=ʔyo|| 'be'. This morpheme appears to be cognate with the Central Pomo word *yo-* 'go' (Mithun 1993: 124). If it does descend from an earlier verb of motion, it has not preserved any semantic traces. This auxiliary most frequently occurs as a second-position clitic, as seen in (421), where it follows the question word 'when' (the auxiliary is in bold).

(421) Example of ||yo|| ~ ||=ʔyo|| AUX as a second-position clitic
búṭ:eʔyómt̪o [ʔ]ahčáči[y] (H ms.)
*buṭ:e**ʔyo**mt̪o ʔahčačiy*
/buṭ:e=ʔyo=mt̪o ʔahčačiy-Ø/
when=AUX=2SG.PAT awake-PFV
'when did you wake up'

When it follows the pro-verb *ha:mini-* it may be suffixed with the quotative evidential, which sets off the entire following sentence as hearsay, as seen in (422) (the auxiliary is in bold).

(422) Example of ||yo|| ~ ||=ʔyo|| AUX suffixed with ||-do|| QUOTATIVE EVIDENTIAL
ha:miní:li yódo miy[:]a[ṭʰ]kʰan bíʔdu čóhšin (H I: 1)
*ha:mini:li **yo**do miy:aṭʰkʰan biʔdu čohšin*
/ha:mini-:li yo-do miy:a-ṭʰkʰan-Ø biʔdu čohšin-Ø/
and.then-D.SEQ AUX-QUOT 3-spouse-AGT acorn pound-PFV
'Then, it is said, his wife was pounding acorns[.]'

The auxiliary ||yo|| ~ ||=ʔyo|| may also be suffixed with irrealis affixes, such as the future ||-kʰ:e||. It may be used in such a combination to form a predicate adjective, as shown in (423).

(423) Example of ||yo|| ~ ||=ʔyo|| AUX forming a predicate adjective
kac:i yokʰ:e (W: OF)
/kac:i yo-kʰ:e/
cold AUX-FUT
'it will be cold'

2.8.7. Particles or Other Minor Word Classes

In addition to the foregoing word classes, there are several small words, most of which are function words and may be clitics (at least optionally). These include the question words *cet̪̓* 'how', *but̪:e* 'when', *met̪̓bu* 'how many', *he:ʔey* 'where', and *he:met̪̓* 'why', which function as pronouns when not combined with the interrogative morpheme ||ka|| ~ ||=ʔka||. The word *ʔiy:o-* 'under', which is not an enclitic like most morphemes in the language which represent location, fits in this catch-all class of function words. Additional words (which are often clitics) that should be included in this section are ||ṭa|| ~ ||=ṭa|| EMPHATIC and ||ṭ̓o|| ~ ||=ṭ̓o|| CONTRASTIVE.

2.9. THE NOUN PHRASE

Noun phrases in Southern Pomo are composed of a noun (whether a monomorphemic noun or one derived from another word class) and its modifiers, which are generally demonstratives, descriptive adjectives, another noun (as a possessive), or numerals. Within the noun phrase, demonstratives, when present, precede the noun, and adjectives, when present, generally follow the noun; numerals may come before or after the noun. When a noun phrase is a nominalized clause, the elements within the nominalized clause show the same word order as regular clauses (SOV). Following are some of the most frequently encountered orderings within NPs in Southern Pomo. This list is not meant to be exhaustive, nor should the statements made be construed as absolutes.

1. $[\text{N}]_{\text{NP}}$
   A noun phrase may consist of a single noun with no modifiers or enclitics.
2. $[\text{N-POSS N}]_{\text{NP}}$
   A noun with the possessive suffix (behaving as an adjective) precedes the possessed noun with the NP.
3. $[\text{DEM N}]_{\text{NP}}$
   Demonstratives precede the nouns they modify within the NP.
4. $[\text{N Adj}]_{\text{NP}} \sim [\text{Adj N}]_{\text{NP}}$
   Adjectives often follow the nouns they modify within the NP, but they may also precede them; no difference in meaning on the basis of this ordering difference has been detected.
5. $[\text{N Num}]_{\text{NP}}$
   Numerals generally follow the nouns they modify within the NP.
6. $[\text{DEM N Adj}]_{\text{NP}}$
   When both a demonstrative and an adjective are modifiying the noun, the demonstrative precedes and adjective follows within the NP.
7. $[\text{N Adj Adj V}]\text{=nominalizing.enclitic(s)}_{\text{NP}}$
   NPs which are composed of a nominalized clause and its arguments show the same ordering as a standard clause: core arguments, if any are present, precede the verb; descriptive adjectives (and other modifiers) remain in their usual positions relative to the nouns they modify; the entire clause is nominalized by a nominal enclitic.

Whereas individual nouns in Southern Pomo have very little morphological complexity, NPs in the language may be marked with a large number of enclitics. These enclitics include case-marking morphemes, determiners (which are conflated with case), a collectivizing suffix, and various oblique markers (mainly locatives). Each of these enclitics is briefly introduced below.

2.9.1. Case-Marking NP Enclitics

The agent/patient case system may be marked on animate NPs. In addition to the core agentive and patient cases, NPs may be marked for the vocative case, and a variety of oblique cases, including the ablative, the instrumental, the comitative, and the locative (there are several locative enclitics, but only one which is treated herein as case-marking enclitic). Each subgroup of case-marking NP enclitics is discussed in the following sections.

2.9.1.1. *Agent/Patient Case-Marking Enclitics*

Animate nominals in Southern Pomo may be marked with case-marking morphemes in an agent/patient system. In transitive clauses, the least affected animate argument may take the agentive case, and the most affected argument may take the patient case; in intransitive clauses, the single argument may be in either case (agentive case if not greatly affected by the event; patient case if greatly affected by the event). Unlike the complex system of case-marking suffixes observed in the kinship terms and pronouns, there is only a single agentive case enclitic and a single patient case enclitic used on NPs.

||=yey|| =yey AGENTIVE CASE

This enclitic may be attached to NPs which have an animate noun as their head on the basis of the semantic criteria laid out in the previous paragraph. The agentive case-marking enclitic for NPs is homophonous with the plural agentive case-marking suffix of the kinship terms; however, unlike in the kinship terms, where ||-yey|| is a portmanteau suffix combing the historic *-ya PLURAL and the agentive case, the agentive case marker on NPs is an enclitic with no inherent number. An example of this enclitic is given in (424); note that the non-agentive argument of the transitive verb ‘marry’ does not have any case-marking morphology (the agentive case is in bold, and the NP to which it is attached is set off by brackets).

(424) Example of agentive case-marking enclitic ||=yey||

kʰáʔbekʰáčʰyey dó:lon čóh:on (H VI: 1)

*[kʰaʔbekʰač̓]**yey** do:lon čoh:on*

/kʰaʔbekʰač̓=yey	do:lon	čoh:on-Ø/
raptor.species=AGT	bobcat	marry-PFV

‘Fish Hawk married Wildcat’

As already stated, the agentive case may be used on the single argument of an intransitive verb if that argument is not greatly affected by the event, as seen in (425) (with the agentive case in bold and the NP to which it is attached set off by brackets).

(425) Example of ||=yey|| on the single argument of an intransitive verb (H VIII: 2)

k^{h}aʔbéyey hó:liw

*[k^{h}aʔbe]**yey** ho:liw*

/k^{h}aʔbe=yey ho:li-w/

rock=AGT leave-PFV

'Rock [Man] went off.'

||=yčon|| =yčon ~ =čon ~ =:čon PATIENT CASE

This case-marking enclitic may be applied to the single animate argument of an intransitive clause if that argument is greatly affected by the action; it may be applied to the most affected animate argument in a transitive clause. Examples are given in (426) and (427) (with the patient case enclitic in bold and the NP to which it is attached set off with brackets).

(426) Patient case enclitic ||=yčon|| on single argument of intranstitive verb (H VIII)

ha:mini(:)ba k^{h}aʔbéyčon sí:ma mí:ṭiw

*ha:miniba [k^{h}aʔbe]**yčon** si:ma mi:ṭiw*

/ha:mini-ba k^{h}aʔbe=yčon si:ma mi:ṭi-w/

and.then-S.SEQ rock=PAT sleep lie-PFV

'Having done so, Rock [Man] went to sleep.'

(427) ||=yčon|| on most affected argument of transtitive verb (H VI: 3)

ha:mini:li k^{h}áʔbek^{h}áč:on ċa:yíyey [ʔ]uht̯éht̯ew,

*ha:mini:li [k^{h}aʔbek^{h}ač]**čon** ċa:yiyey ʔuht̯eht̯ew*

/ha:mini-:li k^{h}aʔbek^{h}ač=čon ċa:yi=yey ʔuht̯e-ht̯e-w/

and.then-D.SEQ raptor.species=PAT scrubjay=AGT tell ~ tell-PFV

'They having done so, the Jay told Fish Hawk'

2.9.1.2. *Oblique Case-Marking Enclitics*

The remaining case-marking enclitics do not attach to NPs which are core arguments. Oblique case-marking enclitics include the vocative, the possessive, the comitative, the instrumental, the ablative, and the locative. Following is discussion of each.

||=yčo|| =yčo ~ =:čo: ~ =yčow(?) VOCATIVE

The vocative is used for direct address. The allomorphs listed might be the result of transcription errors or idiolectal variation. An example of the vocative enclitic is given in (428) (with the vocative morpheme in bold and the NP to which it is attached set off with brackets).

(428) Example of the vocative enclitic ||=yčo|| (H VI: 15)
[ʔ]ám:ačahṯimúyčo
*[ʔam:a čahṯimu]**yčo***
/ʔam:a čahṯi-mu[180]=yčo/
earth exist-second.person?=VOC
'[**O**] Earth lying extended[!]'

||=čo:kʰe|| =čo:kʰe BENEFACTIVE ~ POSSESSIVE

The possessive enclitic is used for alienable possession and as a benefactive (see §2.9.1). An example of this morpheme is given in (429) (with the possessive enclitic in bold and the NP to which it is attached set off by brackets).

(429) Example of possessive enclitic ||=čo:kʰe||
čú:maṭ̓čó:kʰe šiʔmíʔwan (H VIII: 4)
*[ču:maṭ̓]**čo:kʰe** šiʔmiʔwan*
/ču:maṭ̓=čo:kʰe šiʔmi=ʔwan/
gray.squirrel=POSS bow=DET.OBJ
'Squirrel**'s** bow'

||=k̓o|| =k̓o COMITATIVE

The comitative enclitic is applied to NPs and strictly supplies a comitative meaning; it is not an instrumental or an associative. This enclitic may also attach to kinship terms and pronouns. An example is given in (430) (with the comitative in bold and the NP to which it is attached set off with brackets).

(430) Example of comitative enclitic ||=k̓o||
núp[ʰ]:e nóp[ʰ]:ow ka:wíya bahṭʰék̓o (H V: 1)
*nupʰ:e nopʰ:ow [ka:wiya bahṭʰe]$_{NP}$**k̓o***

/nup^{h}:e nop^{h}:o-w ka:wi-ya bahṭ^{h}e=k̓o/
striped.skunk sev.dwell-PFV child-PL big.COLL=COM
'Skunk Woman lived, **with** many children'

||=wi|| =wi INSTRUMENTAL

The instrumental enclitic has two different meanings, at least in English translation. When applied to objects which are susceptible to being manipulated and cannot be used as a container, ||=wi|| has a true instrumental meaning (e.g., *t̪^{h}an:a=wi* hand=INSTR 'with hand(s)'); when applied to a location or container, ||=wi|| has a locative meaning, which is roughly 'at' for places (e.g., *čol:i-k:o=wi* blackbird-field=INSTR 'at blackbird field', the original name for the village that is now Windsor, California) and 'in' for containers (e.g., č^{h}eʔ:et̪may=wi basket=INSTR 'in the basket'). When applied directly to a handful of words, such as 'hand', this enclitic is transcremental (e.g., *t̪^{h}a:na* 'hand' but *t̪^{h}an:a=wi* 'with hand'); however, the laryngeal increment of such words is unaffected if they are not the portion of the NP to which ||=wi|| is directly attached; see the example 'with two hands' in (431). This morpheme is given in examples in (431) and (432) (the instrumental is in bold; its translation is also in bold).

(431) Example of instrumental ||=wi|| with true instrumental meaning
t̪[^{h}]a:na ʔak^{h}:owi da:ṭ^{h}ow (H EA: 4a)
*[t̪^{h}a:na ʔak^{h}:o]$_{NP}$**wi** da:ṭ^{h}ow*
/t̪^{h}a:na ʔak^{h}:o=wi da:ṭ^{h}o-w/
hand two=INSTR scrape-PFV
'scrapes it off **with** both hands'

(432) Example of instrumental ||=wi|| with locative meaning
čó:low:i [ʔ]ahk^{h}a [ʔ]ohčóba, (H VI: 6)
*[čo:low]$_{NP}$**wi** ʔahk^{h}a ʔohčoba,*
/čo:low=wi ʔahk^{h}a ʔohčo-ba/
baby.bath.basket=INSTR water place.shapeless.mass-S.SEQ
'having put water **into** a baby-bath basket'

||=t̪on|| =t̪on LOCATIVE 'on'

This morpheme means 'on'. It may be used to show more than just location. Example (433) gives two instances of this morpheme, including one in which it does not indicate actual location (||=t̪on|| is in bold, and its translation is also in bold).

(433) Examples of ||=t̪on|| 'on'

ʔač:ay=t̪on (O I: 6)		čún:am háyt̪on (H IV: 6)
*[ʔač:ay]**t̪on***		*[čun:am hay]**t̪on***
/ʔač:ay=t̪on/	/čun:am	hay=t̪on/
man=LOC	drift	wood=LOC
'**over** the man'		'[**on**] driftwood'

||=t̪ow|| =t̪ow ABLATIVE

The ablative enclitic is used to indicate origin ('from') and can be combined with the question word *he:ʔey* 'where' to form *he:t̪ow* 'whence'. An example of this enclitic is given in (434) (with the ablative and its translation in bold).

(434) Example of ||=t̪ow|| ABLATIVE

[ʔ]ak^{h}:a:nát̪ow [ʔ]ek^{h}:elkó:le (H ms.)

*[ʔak^{h}:a:na]**t̪ow**[181] ʔek^{h}:elko:le*

/ʔak^{h}:a-:na=t̪ow ʔe-k^{h}:e-lko:-le/

water-LOC=ABL with.body-move-DIR-PL.IMP

'in-law move **out of** water [!]'

2.9.1.3. *Subject/Object Case-Marking Determiner Enclitics*

Noun phrases in Southern Pomo have an additional type of case-marking, one not found in the pronouns and kinship terms. NPs, whether animate or not, may have determiner enclitics attached to them which indicate subject or object in addition to indicating their use as determiners. There is a two-way split between the pair ||=ʔwam:u|| DETERMINER.SUBJECT and ||=ʔwan|| DETERMINER.OBJECT, both of which are most often translated as 'the' in the records, and the pair ||=ʔyo:mu|| DETERMINER.SUBJECT and ||=ʔyowan|| DETERMINER.OBJECT, which are variously translated as 'the' or 'the aforementioned' in the records. The exact nature of the semantics of these morphemes is not well understood. The extant glosses are too vague to make a precise distinction between the two sets, and as it is impossible to obtain native speaker intuitions, these glosses are not susceptible to improvement.

These clitics probably descend from the following combinations at an earlier stage in the language:[182]

*ʔe COPULA + *-wa FACTUAL.EVIDENTIAL + *ham:u 3SG.AGT > *=ʔwam:u*
*ʔe COPULA + *-wa FACTUAL.EVIDENTIAL + *-l PATIENT > *=ʔwan*
*ʔe COPULA + *yo- 'go' + *-wa FACTUAL.EVIDENTIAL + *ham:u 3SG.AGT > *=ʔyo:mu*
*ʔe COPULA + *yo- 'go' + *-wa FACTUAL.EVIDENTIAL + *-l PATIENT > *=ʔyowan*

Each of these enclitics is described in the subsections that follow.

||=ʔwam:u|| =ʔwam:u ~ =wam:u DETERMINER.SUBJECT

This enclitic may be attached to NP that is the subject of a clause. Subject is here defined as the sole argument of intransitive verbs and the least patent-like core argument of transitive verbs. Examples are given in (435) and (436) (with the enclitic and its translations in bold).

(435) ||=ʔwam:u|| on least patient-like core argument of transitive verb (H VIII: 4)
čú:maṭ̓wám:u hoʔ[:]ówi biʔk̓ik̓:iw šiʔmiʔwan
*[ču:maṭ̓]**wam:u** hoʔ:owi biʔk̓ik̓:iw šiʔmiʔwan*

/ču:maṭ̓=wam:u	hoʔ:o=wi	biʔk̓i-k̓:i-w	šiʔmi=ʔwan/
gray.squirrel=DET.SUBJ	teeth=INSTR	gnaw ~ ITER-PFV	bow=DET.OBJ

'**the** Squirrel gnawed it with his teeth, the bow.'

(436) ||=ʔwam:u|| on the single argument of intransitive verb (H V: 7, 8)
kʰaʔbéʔwam:u [ʔ]iy:ót̯ow čí:yow.
*[kʰaʔbe]**ʔwam:u** ʔiy:ot̯ow či:yow*

/kʰaʔbe=ʔwam:u	ʔiy:o=t̯ow	či:yo-w/
rock=DET.SUBJ	under=ABL	stay-PFV

'Rock [Man] sat below.'

||=ʔwan|| =ʔwan ~ =wan DETERMINER.OBJECT

This enclitic is the one most commonly translated with 'the' in the records. It is commonly found on both animate and inanimate NPs. Examples are given in (437)–(439) (with the enclitic and its translations in bold; the NPs to which it is attached are set off with brackets).

(437) ||=ʔwan|| DET.OBJECT on animate NP
há:miní(:)ba baʔ[:]áywan hódʔómhuy (H I: 2)
*ha:miniba [baʔ:ay]**wan** hodʔomhuy*
/ha:mini-ba baʔ:ay=wan hodʔo-mhuy-Ø/
and.then-S.SEQ woman=DET.OBJ handle-RECIP-PFV
'Then (he) made love to **the** woman'

(438) ||=ʔwan|| DET.OBJECT on inanimate NP (H ms.)
čʰeʔ[:]eṭmáywan šuhkʰečí:le
*[čʰeʔ:eṭmay]**wan** šuhkʰ**eči:le***
/čʰeʔ:eṭmay=wan šu-hkʰe-či:-le/
basket=DET.OBJ by.pulling-move-REFL-PL.IMP
'2 move basket closer to self!'

(439) ||=ʔwan|| DET.OBJECT on inanimate NP (H VIII: 4)
čú:maṭwám:u hoʔ[:]ówi biʔk̓ik̓:iw šiʔmiʔwan
*ču:maṭwam:u hoʔ:owi biʔk̓ik̓:iw[šiʔmi]**ʔwan***
/ču:maṭ=wam:u hoʔ:o=wi biʔk̓i-k̓:i-w šiʔmi=ʔwan/
gray.squirrel=DET.SUBJ teeth=INSTR gnaw~ITER-PFV bow=DET.OBJ
'the Squirrel gnawed it with his teeth, **the** bow.'

||=ʔyo:mu|| =ʔyo:mu ~ =yo:mu DETERMINER.SUBJECT 'aforementioned'

This enclitic, like ||=ʔwam:u||, is placed on a NP that is the subject of the verb, as shown in (440a) (with the enclitic and its translation in bold; the NP to which it is attached is set off by brackets).

(440a) Example of ||=ʔyo:mu|| DET.SUBJECT (H IX: 9)
ší:ba:ṭ[ʰ]aw ka:wíyaʔyó:mu hám:i kúṭ:u
*[ši:ba:ṭʰaw ka:wiya]**ʔyo:mu** ham:i kuṭ:u*

/ši:ba:ṯʰaw[183] ka:wi-ya=ʔyo:mu ham:i kuṭ:u/
poor child-PL=DET.SUBJ there just

čʼa:ṯúṯ:ow čʰí:lan šú:new.
čʼa:ṯuṯ:ow čʰi:lan šu:new
/čʼa:-ṯuṯ=ṯow čʰi:lan šu-:ne-w/
one-side?=ABL tumpline with.pulling-grasp-PFV
'**The** poor children stretched the tump-line there just on one side.'

||=ʔyowan|| =ʔyowan ~ =yowan DETERMINER.OBJECT 'aforementioned'

This enclitic may be attached to a NP that is the object of verb. It is not clear how it differs from ||=ʔwan|| in terms of semantics, but Oswalt occasionally translates NPs with this enclitic with the gloss 'that aforementioned . . .', as in (440b) (where the enclitic and its translation are in bold; the NP to which it is attached is set off with brackets).

(440b) Example of ||=ʔyowan|| DET.OBJECT (O I: 19)
pʰa:la baʔ:ay( )yowan kahsakʼ
pʰa:la [baʔ:ay]**yowan** kahsakʼ
/pʰa:la baʔ:ay=yowan kahsak-Ø/
also woman=DET.OBJ desert-PFV
'he also deserted **that aforementioned** woman'

This enclitic may also be used to nominalize clauses, especially those which function as obliques, as in (441).

(441) Example of ||=ʔyowan|| DET.OBJECT nominalizing clause (H VIII: 2)
čú:maṭʼyey hó:liw
ču:maṭʼyey ho:liw
/ču:maṭʼ=yey ho:li-w/
gray.squirrel=AGT leave-PFV

[ʔ]aṯ:íyey daʔṯʼámhukʰ:eʔyowanṯóŋhkʰay
*[ʔaṯ:iyey daʔṯʼamhukʰ:e]**ʔyowan**ṯonhkʰay*
/ʔaṯ:i-yey daʔṯʼa-mhu-kʰ:e=ʔyowan=ṯonhkʰay/

3C-PL.AGT find-RECIP-FUT=DET.OBJ=toward
'Squirrel went off to where they will meet each other'

2.9.2. Other NP Enclitics

This section introduces the remaining NP enclitics, many of which have locative meanings which are handled by adpositions in other languages.

2.9.2.1. The collectivizer enclitic ||=hča||

This enclitic is often translated as a plural or as 'a bunch/group'. It appears to mark groups as a collective and might have grammaticized from the word ʔahča 'house' (perhaps something like 'X's house(hold)' > 'X=house(hold)' > 'X=COLL'). Examples follow (with the enclitic and its translation in bold).

(442) Example of ||=hča|| COLL (H VI: 11)
[ʔ]ak^{h}:óhčaʔ( )waʔya čoh:ók^{h}:e
*[ʔak^{h}:o]**hča**ʔwaʔya čoh:ok^{h}:e*
/ʔak^{h}:o=hča=ʔwa=ʔya čoh:o-k^{h}:e/
two=COLL=COP.EVID=1PL.AGT marry-FUT
'We'll **both** marry him.'

This enclitic may attach to a NP that already has plural marking, and it is also unusual in that it may be marked for case. It takes the ||-n|| allomorph of the patient case, as seen in (443).

(443) Example of ||=hča-n|| (H EA: 9a)
ha:meṭna ʔa: hinṯilku [ʔ]ahṭ^{h}i[y] [ʔ]am:aʔwan
ha:meṭna ʔa: hinṯilku ʔahṭ^{h}iy ʔam:aʔwan
/ha:meṭna ʔa: hinṯilku ʔahṭ^{h}iy ʔam:a=ʔwan
thus 1SG.AGT Indian big.DISTR thing=DET.OBJ[184]

kuʔmu ʔawi:k^{h}e ka:wiyaʔwanhčan [ʔ]uhṯehṯe:ṯ^{h}oṯ.
*kuʔmu [ʔawi:k^{h}e ka:wiyaʔwan]**hčan** ʔuhṯehṯe:ṯ^{h}oṯ*
/kuʔmu ʔawi-:k^{h}e ka:wi-ya=ʔwan=hča-n ʔuhṯehṯe:=ṯ^{h}oṯ/
whole 1SG.OBL-POSS child-PL=DET.OBJ=COLL-PAT tell=NEG
'That's why I never told my kid**s** everything about Indian things'

2.9.2.2. *Locative Enclitics*

These enclitics, unlike ||=t̪on||, refer solely to physical location. Each is discussed separately.

||=k^{h}a:ni|| =k^{h}a:ni 'within'

This enclitic indicates a location within something, as shown in (444) (the enclitic is in bold; the NP to which it is attached is set off by brackets).

(444) Example of ||=k^{h}a:ni|| 'within' (H EA: 35a)
mi:t̪o šiʔbak^{h}a:ni duhṭ^{h}an k^{h}aṭ:ič̓aw
*[mi:t̪o šiʔba]**k^{h}a:ni** duhṭ^{h}an k^{h}aṭ:ič̓aw*
/mi:t̪o   šiʔba=k^{h}a:ni   duhṭ^{h}an-Ø   k^{h}aṭ:ič̓aw/
2SG.PAT   body=LOC   pain-PFV   bad
['within your body (it) badly hurts']

||=li|| =li 'at'

This enclitic indicates a static location without reference to the NP being in, on, or atop something. It is most commonly translated with 'at', as in (445) (with the enclitic in bold; the NP to which it is attached is set off with brackets).

(445) Example of ||=li|| 'at' (O I: 11)
niba ʔyodo ham:i ʔat̪:iyey nop^{h}:o:=li
*nibaʔyodo[ham:i [ʔat̪:iyey nop^{h}:o:]**li***
/ni-ba=ʔyo-do   ham:i   ʔat̪:i-yey   nop^{h}:o-:=li/
and.then-S.SEQ=AUX-QUOT   there   3C-PL.AGT   live-PFV?=at
'Then, it is said, there where they were living'

||=li=k^{h}ač|| =nhk^{h}ay ~ =nhk^{h}č (?) '-ward'

This enclitic indicates direction and is applied to obliques within sentences which have a verb of motion as the main verb. It is conveniently translated into English as '-ward'; examples follow (with the enclitic and its translation in bold; the NPs to which it attaches are set off with brackets).

(446) Example of ||=li=kʰač|| *=nhkʰay* '-ward' (H ms.)

ká:liŋhkʰay ha:čaṭkáčin [ʔ]ám:aŋhkʰay ha:čaṭláwa

*[ka:li]**nhkʰay** ha:čaṭkačin [ʔam:a]**nhkʰay** ha:čaṭlawa*

/ka:li=nhkʰay	ha:ča-ṭ-kač-in	ʔam:a=nhkʰay	ha:ča-ṭ-la-wa/
up=ward	fly-PL.ACT-DIR-S.SEQ	earth=ward	fly-PL.ACT-DIR-EVID

'bird keeps flying up[**ward**] and flying down[**ward**]'

||=ṭon=kʰač|| =ṭonhkʰay 'toward'

This enclitic appears to carry the same meaning as '-ward' in (446). An example is given in (447) with a nominalized clause.

(447) Example of ||=ṭon=kʰač|| *=ṭonhkʰay* (H VIII: 2)

[ʔ]aṭ:íyey daʔṭ̓ámhukʰ:eʔyowanṭóŋhkʰay

*[ʔaṭ:iyey daʔṭ̓amhukʰ:eʔyowan]**ṭonhkʰay***

/ʔaṭ:i-yey	daʔṭ̓a-mhu-kʰ:e=ʔyowan=ṭonhkʰay/
3C-PL.AGT	find-RECIP-FUT=DET.OBJ=toward

'**to** where they will meet each other'

||=sa:ma|| =sa:ma 'beside; near'

This morpheme is translated as 'next', 'near', 'beside'. An example is given in (448).

(448) Example of ||=sa:ma|| 'beside; near' (H EA: 43a)

kʰa:le( )sa:ma

*[kʰa:le]**sa:ma***

/kʰa:le=sa:ma/

tree=beside

['beside a tree']

||=wa:ni|| =wa:ni 'inside'

This enclitic means 'inside', as seen in (449).

(449) Example of ||=wa:ni|| (H VIII: 8)

k̓ohṭokʰṭowá:ni [ʔ]íhčok̓ ču:máṭyey kʰaʔbéyčon.

*[k̓ohṭokʰṭo]**wa:ni** ʔihčok̓ ču:maṭyey kʰaʔbeyčon*

/k̓oht̪ok^{h}t̪o=wa:ni ʔihčok̓-Ø ču:maṭ=yey k^{h}aʔbe=yčon/
base.of.neck=LOC shoot-PFV gray.squirrel=AGT rock=PAT
'[He] shot him **in** the soft spot between the collarbones, [Gray] Squirrel (did it) to Rock [Man].'

||win:a|| ~ ||=win:a|| 'atop'

This morpheme is often written as a separate word. An example is given in (450).

(450) Example of ||win:a|| ~ ||=win:a|| 'atop' (H ms.)
k^{h}áʔbe č̓á:ʔa( )wín:a ba:néman
*[k^{h}aʔbe č̓a:ʔa]**win:a** ba:neman*
/k^{h}aʔbe č̓a:ʔa win:a ba:neman/
rock one atop put.one.nonlong.object-ESSIVE-SG.IMP
'put a rock **on** it'

||=nhi|| ~ ||-:ni|| LOCATIVE 'in; beneath(?)'

This clitic is poorly understood. The two recorded forms do not come from different dialects. Halpern recorded this as /-:ni/ from Annie Burke and as /-nhi/ from Burke's daughter, Elsie Allen. Examples are provided in (451).

(451) Examples of ||-nhi|| ~ ||-:ni|| 'in; beneath'

šaʔk̓anhi (H EA: 43a)	k^{h}á:lešk̓á:ni (H V: 14)
*[šaʔk̓a]**nhi***	*[k^{h}a:lešk̓a]**:ni***
/šaʔk̓a-nhi/	/k^{h}a:le-šk̓a=:ni/
black-LOC	tree-black=LOC
'in the shade'	'in the shade of a tree'

2.9.2.3. *Miscellaneous NP Enclitics*

These enclitics express things that are often handled with adverbs or verbs in other languages. Each is discussed individually below.

||=hlaw|| =hlaw 'too, also'

This enclitic is used for 'too, also', as shown in (452) (the clitic and its translation are in bold; the NP to which it is attached is set off by brackets).

(452) Example of ||=hlaw|| ‘too, also’
[ʔ]í[y]haʔwánhlaw (H V: 26)
*[ʔiyhaʔwan]**hlaw***
/ʔiyha=ʔwan=hlaw/
bone=DET.OBJ=too
‘bones and all’

||=V:meṭ̓|| =:meṭ̓ ‘like, same as’

This enclitic means ‘like, same as’, as shown in example (453), where the clitic is in bold and the constituent to which it is attached is set off by brackets. This clitic is functionally an equative case marker on NPs, especially kinship terms—see example (10)—but it attaches to verbs as well, as follows.

(453) Example of ||=V:meṭ̓|| ‘like, same as’ (O I: 17e)
mi:t̪o p^{h}a[:]la ha:meṭ̓( )wa ʔma čaht̪inčik^{h}:e,
mi:t̪o p^{h}a:la ha:meṭ̓wa ʔma čaht̪inčik^{h}:e,
/mi:t̪o p^{h}a:la ha:meṭ̓=wa ʔma čaht̪in-či-k^{h}:e/
2SG.PAT also thus=COP.EVID thing[185] happen-SEM?-FUT

ʔat̪:o ʔam:a čaht̪inwa( ):meṭ̓.
*[ʔat̪:o ʔam:a čaht̪inwa]**:meṭ̓***
/ʔat̪:o ʔam:a čaht̪in=wa=:meṭ̓/
1SG.PAT thing happen=COP.EVID=like
‘That same thing will happen to you, as happened to me.’

||=t̪on=k^{h}le|| =t̪onhk^{h}(l)e ‘some of’

This enclitic means ‘some of’ and has a partitive meaning that is not a part of the semantics of the non-numeral quantifier *beṭ̓bu* ‘some’. An example is given in (454) with the enclitic and its translation in bold (the NP to which it is attached is set off with brackets).

(454) Example of ||=t̪on=k^{h}le|| =*t̪onhk^{h}le* ‘some of’ (O D: EA)
<mi?di$ wan ton(h)k^hle mihnatin>
*[miʔdišwan]**t̪onhk^{h}le** mihnat̪in*
/miʔdiš=wan=t̪onhk^{h}le mi-hnat̪-in/

nut=DET.OBJ=some by.reckoning-try-SG.IMP
'Test **some of** the nuts by cracking (to see if good inside)!'

||t̪i-|| ~ ||=t̪i-|| INCHOATIVE

This morpheme is often transcribed as an independent word when it has suffixes affixed to it. When it is unaffixed, it is often written together with the preceding NP. This morpheme indicates a change of state, as seen in the examples that follow (where the inchoative is in bold).

(455) Example of ||t̪i|| ~ ||=t̪i|| INCH with affixes (H VI: 6)
[ʔ]ahkʰá [ʔ]oh:o t̪ikʰt̪i.
[ʔahkʰa ʔoh:o] ***t̪i****kʰt̪i.*
/ʔahkʰa ʔoh:o t̪i-kʰ-t̪i/
water fire INCH-CAUS-FUTURE.INTENTIVE
'in order to have the water become hot'
['in order to make it become hot water']

(456) Example of ||t̪i|| ~ ||=t̪i|| INCH without affixes (H V: 37)
nup[ʰ]:ét̪i
*nupʰ:e****t̪i***
/nupʰ:e=t̪i/
striped.skunk=INCH
'they turned into skunks'

2.9.3. Alienable and Inalienable Possession

The possessive prefixes of the kinship terms have already been discussed (§2.8.1.3.1), and they are not considered in this section. The suffix ||-:kʰe|| POSSESSIVE has two specific uses: (1) it indicates alienable possession; and (2) it is used as a benefactive. Examples of each of these usages are given in (457)–(459).

(457) ||-:kʰe|| POSSESSIVE used for alienable possession of animate (H EA: 9a)
ha:meṭna ʔa: hint̪ilku [ʔ]ahṭʰi[y] [ʔ]am:aʔwan
ha:meṭna ʔa: hint̪ilku ʔahṭʰiy ʔam:aʔwan
/ha:meṭna ʔa: hint̪ilku ʔahṭʰiy ʔam:a=ʔwan
thus 1SG.AGT Indian big.DISTR thing=DET.OBJ[186]

ku?mu ?awi:kʰe ka:wiya?wanhčan [?]uhṭehṭe:ṭʰoṭ.
*ku?mu ?awi:**kʰe** ka:wiya?wanhčan ?uhṭehṭe:ṭʰoṭ*
/ku?mu ?awi-:kʰe ka:wi-ya=?wan=hča-n ?uhṭehṭe:=ṭʰoṭ/
whole 1SG.OBL-POSS child-PL=DET.OBJ=COLL-PAT tell=NEG
'That's why I never told **my** kids everything about Indian things'

(458) ||-:kʰe|| POSSESSIVE used for alienable possession of a man-made thing
[?]á:baċe:kʰe [?]ahčaṭóŋhkʰay hó:liṭi?dú:na (H ms.)
*?a:baċe:**kʰe** ?ahčaṭonhkʰay ho:li**ṭi?du**:na*
/?a:-ba-ċ-e-:kʰe ?ahča=ṭonhkʰay ho:li-ṭi?du-:na/
1-fa's.fa-GS-OBL-POSS house=toward leave-FUT.INTENT-FIRST.PERSON
'I am going to my fa[ther's] fa[ther]**'s** house after a while'

(459) ||-:kʰe|| POSSESSIVE used as a benefactive suffix (H III: 1)
míp[ʰ]:ak:i[:]kʰe yúh[:]u [?]ohčóyaw
*mipʰ:ak:i:**kʰe** yuh:u ?ohčoyaw*
/mi-pʰ:ak-ki-:kʰe yuh:u ?ohčo-ya-w/
2-son-GS-POSS pinole put.shapeless.mass-DEFOC-PFV
'They have put up pinole **for** your son.'

Virtually everything that is not a part of an individual may be alienably possessed (e.g., food, man-made items, children, spouses, things). Body parts and names, however, are always inalienably possessed, which is indicated by the use of the patient case form of a pronoun with no possessive suffix, as follows.[187]

(460) Use of patient case to show inalienable possession
?aṭ:o ?i:šan duhṭʰan (W: OF)
/?aṭ:o ?i:šan duhṭʰan-Ø/
1SG.PAT arm hurt-PFV
'my arm hurts'

(461) Use of patient case to show inalienable possession
mi:ṭo ?ahši:yaw hi?du?čenṭʰoṭwa?a (H ms.)[188]
/mi:ṭo ?ahši:yaw hi?du?čen=ṭʰoṭ=wa=?a/
2SG.PAT name know=NEG=COP.EVID=1SG.AGT
['I don't know your name']

THREE

Sentence Structure

Southern Pomo clauses are composed of single predicates, including verbs (the most common predicates), predicate nominals, and predicate adjectives. Southern Pomo sentences are composed of one or more clauses. Southern Pomo verbs do not have any obligatory person marking, and if the suffixes ||-V:na|| FIRST.PERSON and ||-:mu|| SECOND.PERSON are not accepted as person-marking morphemes, Southern Pomo verbs have no person marking whatsoever. Southern Pomo clauses, however, often lack any overt mention of any argument (via full NP or pronoun), and it is often only context and the use of coreferential devices (switch-reference suffixes, third-person coreferential pronouns, and kinship prefixes) which allow for the identification of who does what to whom in the clauses of a sentence.

Because a verb need not surface with any overt arguments and no person-marking affixes, it is often the case that verbs that may be syntactically transitive may also surface with only one overt argument or none. The definition of transitivity is not without difficulty. Dixon takes the position that it is purely a syntactic phenomenon:

> *Transitivity is a syntactic matter.* When a clause is said to have a certain transitivity value, and when a verb is said to show certain transitivity possibilities, these are syntactic—not semantic—specifications. (Dixon 2010b: 116)

This definition is useful: English verbs like 'hear' are clearly syntactically transitive (as Dixon notes), but semantically—if transitivity is treated as a semantic and not a syntactic phenomenon—the verb 'hear' does not share much with more prototypical transitive verbs (e.g., 'kill'). I adopt a modified form of the preceding definition of transitivity—a language-specific definition—that fits with the nature of Southern Pomo sentence structure. The transitivity of a Southern Pomo verb is purely a *lexical matter* (to borrow some of Dixon's phraseology) in the sense that it is not possible to predict transitivity via semantics, and the ability or inability of a verb to surface with one or more than one core argument is lexically determined: a verb is transitive or intransitive on the basis of how that word *may* behave syntactically.

The distinctions drawn between different transitivity types, then, are among verbs which may surface with three core arguments (ditransitives), verbs which may surface with no more than two core arguments (transitives), and verbs that may surface with only one core argument (intransitives). Any of these three types of verbs may surface with fewer arguments than the maximum amount by which they are assigned to a transitivity type.

The following subsections on intransitives, transitives, and ditransitives are solely devoted to a discussion of verbs which maximally surface with one, two, or three core arguments, respectively.[1] The overt marking of core arguments via pronominal enclitics is not considered in the following examples, as the order of the enclitics, which are second-position (Wackernagel) clitics, is dictated by the number of constituents which precede the verb: any constituent may bear these clitics, and their location relative to the verb (whether before or after) is largely predictable.

3.1. INTRANSITIVES

Intransitive verbs are defined as those verbs which may take no more than one core argument. Intransitive verbs are preceded by their single argument (S), if that argument is overtly present as a full NP. However, the order VS is also to be found. Examples of two prototypical intransitive verbs, ||hu:w-|| ‘go’ and ||ho:li-|| ‘leave’, are given below.

(462) SV intransitive clause (H VIII: 2)
kʰaʔbéyey hó:liw
[kʰaʔbeyey]$_{S}$ *ho:liw*
||kʰaʔbe=yey ho:li-w||
/kʰaʔbe=yey ho:li-w/
rock=AGT leave-PFV
‘Rock [Man] went off.’

(463) VS intransitive clause (H I: 21)
hó:liw lik̓lísyey
ho:liw [lik̓lisyey]$_S$
/ho:li-w lik̓lis=yey/
leave-PFV raptor.species=AGT
'(He) went off, Sparrowhawk'

The following example is of a bi-clausal sentence. The first verb is dependent upon the final main verb, the intransitive verb ||hu:w-|| 'go', and no overt argument is present anywhere within the sentence (nor is there any other morphological indication within the sentence of who the argument(s) is/are, though the switch-reference suffix on the dependent verb indicates that the unexpressed argument(s) is/are shared by both verbs).

(464) V intransitive clause (H VI: 17)
ča:dédun hwád:u
ča:dedun hwad:u
||ča:de-ad-Vn hu:w-aded-u||
/ča:de-d-un hw-ad:-u/
look-DIR-S.SIM go-DIR-PFV
'He walked around looking around.'

3.2. TRANSITIVES

Transitive verbs are defined as those verbs which may take no more than two core arguments. Transitive verbs are generally preceded by their single arguments (A and O), if any argument is overtly present as a full NP. The following orders of a transitive verb and its overtly present core arguments are attested: AOV, OAV, VAO, OV, AV, and V. Examples of transitive verbs are given in (465)–(467) (the transitive verbs are in bold in the text and translation).

(465) AOV transitive clause
miy[:]á[ṭʰ]kʰan wéč:é(:)yčon bé:new míṭ:iw (H I: 6)
*[miy:aṭʰkʰan]$_A$ [weč:eyčon]$_O$ **be:new** miṭ:iw*

/miy:a-ṭ^{h}k^{h}an-Ø weč:e=yčon be-:ne-w miṭ:i-Ø-w/
3-spouse-AGT barn.owl=PAT with.arms-grasp-PFV lie-DIFFUSE-PFV
'his wife was lying **hugging** Screech-owl'

(466) OAV transitive clause (H VI: 3)
ha:mini:li k^{h}áʔbek^{h}áč:on c̓a:yíyey [ʔ]uhṯéhṯew,
ha:mini:li [k^{h}aʔbek^{h}ač:on]$_{O}$ [c̓a:yiyey]$_{A}$ ***ʔuhṯehṯew***
/ha:mini-:li k^{h}aʔbek^{h}ač=čon c̓a:yi=yey ʔuhṯe-hṯe-w/
and.then-D.SEQ raptor.species=PAT scrubjay=AGT tell~tell-PFV
'They brought in the fish. They having done so, the Jay **told** Fish Hawk'

(467) VAO transitive clause (H VIII: 8)
k̓ohṯok^{h}ṯowá:ni [ʔ]íhčok̓ ču:máṭyey k^{h}aʔbéyčon.
k̓ohṯok^{h}ṯowa:ni ***ʔihčok̓*** *[ču:maṭyey]$_{A}$ [k^{h}aʔbeyčon]$_{O}$*
/k̓ohṯok^{h}ṯo=wa:ni ʔihčok̓-Ø ču:maṭ=yey k^{h}aʔbe=yčon/
base.of.neck=LOC shoot-PFV gray.squirrel=AGT rock=PAT
'[He] **shot** him in the soft spot between the collarbones, [Gray] Squirrel (did it) to Rock [Man].'

The example that follows has the NP *biʔdu čohšin=wan* 'acorn pound=the' as the O of the transitive verb šu:k^{h}aw 'finish'; there is no overt A in the clause.

(468) OV transitive clause (H I: 1)
ma:číl:e bíʔdu čóhšinwan šú:k^{h}aw
ma:čil:e [biʔdu čohšinwan]$_{O}$ ***šu:k^{h}aw***
/ma:či-l:e biʔdu čohšin-Ø=wan šu:k^{h}a-w/
day-mid acorn pound-PFV=DET.OBJ finish-PFV
'(at) noon (she) **finished** pounding acorns.'
[lit: 'At midday (she) **finished** the acorn pounding/pounding of acorns.']

The next example presents a multi-clause sentence without a single core argument overtly present. Three of the five verbs in this sentence are transitive: *daʔṭa-* 'to find or encounter someone or something', *čoh:om-* 'to marry someone', and *šudʔe-* 'to drag someone or something'.

(469) Transitive clauses with no overt core arguments present (O I: 9)

ʔaṯ:i=ṯon mi:mačen, či:yowen,

ʔaṯ:iṯon mi:mačen, či:yowen,

||ʔaṯ:i=ṯon mi:mač-en či:yo-en||

/ʔaṯ:i=ṯon mi:mač-en či:yo-wen/

3C.SG=LOC cry-D.SIM sit-D.SIM

daʔṯ̓aba, čoh:omba, šudʔeduy.

daʔṯ̓aba, čoh:omba, šudʔeduy.

||daʔṯ̓a-ba čoh:oN-ba šu-ʔde-aduč-Ø||

/daʔṯ̓a-ba čoh:om-ba šu-dʔe-duy-Ø/

find-S.SEQ marry-S.SEQ by.pulling-move-DIR-PFV

'Having found her sitting, crying for him, he married her and led her away.'

3.3. DITRANSITIVES

Ditransitive verbs, such as the verb for 'to give', may take three core arguments (if the indirect object is treated as a core argument). The attested order is A IO V O. In the following example, the ditransitive verb *ʔoh:o-* 'to give (long object or contained mass)' appears with its three arguments present as full NPs (the ditransitive verb is in bold in the text and translation; each argument is marked as A, O, or IO and bracketed off in the text).

(470) A IO V O transitive clause (H VIII: 3)

kʰaʔbéyey čú:maṭ̓čon [ʔ]óh:ow [ʔ]aṯ:í:kʰe ċú:ʔu.

[kʰaʔbeyey]$_A$ [ču:maṭ̓čon]$_{IO}$ ***ʔoh:ow*** *[ʔaṯ:i:kʰe ċu:ʔu]$_O$*

/kʰaʔbe=yey ču:maṭ̓=čon ʔoh:o-w ʔaṯ:i-:kʰe ċu:ʔu/

rock=AGT gray.squirrel=PAT give-PFV 3C.SG-POSS arrow

'Rock [Man] **handed** his arrow to Squirrel.'

3.4. GRAMMATICAL RELATIONS

Southern Pomo is a case-marking language. Pronouns, kinship terms, and highly animate common nouns (e.g., humans, some animals, plants, anthropomorphized weather events) are marked according to an agent/

patient case-marking system. The agent/patient case system of Southern Pomo is identical to the one reported for Central Pomo by Mithun (1991). The basics of the system are laid out in the next section. For a detailed list of all the agent/patient case-marking morphemes, consult the following sections: (§2.8.2) for the pronouns (personal and demonstrative); (§2.8.1.3.5) for the kinship terms; and (§2.9.1) for NP enclitics.

3.4.1. Agent/Patient Case System

The defining feature of the Southern Pomo (and Central Pomo) agent/patient case-marking system is the marking of the single argument of intransitive verbs in the agentive or patient case on the basis of whether or not the argument is affected. For the core arguments of transitive verbs, the most agent-like argument takes the agentive case and the least agentive argument takes the patient case. In Southern Pomo it is also possible to mark both arguments of certain verbs of emotion (e.g., *yaʔčʰo-* 'to not like' and *čun:a-* 'to tire or exhaust') with the patient case. Agent/patient case marking is only obligatory in the pronouns and kinship terms. It is optional on NPs with animate heads.

When both core arguments of a transitive verb are overtly present (and animate), the most agentive argument takes the agentive case; the least agentive argument takes the patient case. The actual semantic roles of the argument marked by the patient case vary from experiencer/undergoer/recipient to highly affected patient. Examples (471)–(473), which are repeated elsewhere in the text, give three different transitive clauses with agent/patient case marking on the arguments. Note that it is often the case marking alone that disambiguates who does what to whom. (The case-marking morphemes are in bold; the arguments marked for case are subscripted with AGT or PAT in the translation.)

(471) Agent/patient case on NPs of transitive verb (H I: 6)

miy[:]á[ṭʰ]kʰan wéč:é(:)yčon bé:new míṭ:iw

miy:aṭʰkʰan-**Ø** weč:e**yčon** be:new miṭ:iw

/miy:a-ṭʰkʰan-Ø	weč:e=yčon	be-:ne-w	miṭ:i-Ø-w/
3-spouse-AGT	barn.owl=PAT	with.arms-grasp-PFV	lie-DIFFUSE-PFV

'his wife$_{\text{AGT}}$ was lying hugging Screech-owl$_{\text{PAT}}$'

(472) Agent/patient case on NPs of transitive verb (H VI: 3)
ha:mini:li kʰáʔbekʰáč:on ċa:yíyey [ʔ]uht̯éht̯ew,
*ha:mini:li kʰaʔbekʰač**:on** ċa:yi**yey** ʔuht̯eht̯ew*
/ha:mini-:li kʰaʔbekʰač=čon ċa:yi=yey ʔuht̯e-ht̯e-w/
and.then-D.SEQ raptor.species=PAT scrubjay=AGT tell~tell-PFV
'They brought in the fish. They having done so, the Jay$_{\text{AGT}}$ told Fish Hawk$_{\text{PAT}}$'

(473) Agent/patient case on NPs of transitive verb (H VIII: 8)
k̓oht̯okʰt̯owá:ni [ʔ]íhčok̓ ču:máṭ̓yey kʰaʔbéyčon.
*k̓oht̯okʰt̯owa:ni ʔihčok̓ ču:maṭ̓**yey** kʰaʔbe**yčon***
/k̓oht̯okʰt̯o=wa:ni ʔihčok̓-Ø ču:maṭ̓=yey kʰaʔbe=yčon/
base.of.neck=LOC shoot-PFV gray.squirrel=AGT rock=PAT
'[He] shot him in the soft spot between the collarbones, [Gray] Squirrel$_{\text{AGT}}$ (did it) to Rock [Man]$_{\text{PAT}}$.'

In example (474) the ditransitive verb *ʔoh:o-* 'give' has three arguments, but it is only the animate arguments to which agent/case marking applies. In this case the recipient, as the most affected animate argument, is marked in the patient case.

(474) Agent/patient case on NPs of ditransitive verb (H VIII: 3)
kʰaʔbéyey čú:maṭ̓čon [ʔ]óh:ow [ʔ]at̯:í:kʰe ċú:ʔu.
*kʰaʔbe**yey** ču:maṭ̓**čon** ʔoh:ow ʔat̯:i:kʰe ċu:ʔu*
/kʰaʔbe=yey ču:maṭ̓=čon ʔoh:o-w ʔat̯:i-:kʰe ċu:ʔu/
rock=AGT gray.squirrel=PAT give-PFV 3C.SG-POSS arrow
'Rock [Man]$_{\text{AGT}}$ handed his arrow to Squirrel$_{\text{PAT}}$.'

A few verbs of emotion which express actions or states over which none of the arguments has any control may have both arguments in the patient case. The examples of this phenomenon are limited, and a first-person argument seems to be present in all of them. An illustration of this is given in (475).

(475) Verb of emotion with two arguments marked in patient case (O D)
<yaʔcʌhowa ʔto mi*to.>
*yaʔčʰowa**ʔt̯o mi:t̯o***

/yaʔčʰo-wa=ʔṯo mi:ṯo/
not.want-EVID=1SG.PAT 2SG.PAT
'I$_{PAT}$ don't like you$_{PAT}$.'

When the single argument of an intransitive verb is animate and has some control over the action or is not significantly affected, the agentive case may be used, as in (476) (the agentive case marker is in bold; the case-marked argument is indicated in the translation with subscript).

(476) Example of agentive case with intransitive verb (H VIII: 2)
kʰaʔbéyey hó:liw
*kʰaʔbe**yey** ho:liw*
||kʰaʔbe=yey ho:li-w||
/kʰaʔbe=yey ho:li-w/
rock=AGT leave-PFV
'Rock [Man]$_{AGT}$ went off.'

When the single argument of an intransitive verb is animate and has little control over the action or is significantly affected by it, the patient case may be used. In example (477) 'Rock [Man]' falls asleep and is marked with the patient case for his being affected by the activity and his lack of control over falling asleep. (The patient case marker is in bold; the case-marked argument is indicated in the translation with subscript.)

(477) Example of patient case on single argument of intransitive verb (H VIII: 8)
ha:mini(:)ba kʰaʔbéyčon sí:ma mí:ṭiw
*ha:miniba kʰaʔbe**yčon** si:ma mi:ṭiw*
/ha:mini-ba kʰaʔbe=yčon si:ma mi:ṭi-w/
and.then-S.SEQ rock=PAT sleep lie-PFV
'Having done so, Rock [Man]$_{PAT}$ went to sleep.'

In (478) this same 'Rock [Man]' has no control over his dying after having been shot by the narrative's protagonist and is therefore marked with the patient case. (The patient case marker is in bold; the case-marked argument is indicated in the translation with subscript.)

(478) Example of patient case on single argument of intransitive verb (H VIII: 9)

ha:mini:li kʰaʔbéyčon k̓ál:aw.

*ha:mini:li kʰaʔbe**yčon** k̓al:aw*

||ha:mini-:li kʰaʔbe=yčon k̓al:a-w||

/ha:mini-:li kʰaʔbe=yčon k̓al:a-w/

and.then-D.SEQ rock=PAT die-PFV

'He having done so, Rock $[\text{Man}]_{\text{PAT}}$ died.'

3.4.2. Subject/Object Determiner Enclitics

Though the agent/patient case system described is a robust part of Southern Pomo grammar and is quite conspicuous in clauses with animate arguments, another corner of the language is unconcerned with agent/patient case marking and has grammaticized case-marking enclitics which are attached to NPs on the basis of nominative/accusative case distinctions. Nominative/accusative is hereafter marked as subject/object for convenience and because subject is a relevant category elsewhere in the language (e.g., in the switch-reference system). The definition of subject used herein is language-specific: the subject is the single core argument of an intransitive verb or the least patient-like argument of an intransitive verb. Thus the definition of subject is strictly syntactic with regard to intransitive clauses; it is semantic with regard to transitive clauses (there being no fixed word order upon which to hang a syntactic definition).

These enclitics are actually determiners which indicate definiteness and identifiability in addition to subject or object case, but the specifics of their semantic contribution as determiners are not fully understood at this time. The case-marking functions of these NP enclitics are explored in the remainder of this section. Many of the examples are repeated from the earlier discussion of the shapes of these clitics and their diachronic development (see §2.9.1.3). Table 46 summarized these subject/object case-marking enclitics.[2]

Whereas the agent/patient case markers are sensitive to animacy and—in intransitive clauses—affectedness, the subject/object case-marking determiner enclitics are not sensitive to affectedness or animacy: both animate and inanimate NPs may be marked with the subject/object deter-

Table 46. Subject/object case-marking determiner enclitics

	Subject case	**Object case**
'the'	*=ʔwam:u*	*=ʔwan*
'the aforementioned'	*=ʔyo:mu*	*=ʔyowan*

miner enclitics, and when these clitics are attached to the single argument of an intransitive verb, the subject case forms are employed regardless of the level of control or affectedness. In the following sections the specifics of this distribution are laid out with examples.

||=ʔwam:u|| DET.SUBJ 'the' and ||=ʔyo:mu|| DET.SUBJ 'the aforementioned'

These clitics may be attached to the least patient-like argument of a transitive verb to mark it as definite and the subject, as seen in (479) and (480) (the subject-marking clitics are in bold in the text; the translations of the NPs to which they are attached are in bold).

(479) ||=ʔwam:u|| on least patient-like core argument of transitive verb (H VIII: 4)

čú:maṭ̓wám:u hoʔ[:]ówi biʔk̓ik̓:iw šiʔmiʔwan

*ču:maṭ̓**wam:u** hoʔ:owi biʔk̓ik̓:iw šiʔmiʔwan*

/ču:maṭ̓=wam:u	hoʔ:o=wi	biʔk̓i-k̓:i-w	šiʔmi=ʔwan/
gray.squirrel=DET.SUBJ	teeth=INSTR	gnaw~ITER-PFV	bow=DET.OBJ

'**the Squirrel** gnawed it with his teeth, the bow.'

(480) ||=ʔyo:mu|| on most patient-like core argument of transitive verb (H V: 11)

ma: nup[ʰ]:é baʔ[:]áy:o:mu k̓as[:]ísiʔyowan dóṭ̓:ow

*ma: nupʰ:e baʔ:ay**:o:mu** k̓as:isiʔyowan doṭ̓:ow*

/ma:	nupʰ:e	baʔ:ay=yo:mu	k̓as:isi=ʔyowan	do-ṭ̓:o-w/
DEM	striped.skunk	woman=DET.SUBJ	elk=DET.OBJ	by.finger-skin-PFV

'**This Skunk woman** skinned the Elk.'

||=ʔwan|| DET.OBJ 'the' and ||=ʔyowan|| DET.OBJ 'the aforementioned'

These clitics may be attached to the most patient-like argument of a transitive verb to mark it as definite and the object, as seen in (481) and (482), which are repeated from the preceding versions. (The object-marking clitics are in bold in the text; the translations of the NPs to which they are attached are in bold.)

(481) ||=ʔwan|| on the most patient-like core argument of transitive verb (H VIII: 4)

čú:maṭ̓wám:u hoʔ[:]ówi biʔk̓ik̓:iw šiʔmiʔwan

*ču:maṭ̓wam:u hoʔ:owi biʔk̓ik̓:iw šiʔmi**ʔwan***

/ču:maṭ̓=wam:u hoʔ:o=wi biʔk̓i-k̓:i-w šiʔmi=ʔwan/

gray.squirrel=DET.SUBJ teeth=INSTR gnaw~ITER-PFV bow=DET.OBJ

'the Squirrel gnawed it with his teeth, **the bow**.'

(482) ||=ʔyowan|| on the most patient-like core argument of transitive verb (H V: 11)

ma: nup[ʰ]:é baʔ[:]áy:o:mu k̓as[:]ísiʔyowan dóṭ̓:ow

*ma: nupʰ:e baʔ:ay:o:mu k̓as:isi**ʔyowan** doṭ̓:ow*

/ma: nupʰ:e baʔ:ay=yo:mu k̓as:isi=ʔyowan do-ṭ̓:o-w/

DEM striped.skunk woman=DET.SUBJ elk=DET.OBJ by.finger-skin-PFV

'This Skunk woman skinned **the Elk**.'

When the subject/object clitics are attached to the single argument of an intransitive verb, only the subject-marking clitics ||=ʔwam:u|| and ||=ʔyo:mu|| may be used, as seen in (483)–(485) (the object-marking clitics are in bold in the text; the translations of the NPs to which they are attached are in bold).

(483) ||=ʔwam:u|| on the single argument of intransitive verb (H V: 7, 8)

kʰaʔbéʔwam:u [ʔ]iy:ót̯ow čí:yow.

*[kʰaʔbe]**ʔwam:u** ʔiy:ot̯ow či:yow*

/kʰaʔbe=ʔwam:u ʔiy:o=t̯ow či:yo-w/

rock=DET.SUBJ under=ABL stay-PFV

'**Rock [Man]** sat below.'

(484) ||=ʔyo:mu|| on the single argument of intransitive verb (H V: 6)

nup[ʰ]:é baʔ[:]ay( )yó:mu miṭ:iw

*nupʰ:e baʔ:ay**o:mu** miṭ:iw*

/nupʰ:e ba?:ay=yo:mu miṭ:i-w/
striped.skunk woman=DET.SUBJ lie-PFV
'**That Skunk woman** lay (there).'

Example (485) presents a connected stretch of narrative discourse made up of three sentences. Each sentence ends with a finite verb suffixed with the perfective. The protagonist of the story from which this selection comes is the father of the child who is mentioned in each sentence. In each sentence, the NP 'child' is marked with either ||=ʔwan|| DET.OBJ or ||=ʔwam:u|| DET.SUBJ. The subject/object case-marking enclitics are in bold; the NPs—all 'child'—to which they are attached are in bold in the translation; and the three sentences have been subdivided into (485a–c) for ease of reference.

(485a) ||=ʔwam:u|| DET.SUBJ and ||=ʔwan|| DET.OBJ in multi-clause sentence (H I: 21)
muʔṭ̪á:li ká:wiʔwan čuh:úkaw,
*muʔṭ̪a:li ka:wi**ʔwan** čuh:ukaw*
/muʔṭ̪a-:li ka:wi=ʔwan čuh:u-ka-w/
cook-D.SEQ child=DET.OBJ eat-CAUS-PFV
'when (it) was cooked (he) fed **the child**.'

(485b) bihsúmbakʰmá:yow ká:wiʔwam[:]u sí:ma mí:ṭiw.
*bihsumbakʰma:yow ka:wi**ʔwam:u** si:ma mi:ṭiw*
/bi-hsum-ba=kʰma:yow ka:wi=ʔwam:u si:ma mi:ṭi-w/
with.lips-stop-S.SEQ child=DET.SUBJ sleep lie-PFV
'After (he) had finished eating, **the child** went to sleep.'

(485c) ha:miní:li mí(:)y[:]ame ká:wiʔwan čóh:oy.
*ha:mini:li miy:ame ka:wi**ʔwan** čoh:oy*
/ha:mini-:li miy:a-me-Ø ka:wi=ʔwan čoh:oy-Ø/
and.then-D.SEQ 3-father-AGT child=DET.OBJ sleep.next.to-PFV
'Then his father slept with **the child**.'
[Lit: '(485a) After (it) cooked, (the child's father) fed the child. (485b) After (the child) finished eating, the child fell asleep. (485c) And then his (the child's) father slept with the child.']

In (485b), the single argument of the intransitive verb ‘sleep’ is ‘child’, which is marked with ||=ʔwam:u|| DET.SUBJ. Compare this with (477) from the earlier discussion of agent/patient case marking (§3.4.1), which is repeated in (486):

(486) Example of patient case on single argument of intransitive verb (H VIII: 8)
ha:mini(:)ba kʰaʔbéyčon sí:ma mí:ṭiw
*ha:miniba kʰaʔbe**yčon** si:ma mi:ṭiw*
/ha:mini-ba kʰaʔbe=yčon si:ma mi:ṭi-w/
and.then-S.SEQ rock=PAT sleep lie-PFV
‘Having done so, Rock [Man]$_{\text{PAT}}$ went to sleep.’

Both (485b) and (486) involve a single argument of the verb ‘sleep’ that is animate. The agent/patient case-marking system codes the animate single argument of (486) in the patient case because ‘Rock [Man]’ has no control over his falling asleep and is highly affected by the activity. However, in (485b) the subject/object case-marking system codes the animate single argument as a subject—the level of control/affectedness is irrelevant.

The subject/object case-marking enclitics differ from the agent/patient case-marking system in another crucial way: these enclitics may attach to inanimate noun phrases, as seen in (487) and (488) (the case-marking enclitics are in bold in the text; the translations of the NPs to which they are attached are in bold).

(487) ||=ʔwan|| DET.OBJECT on inanimate NP (H VIII: 4)
čú:mat̪wám:u hoʔ[:]ówi biʔk̓ik̓:iw šiʔmiʔwan
*ču:mat̪wam:u hoʔ:owi biʔk̓ik̓:iw šiʔmi**ʔwan***
/ču:mat̪=wam:u hoʔ:o=wi biʔk̓i-k̓:i-w šiʔmi=ʔwan/
gray.squirrel=DET.SUBJ teeth=INSTR gnaw~ITER-PFV bow=DET.OBJ
‘the Squirrel gnawed it with his teeth, **the bow**.’

(488) ||=ʔwan|| DET.OBJECT on inanimate NP (H ms.)
čʰeʔ[:]et̪máywan šuhkʰečí:le
*čʰeʔ:et̪may**wan** šuhkʰeči:le*
/čʰeʔ:et̪may=wan šu-hkʰe-či:-le/

basket=DET.OBJ by.pulling-move-REFL-PL.IMP
'2 move **basket** closer to self!'

The two systems—agent/patient and subject/object—may combine, in which case the agent/patient case-marking morphemes offer strictly clause-level information (e.g., the animacy of the arguments of the verb and the degree of control and affectedness related to the animate arguments); the subject/object case-marking enclitics, however, offer both clause-level information (which argument is the subject) and broader discourse-level information as determiners indicating some sort of identifiability or discourse relevance relating to whether or not the NP has been previously mentioned or is otherwise an understood part of the discourse. Table 47 summarizes the split between agent/patient case-marking system and the subject/object case-marking enclitics.

The above table is somewhat of a simplification. I have few clear examples of inanimate arguments marked with the subject case-marking enclitics ||=ʔwam:u|| and ||=ʔyo:mu||. This could be the result of a prohibition on such marking, the effect of an incomplete database, or, most likely, it could be explained by the fact that inanimate arguments are much less likely to be doing anything. Remember that all these case-marking strategies are optional on common nouns, and it is often the case that an inanimate argument lacks any case marking whatsoever.

3.5. VOICE AND VALENCE-RELATED CONSTRUCTIONS

Southern Pomo uses affixation for valence-related constructions. Each of these affixes is discussed elswhere, and this section summarizes the system of valence-changing affixes with reference to the relevant sections in which more detailed examples can be found.

There are four productive valence-changing suffixes: ||-ka-|| CAUSATIVE, ||-č̓-|| ~ ||-čič̓-|| REFLEXIVE, ||-mhuč̓-|| RECIPROCAL, and ||-ya|| DEFOCUS (see §2.8.3.2.5 for a discussion of all four of these suffixes). To this list might be added ||-č-|| SEMELFACTIVE, which is used to derive transitive verbs to a limited extent (see §2.8.3.2.6).

The causative suffix is the only method (uncovered to date) by which causative constructions are formed in Southern Pomo. There is no peri-

Table 47. Summary of agent/patient and subject/object case-marking systems

Clause type →		Transitive verb		Intransitive verb			
Animacy →		Animate arguments	Inanimate arguments	Animate arguments			Inanimate arguments
Case-marking type ↓				volitional, not affected, e.g., 'go', 'swim'	not volitional, not affected, e.g., 'be tall', 'be strong'	affected, not volitional, e.g., 'be cold', 'be angry'	
Agent/patient		A-*yey* (agent) O-*yčon* (patient)	N/A	S-*yey* (AGENT)		S-*yčon* (PATIENT)	N/A
Subject/object	'the'	A=*ʔwam:u* (DET.SUBJECT) O=*ʔwan* (DET.OBJECT)		S=*ʔwam:u* (DET.SUBJECT)			
	'the aforementioned'	A=*ʔyo:mu* (DET.SUBJECT) O=*ʔyowan* (DET.OBJECT)		S=*ʔyo:mu* (DET.SUBJECT)			

phrastic construction (e.g., make/force/cause X to do . . .), and words which are inherently causative in English, such as 'teach' and 'feed', are simply derived by the causative suffix (e.g., *čuh:u-* 'eat' vs. *čuh:u-ka-* 'feed'). The causative is also used to express allowance ('let').

Oswalt notes that the Kashaya, Central Pomo, and Southern Pomo may use the causative suffix to indicate switch-reference in certain constructions (1976a, 26). In Kashaya such constructions are specifically reported for "certain verbs of volition or emotional attitude" (Oswalt 1983, 285–86). The following Kashaya examples of this phenomenon are adapted from Oswalt (1983, 285).

(489) Use of causative in Kashaya to indicate lack of shared subject across clauses

[without causative: both verbs have same subject]

ʔa	*mul*	*čʰiʔdimáʔ*	*da:qaʔ*
I	that	carry-in	want

'I want to carry that in'

[with causative *-qa-* (in bold): each verb has different subject]

ʔa	*mul*	*čʰiʔdimáčʰ**qa**:*	*da:qaʔ*
I	that	carry-in-CAUS	want

'I want someone else to carry that in'

I have no similar examples for Southern Pomo, but Oswalt's passing reference to such constructions as a part of Southern Pomo grammar warrant the assumption that such constructions are a part of the language.

3.6. TENSE/ASPECT/MODALITY AND EVIDENTIALS

All Southern Pomo main verbs (i.e., verbs which are not dependent verbs) are marked with a TAM suffix. Within the TAM suffixes, there is a strict division between realis and irrealis: tense and modality suffixes are all irrealis; aspectual suffixes are all realis. There are also several evidential suffixes which may occupy the same slot on the verb as the TAM suffixes. All of these affixes are discussed elsewhere, and this section provides a brief summary with reference to the relevant sections in which more detailed examples can be found.

Tense is restricted to two future suffixes, a general future and a future intentive, and is not a robust category within the language (see §2.8.3.3.1 for examples). Modal suffixes include a conditional, a hortative, two imperatives, and a prohibitive; there is also an optative enclitic (see §2.8.3.3.3 for a discussion with examples). Aspectual suffixes include a perfective (the citation form of verbs), an imperfective, and a habitual (see §2.8.3.3.2 for a list of these morphemes together with examples); there is also an iterative, which is indicated with reduplication (see §2.8.3.2.3), and a semelfactive, which may be used for punctual aspect, though it is more often used idiosyncratically to derive transitive verbs (see §2.8.3.2.6). Evidential suffixes included a quotative, an aural, an inferential, a factual/visual, and a performative. These suffixes are not obligatory and, when present, are often not found on more than one verb in a sentence (see §2.8.3.3.4 for a discussion of the evidentials together with examples).

The switch-reference suffixes, which are restricted to dependent verbs which do not take TAM suffixes, mirror the TAM system. Realis dependent verbs are marked for same or different subject and perfective or imperfective aspect (sequential versus simultaneous action); irrealis dependent verbs are marked differently than realis ones but do not include an aspectual distinction (see §2.8.3.3.7 and §3.10.2 for discussion of the dependent clause markers).

3.7. CONSTITUENT ORDER

The constituents of a clause in Southern Pomo are not rigidly ordered; however, there are common patterns, and it is possible to make some useful observations about the more common ordering possibilities. Word order and constituent order are not necessarily the same thing, and it should be borne in mind that examples showing words relative to other words do so as words which are also constituents (e.g., a NP made of up of a single word is still a NP). Before discussing the more robust patterns of constituent ordering, the following cautionary words bear repeating:

> The most insidious fad which has infiltrated linguistics during past decades is the idea that every language has an underlying structure involving a fixed order of phrasal constituents (often mislabeled 'word order'),

> and that the ordering of elements is one of the (or is the) most fundamental typological feature(s) of a language. (Dixon 2010a: 71)

This section is not meant to add to the "insidious fad" of word-order madness, and the following brief statements should be taken as broad generalizations that are true of much of the data for Southern Pomo. Throughout the remainder of the discussion, S = single argument of an intransitive verb, A = subject (or least patient-like argument) of a transitive verb, and O = object (or most patient-like argument) of a transitive verb.

Southern Pomo is a predicate-final language. It is rare for a clause to contain more than one overt argument. Indeed, in lengthy narratives, it is possible to find two or more clauses back to back without any core arguments overtly expressed with NPs. When a core argument of a verb is overtly expressed within a clause, it generally precedes the verb, whether it is the single argument of an intransitive verb or the A or O argument of a transitive verb.[3] When a transitive verb has two arguments overtly present as full NPs, one possible ordering of these constituents is AOV. Because Southern Pomo is a case-marking language, there is no need for fixed ordering of overt arguments of transitive verbs, and the order OAV is also attested, as is the order VAO. However, there is reason to believe that orderings other than AOV are not merely free-ranging variants with no ordering privileged over another. Examples of these four constituent orders follow: SV, AOV, OAV, and VAO.

(490) Example of SV constituent ordering
ha:mini(:)ba kʰaʔbéyčon sí:ma mí:ṭiw (H VIII: 8)
ha:miniba [kʰaʔbeyčon]$_{S}$ si:ma mi:ṭiw

/ha:mini-ba	kʰaʔbe=yčon	si:ma	mi:ṭi-w/
and.then-S.SEQ	rock=PAT	sleep	lie-PFV

'Having done so, Rock [Man] went to sleep.'

(491) Example of AOV constituent ordering
miy[:]á[ṭʰ]kʰan wéč:é(:)yčon bé:new míṭ:iw (H I: 6)
[miy:aṭʰkʰan]$_{A}$ [weč:eyčon]$_{O}$ be:new miṭ:iw

/miy:a-ṭʰkʰan-Ø	weč:e=yčon	be-:ne-w	miṭ:i-Ø-w/

3-spouse-AGT barn.owl=PAT with.arms-grasp-PFV lie-DIFFUSE-PFV
'his wife was lying hugging Screech-owl'

In example (492) the ordering of the NPs is different, but the agent/patient case-marking enclitics remove any potential ambiguity.

(492) Example of OAV constituent ordering
ha:mini:li kʰáʔbekʰáč:on ċa:yíyey [ʔ]uhṭéhṭew, (H VI: 3)
ha:mini:li [kʰaʔbekʰač:on]$_O$ [ċa:yiyey]$_A$ ʔuhṭehṭew
/ha:mini-:li kʰaʔbekʰač=čon ċa:yi=yey ʔuhṭe-hṭe-w/
and.then-D.SEQ raptor.species=PAT scrubjay=AGT tell~tell-PFV
'They brought in the fish. They having done so, the Jay told Fish Hawk'

There are good, discourse-based reasons to suspect that the OAV ordering in (492) is not in free variation with the AOV ordering of the previous example. In (492) the narrative is about 'Fish Hawk', and 'Jay' is not actually a character of any importance beyond this cameo appearance. The OAV ordering in (492) is therefore being used to focus on the protagonist of the tale. In (493) the order of the NPs relative to one another is AO, but they are given after the verb.

(493) Example of VAO constituent ordering
k̓ohṭokʰṭowá:ni [ʔ]íhčok̓ ču:máṭyey kʰaʔbéyčon. (H VIII: 8)
k̓ohṭokʰṭowa:ni ʔihčok̓ [ču:maṭyey]$_A$ [kʰaʔbeyčon]$_O$
/k̓ohṭokʰṭo=wa:ni ʔihčok̓-Ø ču:maṭ=yey kʰaʔbe=yčon/
base.of.neck=LOC shoot-PFV gray.squirrel=AGT rock=PAT
'[He] shot him in the soft spot between the collarbones, [Gray] Squirrel (did it) to Rock [Man].'

In (493) Halpern's free translation suggests that the addition of the A and O arguments was an afterthought on the part of the speaker in order to remove potential confusion about who shot whom, and this seems right. The discourse context for example (493) is a multi-clause sentence in which '[Gray] Squirrel', the protagonist of the narrative, is not mentioned for several clauses leading up to his shooting of 'Rock [Man]', a serious event about which the speaker did not want to risk confusion for her listeners. If

Table 48. Bound negative pronouns and negative response particle

‖-t̪ʰ-‖	‖-t̪ʰe-‖	‖-t̪ʰen-‖	‖-t̪ʰu-‖	‖=t̪ʰoṭ‖~‖=t̪ʰoṭ‖	‖t̪ʰe:‖
NEGATIVE (IRREALIS?)	NEGATIVE (REALIS?)	NEGATIVE IMPERFECTIVE	PROHIBITIVE (SINGULAR)	NEGATIVE (PERFECTIVE?)	NEGATIVE RESPONSE PARTICLE

the foregoing examples are accepted, Southern Pomo does have a default constituent order for NPs that are also core arguments: SV in intransitive clauses and AOV intransitive clauses. Deviations from AOV order might have functional motivations and might be used for topic continuity, focus, or to disambiguate a clause that would otherwise have surfaced without overt arguments.

3.8. NEGATION

Negation is handled in two ways: (1) through bound morphemes (and one free particle), all of which begin with the phoneme /t̪ʰ/; and (2) by means of lexical words with an inherently negative meaning. These types are discussed in the next two sections.

3.8.1. Bound Negative Morphemes (and Response Particle)

This type of negation is by far the most prevalent in the extant records. The negative suffixes, enclitics, and negative response particle have already been discussed, and examples of each negative morpheme can be found in the relevant section (§2.8.3.3.5). Table 48 lists the recorded bound negative morphemes and the negative response particle.[4]

Examples of each of the bound negative morphemes are repeated below.

(494) Example of ‖-t̪ʰ-‖-t̪ʰ-NEGATIVE

čáhnu k̓óʔdi čánhodent̪[ʰ]í:baʔwáʔa (H ms.)

čahnu k̓oʔdi čanhodent̪ʰi:baʔwaʔa

/čahnu k̓oʔdi čanho-den-t̪ʰ-i:ba=ʔwa=ʔa/

speech good speak-DIR-NEG-COND=COP.EVID=1SG.AGT

'I can't talk well.'

(495) Example of ||-t̯^{h}e-|| NEGATIVE
hudʔat̯^{h}é( )[ʔ]t̯o mí:t̯o. (H I: 25)
*hudʔa**t̯^{h}e**ʔt̯o mi:t̯o*
/hudʔa-t̯^{h}e=ʔt̯o mi:t̯o/
want-NEG=1SG.PAT 2SG.PAT
'I don't want you.'

(496) Example of ||-t̯^{h}en-|| NEGATIVE.IMPERFECTIVE
sí:ma mí:ṭit̯^{h}enṭ̓óʔt̯o dúw:e (H VIII: 2)
*si:ma mi:ṭi**t̯^{h}en**ṭ̓oʔt̯o duw:e*
/si:ma mi:ṭi-t̯^{h}en=ṭ̓o=ʔt̯o duw:e/
sleep lie-NEG.IPFV=CONTRAST=1SG.PAT night
'I can't sleep (at) night.'

(497) Example of ||-t̯^{h}u-|| PROHIBITIVE in command to one person
mi:mák^{h}t̯[^{h}]u mádan (H ms.)
*mi:mak^{h}**t̯^{h}u** madan*
/mi:ma-k^{h}-t̯^{h}u mad-an/
cry-CAUS-PROH 3SG.F-PAT
'don't make her cry'

(498) Example of ||-t̯^{h}u-|| PROHIBITIVE in command to more than one person
bé:nemhút̯[^{h}]le (H ms)
*be:nemhu**t̯^{h}**le*
/be-:ne-mhu-t̯^{h}-le/
with.arms-grasp-RECIP-PROH-PL.IMP
'2 don't hug e[ach] o[ther]!'

(499) ||=t̯^{h}oṭ̓|| ~ ||=t̯^{h}ot̯̓|| NEGATIVE (PERFECTIVE?) negating verb
ʔa:ʔa k^{h}at̯:aduk^{h}:et̯^{h}oṭ̓ (W: OF)
/ʔa:ʔa k^{h}at̯:-adu-k^{h}:e=t̯^{h}oṭ̓/
1SG.AGT run-DIR-FUT=NEG
'I didn't run away'

(500) ||=t̪ʰot̪̓|| ~ ||=t̪ʰot̪̓|| NEGATIVE (PERFECTIVE?) negating predicate nominal
[ʔ]á:čaċyey( )t̪[ʰ]ot̪̓wa (H ms.)
*ʔa:čaċyey**t̪ʰot̪̓**wa*
/ʔa:-ča-ċ-yey=t̪ʰot̪̓=wa/
1-mother's.father-GS-PL.AGT=NEG=COP.EVID
'they are not my mo[ther's] fa[ther]s.'

3.8.2. Words with Inherently Negative Meaning

This section highlights three verbs which have inherently negative meaning.

||ʔačʰ:o-|| ~ ||ʔahčʰo-|| NEGATIVE EXISTENTIAL

This verb stem literally means 'there is none' when suffixed with the perfective.[5]

(501) Example of ||*ʔačʰ:o-*|| NEGATIVE.EXISTENTIAL with perfective suffix
kʰaʔbeʔkʰe ʔačʰ:ow (W: OF)
/kʰaʔbe=ʔkʰe ʔačʰ:o-w/
rock=1SG.POSS NEG.EXISTENTIAL-PFV
'I have no money'

(502) Example of ||*ʔačʰ:o-*|| NEGATIVE.EXISTENTIAL with perfective suffix
há:miní:li miy[:]a[t̪ʰ]kʰan ʔačʰ:ow (H I: 3)
ha:mini:li miy:at̪ʰkʰan ʔačʰ:ow
/ha:mini-:li miy:a-t̪ʰkʰan-Ø ʔačʰ:o-w/
and.then-D.SEQ 3-spouse-AGT NEG.EXISTENTIAL-PFV
'Then his wife was not there'

When suffixed with ||-č-ka-|| SEMELFACTIVE-CAUSATIVE, it becomes a transitive verb with the meaning 'to wear out' (lit: 'to cause to become nonexistent'), and it surfaces with the laryngeal increment /h/ to the left of the root consonant, as shown in (503).

(503) Example of ||ʔahčʰo-č-ka-|| NEG.EXISTENTIAL-SEM-CAUS-
<tada*pu ?ahc^ho*kaw.> (O D: ED)
t̪ada:pu ʔahčʰo:kaw

/t̪ada:pu ʔahčʰo-:-ka-w/
clothes NEG.EXISTENTIAL-SEM-CAUS-PFV
'(He) wore out his clothes.'

When suffixed with ||-čič̓-|| REFLEXIVE~INCEPTIVE, it means 'to die' (lit: 'oneself to come not to exist'), and it surfaces with the laryngeal increment /h/ to the left of the root consonant, as shown in (504).

(504) Example of ||ʔahčo-čič̓-|| NEG.EXISTENTIAL-REFLEXIVE
<ʔahcʌhociy> (O D: ED)
ʔahčʰočiy
/ʔahčʰo-čiy-Ø/
NEG.EXISTENTIAL-REFL-PFV
'to die'

||yaʔčʰo-|| 'to not like, not want'

This word violates the expected pattern of laryngeal augments, and it seems likely that it is (or was) a compound with ||ʔačʰ:o-|| NEG.EXISTENTIAL as its second component. However, there is no obvious source for the first syllable, and it is best treated as a monomorphemic word synchronically. Examples follow.

(505) Example of ||yaʔčʰo-|| 'to not like, not want'
<yaʔcʌhowa ʔto mi*to.> (O D: EA)
yaʔčʰowaʔt̪o mi:t̪o
/yaʔčʰo-wa=ʔt̪o mi:t̪o/
not.want-EVID=1SG.PAT 2SG.PAT
'I don't like you.'

(506) Example of ||yaʔčʰo-|| 'to not like, not want'
<ʔat*o yaʔcʌhowa.> (O D: EA)
ʔat̪:o yaʔčʰowa
/ʔat̪:o yaʔčʰo-wa/
1SG.PAT not.want-EVID
'I don't want it (dislike).'

||laʔbač-|| 'be unable to do'

This word is used for inability. The conditional suffix ||-V:ba|| may be used to show ability, and this suffix, when negated, is translated as 'can ~ could not/will ~ would not'. Whether this word is equivalent to a negated verb with the conditional is unknown. Examples follow.

(507) Example of ||laʔbač-|| 'to be unable'
<beh$e bo*?odenti ?to la?bay> (O D: ED)
behše bo:ʔodenti̯ʔt̯o laʔbay
/behše bo:ʔo-den-t̯i̯=ʔt̯o laʔbay-Ø/
deer hunt-DIR-FUT.INTENT=1SG.PAT be.unable-PFV
'I don't know how to hunt deer'

(508) Example of ||laʔbač-|| 'to be unable'
čáhnu láʔbaywáʔt̯o (H ms.)
čahnu laʔbaywaʔt̯o
/čahnu laʔbay=wa=ʔt̯o/
speech be.unable=COP.EVID=1SG.PAT
'I don't know how to talk'

3.9. QUESTIONS

All questions are formed by means of the interrogative morpheme ||ka|| ~ ||=ʔka||. This morpheme is used for all types of questions, including polar questions, and is also attached to the interrogative pronoun *čaʔ:a(t̯o)* 'who(m)' and all other question words (*cet̯̓* 'how', *ba:k̓o* 'what', *but̯:e* 'when', *he:ʔey* 'where', *he:met̯̓* 'why', and *met̯̓bu* 'how many') when they are used as interrogatives. Question words come first within the interrogative clause, and it is to them that the second position clitic ||ka|| ~ ||=ʔka|| attaches. Examples are given in (509)–(512).

(509) Interrogative ||ka|| ~ ||=ʔka|| with *čaʔ:a* 'who'
čaʔ[:]áʔkam:u [ʔ]át̯ʰ:a [ʔ]ahsóduy (H ms.)
čaʔ:aʔkam:u ʔat̯ʰ:a ʔahsoduy
/čaʔ:a=ʔka=m:u ʔat̯ʰ:a ʔahso-duy-Ø/

who=INTER=3SG gravel throw.many.small-DIR-PFV
'who threw the gravel[?]'

(510) Interrogative ||ka|| ~ ||=ʔka|| with *čaʔ:at̯o* 'whom'
čaʔ:at̯oʔkaʔma dihkaw (Halpern 1984: 7)
čaʔ:at̯oʔkaʔma dihkaw
/čaʔ:a-t̯o=ʔka=ʔma dihka-w/
who-PAT=INTER=2SG.AGT give.one-PFV
'to whom did you give it?'

(511) Interrogative ||ka|| ~ ||=ʔka|| with *he:ʔey* 'where'
he:ʔeykaʔma ho:li:mu (W: OF)
/he:ʔey=ka=ʔma ho:li-:mu/
where=INTER=2SG.AGT leave-SECOND.PERSON
'Where are you going?'

(512) Interrogative ||ka|| ~ ||=ʔka|| with *cet̯'* 'how'
*cet̯' kaʔ*ma (W: OF)
/cet̯' ka=ʔma/
how INTER=2SG.AGT
'How are you?' (used for 'hello')

When there is no question word present, ||ka|| ~ ||=ʔka|| attaches to the first large constituent and may be followed by pronominal enclitics, as seen in (513)–(515).

(513) Interrogative ||ka|| ~ ||=ʔka|| attached to verb
[ʔ]ahnat̯í:baʔkáʔma (H ms.)
ʔahnat̯i:baʔkaʔma
/ʔa-hnat̯-i:ba=ʔka=ʔma/
with.leg-try-COND=INTER=2SG.AGT
'are you going to try it w[ith] heel?'

(514) Interrogative ||ka|| ~ ||=ʔka|| attached to adverb
ma:liʔkaʔya das:ékʰ:e (H V: 11)
ma:liʔkaʔya das:ekʰ:e

/ma:li=ʔka=ʔya das:e-k^{h}:e/
here=INTER=1PL.AGT wash-FUT
'shall we wash it here?'

(515) Interrogative ||ka|| ~ ||=ʔka|| attached to nominal
midʔikí:k^{h}eʔka[ ]má:mu (H ms.)
midʔiki:k^{h}eʔka ma:mu
/mi-dʔi-ki-:k^{h}e=ʔka ma:mu/
2-older.sister-GS-POSS=INTER DEM
'is this your sister's?'

There is a possibility that ||ka|| ~ ||=ʔka|| might be restricted to questions about things that are only possible (irrealis) or unknown. Examples (516) and (517) both begin with the question word *but̪:e* 'when'; however, the second example shows this word followed by the auxiliary ||yo|| ~ ||=ʔyo|| without the interrogative clitic. The translation suggests the speaker knew the addressee had awoken at some point (a logical situation). Perhaps questions about details of known events are not formed with ||ka|| ~ ||=ʔka||. The data are too few at this time to know whether the following pair reflect a robust pattern, one that would easily be missed by most elicitation, or simply a case of variation among speakers.

(516) Interrogative ||ka|| ~ ||=ʔka|| attached to *but̪:e* 'when'
but̪:e kaʔma čoh:onhk^{h}e (W: OF)
||but̪:e ka=ʔa:ma čoh:oN-k^{h}:e||
/but̪:e ka=ʔma čoh:onh-k^{h}e/
when INTER=2SG.AGT marry-FUT
'when will you get married?'

(517) *but̪:e* 'when' as question without interrogative ||ka|| ~ ||=ʔka||
bút̪:eʔyómt̪o [ʔ]ahčáči[y] (H ms.)
but̪:eʔyomt̪o ʔahčačiy
/but̪:e=ʔyo=mt̪o ʔahčačiy-Ø/
when=AUX=2SG.PAT awake-PFV
'when did you wake up[?]'

There are two response particles which may be used in reply to a yes/no question: *hiy:o* 'yes' (sometimes recorded as *hiy:ow*); or *t̪ʰe:* 'no'. Examples of recorded exchanges with the response particles are given in (518) and (519).

(518) Example of *hiy:o* positive response particle

Question: mabʔaċé:k̓oʔkáʔma (H ms.)
mabʔaċe:k̓oʔkaʔma
/ma-bʔa-ċ-e:=k̓o=ʔka=ʔma/
3C-father's.father-GS-OBL=COM=INTER=2SG.AGT
'have you a gr.fa.[?]'

Answer: híy:o mábʔaċé:k̓oʔwáʔa (H ms.)
hiy:o mabʔaċe:k̓oʔwaʔa
/hiy:o ma-bʔa-ċ-e:=k̓o=ʔwa=ʔa/
yes 3C-father's.father-GS-OBL=COM=COP.EVID=1SG.AGT
'yes I have a gr.fa.'

(519) Example of *t̪ʰe:* negative response particle (W: OF)

Elsie Allen: *pʰal:aʔčaykaʔma*
/pʰal:aʔčay=ka=ʔma/
white.person=INTER=2SG.AGT
'Are you a white person?'

Olive Fulwider: *t̪ʰe: ʔahčahčaywaʔa*
/t̪ʰe: ʔahčahčay=wa=ʔa/
no Indian=COP.EVID=1SG.AGT
'No, I'm Indian.'

3.10. CLAUSE COMBINATIONS

There are four types of clause combining to be found in Southern Pomo: (1) complement clauses, which are a very small component of the grammar; (2) multi-clause sentences with one main verb and one or more dependent verbs marked with switch-reference suffixes, which are very common in narrative texts; (3) nominalized clauses which behave as arguments of a main verb; and (4) clause coordination, which is generally marked by means of the switch-reference suffixes, and what would be translated as coordinate clauses in English are therefore most often handled with dependent verbs marked with switch-reference suffixes in relation to a main verb with TAM marking—there is no known word for 'and' in Southern Pomo—however, there is one true conjunction (actually a disjunction), *he:* 'or', which may be used to conjoin two main verbs. Each of these types of clause combining is discussed in following sections.

3.10.1. Complement Clauses

Thomas Payne (citing Noonan 1985) notes that one definition of "a prototypical complement clause is a clause that functions as an argument (subject or object) of some other clause" (Payne 1997: 313). If this definition is accepted (depending upon the working definition of clause versus nominalized clause), then it could be argued that Southern Pomo nominalized clause constructions discussed later (§3.10.3) are a type of complement clause strategy. Such an analysis is not accepted here, however, and a narrower definition must be sought. Dixon states that "all languages have a set of 'complement-taking verbs'" and lists 'see', 'think', 'know', and 'like' as typical examples of such verbs; he also notes that "there are languages whose grammars have no instance of a clause filling a core argument slot in a higher clause," languages which use what he terms "complementation strategies," such as serial verb constructions, relative clause constructions, clause nominalization, and "complementation strategies involving linked clauses," such as juxtaposition of clauses, clause chaining, and "purposive linking" (Dixon 2010b: 405). Whatever the merits of the various proposed categories of complementation and complementation strategies, this work restricts the use of the term to constructions involving a handful of verbs of utterance or perception, such as 'say', 'want', and 'feel', which fit into the category of complement-taking verbs listed by Dixon (hereafter abbreviated as CTVs).

Many of the epistemic functions handled by verbs of utterance or perception in English (and other languages) are rendered in Southern Pomo by means of the evidential suffixes or other bound morphology (e.g., the optative enclitic ||=ʔšen||). Thus the number of CTVs of the sort considered in this section is smaller in the language than might otherwise be the case.

Southern Pomo CTVs may be in a multi-clause sentence without any morphological indication of subordination, dependency, nominalization, or any other type of morphological marking that might be construed as overtly indicating clause combining. The only structural hint that CTVs take the adjacent clause as an argument is constituent order: Southern Pomo is an AOV language, and multi-clause sentences with CTVs typically have the complement clause precede the CTV, in OV order, as shown in examples that follow (where the complement clauses are set off by brackets and labeled with a subscript C).

(520) Example of CTV *hiʔduʔč̓edu-* 'to know' with complement clause
čáhnu čanhódu híʔduʔč̓eduʔwám:u (H ms.)
[čahnu čanhodu]$_{C}$ hiʔduʔč̓eduʔwam:u
/čahnu čanho-du hiʔduʔč̓edu=ʔwa=m:u/
speech speak-IPFV know=COP.EVID=3SG
'he knows how to talk'

An example of the CTV *hudʔa-* 'to want, like' is given in (521).

(521) Example of CTV *hudʔa-* 'to want, like' with complement clause
[ʔ]a:mayá:k̓o mí:ṭiw hudʔá:t̪ʰot̪̓ ṭáʔt̪o (H ms.)
[ʔa:maya:k̓o mi:ṭiw]$_{C}$ hudʔa:t̪ʰot̪̓ ṭaʔt̪o
/ʔa:maya=:k̓o mi:ṭi-w hudʔa:=t̪ʰot̪̓ ṭa=ʔt̪o/[6]
2PL.AGT=COM lie-PFV want=NEG EMPH=1SG.PAT
'I don't like to sleep w. ye'

The CTV *nih:i- ~ nihi- ~ hnih- ~ hni- ~ ni-* 'say' follows the same pattern as the CTVs seen in (520) and (521); however, it shows the peculiarity that when the complement clause is about the speaker, the CTV takes the reflexive suffix ||-č̓-||, as shown in (522).

(522) Example of CTV *nih:i- ~ nihi- ~ hnih- ~ hni- ~ ni-* 'say' with reflexive suffix
<?it∧h*in ho*liw hnic'a.> (O D)
[ʔit̪ʰ:in ho:liw]$_{C}$ hnič̓a

/ʔit̯^{h}:in   ho:li-w   hni-č̓-a/

early   leave-PFV   say-REFL-EVID

'He said he had gone there.'

Unlike the CTVs discussed thus far, the verb *labʔay-* 'to be unable' does have overt morphology on the complement clause. The complement clause with this verb must be inflected with the future intentive suffix *-t̯i-*, as shown in (523).

(523) Example of complement clause with *laʔbay-* 'to be unable'

<beh$e bo*?odenti ?to la?bay>   (O D: ED)

[behše bo:ʔodent̯i]$_{C}$ ʔt̯o laʔbay

/behše   bo:ʔo-den-t̯i=ʔt̯o   laʔbay-Ø/

deer   hunt-DIR-FUT.INTENT=1SG.PAT   be.unable-PFV

'I don't know how to hunt deer'

The preceding example is similar to sentences in which the future intentive has a purposive meaning ('in order to'), as seen in (524).

(524) Multi-clause sentence with purposive verb suffixed with future intentive

ka:wi ʔa: čuh:ukat̯i ho:li:na   (W: OF)

/ka:wi   ʔa: čuh:u-ka-t̯i   ho:li-:na/

child   1SG.AGT   eat-CAUS-FUT.INTENT   leave-FIRST.PERSON

'I'm going to feed my baby'

Though these two examples with the future intentive suffix are superficially similar, they are actually quite different. The use of the future intentive with *laʔbay-* 'to be unable' is automatic; its selection is not based on semantics. The future intentive in the preceding expresses real purpose and near future semantics; it is not merely an automatic feature required by a CTV.

It is possible that the use of the future intentive suffix stretches across a cline: on one end, CTVs (such as *laʔbay-* 'to be unable') demand its presence on complement clauses; on the other end, it is used purely for its semantic contributions as a near future and purposive suffix with no need to be combined with another clause.

Table 49. Switch-reference suffixes

	Same subject	Different subject
Sequential	||-ba||	||-:li||
Simultaneous	||-Vn||	||-en||
Irrealis	||-pʰi||	||-pʰla||

Table 50. Additional morphemes treated as switch-reference markers by Oswalt

	Same subject	Different subject
Oppositive	||=ʔnat̪i||	||-et̪i||
Inferential	||-mna||	||-ben||

3.10.2. Switch-Reference

Southern Pomo has a rich system of switch-reference suffixes. These suffixes, like their cognates in the neighboring sister languages of Kashaya and Central Pomo, mark verbs as being dependent, indicate the temporal ordering of dependent verbs in relation to a main verb, and whether the main verb is realis or irrealis. The Southern Pomo affixes follow the same pattern reported for Kashaya, in which all dependent verbs are marked in relation to the main verb, a system which differs from the switch-reference systems reported for other parts of the world, especially New Guinea (Roberts 1988). Unlike the cognate morphemes in Central Pomo, where the closeness of the relationship between events appears to be the sole consideration, the Southern Pomo suffixes indicate whether the subject of the dependent verb is coreferential or disreferential with that of the main verb. Table 49 gives the six most common switch-reference suffixes.

Oswalt also reports four additional switch-reference morphemes, which are given in table 50.

These are not considered further as there are very few examples of ||-mna||, ||=ʔnat̪i|| is a clitic rather than an affix and not clearly part of the larger system, and the different subject morphemes in table 50 are rare-to-nonexistent in the corpus. The remainder of this section focuses on the well-attested switch-reference suffixes laid out in table 49.

Table 51. Southern Pomo switch-reference suffixes and cognates

	Realis				**Irrealis**	
	Sequential		Simultaneous			
	Same	Different	Same	Different	Same	Different
Kashaya	*-ba*	*-. . . li*	*-in ~ -an ~ -on ~ -un ~ -n*	*-em ~ -wem*	$-p^{h}i \sim -\check{c}^{h}i \sim -hi$	$-p^{h}ila \sim -\check{c}^{h}ila \sim -hila$
Central Pomo	*-ba*	*=li*	*-in*	*=da*	*-hi*	*=hla*
Southern Pomo	*-ba*	*-:li ~ -:ni*	*-in ~ -an ~ -on ~ -un ~ -n*	*-en ~ -wen*	$-p^{h}i$	$-p^{h}la$

Switch-reference systems have been described for three of the Pomoan languages: Kashaya, Central Pomo, and Southern Pomo. The switch-reference morphemes of Southern Pomo are remarkably similar in form to those of both Kashaya and Central Pomo. Table 51 gives the Southern Pomo switch-reference from table 49 together with those for Kashaya and Central Pomo.

As shown in table 51, the Southern Pomo forms are clearly cognate with those of both Central Pomo and Kashaya.[7] Oswalt (1983) analyzes the Kashaya system as one of switch-reference marking with dependent verbs being marked in relation to a main verb. He terms this system as a sentential focal reference one: dependent verbs in Kashaya are marked with switch-reference suffixes which indicate whether each dependent verb shares its subject with one main verb—dependent verbs are not marked in relation to one another.[8] Mithun, basing her analysis on data from spontaneous speech, finds that the primary function of the dependent clause markers of Central Pomo listed in the preceding table, which are cognate with the Kashaya switch-reference markers, is one of clause combining (Mithun 1993: 119). Also, she concludes that these markers in Central Pomo, unlike their Kashaya cognates, do not track subjects or agents; rather, they are primarily used to "specify relations between actions, states, or events, not participants . . . [and] mark same versus different eventhood, rather than same versus different subject" (1993: 134).

Oswalt (1978) provides the only published description of the Southern Pomo switch-reference system. He analyzes the Southern Pomo system of dependent markers as consisting of "pairs of subordinating verbal suffixes ... indicat[ing] that the agent [=subject] of the subordinate verb is the same as that of the superordinate ... [or] different" (Oswalt 1978: 12). This analysis appears similar to his analysis of Kashaya (minus any reference to sentential focus). However, unlike his detailed and thoroughly explained analysis of the Kashaya system, Oswalt's analysis of switch-reference in Southern Pomo does not include significant amounts of detail and examples.

Careful investigation shows that the Southern Pomo switch-reference suffixes do function as described by Oswalt. Dependent verbs are marked with these suffixes in relation to a single main verb, just as Oswalt describes for the sentential focus system of Kashaya. The main verb is most often final in the sentence, but it need not be in that position. Dependent verbs are therefore not marked as having a subject the same as or different from that of a following dependent verb.

The following sections flesh out the switch-reference system. The six suffixes from table 49 are introduced as pairs, and the basics of the system are laid out. Each pair of switch-reference suffixes is introduced together with examples. It should be noted at the outset, however, that the 'main verb', though usually represented by a sentence-final verb in the data, is not always final. The main verb carries TAM marking, whereas the dependent verbs marked with switch-reference suffixes do not carry such marking, but are marked as dependent upon the main verb for TAM information.[9]

3.10.2.1. Same Subject and Different Subject Sequential Suffixes

||-ba|| -ba SAME SUBJECT SEQUENTIAL (S.SEQ)

||-:li|| -:li ~ -:ni DIFFERENT SUBJECT SEQUENTIAL (D.SEQ)

These suffixes attach after all other suffixes on dependent verbs and mark them as having been completed prior to the action of the main verb. Examples of both are given in (525)–(526) (where verbs marked with *-ba* and *-:li* and their glossing and translation are in bold).

(525) Example of ||-ba|| (H VI: 3)
šin:ák^{h}le héʔ[:]e ***p[^{h}]aʔč̓iba*** *ma:ṭíkin,*
šin:ak^{h}le heʔ:e ***p^{h}aʔč̓iba*** *ma:ṭikin*
||šin:a-k^{h}le heʔ:e p^{h}a-ʔč̓i-ba maH-ṭi-ki-n||

/šin:a-kʰle	heʔ:e	pʰa-ʔc̓i-ba	ma-:ṭ̓i-ki-n/
head-crown	hair	**with.hand-grab-s.SEQ**	3C-younger.sibling-GS-PAT

ká:liŋhkʰay huʔ[:]ú:čin nih[:]iw.

ka:linhkʰay huʔ:u:čin nih:iw

||ka:li=li=kʰač huʔ:uy-t̪-č-Vn nih:i-w||[10]

/ka:li-nhkʰay	huʔ:u-:-č-in	nih:i-w/
up-ward	face-DENOM-SEM-SG.IMP	say-PFV

‘**Having grabbed** the hair on top of his head, he said to his y[ounger] bro[ther], ‘Look upwards.”

(526) Example of ||-ba|| and ||-:li|| (H VI: 12)

hám:un hniba duw:é:li

*ham:un **hniba duw:e:li***

||ham:u-n nih:i-ba duw:eč-:li||[11]

/ham:u-n	hni-ba	duw:e-:li/
3SG-PAT	**say-S.SEQ**	**night.falls-D.SEQ**

č̓á:t̪on mis:íbo mí:ṭiw.

č̓a:t̪on mis:ibo mi:ṭiw

||č̓a:ʔa=t̪on mis:ibo mi:ṭi-w||

/č̓a:=t̪on	mis:ibo	mi:ṭi-w/
one=LOC	three	lie-PFV

‘**Having said** this, **when night came on**, (the) three lay down in one (place).’

3.10.2.2. Same Subject and Different Subject Simultaneous Suffixes

||-Vn|| -in ~ -an ~ -on ~ -un ~ -n SAME SUBJECT SIMULTANEOUS (S.SIM)

and ||-en|| -en ~ -wen DIFFERENT SUBJECT SIMULTANEOUS (D.SIM)

These suffixes attach to dependent verbs after all other suffixes and indicate that the action occurred simultaneously with that of the main verb. Examples of each are given in (527)–(528b) (where ||-Vn|| and ||-en|| and their glossing and translation are in bold).

(527) Example of ||-Vn|| S.SIM (H VI: 17)

ča:dédun hwád:u

***ča:dedun** hwad:u*

||ča:de-ad-Vn hu:w-aded-u||
/ča:de-d-un hw-ad:-u/
look-DIR-S.SIM go-DIR-PFV
'He walked around **looking around**.'

(528a) Example of ||-en|| D.SIM (H VIII: 4)
má:mu k^{h}aʔbéyey wí:miŋhk^{h}áyʔden
ma:mu k^{h}aʔbeyey ***wi:minhk^{h}ayʔden***
||ma:mu k^{h}aʔbe=yey wi:mi=li=k^{h}ač-wad-en||
/ma:mu k^{h}aʔbe=yey wi:mi-nhk^{h}ay-ʔd-en/
DEM rock=AGT **there-ward-HAB-D.SIM**[12]
'**While** this Rock **was facing towards there**,'

(528b) čú:maṭwám:u hoʔ[:]ówi biʔk̓ik̓:iw šiʔmiʔwan
ču:maṭwam:u hoʔ:owi biʔk̓ik̓:iw šiʔmiʔwan
||ču:maṭ=ʔwam:u hoʔ:o=wi biʔk̓i-R-w šiʔmi=ʔwan||
/ču:maṭ=wam:u hoʔ:o=wi biʔk̓i-k̓:i-w šiʔmi=ʔwan/
gray.squirrel=DET.SUBJ teeth=INSTR Gnaw ~ ITER-PFV bow=DET.OBJ
'the Squirrel gnawed it with his teeth, the bow.'

3.10.2.3. Same Subject and Different Subject Irrealis Suffixes

||-p^{h}i|| -p^{h}i SAME SUBJECT IRREALIS (S.IRR)

||-p^{h}la|| -p^{h}la DIFFERENT SUBJECT IRREALIS (D.IRR)

These suffixes indicate that the event expressed by the dependent clause would occur prior to an irrealis main clause, which may be suffixed with a future, an imperative, or the conditional. Examples of each these switch-reference suffixes are given in (529) and (530) (where ||-p^{h}i|| and ||-p^{h}la|| and their glossing and translation are in bold).

(529) Example of ||-p^{h}i|| S.IRR (H II: 1)
k^{h}aʔ[:]á:le[ʔ]waʔ( )máya kú:lun hó:lip[^{h}]i
k^{h}aʔ:a:leʔwaʔmaya ku:lun ***ho:lip^{h}i***
||k^{h}aʔ:a:le=ʔwa=ʔa:maya ku:lu-n ho:li-p^{h}i||
/k^{h}aʔ:a:le=ʔwa=ʔmaya ku:lu-n ho:li-p^{h}i/
tomorrow=COP.EVID=2PL.AGT outside-GOAL **leave-S.IRR**

baʔ[:]á:yey híʔbu [ʔ]ehčʰékʰ[:]e
baʔ:a:yey hiʔbu ʔehčʰekʰ:e
||baʔ:ay=yey hiʔbu ʔehčʰe-kʰ:e||[13]
/baʔ:a:=yey   hiʔbu   ʔehčʰe-kʰ:e
woman=AGT   potato   dig-FUT
'Tomorrow, you women **will go** to the outside and dig wild potatoes'

(530) Example of ||-pʰla|| D.IRR   (H V: 26)
mič:áċyey mehšekʰ[:]éʔwa
mič:aċyey mehšekʰ:eʔwa
||miH-ča-ċ-yey mi-hše-kʰ:e=ʔwa||
/mi-č:a-ċ-yey   me-hše-kʰ:e=ʔwa/
2-mother's.father-GS-PL.AGT   with.nose-smell-FUT=COP.EVID

[ʔ]á:maya híʔṭa das:ép[ʰ]la.
ʔa:maya hiʔṭa ***das:epʰla***
||ʔa:maya hiʔṭa da-s:e-pʰla||
/ʔa:maya   hiʔṭa   da-s:e-pʰla/
2PL.AGT   nearby   **with.palm-wash-D.IRR**
'Your grandfathers will smell (it) **if** you **wash** them nearby.'

3.10.2.4. *The ha:mini- Construction*

In addition to the switch-reference suffixes on dependent verbs, Southern Pomo contains a pro-verb, *ha:mini-* (and its dialectal variant *ni-*), which links sentences together. This pro-verb can be roughly translated as 'and then' or 'and it came to pass'. Switch-reference markers suffixed to *ha:mini-* relate anaphorically to the last clause of the previous sentence and cataphorically to the first clause of the following sentence. Examples (531) and (532) show two sentences linked by the pro-verb *ha:mini-* with the S.SEQ suffix ||-ba||.

(531) Example of *ha:mini*-with ||-ba|| S.SEQ   (H V: 3)
mú:kʰel( )háywan mú:kʰen.
mu:kʰelhaywan mu:kʰen
||mu-:kʰeN-ʔah:ay=ʔwan mu-:kʰeN-Ø||

/mu-:kʰel-hay=wan	mu-:kʰen-Ø/
object.thru.air-sev.slide-wood=DET.OBJ	object.thru.air-sev.slide-PFV

ha:miní(:)ba [ʔ]íhmin.
***ha:miniba** ʔihmin*
||ha:mini-ba ʔihmiN-Ø||

/ha:mini-ba	ʔihmin-Ø/
and.then-S.SEQ	sing-PFV

‘they went off, scaling their scaling-sticks. **Having done so**, they sang.’

(532) Example of *ha:mini-* with ||-:li|| D.SEQ (H VI: 3)
[ʔ]ahšáʔwan [ʔ]áč:a mí:hat̪ak̓.
ʔahšaʔwan ʔač:a mi:hat̪ak̓
||ʔahša=ʔwan ʔahča-Ø mi:ha<t̪a>k-Ø||

/ʔahša=ʔwan	ʔač:a-Ø	mi:ha<t̪a>k̓-Ø/
fish=DET.OBJ	house-DIFFUSE	bring<PL.ACT>-PFV

ha:mini:li kʰáʔbekʰáč:on c̓a:yíyey [ʔ]uht̪éht̪ew,
***ha:mini:li** kʰaʔbekʰač:on c̓a:yiyey ʔuht̪eht̪ew*
||ha:mini-:li kʰaʔbekʰač=yčon c̓a:yi=yey ʔuht̪e-ř-w||

/ha:mini-:li	kʰaʔbekʰač=čon	c̓a:yi=yey	ʔuht̪e-ht̪e-w/
and.then-D.SEQ	raptor.species=PAT	scrubjay=AGT	tell~tell-PFV

‘They brought in the fish. **They having done so**, the Jay told Fish Hawk’

The *ha:mini-* construction is unique. It combines sentences. The switch-reference suffixes on regular verbs (i.e., not on the pro-verb *ha:mini-*) combine clauses into a single sentence. Hereafter, the examples of switch-reference suffixes are restricted to those applied to regular verbs as part of their being combined into a single sentence, unless otherwise noted.

3.10.2.5. The Basics of the Switch-Reference System

In the following subsections I lay out the nature of the switch-reference system in Southern Pomo:

(i) The system is not sensitive to the agent/patient case-marking system found on animate arguments.

(ii) It does not indicate the closeness or lack of closeness between events (as in Central Pomo).
(iii) It is sensitive to the category of subject, and it is subjects which are marked as being shared or not shared with the TAM-bearing main verb.
(iv) Switch-reference suffixes may occur without any core arguments being overtly present in the sentence.
(v) Dependent verbs are marked with switch-reference suffixes in relation to a single main verb, and they are not marked in relation to other dependent verbs (as reported for other languages).

3.10.2.6. Summary of Switch-Reference System

Southern Pomo makes use of switch-reference suffixes to mark dependent verbs. Unlike their cognates in neighboring Central Pomo, the Southern Pomo switch-reference suffixes do not mark events as being more closely or loosely bound. The switch-reference suffixes of Southern Pomo perform two principal functions:

(1) They mark one or more clauses as dependent upon a single main verb.
(2) They mark dependent verbs as having either the same or a different subject (defined here as the least affected core argument of a clause, whether expressed or implied) as the main verb; they do not mark same or different subject with respect to another dependent verb.

The Southern Pomo dependent clause suffixes thus behave like the sentential focus reference system of Kashaya (Oswalt 1983). The Southern Pomo switch-reference system therefore differs substantially from the types of switch-reference marking reported from some languages, especially those in New Guinea (Roberts 1988; MacDonald 1990), where medial verbs within sometimes lengthy chains are marked as having the same or different subject with respect to a following medial verb.

One potential explanation for the differences between the two systems is the number of medial verbs that may be strung together in languages with switch-reference marking on dependent verbs relative to adjacent verbs (such as in some well-studied New Guinea languages) versus the number of dependent verbs that may be strung together in Southern Pomo. The Southern Pomo data upon which this study is based rarely show chunks of discourse with more than two or three dependent verbs relating to a main verb. Descriptions of New Guinea languages, by contrast, report the possibility of much longer strings of medial verbs.

If Southern Pomo dependent clauses were strung together in much longer chains preceding a main verb, it seems likely that both speaker and listener might be unduly burdened by a sentential focus reference system. The Southern Pomo system requires the speaker to know the subject of the main verb from the beginning of the first dependent verb, which would be nigh impossible with clause chains of five or more dependent verbs. However, Southern Pomo speakers, using but few dependent clauses per sentence, do not appear to labor under any such burden. The relative frequency with which finite verbs appear in Southern Pomo narratives—the genre where the longest possible clause chains might be expected—shows that Southern Pomo speakers need to use relatively few dependent verbs per main (finite) verb, which, in turn, makes possible a sentential focus system in which each dependent verb is marked with reference to the main verb, not in relation to a neighboring dependent verb.

3.10.3. Nominalized Clauses

Southern Pomo clauses may be nominalized by means of NP enclitics in order to serve as core arguments of another verb or as nominal obliques. Nominalized clauses without a nominal head (overtly present or understood) may function as the core argument of another verb. Nominalized clauses which include a nominal head (either overtly present or understood) may serve as the core argument of another verb and additionally function as internal-head (circumnominal) restrictive relative clauses. There is no evidence for non-restrictive relative clauses in the language. Two finite clauses may be juxtaposed without any dependent verb morphology or nominalizing morphology; such clauses mirror the nominalized internal-head relative clauses in every way but the lack of nominalizing morphology. In at least some instances, such constructions might be analyzed as internal-head relative clauses which lack overt morphology but do fit the syntactic patterns of an argument of another verb. These are included within the section on nominalizaton despite their lacking overt nominalizing morphology. The following abbreviations are used throughout the remainder of this section:

A = subject of a transitive clause
O = object of a transitive clause
S = single argument of an intransitive clause
OBL = non-core argument (oblique)
RC = relative clause

Each of the three types of clause nominalization is discussed in the following sections.

3.10.3.1. Nominalized Clauses Which Are Not Relative Clauses

Verbs may be nominalized to serve as the core argument of another verb or as an oblique. If there is no nominal head in the nominalized verb (overt or understood)—whether or not there is an overt nominal argument within the nominalized clause—then the nominalized verb does not function as a relative clause. Nominalized verbs which serve as core arguments do so as objects (though this observation might be biased by my database and should be accepted with caution).

Nominalization is accomplished by means of the case-marking and locative NP enclitics discussed earlier (§2.9.1). The patient case enclitic ||=yčon|| does not appear to be used to nominalize a verb which will not be part of a relative clause.[14] The enclitics ||=ʔwan|| DET.OBJ and ||=ʔyowan|| may be used to mark the clause as the core argument of another verb. These clitics may also be combined with additional enclitics (generally the locative NP enclitics) to form an oblique NP from a verb. The locative NP enclitics, when attached to a clause, always create an oblique NP. An example of a nominalized clause serving as the core argument of another clause is given in (533).

(533) Nominalized clause as core argument of a verb (H I: 1)
ma:číl:e bíʔdu čóhšinwan šú:kʰaw
ma:čil:e [biʔdu čohšinwan]$_O$ šu:kʰaw
/ma:či-l:e biʔdu čohšin-Ø=wan šu:kʰa-w/

day-mid acorn pound-PFV=DET.OBJ finish-PFV
'(at) noon (she) finished pounding acorns.'
[lit: 'At midday (she) finished the acorn pounding/pounding of acorns.']

The head of the preceding nominalized clause is not 'acorns', and the clause does not serve to disambiguate which acorns out of all acorns in the world were pounded.

3.10.3.2. Nominalized Clauses Which Function as Relative Clauses

The definition of relative clause used herein is taken from Comrie (1989: 143):

> A relative clause . . . consists necessarily of a head and a restricting clause. The head itself has a certain potential range of referents, but the restricting clause restricts this set by giving a proposition that must be true of the actual referents of the over-all construction.

Comrie notes that there must be "some construction or constructions *correlating highly*" with this definition within a language in order to claim it has relative clauses (1989: 144). A subset of nominalized clauses in Southern Pomo fit the criteria for relative clauses. They have a nominal head (overt or understood) that is restricted—set off from other nominals—by the nominalized clause. Specifically, the relative clause construction in Southern Pomo is of the internal-head (circumnominal) variety: the head noun is expressed inside the relative clause in the relative order where it would be found in a main clause; the head is not overtly present in the main clause (Comrie 1989: 145–46). When a nominalized clause functions as a relative clause as part of the core argument of the main verb, it is of the non-reduction type, and the head noun is overtly present and unreduced in the nominalized clause (though, as stated before, such an assertion might be too specific and is subject to change as more data are processed). Nominalized clauses functioning as relative clauses that are oblique arguments of a main verb generally are not of the non-reduction type: they do not have an overt nominal (the understood nominal in such cases is most often 'place/location').

There are two overt morphological manifestations of this relative clause construction in Southern Pomo: (1) a nominal enclitic is attached to the end of the clause that functions as an internal-head relative clause; or (2) a third-person coreferential device (either one of the third-person coreferential pronouns or a kinship term with the third-person-coreferential prefix) is present within the internal-head relative clause. There is also a potential morphological distinction between nominalized clauses which function as relative clauses (at least those which function as the core argument of a main clause) and nominalized clauses which are not also relative clauses (i.e., which do not restrict a nominal head). If the head noun of a relative clause is animate, it is possible to nominalize the clause by means of the patient case enclitic ||=yčon||; this is in contradistinction to simple nominalized clauses, which may be nominalized with the object-marking determiner enclitics but which may not take the agent/patient case-marking morphemes. Examples of internal-head relative clauses with nominalizing morphology follow. In each example, the nominalized constituent that is also an internal-head relative clause is set off by brackets, and its role as O or OBL is indicated with subscripts.

(534) Example of nominalized clause functioning as internal-head RC (H I: 4)
[ʔ]at̪[:]i ċíht̪a mí:hak̓( )want̪óŋhkʰle muʔt̪̓ákaw.
[ʔat̪:i ċiht̪a mi:hak̓want̪onhkʰle]$_{\text{RC:O}}$ *muʔt̪̓akaw*

/ʔat̪:i	ċiht̪a	mi:hak̓-Ø=wan=t̪onhkʰle	muʔt̪̓a-ka-w/
3C.SG.AGT	bird~game	bring-PFV=DET.OBJ=some.of	cook-CAUS-PFV

'(he) cooked some of the game that he had brought in.'

In the preceding example the head noun is 'game', and the RC restricts the interpretation of this noun to only the game which had been brought in. This example highlights several features of this relative clause construction in the language. Note the use of *ʔat̪:i* 3COREFERENTIAL.SINGULAR.AGENTIVE, which indicates that the third-person subject responsible for the bringing of the game is the same as the subject of the main clause 'cause to cook'. As already stated, a coreferential pronoun or kinship prefix is generally (possibly always) present within a nominalized clause that is also a relative clause.

Two other features of the preceding example bear mentioning. Note that it is the enclitic *=wan* DET.OBJ that nominalizes the clause, and the partitive enclitic *=t̪onhkʰle* 'some.of' is attached to the NP made by *=wan* DET.OBJ. Also note that the verb within the relative clause is glossed as taking finite morphology: it is suffixed with the post-consonantal -Ø allomorph of the perfective suffix. The zero allomorph is not convincing evidence that clauses keep their finite inflection when nominalized. Example (535) gives another nominalized clause which functions as relative clause, and the verb within that nominalization, *ʔačʰ:a-* 'to catch', is vowel-final and takes the *-w* allomorph of the perfective suffix, which provides unequivocal evidence that the nominalized clause retains its finite inflection within relative clause constructions.[15]

(535) Example of nominalized clause functioning as internal-head RC (H I: 17)
ʔat̪:í:kʰe ċíht̪a [ʔ]ačʰ:áw:an dóhlok̓
[ʔat̪:i:kʰe ċiht̪a ʔačʰ:aw:an]$_{RC:O}$ *dohlok̓*
/ʔat̪:i-:kʰe ċiht̪a ʔačʰ:a-w=wan dohlo-k̓-Ø/
3C.SG-POSS bird~game catch-PFV=DET.OBJ take.off-DIR-PFV
'(He) took off his own game that (he) had caught'

Note that the use of the possessive form of the third-person coreferential pronoun in (535) indicates that the possessor of the head noun of the relative clause is coreferential with the subject of the main verb. This sentence therefore has no overt mention of the subject of either the nominalized clause or the main clause.

Two possible features of Southern Pomo relative clauses have been mentioned without exemplification: (1) a kinship term with a coreferential prefix may be used instead of a third-person coreferential pronoun within the relative clause; and (2) a relative clause that has as its head an animate noun may take the patient case enclitic ||=yčon|| for nominalization. Both of these phenomena are present in example (536) (note that the verb 'tell' is transitive and does take an object).

(536) RC with animate argument and patient case nominalization
mák:aċ ší:ba:t̪[ʰ]aw mát̪ʰ:i mit̪:í:čon [ʔ]uht̪éht̪ew (H IX: 8)
[mak:aċ ši:ba:t̪ʰaw mat̪ʰ:i mit̪:i:čon]$_{RC:O}$ *ʔuht̪eht̪ew*

/ma-k:a-ċ-Ø šiːba:t̪ʰaw mat̪ʰ:i mit̪:i-Ø=:čon ʔuht̪eht̪e-w/
3C-mo.mo.-GS-AGT poor blind lie-DIFFUSE=PAT[16] tell-PFV
'[They] told their poor blind grandmother who was lying (there)'

Note that the use of the third-person-possessed kinship prefix ||maH-|| *ma-* indicates that the possessor of the noun head of the relative clause ('their poor blind grandmother') is coreferential with the subject of the main verb 'tell'. Because it is the grandmother whom they tell who is the head noun of the relative clause, the patient case enclitic is used to indicate her highly animate status.

Thus far the examples of relative clauses have included only those nominalized clauses which are core arguments of a main verb. Example (537) illustrates a nominalized clause that functions as an oblique. Note that the pattern seen in (537) fits into the so-called gap type of relative clause: there is no "overt indication of the role of the head within the relative clause" (Comrie 1989: 151). This is quite unlike the nominalized clauses seen earlier, which function as core arguments of a main verb and have the noun head of the relative clause overtly present.

(537) Gap-type RC as oblique nominalization (H VIII: 2)
čú:mat̪yey hó:liw [ʔ]at̪:íyey daʔt̪ámhukʰ:eʔyowant̪óŋhkʰay
ču:mat̪yey ho:liw [ʔat̪:iyey daʔt̪amhukʰ:eʔyowant̪onhkʰay]$_{RC:OBL}$
/ču:mat̪=yey ho:li-w ʔat̪:i-yey daʔt̪a-mhu-kʰ:e=ʔyowan=t̪onhkʰay/
squirrel=AGT leave-PFV 3C-PL.AGT find-RECIP-FUT=DET.OBJ=toward
'Squirrel went off to where they will meet each other'

The understood head of (537) is the physical location where 'Squirrel' will meet with the antagonist (Rock Man), though this is nowhere explicitly mentioned within the nominalized clause. Note that this example is otherwise quite similar to the previous relative clause examples: it makes use of a third-person coreferential pronoun, and the nominalized verb retains its inflectional morphology (i.e., the clause, were it to be stripped of the nominalizing enclitics, could stand alone as a fully grammatical sentence). And, as seen earlier, the locative enclitic *=t̪onhkʰay* 'toward' is added after a nominalizing object-marking determiner enclitic, which is *=ʔyowan* in this case.

3.10.3.3. Juxtaposed Clauses Which May Function as Relative Clauses

In addition to the robust strategies for forming internal-head relative clauses which were discussed in the previous section, there are examples of what appear to be single sentences composed of two finite verbs. These examples do show any verbal morphology that would indicate one verb is dependent upon or embedded within another verb. Before specific examples of this phenomenon are introduced, it is worthwhile to repeat an example from the previous section, which is given in (538).

(538) Example of nominalized clause functioning as internal-head RC (H I: 17)

ʔat̪:í:k^{h}e c̓íht̪a [ʔ]ač^{h}:áw:an dóhlok̓

[ʔat̪:i:k^{h}e c̓iht̪a ʔač^{h}:aw:an]$_{RC:O}$ dohlok̓

/ʔat̪:i-:k^{h}e	c̓iht̪a	ʔač^{h}:a-w=wan	dohlo-k̓-Ø/
3C.SG-POSS	bird~game	catch-PFV=DET.OBJ	take.off-DIR-PFV

'(He) took off his own game that (he) had caught'

The narrative from which the preceding example comes is quite repetitive. The same events (a quarrel between jilted lovers who eventually transform into animal species) are repeated over and over again. This somewhat tedious oral literature device has the happy side effect that the speaker is given the opportunity to produce slight variations in what are functionally the same statements. Compare (538) with the following example from the same text in (539).

(539) Possible RC with juxtaposed finite clauses and no nominalization (H I: 21)

c̓íht̪a [ʔ]áč^{h}:aw dólhow

c̓iht̪a ʔač^{h}:aw dolhow

/c̓iht̪a	ʔač^{h}:a-w	dolho-w/
bird~game	catch-PFV	take.off-PFV

'(the) game (he) caught (he) took off'

The two clauses in (539) above have exactly the same verb stems as found in (538). In fact, they describe the same thing. The character repeatedly returns to traps to retrieve small game. Example (539) appears to have no overt indication that it might include a relative clause: there is no nominalized verb, nor is there a coreferential pronoun or kinship prefix. Yet the meaning of these two clauses does not appear to be one of '(he) caught game; (he) took (them) off'; rather, the verb 'catch-PFV' is restricting the interpretation of the noun 'bird ~ game' to only those which were caught in the trap. If this example is viewed in the larger discourse chunk of which it is a part, it is even more evident that it functions as a relative clause. Examples (540a–d) give (539) in context (it is broken down into subparts for easy reference).

(540a) The discourse context for example (539) (H I: 21)
hó:liw lik̓lísyey
ho:liw lik̓lisyey
/ho:li-w lik̓lis=yey/
leave-PFV raptor.species=AGT
'(He) went off, Sparrowhawk,

(540b) [ʔ]at̪:i ċiht̪a mín:an( )yowan( )t̪óŋhk^{h}ay,
[ʔat̪:i ċiht̪a min:anyowant̪oŋhk^{h}ay]$_{RC:OBL}$
/ʔat̪:i ċiht̪a min:an-Ø=yowan=t̪oŋhk^{h}ay/
3C.SG.AGT bird~game trap-PFV=DET.OBJ=toward
'to the game that he himself trapped;'

(540c) ċíht̪aʔwan dólhow,
ċiht̪aʔwan dolhow
/ċiht̪a=ʔwan dolho-w/
bird~game=DET.OBJ take.off-PFV
'(he) took the game off the snares;'

(540d) ċíht̪a [ʔ]áč^{h}:aw dólhow
ċiht̪a ʔač^{h}:aw dolhow
/ċiht̪a ʔač^{h}:a-w dolho-w/
bird~game catch-PFV take.off-PFV
'(the) game (he) caught (he) took off.'

A careful investigation of (540a–d) reveals two things: (1) the normal relative clause strategy is employed in (540b) to form an oblique ('to the game that he himself trapped'); and (2) the utterance in (540d) is presented as a clarification of (540c) as to which game were taken from traps. This leaves no room for an interpretation of (540d) other than that of a relative clause strategy: the game animals are being restricted to only those caught (in the traps) from all other game animals.

But is this a relative clause strategy with no overt morphology? If the clause from (540c) is examined, it will be seen that it is identical to the forms of (540d) in all but two ways. Both of these are repeated below (with same numbering).

(540c) (repeated from above)
číhṯaʔwan dólhow,
čihṯaʔwan dolhow
/čihṯa=ʔwan dolho-w/
game=DET.OBJ take.off-PFV
'(he) took the game off the snares'

(540d) (repeated from above)
číhṯa [ʔ]áč^h:aw dólhow
čihṯa ʔač^h:aw dolhow
/čihṯa ʔač^h:a-w dolho-w/
game catch-PFV take.off-PFV
'(the) game (he) caught (he) took off.'

As can be seen, (540c) differs from (540d) in having only one verb (it does not have the verb 'catch' following 'game') and in the presence of the object-marking determiner enclitic *=ʔwan* on the noun 'game'. This last difference is important: (540d) shows no nominalizing morphology on the verb, but it also lacks any case-marking morphology on the noun 'game'. Recall that all case-marking morphology outside the pronouns and kinship terms is represented by enclitics that attach to constituents larger than the phonological word. Nominalized clauses are, by definition, NPs, and it is only at the end of the NP that a case-marking enclitic may attach. In other words, the lack of any nominal enclitics on 'game' in (540d) is evidence that it is within a larger NP, albeit one with no unambiguous overt morphological indication of its nominal status. Example (541) comes from later in the same narrative and shows the same game-collection event with an internal-head relative clause composed of juxtaposed finite verbs with no nominal enclitics present on the head noun; however, this example includes a coreferential pronoun as part of the relative clause and therefore shows more similarity to those seen in the relative clauses with overt clause nominalization.

Table 52. Summary of nominalized clause types

	Nominalized clauses which are not RCs	**Nominalized clauses which are RCs**		**Juxtaposed clauses which may function as RCs**
		As core argument	As oblique	
Overt nominalizing morphology on clause	Yes	Yes	Yes	No
Functions as a relative clause	No	Yes	Yes	Yes
Internal-head, non-reduction type	N/A	Yes	No	Yes
Internal-head, gap type	N/A	No	Yes	No
RC includes coreferential pronoun or kinship prefix	N/A	Yes (optional?)	Yes (optional?)	Optional

(541) RC with juxtaposed finite verbs and coreferential pronoun (H I: 23)

[ʔ]at̯:í:kʰe ċíht̯a [ʔ]áčʰ:aw dólhow

[ʔat̯:i:kʰe ċiht̯a ʔačʰ:aw]$_{RC:O}$ *dolhow*

/ʔat̯:i:kʰe ċiht̯a ʔačʰ:aw dolhow/

3C.SG-POSS bird~game catch-PFV take.off-PFV

'(He) took off his own game (that he) caught'

Juxtaposition of two finite verbs without any nominalizing morphology, then, may be used as a relative clause formation strategy. Note that it is not just the lack of nominal morphology on the noun head of the relative clause that suggests a NP analysis for the first clause in (541). Southern Pomo is an AOV language (AV and OV), and the object of a transitive verb generally comes immediately before the verb. The juxtaposed clauses in (541), which show no argument between the verbs, fit the syntax of an OV sentence type.

3.10.3.4. Summary of Clause Nominalization Strategies

The different clause nominalization types discussed thus far, including both relative clause strategies and more basic clause nominalization, are summarized in table 52.

3.10.4. Coordination

In addition to the types of clause combination already discussed, such as switch-reference suffixes and the oppositive enclitic ||=ʔnat̪i|| 'but; however', clauses may be linked by the conjunction (really a disjunction) word *he:* 'or', as seen in (542) (with *he:* and its translation in bold).

(542) Example of two clauses linked by *he:* 'or' (O I: 24)

miy:ame miy:at̪ʰe he:miniw

miy:ame miy:at̪ʰe he:miniw

/miy:a-me-Ø	miy:a-t̪ʰe-Ø	he:mini-w/
3-father-AGT	3-mother-AGT	how.do-PFV

diʔbuw he: muʔk̓ukaw.

diʔbuw ***he:*** *muʔk̓ukaw*

/diʔbu-w	he:	mu-ʔk̓u-ka-w/
bury-PFV	or	with.heat-finish-CAUS-PFV

'Her father and mother somehow buried **or** cremated her.'

Example (542) also highlights the main method of conjoining nominals: *miy:ame* 'her father' and *miy:at̪ʰe* '[her] mother' are simply listed one after the other with no conjunction or bound morphemes to indicate the relationship.

APPENDIX 1

2012 Visit with Olive Fulwider and Photographs

Between mid-fall of 2011 and mid-spring 2014, I served as the language project coordinator for the Dry Creek Rancheria Band of Pomo Indians, in which role I taught Southern Pomo classes on a weekly basis and managed language content on the Dry Creek Rancheria's official website. Some of my students were closely related to the tribe's last fluent speaker, Olive Fulwider, who had developed dementia by this time.

In 2012, after approximately a year of classes, I arranged for me and two of my students to visit Olive and her daughter and stepdaughter at Olive's home. We visited with the express intent of learning how to ask 'when will . . . ?' and 'do you have . . . ?' questions. Because of Mrs. Fulwider's advanced age and dementia, we knew that we might not be able to obtain anything. However, we were able to hear quite a bit of language during the visit, including 'when will . . . ?' questions and 'do you have . . . ?' questions. I maintained a closed language group on an online social media platform, and I posted transcriptions of the day's visit to this site, the retranscriptions of which follow.

but̪:e kaʔma čoh:onhk^{h}e	'when will you get married?'
ʔit̪^{h}:inwaʔa čoh:ondedu	'I'm already married' (lit: early is I married)
ʔayha ʔom:it̪^{h}oṭ̓ p^{h}al:aʔčay ya:la ʔom:iw	'(you) don't understand the Indian (language); (you) only understand the whiteman's (language)'
ma:kina p^{h}ad:ed:u	'to drive (a) car'
ši:bat̪^{h}yaw ceṭ̓ ne:nek^{h}:et̪^{h}oṭ̓	(not 100% sure, might be 'pathetic how (you?) cannot be taught'
ʔaṭ^{h}:ew	'to spread (a blanket); a large blanket/quilt'
si:lišk̓a	'black-ass'
hay:u(ʔ)kamk^{h}e	'do you have a dog?'
ʔayt̪o kac̓e	'ouch!' (lit: ow! me mother's mother!)

PHOTOGRAPHS

These photographs include pictures of the last fluent speaker of Southern Pomo, Olive Fulwider of the Dry Creek Rancheria Band of Pomo Indians, her relatives, traditional foods from a Southern Pomo language and culture camp, and students from Southern Pomo classes held in Santa Rosa, California. (All photos courtesy of the author.)

Photo 1. Olive Fulwider (Na:hoʔmen) with Joshua Walker (Biʔdu). Photo taken ca. 2003 at a family reunion for the relatives of the late Nellie Cordova (Ṭ^{h}ak̓men), the youngest sibling of Mrs. Fulwider.

Photo 2. Olive Fulwider (Na:hoʔmen) with Nathan Walker (K^{h}aʔbe). Photo taken at Olive Fulwider's home in Santa Rosa, California, in 2006. It was during this visit that Mrs. Fulwider exclaimed, "ʔahčahčay mahṭ^{h}e:meṭ̓" 'Indian like his own mother' upon seeing Nathan for the first time.

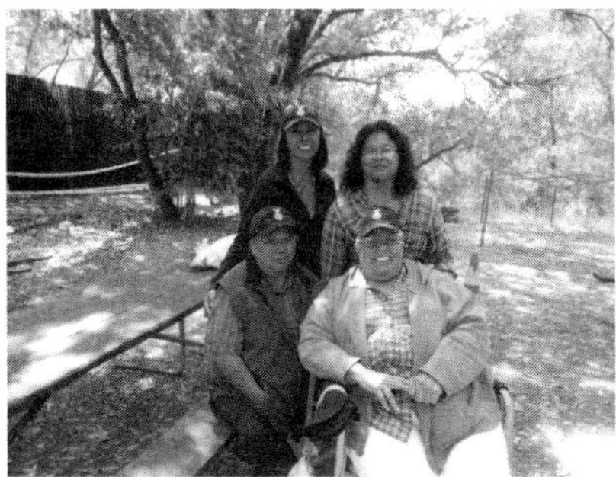

Photo 3. Dry Creek elders at language and culture day camp ca. 2013. *Top row, left to right*: Cheryl Bowden (Olive Fulwider's first cousin), Yvonne Gonzales, daughter of Nellie Cordova (Olive Fulwider's sister). *Bottom row, left to right*: Olivia Altizen, daughter of Nellie Cordova (Olive Fulwider's sister), and Irene Fox, a descendant of Elizabeth Dollar. Cheryl Bowden attended Southern Pomo classes for the duration of the period between 2011 and 2014 when they were offered by the Dry Creek Rancheria. At this camp she and several other students helped model words and phrases for youth who had come to experience traditional foods. The camp was held at a campground on the Russian River.

Photo 4. Language signage from language and culture day camp ca. 2013. Special signs were made to teach youth words for traditional foods. Here, *bahkay* berries have been used to make a mild drink.

Photo 5. Traditional *ʔo:ṭʰono* (dried seaweed) and tortillas. *ʔo:ṭʰono* is now fried and served with tortillas at most gatherings where it is offered. Photo taken ca. 2013 at the language and culture day camp.

Photo 6. Language signage and traditional *ʔo:ṭ^{h}ono* (dried seaweed). During a set time each year, tribal members go to the coast to collect seaweed. The seaweed is taken by hand from rocks just off of the rocky beaches. The wet seaweed is first cleaned of bugs and then set to dry in the sun on the rocks before being brought home to dry for an extended period of time. Photo taken ca. 2013 at the language and culture day camp.

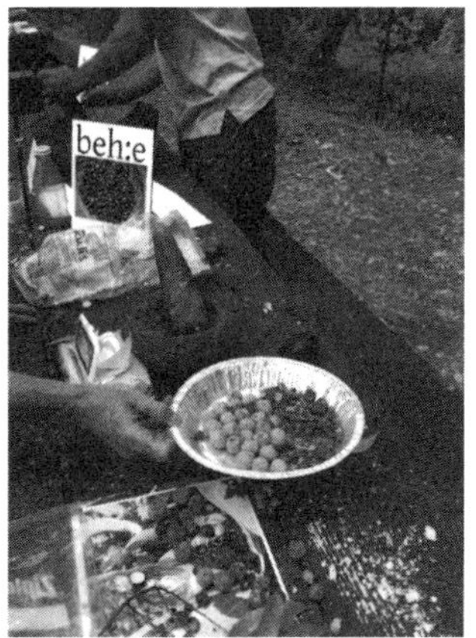

Photo 7. *K^{h}aʔbeṭ̓le* 'stone mortar', *dok:o* 'pestle', and *beh:eč^{h}ni* 'bay nut candy'. This picture was taken ca. 2013 at the language and culture day camp held for Dry Creek Pomo youth. The stone *k^{h}aʔbeṭ̓le* and *dok:o* are used to pulverize the roasted *beh:e* 'bay nuts' (from the California laurel). The grounds are then rolled into balls, and in modern iterations, may be combined with maple syrup or chocolate. These candies provide a weak buzz, the effect of which is similar to that experienced after imbibing a strongly caffeinated drink.

Photo 8. *Beh:e* 'bay nut' grounds at language and culture youth camp ca. 2013.

Photo 9. *Si:lun* 'bread' at language and culture youth camp ca. 2013. Traditional bread was made with acorn flour. The word *si:lun*, however, came to be applied to any bread.

Photo 10. *Ma:kʰa* 'salmon' cooking at language and culture youth camp ca. 2013.

Photo 11. Michael Racho, former Dry Creek Rancheria chairman. Michael Racho is the son of the late Nellie Cordova, Olive Fulwider's youngest sister. He was the chairman of the Dry Creek Rancheria Band of Pomo Indians in the late 1990s. Here he is displaying a necklace he was commissioned to make by the Western Institute for Endangered Language Documentation ca. 2014. The necklace includes a small *duʔk̓aš* 'abalone' shell.

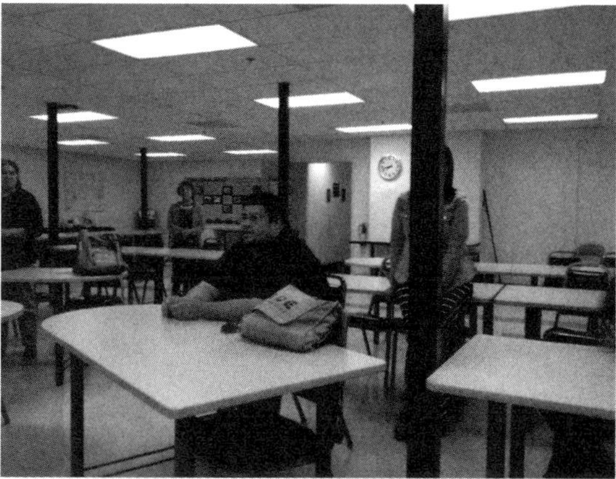

Photo 12. Southern Pomo classes held by WIELD at the CIMCC in 2014. Southern Pomo classes at the Dry Creek Rancheria ended in early spring of 2014, and the semester was continued under the direction of the Western Institute for Endangered Language Documentation (WIELD), which negotiated the use of facilities at the California Museum and Cultural Center (CIMCC) in Santa Rosa, California. In this picture, Ramón Billy of the Hopland Rancheria is seated at a desk.

Photo 13. Southern Pomo orthography in use during classes at CIMCC. In this picture, Anthony England of the Dry Creek Rancheria is using an interactive board to read and write in Southern Pomo.

Photo 14. Nellie Cordova's granddaughter and family ca. 2017. *Bottom row, left to right*: Nathan Walker (Kaʔbe), Christopher Walker (Bu:ṭaka), Jenny Walker (Kic:idu), Maayu Walker (<Maayu> is the Anglicization of Ma:yu). Joshua Walker (Biʔdu) is standing behind. Jenny Walker is the granddaughter of Nellie Cordova (T^{h}ak̓men), the younger sister of Olive Fulwider (Na:hoʔmen).

APPENDIX 2

Sample Text

The story of *kʰaʔbe ʔač:ay* 'rock man' and *ču:maṭ* 'gray squirrel' is the eighth narrative spoken by Annie Burke, a Cloverdale speaker, and collected and transcribed by Abraham Halpern, and cited as (H VIII) throughout the grammar. This text has been chosen for inclusion in this grammar for several reasons: (1) it is perhaps the clearest example of agent/patient case marking on common nouns; (2) its restriction to two characters allows language learners to observe the switch-reference system more clearly (e.g., most clauses have either 'rock man' or 'gray squirrel' as their subject, and it is fairly easy to track when the subject changes); and (3) it was the primary text studied by members of the Dry Creek Rancheria's Southern Pomo language classes.

The text is provided here in two forms. The first is a cleaned-up version entirely in my orthography (and thus there are no accent marks to show stress), and it is this version of the text that should prove most useful to language revitalization efforts and interested scholars seeking a complete narrative. The glossing and free translation of this version are my own. I have kept the morpheme-by-morpheme glossing to a minimum. Instrumental prefixes are not parsed as they are largely idiosyncratic in meaning when combined with verb roots; the prefix+root verb stems are therefore glossed as though they are monomorphemic words. The phonological changes that affect morphemes are not indicated; rather, morpheme breaks are indicated without any indication of the underlying forms of affixes. In addition to Halpern's original numbering, I have added sentence-by-sentence numbering (e.g., 1.2, 1.3, etc.) for ease of reference; this additional numbering is based largely on Halpern's use of punctuation in his transcription and free translation.

My free translation is provided in three places: (1) after each sentence; (2) after all sentences in each section; and (3) after the entire text. It is hoped that the redundant presence of free translations through the text will allow learners to work through the narrative in the original Southern Pomo without becoming lost. It should be noted that I do not capitalize the translations for *ču:maṭ̓* 'gray squirrel' and *k^haʔbe ʔač:ay* 'rock man' because they are not unique personal names, though they are anthropomorphic mythological characters whose deeds would have been widely known. Note also that several verbs with 'rock man' as their subject have slightly different glosses than are used for the same morphemes in the body of the grammar (e.g., the instrumental prefix ||di-|| in this story is often translated together with its root with a 'by body' meaning). This is because the specifics of the story allow for a narrower interpretation of the semantics of these switch-reference+root verb stems.

The second rendering of this text is a transliteration of Halpern's original unpublished version of the text in both Southern Pomo and English. It is from this transliteration of Halpern's transcription and translation that examples of (H VIII) have been used throughout the grammar. In this version, only items bracketed [ ] have been added by me. I use ( ) to indicate a space or phone in Halpern's transcript that I believe to be incorrect. Everything else, in English or Southern Pomo, is present in Halpern's original (albeit in his orthography).

(1.1) *ču:maṭ̓yey č̓a:šba kul:u hwademʔdu,*

ču:maṭ̓=yey	č̓a:šba	kul:u-Ø[1]	hw-adem-ʔdu
gray.squirrel=AGT	always	outside-DIFFUSE	go-DIR-HAB

k̓ay:ama či:yow.

k̓ay:ama	či:yo-w
alone	stay-PFV

'Gray squirrel always went around outside. (He) stayed alone.'

(1.2) *ma: k^haʔbe ʔač:aywan daʔt̪̓aw kul:u.*

ma:	k^haʔbe	ʔač:ay=wan	daʔt̪̓a-w	kul:u
DEM	rock	man=DET.OBJ	encounter-PFV	outside

'(He) found this rock man outside.'

(1.3) *kʰaʔbe ʔač:ay:ey ʔe: maʔkaʔma he:t̯ow k̓a:de*

kʰaʔbe	ʔač:ay=yey	ʔe:	ma=ʔka=ʔma	he:t̯ow	k̓a:-de
rock	man=AGT	EXCLAMATION	DEM=INTER=2SG.AGT	whence	friend-VOC

ʔahčahčey daʔt̯aw hudʔakaywaʔa, k̓a:de.

ʔahčahčey	daʔt̯a-w	hudʔa-ka-y=wa=ʔa	k̓a:-de
people[2]	encounter-PFV	want-CAUS-REFL= COP.EVID=1SG.AGT	friend-VOC

'Rock man (said), "Hey, where have you come from, friend?"
I want to find people, friend.'

(1.4) *ʔahka hodʔo:t̯i k̓a:de ʔa: ʔahčahčey daʔt̯aw hudʔakaywa.*

ʔahka	hodʔo:-t̯i	k̓a:-de	ʔa:	ʔahčahčey
gamble	handle	friend-VOC	1SG.AGT	people

daʔt̯a-w	hudʔa-ka-y=wa
encounter-PFV	want-CAUS-REFL=COP.EVID

'In order to gamble, I want to find people.'

(1.5) *hiy:o k̓oʔdiʔwa, ʔat̯:o pʰa:la kʰač̓:aw hit̯:aduw:a k̓ay:ama či:yon.*

hiy:o	k̓oʔdi=ʔwa	ʔat̯:o	pʰa:la	kʰač̓:aw	hit̯:adu-w=wa
yes	good=COP.EVID	1SG.PAT	also	bad	feel-PFV=COP.EVID

k̓ay:ama	či:yo-n
alone	stay-S.SIM

'Yes, it is good. I am also feeling bad, staying alone.'

(1.6) *ʔa: pʰa:la ʔahčahčey daʔt̯aw hudʔakay.*

ʔa:	pʰa:la	ʔahčahčey	daʔt̯a-w	hudʔa-ka-y
1SG.AGT	also	people	encounter-PFV	want-CAUS-REFL

'I also want to find people.'

(1.7) *hiy:o ʔahkaʔwaʔya hodʔokʰ:e, ċu:ʔuʔwaʔya*

hiy:o	ʔahka=ʔwa=ʔya	hodʔo-kʰ:e	ċu:ʔu=ʔwa=ʔya
yes	gamble=COP.EVID=1PL.AGT	handle-FUT	arrow=COP.EVID=1PL.AGT

šuhnamhuk^h:e.
šuhna-mhu-k^h:e
try.by.pulling-RECIP-FUT
'Yes, we shall gamble; we shall try the bows [lit. 'arrow'] by pulling (them).'

(1.8) *hiy:o k̓oʔdiʔwa.*

hiy:o	k̓oʔdi=ʔwa
yes	good=COP.EVID

'Yes, it is good.'

(1.9) *ma:liʔwaʔya k^{h}aʔ:a:le daʔt̯amhuk^h:e k̓a:de.*

ma:li=ʔwa=ʔya	k^{h}aʔ:a-:le	daʔt̯a-mhu-k^h:e	k̓a:-de
here=COP.EVID=1PL.AGT	morning-mid[3]	encounter-RECIP-FUT	friend-VOC

'We shall meet each other here in the morning, friend.'

(1.10) *ʔit̯^{h}:inwaʔya daʔt̯amhuk^h:e.*

ʔit̯^{h}:in=wa=ʔya	daʔt̯a-mhu-k^h:e
early=COP.EVID=1PL.AGT	encounter-RECIP-FUT

'We shall meet each other early.'

(1.11) *hiy:o ma:liʔwaʔa kahkot̯ik^h:e.*

hiy:o	ma:li=ʔwa=ʔa	kahkot̯i-k^h:e
yes	here=COP.EVID=1SG.AGT	arrive-FUT

'Yes, I shall arrive here.'

(1.12) *hiy:o ʔa: p^{h}a:la ma:li kahkot̯ik^h:e, ma:liʔwaʔya daʔt̯amhuk^h:e.*

hiy:o	ʔa:	p^{h}a:la	ma:li	kahkot̯i-k^h:e
yes	1SG.AGT	also	here	arrive-FUT

ma:li=ʔwa=ʔya	daʔt̯a-mhu-k^h:e
here=COP.EVID=1PL.AGT	encounter-RECIP-FUT

'Yes, I too shall arrive here; we shall meet each other here.'

(1.1) Gray squirrel always went around outside. (He) stayed alone. (1.2) (He) found this rock man outside. (1.3) Rock man (said), "Hey, where have you come from, friend? I want to find people, friend. (1.4) In order to gamble, I want to find people." (1.5) [Gray squirrel replied,] "Yes, it is good. I am also feeling bad, staying alone. (1.6) I also want to find people." (1.7) [Rock man said,] "Yes, we shall gamble; we shall try the bows [lit. 'arrow'] by pulling (them)." (1.8) [Gray squirrel replied,] "Yes, it is good. (1.9) We shall meet each other here in the morning, friend. (1.10) We shall meet each other early." (1.11) [Rock man replied,] "Yes, we shall arrive here." (1.12) [Gray squirrel said,] "Yes, I too shall arrive here; we shall meet each other here."

(2.1) *ču:maṭ̓yey ʔahčanhkʰay ho:liw.*
ču:maṭ̓=yey ʔahča=nhkʰay ho:li-w
gray.squirrel=AGT house=ward go[4]-PFV
'Gray squirrel went toward home.'

(2.2) *kʰaʔbeyey pʰa:la ho:liw, ʔahčanhkʰay.*
kʰaʔbe=yey pʰa:la ho:li-w ʔahča=nhkʰay
rock=AGT also go-PFV house=ward
'Rock (man) also went toward home.'

(2.3) *ču:maṭ̓yey ʔač:a hač̓:ow, ʔat̯:i:kʰe ʔač:a.*
ču:maṭ̓=yey ʔač:a-Ø[5] hač̓:o-w ʔat̯:i-:kʰe ʔač:a-Ø
gray.squirrel=AGT house-DIFFUSE arrive-PFV 3C.SG-POSS house-DIFFUSE
'Gray squirrel arrived at home, at his own home.'

(2.4) *duw:ey*
duw:e-y
night-SEM
'Night fell.'

(2.5) *mi:ṭiw*
mi:ṭi-w
lie-PFV
'(He) lay down.'

(2.6) *kʰaʔ:ašk̓aden kʰaʔbeyey t̯o:biy, ču:maṭ̓yey t̯o:biy.*
kʰaʔ:ašk̓aden kʰaʔbe=yey t̯o:-biy-Ø ču:maṭ̓=yey t̯o:-biy-Ø
morning rock=AGT rise-DIR-PFV gray.squirrel=AGT rise-DIR-PFV
'In the morning, rock (man) arose, (and) gray squirrel arose.'

(2.7) *ma: ču:maṭyey ho:liw, ʔat̪:iyey daʔt̪̓amhukʰ:eʔyowant̪onhkʰay.*

ma: ču:maṭ=yey ho:li-w ʔat̪:i-yey
DEM gray.squirrel=AGT go-PFV 3C.SG-PL.AGT

daʔt̪̓a-mhu-kʰ:e=ʔyowan=t̪onhkʰay
encounter-RECIP-FUT=DET.OBJ=toward
'Gray squirrel went toward the place where they were to meet each other.'[6]

(2.8) *kʰaʔbeyey ho:liw,*

kʰaʔbe=yey ho:li-w
rock=AGT go-PFV
'Rock (man) went.'

(2.9) *ču:maṭyey waʔ:a:t̪on hač̓:ow.*

ču:maṭ=yey waʔ:a:=t̪on hač̓:o-w
gray.squirrel=AGT first=LOC arrive=PFV
'Gray squirrel arrived first.'

(2.10) *ham:i či:yow, mač:eč̓in.*

ham:i či:yo-w mač:e-č̓-in
there stay-PFV watch[7]-REFL-S.SIM
'(He) stayed there and waited.'

(2.11) *kʰaʔbeyey kahkot̪iy.*

kʰaʔbe=yey kahkot̪iy-Ø
rock=AGT arrive-PFV
'Rock (man) arrived.'

(2.12) *ʔit̪ʰ:inkaʔma hwad:u k̓a:de, kʰaʔbeyey.*

ʔit̪ʰ:in=ka=ʔma hwa-d:-u k̓a:-de kʰaʔbe=yey
early=INTER=2SG.AGT go-DIR-PFV friend-VOC rock-AGT
'"Do you walk about (so) early, friend?" Rock (man said).'

(2.13) *ču:maṭyey, hiy:o, si:ma mi:ṭit̪ʰenṭoʔt̪o duw:e, ʔahka hudʔan.*

ču:maṭ=yey hiy:o si:ma mi:ṭi-t̪ʰen-ṭo=ʔt̪o
gray.squirrel=AGT yes sleep lie-NEG.IPFV=CONTRASTIVE=1SG.PAT

duw:e	ʔahka	hudʔa-n
night	gamble	want-S.SIM

'Gray squirrel (said), "Yes, I could not sleep (during the) night (because of my) wanting to gamble!"'

(2.1) Gray squirrel went toward home. (2.2) Rock (man) also went toward home. (2.3) Gray squirrel arrived at home, at his own home. (2.4) Night fell. (2.5) (He) lay down. (2.6) In the morning, rock (man) arose, (and) gray squirrel arose. (2.7) Gray squirrel went toward the place where they were to meet each other.[8] (2.8) Rock (man) went. (2.9) Gray squirrel arrived first. (2.10) (He) stayed there and waited. (2.11) Rock (man) arrived. (2.12) "Do you walk about (so) early, friend?" Rock (man said). (2.13) Gray squirrel (said), "Yes, I could not sleep (during the) night (because of my) wanting to gamble!"

(3.1) *ču:maṭ̓yey kaʔbeyčon ʔa:ma wayiʔwaʔkʰe c̓u:ʔu šuhnakʰ:e.*

ču:maṭ̓=yey	kaʔbe=yčon	ʔa:ma	wayi=ʔwa=ʔkʰe	c̓u:ʔu
gray.squirrel=AGT	rock=PAT	2SG.AGT	first=COP.EVID= 1SG.POSS	arrow

šuhnakʰ:e.

šuhna-kʰ:e

try.by.pulling-FUT

'Gray squirrel (said) to rock (man), "You will try pulling my arrow [lit. 'bow'] first."'

(3.2) *hiy:o.*

hiy:o

yes

'Yes, (rock man said).'

(3.3) *ʔoh:ow ʔaṭ̯:i:kʰe c̓u:ʔu,*

ʔoh:o-w	ʔaṭ̯:i-:kʰe	c̓u:ʔu
give-PFV	3C-POSS	arrow

kʰaʔbeyey ču:maṭčon ʔoh:ow ʔaṭ:i:kʰe ċu:ʔu.

kʰaʔbe=yey ču:maṭ=čon ʔoh:o-w ʔaṭ:i-:kʰe ċu:ʔu

rock=AGT gray.squirrel=PAT give-PFV 3C-POSS arrow

'(He) gave (him) his own arrow [lit. 'bow']; rock (man) gave his own arrow [lit. 'bow'] to gray squirrel.'

(3.4) *ču:maṭyey, haha ṭeč̓:aw:amkʰe k̓a:de.*

ču:maṭ=yey haha ṭeč̓:aw=wa=mkʰe k̓a:-de

gray.squirrel=AGT haha much=COP.EVID=2SG.POSS friend-VOC

'Gray squirrel (said), "Aha, yours is too much, friend!"'

(3.5) *ṭeč̓:aw ʔahsič̓ duʔṭaw:amkʰe ċu:ʔuʔwam:u k̓a:de.*

ṭeč̓:aw ʔahsič̓ duʔṭa-w=wa=mkʰe ċu:ʔu=ʔwam:u k̓a:-de

much hard feel.by.touch-PFV=COP.EVID=2SG.POSS arrow=DET.SUBJ friend-VOC

"(It) feels too tough, your arrow [lit. 'bow'], friend."

(3.1) Gray squirrel (said) to rock (man), "You will try pulling my arrow [lit. 'bow'] first." (3.2) "Yes," (rock man said). (3.3) (He) gave (him) his own arrow [lit. 'bow']; rock (man) gave his own arrow [lit. 'bow'] to gray squirrel. (3.4) Gray squirrel (said), "Aha, yours is too much, friend!" (3.5) "(It) feels too tough, your arrow [lit. 'bow'], friend."

(4.1) *ma: waʔ:an bedʔeṭway ʔakʰ:ohča.*

ma: waʔ:an bedʔe-ṭway-Ø ʔakʰ:o=hča

DEM now handle?-PL?[9]-PFV two=COLL

'Now they handled (them), both of them.'

(4.2) *ma:mu kʰaʔbeyey wi:minhkʰayʔden ču:maṭwam:u hoʔ:owi biʔk̓ik̓:iw šiʔmiʔwan,*

ma:mu kʰaʔbe=yey wi:mi=nhkʰay-ʔd-en

DEM rock=AGT there=ward-HAB-D.SIM

ču:maṭ=wam:u hoʔ:o=wi biʔk̓i~k̓:i-w šiʔmi=ʔwan

gray.squirrel=DET.SUBJ tooth=INSTR gnaw~ITER-PFV bow-DET.OBJ

'While this rock (man) was (turning away)[10] toward there, gray squirrel gnawed the bow with (his) teeth.'

(4.3) *ma:mu kʰaʔbeyey hi:maʔwan cim cim hnikaw duhnat̯̓dun.*

ma:mu kʰaʔbe=yey hi:ma=ʔwan cim cim hni-ka-w

DEM rock=AGT sinew=DET.OBJ cim cim say-CAUS-PFV

duhnat̯̓-du-n

try.by.touch-HAB-S.SIM

'This rock (man) made the sinew say *cim cim* while continuously trying (it).'

(4.4) *ma:mu kuṭ:u ču:maṭ̓yey biʔk̓ik̓:iw, wi:minhkʰay huʔ:učwaden.*

ma:mu kuṭ:u ču:maṭ̓=yey biʔk̓i~k̓:i-w

DEM just gray.squirrel=AGT gnaw~ITER-PFV

wi:mi=nhkʰay huʔ:uč[11]-wad-en

there=ward face-HAB-D.SIM

'This gray squirrel just gnawed while (rock man) was facing toward there.'

(4.5) *ču:maṭ̓yey kʰaʔbeyčon wey šuhnat̯in k̓a:de,*

ču:maṭ̓=yey kʰaʔbe=yčon wey šuhnat̯-in k̓a:-de

gray.squirrel=AGT rock=PAT now[12] try.by.pulling-SG.IMP friend-VOC

'Gray squirrel (said) to rock (man), "Now try pulling (it), friend!"'

(4.6) *yow hniba šuhnat̯̓, ču:maṭ̓čo:kʰe šiʔmiʔwan.*

yow hni-ba šuhnat̯̓-Ø ču:maṭ̓=čo:kʰe šiʔmi=ʔwan

oh say-S.SEQ try.by.pulling-PFV gray.squirrel=POSS bow=DET.OBJ

'(Rock man) having said "Oh," (he) tried to pull (it), gray squirrel's bow.'

(4.7) *šuč̓:at̯ʰot̯̓,*

šuč̓:a=t̯ʰot̯̓

break.by.pulling=NEG

'(Rock man) did not break it by pulling.'

(4.8) *kuṭ:u ʔah:ay daṭ̓:i:yawmeṭ̓ de:dedu.*

kuṭ:u ʔah:ay daṭ̓:i:-ya-w=meṭ̓ de:de-du

just stick twist-DEFOC-PFV=like Pull ~ handle[13]-IPFV

'(He) just kept pulling (it) like a bendable stick.'

(4.1) Now they handled (them), both of them. (4.2) While this rock (man) was (turning away)[14] toward there, gray squirrel gnawed the bow with (his) teeth. (4.3) This rock (man) made the sinew say *cim cim* while continuously trying (it). (4.4) This gray squirrel just gnawed while (rock man) was facing toward there. (4.5) Gray squirrel (said) to rock (man), "Now try pulling (it), friend!" (4.6) (Rock man) having said "Oh," (he) tried to pull (it), gray squirrel's bow. (4.7) (Rock man) did not break it by pulling. (4.8) (He) just kept pulling (it) like a bendable stick.

(5.1) *kuṭ:u č̓a:šba biʔk̓ik̓:iw ču:maṭ̓yey.*

kuṭ:u   č̓a:šba   biʔk̓i~k̓:i-w   ču:maṭ̓=yey

just   always   gnaw~ITER-PFV   gray.squirrel=AGT

'Gray squirrel just kept gnawing continuously.'

(5.2) *k^{h}aʔbeyey t̯eč̓:aw ʔahsičwa k̓a:de hniba šiʔmiʔwan ʔam:at̯on ha:new*

k^{h}aʔbe=yey   t̯eč̓:aw   ʔahsič=wa   k̓a:-de   hni-ba

rock=AGT   much   hard=COP.EVID   friend-VOC   say-S.SEQ

šiʔmi=ʔwan   ʔam:a=t̯on   ha:ne-w

bow=DET.OBJ   ground=LOC   lay-PFV

'Rock (man) laid the bow on the ground after having said, "(It) is too hard, friend!"'

(5.3) *duhsun,*

duhsun-Ø

quit-PFV

'(He) quit.'

(5.4) *ma: ču:maṭ̓yey ma: šuhnak^{h}:e, kuʔmu biʔk̓ik̓:ibak^{h}ma:yow.*

ma: ču:maṭ̓=yey   ma: šuhna-k^{h}:e

DEM   gray.squirrel=AGT   DEM   try.by.pulling-FUT

kuʔmu   biʔk̓i~k̓:i-ba=k^{h}ma:yow[15]

all   gnaw~ITER-S.SEQ=after

'Gray squirrel tried to pull (the bow) after having gnawed all over (it).'

(5.5) *ma: ču:maṭ̓yey šuhnat̪̓, ʔat̪:i biʔk̓ik̓:iwa:ni šuc̓:aw.*

ma:	ču:muṭ̓=yey	šuhnat̪̓-Ø	ʔat̪:i
DEM	gray.squirrel=AGT	try.by.pulling-PFV	3C.AGT

biʔk̓i~k̓:i=wa:ni	šuc̓:a-w
gnaw~ITER=LOC	break.by.pulling-PFV

'Gray squirrel tried to pull (the bow); he broke (it) by pulling where he was gnawing (it).'

(5.1) Gray squirrel just kept gnawing continuously. (5.2) Rock (man) laid the bow on the ground after having said, "(It) is too hard, friend!" (5.3) (He) quit. (5.4) Gray squirrel tried to pull (the bow) after having gnawed all over (it). (5.5) Gray squirrel tried to pull (the bow); he broke (it) by pulling where he was gnawing (it).

(6.1) *kʰaṭ:ič̓a:čo šuc̓:aw:aʔmaʔkʰe*

kʰaṭ:ič̓a:-čo	šuc̓:a-w=wa=ʔma=ʔkʰe
bad-VOC	break.by.pulling-PFV=COP.EVID=2SG.AGT=1SG.POSS

hi:liʔma	*kaš:okʰ:et̪ʰot̪̓wa*
hi:li=ʔma	kaš:o-kʰ:e=t̪ʰot̪̓=wa
where[16]=2SG.AGt	live-FUT=NEG=COP.EVID

mihyanakʰ:eʔwamt̪aʔa.

mihyana-kʰ:e=ʔwa=mt̪a=ʔa

kill[17]-FUT=COP.EVID=2SG.PAT=1SG.AGt

'O bad (one), you broke my (bow) by pulling! You will not survive anywhere—I will kill you!'

(6.2) *ha:mini:li ču:maṭ̓yey ʔat̪:i:kʰe šiʔmiʔyowan heʔbeba[18] kal:i kʰat̪:akay hač:abiy,*

ha:mini-:li	ču:maṭ̓=yey	ʔat̪:i-:kʰe	šiʔmi=ʔyowan
and.then-D.SEQ	gray.squirrel=AGT	3C-POSS	bow=DET.OBJ
heʔbe[19]-ba	kal:i-Ø	kʰat̪:-akay-Ø	hač:a-biy-Ø
pick.up.long.object-S.SEQ	up-DIFFUSE	run-DIR-PFV	fly[20]-DIR-PFV

'After (rock man) had done so, gray squirrel, having picked up his own bow, ran and fled up (a tree).'

(6.3) *ma: kʰaʔbeyey kʰat̪:aba*[21] *kʰa:leʔyowan dic̓:aw*

ma: kʰaʔbe=yey kʰat̪:a-ba kʰa:le=ʔyowan dic̓:a-w

DEM rock=AGT run-S.SEQ tree=DET.OBJ break.by.body-PFV

'After rock man had run (after gray squirrel), (he) broke the tree with (his) body.'

(6.4) *dihna:ba ma: ču:maṭ̓čok̓o kʰa:leʔyowan ʔahčʰaw.*

dihna:-ba ma: ču:maṭ̓=čo=k̓o kʰa:le=ʔyowan ʔahčʰa-w

try.by.body-S.SEQ DEM gray.squirrel=OBL=COM tree=DET.OBJ fall[22]-PFV

'After having tried the tree with his body, the tree with gray squirrel (in it) fell.'

(6.5) *ma: ču:maṭ̓yey kʰat̪:ad:u pʰal:a kʰa:let̪on kʰat̪:akay.*

ma: ču:maṭ̓=yey kʰat̪:-ad:-u pʰal:a

DEM gray.squirrel=AGT run-DIR-PFV again[23]

kʰa:le=t̪on kʰat̪:-akay-Ø

tree=LOC run-DIR-PFV

'Gray squirrel ran about and ran up another tree.'

(6.6) *kʰa:leʔwan kuʔmu di:lac̓aw, kʰaʔbeyey.*

kʰa:le=ʔwan kuʔmu di-:la-c̓a-w kʰaʔbe=yey

tree=DET.OBJ all by.body-PL.ACT-break-PFV rock=AGT

'Rock (man) broke all of the trees with his body.'

(6.7) *ʔat̪:it̪o šiʔbawi kʰa:le di:lac̓kaw mo:k̓ot̪in.*

ʔat̪:i-t̪o šiʔba=wi kʰa:le di-:la-c̓-ka-w

3C-PAT body=INSTR tree by.body-PL.ACT-break-CAUS-PFV

mo:k̓o[24]-t̪-in

strike-PL.ACT-S.SIM

'With his own body, he struck and broke the trees.'

(6.8) *ha:meṭ̓ nu:haṭ̓duway.*

ha:meṭ̓ nu:hat̪-duway[25]-Ø

thus several.run-?-PFV

'Thus they ran about.'

(6.9) *kʰa:wan ʔahṭʰi:t̪on kʰa:t̪at̪kay,*

kʰa:wan ʔahṭʰi:=t̪on kʰa:t̪a-t̪-kay-Ø

Douglas.fir big.DISTR=LOC run-PL.ACT-DIR-PFV

'(Gray squirrel) kept running up big Douglas fir trees.'

(6.10) *hi:ʔin:at̪i duk:elhe:t̪ʰot̪̓ kʰaʔbeyey, kʰa:wan ʔahṭʰi:wan nat̪i di:laċaw.*

hi:ʔi-n=nat̪i duk:elhe:=t̪ʰot̪̓ kʰaʔbe=yey

DEM-PAT=but hard.to.do=NEG rock=AGT

kʰa:wan ʔahṭʰi:=wan nat̪i di-:la-ċa-w

Douglas.fir big.DISTR=DET.OBJ but by.body-PL.ACT-break-PFV

'None of them was difficult (for) rock (man); (he) broke (each of) the big Douglas fir trees.'

(6.1) O bad (one), you broke my (bow) by pulling! You will not survive anywhere—I will kill you! (6.2) After (rock man) had done so, gray squirrel, having picked up his own bow, ran and fled up (a tree). (6.3) After rock man had run (after gray squirrel), (he) broke the tree with (his) body. (6.4) After having tried the tree with his body, the tree with gray squirrel (in it) fell. (6.5) Gray squirrel ran about and ran up another tree. (6.6) Rock (man) broke all of the trees with his body. (6.7) With his own body, he struck and broke the trees. (6.8) Thus they ran about. (6.9) (Gray squirrel) kept running up big Douglas fir trees. (6.10) None of them was difficult (for) rock (man); (he) broke (each of) the big Douglas fir trees.

(7.1) *ʔahšiyanči:li ʔakʰ:at̪ow nu:hat̪law,*

ʔahšiyan-či-:li ʔakʰ:a=t̪ow[26] nu:hat̪-la-w

evening-SEM-D.SEQ water=ABL several.run-DIR-PFV

'After evening fell, they ran down to the water.'

(7.2) *ham:i waʔ:an ču:maṭ̓yey šahčonhkʰlet̪on pʰil:akay,*

ham:i waʔ:an ču:maṭ̓=yey šahčonhkʰle=t̪on pʰil:-akay-Ø

there now gray.squirrel=AGT sugar.pine=LOC crawl-DIR-PFV

'There, gray squirrel now crawled up onto a sugar pine.'

(7.3) *pʰil:aka:ba ču:maṭyey yuhswe:li ma: kʰa:leʔwam:u dič̓:at̪ʰu.*

pʰil:-aka:-ba   ču:maṭ=yey   yuhswe-:li   ma:
crawl-DIR-S.SEQ   gray.squirrel=AGT   so.be.it[27]-D.SEQ   DEM

kʰa:le=ʔwam:u[28]   di-č̓:a-t̪ʰu
tree=DET.SUBJ   by.body-break-PROH

'After crawling up (the sugar pine), gray squirrel (said), "So be it—do not break this tree with your body!"'

(7.4) *ma: waʔ:an kʰaʔbeyey dihnat̪du kʰa:leʔwan,*

ma: waʔ:an   kʰaʔbe=yey   dihnat̪-du   kʰa:le=ʔwan
DEM   now   rock=AGT   try.by.body-IPFV   tree=DET.OBJ

haʔduwa:=t̪ow   kʰat̪:-ak̓du[29]-n   dihnat̪-du
far=ABL   run-?-S.SIM   try.by.body-IPFV

'Now this rock (man) kept trying the tree with (his) body; from far (back), (rock man) continued to run (at and) try the (tree) with (his) body.'

(7.5) *ma: waʔ:an kʰa:leʔwam:u hič̓:a:t̪ʰot̪.*

ma: waʔ:an   kʰa:le=ʔwam:u   hič̓:a-:[30]=t̪ʰot̪
DEM   now   tree=DET.SUBJ   break.without.agent-?=NEG

'Now this tree did not break (on its own after the damage had been inflicted by rock man).'

(7.6) *duk:elhey.*

duk:elhey-Ø
hard.to.do-PFV

'(Rock man) had difficulty (breaking the tree).'

(7.7) *ha:miniba kʰa:le sa:mat̪in čahčiw.*

ha:mini-ba   kʰa:le   sa:ma-t̪in[31]   čahči-w
and.then-S.SEQ   tree   near-?   sit-PFV

'(Rock man) then sat beside the tree.'

(7.8) *kʰa:leʔwan haṭʰ:ihlaw,*

kʰa:le=ʔwan   haṭʰ:ihla-w
tree=DET.OBJ   by.leg.encircle-PFV

'(He) wrapped (his) legs around the tree.'

(7.9) *ha:miniba kʰa:leʔwan be:new,*

ha:mini-ba	kʰa:le=ʔwan	be:ne-w
and.then-S.SEQ	tree=DET.OBJ	hug-PFV

'Then (rock man) hugged the tree.'

(7.10) *ču:maṭwam:u kal:i čum:aw,*

ču:maṭ=wam:u	kal:i-Ø	čum:a-w
gray.squirrel=DET.SUBJ	up-DIFFUSE	sit[32]-PFV

'Gray squirrel was sitting up (in the tree).'

(7.11) *kʰaʔbeʔwam:u ʔiy:oṯow či:yow.*

kʰaʔbe=ʔwam:u	ʔiy:o=ṯow	či:yo-w
rock=DET.SUBJ	below=ABL	stay[33]-PFV

'Rock (man) sat on the ground beneath (him).'

(7.1) After evening fell, they ran down to the water. (7.2) There, gray squirrel now crawled up onto a sugar pine. (7.3) After crawling up (the sugar pine), gray squirrel (said), "So be it—do not break this tree with your body!" (7.4) Now this rock (man) kept trying the tree with (his) body; from far (back), (rock man) continued to run (at and) try the (tree) with (his) body. (7.5) Now this tree did not break (on its own after the damage had been inflicted by rock man). (7.6) (Rock man) had difficulty (breaking the tree). (7.7) (Rock man) then sat beside the tree. (7.8) (He) wrapped (his) legs around the tree. (7.9) Then (rock man) hugged the tree. (7.10) Gray squirrel was sitting up (in the tree). (7.11) Rock (man) sat on the ground beneath (him).

(8.1) *ha:miniba kʰaʔbeyčon si:ma mi:ṭiw,*

ha:mini-ba	kʰaʔbe=yčon	si:ma	mi:ṭi-w
and.then-S.SEQ	rock=PAT	sleep	lie-PFV

'Rock (man) then fell asleep.'

(8.2) *ha:mini:li ču:maṭyey si:ma mikʰ:o:li ʔam:anhkʰay pʰil:alʔba,*

ha:mini-:li	ču:maṭ=yey	si:ma	mikʰ:o[34]-:li
and.then-D.SEQ	gray.squirrel=AGT	sleep	snore-DS.SEQ

ʔam:a=nhkʰay	pʰil:-alʔ-ba
earth=toward	crawl-DIR-S.SEQ

'(Rock man) having (fallen asleep), gray squirrel, when (rock man) snored, ran down toward the ground.'

(8.3) *kʰaʔbeyey ka:linhkʰay huʔ:uṭmaw,*

kʰaʔbe=yey ka:li=nhkʰay huʔ:u-ṭ-ma-w

rock=AGT up=toward face-DENOM-ESSIVE-PFV

'Rock (man) faced upward.'

(8.4) *k̓ohṭokʰṭowa:ni ʔihčok̓ ču:maṭyey kʰaʔbeyčon.*

k̓ohṭokʰṭo[35]=wa:ni ʔihčok̓-Ø ču:maṭ=yey kʰaʔbe=yčon

base.of.neck=LOC shoot-PFV gray.squirrel=AGT rock=PAT

'(He) shot (him) in the soft spot between the collarbones, gray squirrel (did it) to rock (man).'

(8.5) *ham:i ya:la kʰaʔbe ʔačʰ:ow čahṭin.*

ham:i ya:la kʰaʔbe ʔačʰ:o-w čahṭin-Ø

there only rock NEG.EXISTENTIAL-PFV EXISTENTIAL.VERB[36]

'Only there was no rock there.'

(8.6) *čohčʰiwʔduy.*

čohčʰiwʔduy[37]-Ø

strike.down-PFV

'(Gray squirrel had) struck (him) down.'

(9.1) *ha:mini:li kʰaʔbeyčon k̓al:aw.*

ha:mini-:li kʰaʔbe=yčon k̓al:a-w

and.then-D.SEQ rock=PAT one.die[38]-PFV

'(Gray squirrel) having done so, rock (man) died.'

(9.2) *ha:miniba ma:mu ʔakʰ:aṭow kʰaʔbe ya:laṭi, kʰaʔbeyčon muhlamba.*

ha:mini-ba ma:mu ʔakʰ:a=ṭow kʰaʔbe ya:la=ṭi

and.then-S.SEQ DEM water=ABL rock only=INCH

kʰaʔbe=yčon muhlam[39]-ba

rock-PAT break.up-S.SEQ

'(Rock man) having (died), this (one) only became the rocks on the coast, rock (man) having broken up.'

(9.1.) (Gray squirrel) having done so, rock (man) died. (9.2) (Rock man) having (died), this (one) only became the rocks on the coast, rock (man) having broken up.

COMPLETE FREE TRANSLATION

(1.1) Gray squirrel always went around outside. (He) stayed alone. (1.2) (He) found this rock man outside. (1.3) Rock man (said), "Hey, where have you come from, friend? I want to find people, friend. (1.4) In order to gamble, I want to find people." (1.5) [Gray squirrel replied,] "Yes, it is good. I am also feeling bad, staying alone. (1.6) I also want to find people." (1.7) [Rock man said,] "Yes, we shall gamble; we shall try the bows [lit. 'arrow'] by pulling (them)." (1.8) [Gray squirrel replied,] "Yes, it is good. (1.9) We shall meet each other here in the morning, friend. (1.10) We shall meet each other early." (1.11) [Rock man replied,] "Yes, we shall arrive here." (1.12) [Gray squirrel said,] "Yes, I too shall arrive here; we shall meet each other here."

(2.1) Gray squirrel went toward home. (2.2) Rock (man) also went toward home. (2.3) Gray squirrel arrived at home, at his own home. (2.4) Night fell. (2.5) (He) lay down. (2.6) In the morning, rock (man) arose, (and) gray squirrel arose. (2.7) Gray squirrel went toward the place where they were to meet each other. (2.8) Rock (man) went. (2.9) Gray squirrel arrived first. (2.10) (He) stayed there and waited. (2.11) Rock (man) arrived. (2.12) "Do you walk about (so) early, friend?" Rock (man said). (2.13) Gray squirrel (said), "Yes, I could not sleep (during the) night (because of my) wanting to gamble!"

(3.1) Gray squirrel (said) to rock (man), "You will try pulling my arrow [lit. 'bow'] first." (3.2) "Yes," (rock man said). (3.3) (He) gave (him) his own arrow [lit. 'bow']; rock (man) gave his own arrow [lit. 'bow'] to gray squirrel. (3.4) Gray squirrel (said), "Aha, yours is too much, friend!" (3.5) "(It) feels too tough, your arrow [lit. 'bow'], friend."

(4.1) Now they handled (them), both of them. (4.2) While this rock (man) was (turning away) toward there, gray squirrel gnawed the bow with (his) teeth. (4.3) This rock (man) made the sinew say *cim cim* while continuously trying (it). (4.4) This gray squirrel just gnawed while (rock man) was facing toward there. (4.5) Gray squirrel (said) to rock (man), "Now try pulling (it), friend!" (4.6) (Rock man) having said "Oh," (he) tried to pull (it), gray squirrel's bow. (4.7) (Rock man) did not break it by pulling. (4.8) (He) just kept pulling (it) like a bendable stick.

(5.1) Gray squirrel just kept gnawing continuously. (5.2) Rock (man) laid the bow on the ground after having said, "(It) is too hard, friend!" (5.3) (He) quit. (5.4) Gray squirrel tried to pull (the bow) after having gnawed all over (it). (5.5) Gray squirrel tried to pull (the bow); he broke (it) by pulling where he was gnawing (it).

(6.1) O bad (one), you broke my (bow) by pulling! You will not survive anywhere—I will kill you! (6.2) After (rock man) had done so, gray squirrel, having picked up his own bow, ran and fled up (a tree). (6.3) After rock man had run (after gray squirrel), (he) broke the tree with (his) body. (6.4) After having tried the tree with his body, the tree with gray squirrel (in it) fell. (6.5) Gray squirrel ran about and ran up another tree. (6.6) Rock (man) broke all of the trees with his body. (6.7) With his own body, he struck and broke the trees. (6.8) Thus they ran about. (6.9) (Gray squirrel) kept running up big Douglas fir trees. (6.10) None of them was difficult (for) rock (man); (he) broke (each of) the big Douglas fir trees.

(7.1) After evening fell, they ran down to the water. (7.2) There, gray squirrel now crawled up onto a sugar pine. (7.3) After crawling up (the sugar pine), gray squirrel (said), "So be it—do not break this tree with your body!" (7.4) Now this rock (man) kept trying the tree with (his) body; from far (back), (rock man) continued to run (at and) try the (tree) with (his) body. (7.5) Now this tree did not break (on its own after the damage had been inflicted by rock man). (7.6) (Rock man) had difficulty (breaking the tree). (7.7) (Rock man) then sat beside the tree. (7.8) (He) wrapped (his) legs around the tree. (7.9) Then (rock man) hugged the tree. (7.10) Gray squirrel was sitting up (in the tree). (7.11) Rock (man) sat on the ground beneath (him).

(8.1) Rock (man) then fell asleep. (8.2) (Rock man) having (fallen asleep), gray squirrel, when (rock man) snored, ran down toward the ground. (8.3) Rock (man) faced upward. (8.4) (He) shot (him) in the soft spot between the collarbones, gray squirrel (did it) to rock (man). (8.5) Only there was no rock there. (8.6) (Gray squirrel had) struck (him) down.

(9.1.) (Gray squirrel) having done so, rock (man) died. (9.2) (Rock man) having (died), this (one) only became the rocks on the coast, rock (man) having broken up.

[H VIII]

So. Pomo Text VIII

Rock Man

16:103–17:3

[1]	ču:máṭ̓yey	č’á:šba	kúl:u	hwadémʔdu,	k̓ay:áma
	grey squirrel	always	outside	always goes around	alone

čí:yow./	ma:	kʰáʔbe	[ʔ]ač:áywan	dáʔt̯̓aw	kúl:u./
stays	[blank]	rock	man	he finds	outside

kʰaʔbe	[ʔ]ač:áy:ey	[ʔ]é:	maʔkaʔma	hé:t̯ow	k̓á:de
rock	man	well	now ? you	whence	friend!

[ʔ]ahčahčéy	daʔt̯̓áw	hudʔakaywáʔa,	k̓á:de./
People	find	I want	friend

[ʔ]áhka hodʔó:t̯i	k̓á:de	[ʔ]a:ʔ( )ahčahčéy	daʔt̯̓áw	hudʔakáywa./
in order to gamble	friend!	I people	find	want

híy:o	k̓oʔdíʔwa,	[ʔ]át̯:o	p[ʰ]á:la	kʰáč’:aw	hit̯:adúw:a
Yes	it is good	we [?]	in turn	lonesome, had	feel

k̓ay:áma	čí:yon./
alone	staying

[ʔ]a:	p[ʰ]á:la	[ʔ]ahčahčéy	daʔt̯̓áw	hudʔákay./
I	in turn	people	find	want

híy:o	[ʔ]áhkaʔwaʔya	hodʔókʰ:e,	ċú:ʔuʔ( )waʔya
Yes	we will gamble	[blank]	arrows we

šuhnamhúkʰ:e./	híy:o	k̓oʔdíʔwa.
will try e. o. out	Yes	it's good

má:liʔ waʔya	kʰaʔ[:]á:le	daʔt̯̓amhúkʰ:e	k̓á:de./
here we	in morning	we will meet	friend

[ʔ]it̯[ʰ]:ín( )waʔya	daʔt̯̓amhúkʰ:e./
early we	will meet

hí:yo má:liʔwaʔa kahkot̪íkʰ:e./
Yes here I will arrive

hí:yo [ʔ]a: p[ʰ]á:la má:li kahkot̪íkʰ:e,/ má:liʔ wáʔya daʔṭ̪amhúkʰ:e.
Yes I in turn here will arrive here we will meet

[2] čú:maṭyey [ʔ]ahčáŋhkʰay hó:liw./ kʰaʔbéyey p[ʰ]á:la
[blank] home goes rock also

hó:liw, [ʔ]ahčáŋhkʰay./ čú:maṭyey [ʔ]áč:a háč’:ow, [ʔ]at̪:í:kʰe [ʔ]áč:a./
goes home [blank] home arrives his own home

dúw:ey mí:ṭiw kʰaʔ[:]ašk̓áden kʰaʔbéyey t̪ó:bi[y],
it is night he lies down morning rock gets up

ču:máṭyey t̪ó:bi[y] ,/ ma: čú:maṭyey hó:liw, [ʔ]at̪:íyey
Squirrel gets up now squirrel goes they (selves)

daʔṭ̪ámhukʰ:eʔyowant̪óŋhkʰay./
to where they will meet

kʰaʔbéyey hó:liw, čú:maṭyey waʔ[:]á:t̪on háč’:ow./
rock goes squirrel before, ahead, first arrives

hám:i čí:yow, mač:éč’in./ kʰaʔbéyey kahkót̪i[y]./
there he sits waiting rock arrives

[ʔ]it̪[ʰ]:íŋkaʔ( )ma hwád:u
early ? you walk around

k̓á:de, kʰaʔbéyey./ ču:máṭyey, hí:yo, sí:ma mí:ṭit̪ʰenṭ̪óʔt̪o
friend rock [blank] yes I can’t sleep

dúw:e, [ʔ]áhka húdʔan./
night gambling wanting to

[3] ču:máṭyey kʰaʔbéyčon [ʔ]á:ma wayíʔwaʔkʰe čú:ʔu
squirrel to rock you first my bow

šuhnákʰ:e./ hí:yo. [ʔ]óh:ow [ʔ]at̪:í:kʰe čú:ʔu, kʰaʔbéyey
will try Yes he gives his own bow rock

čú:maṭčon	[ʔ]óh:ow	[ʔ]at̯:í:kʰe	c̓ú:ʔu./	čú:maṭyey,
to squirrel	gives	his own	bow	squirrel

hahá	t̯éč’[:]aw( )wámkʰe	k̓á:de./	t̯éč’[:]aw	[ʔ]ahsič’
aha	too much is yours	friend	too much	hard, tough

duʔt̯aw:ámkʰe	c̓ú:ʔuʔwám:u	k̓á:de./
feels	your bow	friend

[4]

ma:	waʔ[:]an	bedʔéṭway	[ʔ]akʰ:óhča./	má:mu	kʰaʔbéyey
now	this	they handle	both	this	rock

wí:miŋhkʰáyʔden	čú:maṭwám:u	hoʔ[:]ówi
when every time he (turns) this way	squirrel	w. tooth

biʔk̓ik̓:iw	šiʔmiʔwan,/	má:mu	kʰaʔbéyey
he bites, gnaws	the bow	this	rock

hí:maʔwan	cím	cím	hníkaw	duhnáṭ̯dun./	má:mu	kuṭ:u
sinew	[blank]	[blank]	makes it say	always trying it	this	all the time

čú:maṭyey	biʔk̓ík̓:iw,	wí:miŋhkʰay	huʔ[:]učwáden./	ču:máṭyey
squirrel	gnaws	this way	while he always faces	[blank]

kʰaʔbéyčon	wéy	šuhnát̯in	k̓á:de,/	yów	hniba	šúhnat̯,
[blank]	now	try (to pull)!	friend	[blank]	having said	he tries to pull

čú:maṭčó:kʰe	šiʔmíʔwan./	šuc̓:á:t̯[ʰ]ot̯,	kúṭ:u	[ʔ]ah:áy	daṭ:i:yáwmeṭ
squirrel's	bow	he doesn't break it	just	wood	flexible, easily

de:dédu./
he pulls it, handles it

[5]

kúṭ:u	č’á:šba	biʔk̓ík̓:iw	ču:máṭyey./	kʰaʔbéyey
just	all the time	he chews, gnaws	squirrel	rock

t̯éč’:aw	[ʔ]ahsičwa	k̓á:de	hniba	šiʔmíʔwan	[ʔ]ám:at̯on	há:new,
too	hard is	friend!	having said	bow	on ground	he lays

dúhsun,/	ma:	čú:maṭyey	ma:	šuhnák^h:e,	kúʔmu
he quits	now	[blank]	now	will try	all

biʔk̓ík̓:ibak^{h}má:yow./	(or biʔk̓ipk̓íbak^{h}má:yow)/	ma:	čú:maṭyey
after having gnawed up	[blank]	[blank]	[blank]

šúhnat̪,	[ʔ]át̪:i	bíʔk̓ik̓i:wá:ni	šúc̓:aw./
tries, pulls	he self	where he gnawed	he broke it

[6]

k^{h}áṭ:ič'á:čo	šúc̓:awaʔmáʔk^{h}e/	hí:liʔ( )ma	kaš:ók^h:et̪^{h}ót̪wa
nasty one!	you broke mine	where?	will not be safe

mihyanák^h:eʔwamt̪áʔa./	ha:mini:li	čú:maṭyey	[ʔ]at̪:í:k^{h}e
I'm going to kill you	then	squirrel	his own

šíʔmiʔyówan	heʔbé(:)ba	kál:i	k^{h}at̪:ákay	hač:ábi[y],/	ma:	k^{h}aʔbéyey
bow	having taken	up	ran away	[blank]	[blank]	[blank]

k^{h}at̪:á(:)ba	k^{h}a:léʔyowan	díc̓:aw	dihná:ba/
having run	tree	he breaks w. body	having (tried) pushed w. body

ma:	čú:maṭčók̓o	k^{h}a:léʔyowan	[ʔ]áhč^{h}aw./	ma:	čú:maṭyey
[blank]	with squirrel	tree	[blank]	[blank]	[blank]

k^{h}at̪:ád:u,	p[^{h}]ál:a	k^{h}á:let̪on	k^{h}at̪:ákay./	k^{h}a:léʔwan
runs around	again	on tree	runs up	trees

kúʔmu	di:lác̓aw,	k^{h}aʔbéyey./	[ʔ]at̪:ít̪o	šiʔbáwi
all	he breaks	rock	his	w. body

k^{h}á:le	di:lác̓kaw	mo:k̓ót̪in./
tree	he breaks	striking them w. body

há:meṭ	nú:hat̪dúway./	k^{h}á:wan	[ʔ]ahṭ^{h}i:t̪on
thus	they keep running (around)	fir tree	on big ones

k^{h}a:t̪át̪kay,/	hi:ʔin:át̪i	duk:elhé:t̪^{h}ot̪	k^{h}aʔbéyey,
he keeps running up	anyone not	he doesn't find it hard	rock

k^{h}á:wan	[ʔ]ahṭ^{h}í:wan	nát̪i	di:lác̓aw./
fir	big ones	(but) even	he breaks them

[7]

[ʔ]ahšíyančí:li	[ʔ]akʰ:át̪ow	nu:hát̪law,/	hám:i	wáʔ[:]an
when evening comes	at coast	they run down to	here	now

ču:máṭyey	šahčoŋhkʰlét̪on	p[ʰ]il:ákay,/	p[ʰ]íl:aká:ba	čú:maṭyey
[blank]	on (sugar?) pine	he runs up	having run up	squirrel

yúhswé:li [?]	ma:	kʰá:leʔwám:u	dic̓:át̪ʰu./	ma:	waʔ[:]an	kʰaʔbéyey
[blank]	this	tree	don't break it!	and	now	rock

dihnáṭdu	kʰa:léʔwan,	haʔduwá:t̪ow	kʰat̪:ák̓dun
he keeps pushing, bumping w. body	the tree	from far	always running

dihnáṭdu./	ma:	waʔ[:]an	kʰá:leʔwám:u	hic̓:á:t̪ʰoṭ.
he keeps bumping	[blank]	now	the tree	didn't break

duk:élhey./	ha:mini(:)ba	kʰá:le	sá:mat̪in	čáhčiw./
it's hard for him, he can't do it	[blank]	tree	near, beside	he sits down

kʰa:léʔwan	haṭʰ:íhlaw,	ha:mini(:)ba	kʰa:léʔwan	bé:new,/
tree	he puts legs around	then	tree	he hugs

čú:maṭwám:u	kál:i	čúm:aw,	kʰaʔbéʔwam:u	[ʔ]iy:ót̪ow	čí:yow./
squirrel	up	is sitting	[blank]	under	he sits

[8]

ha:mini(:)ba	kʰaʔbéyčon	sí:ma mí:ṭiw,/
then	rock	went to sleep

ha:mini:li	čú:maṭyey	sí:ma	mikʰ:ó:li
then	squirrel	(asleep)	when he snored, started to snore

[ʔ]am:áŋhkʰay	p[ʰ]il:álʔba,	—/	kʰaʔbéyey	ká:liŋhkʰay
to ground	having run down		rock	upwards

huʔ[:]út̪maw,/	k̓oht̪okʰt̪owá:ni	[ʔ]íhčok̓
turns his face	in soft spot between collar bones	shoots

ču:máṭyey	kʰaʔbéyčon./	hám:i	yá:la	kʰáʔbe	[ʔ]áčʰ:ow
squirrel	rock	here	only	rock	was absent

	čáhṭin./	čohčʰiwʔduy./
	(place ?) [in H]	he kills him dead w. first shot

[9]	ha:mini:li	kʰaʔbéyčon	k̓ál:aw./	ha:mini(:)ba	má:mu
	then	rock	dies	then	this

[ʔ]akʰ:áṭow	kʰaʔbé	ya:láṭi,	kʰaʔbéyčon	muhlámba./
on coast	rock	only bécame	rock	having gotten cracked up

[H VIII FREE TRANSLATION]

So. Pomo Text VIII

1. Grey Squirrel always used to go about in the outside. He lived alone. Now he found Rock Man, in the outside.

Rock Man (said), 'Well, now, where (are) you from, friend. I want to find people, friend. In order to gamble, friend, I want to find people.'

'Yes, it is good. I in turn feel lonesome, living alone. I in turn want to find people.'

'Yes, we'll gamble. We'll try each other out in pulling arrows.'

'Yes, it is good.'

'Here we will meet each other in the morning, friend. We will meet each other early.'

'Yes, I will arrive here.'

'Yes, I in turn will arrive here. Here we will meet each other.'

2. Squirrel went off home. Rock in turn went off, home. Squirrel arrived at home, at his home. Night came on. He lay down. In the morning, Rock got up, Squirrel got up. Now, Squirrel went off to where they will meet each other. Rock went off. Squirrel arrived ahead (of Rock). He sat there, waiting. Rock arrived.

'Do you walk around (so) early, friend,' (said) Rock. Squirrel (said), 'Yes, I guess I can't sleep (at) night, desiring gambling.'

3. Squirrel (said) to Rock, 'You will try pulling my arrow first.'

'Yes.'

He handed it to him, his arrow. Rock handed his arrow to Squirrel. Squirrel (said), 'Aha, yours (is) too (tough), friend. It feels awfully tough, this arrow of yours, friend.'

4. Now they kept stretching them, both of them. While this Rock was facing towards there, the Squirrel gnawed it with his teeth, the bow. This Rock made the sinew say 'cim cim', while repeatedly trying it. This Squirrel just gnawed, while (Rock) kept looking towards there.

Squirrel (said) to Rock, 'Now, try pulling it, friend.'

Having said 'Oh. ˇ', he tried pulling it, Squirrel's bow. He didn't break it. He just kept pulling it like a flexible stick.

5. Squirrel just continually gnawed. Rock, having said 'It's too tough, friend,' laid the bow on the ground. He quit. Now, Squirrel tried pulling. He broke it where he gnawed it.

6. 'Dirty thing. ˇ You broke mine. You will not be safe anywhere. I'll kill you.'

He having done so, Squirrel, having picked up his own bow, ran up high (and) ran away.

Now, Rock, having run (after him), having tried to break the tree by pushing with his body—now, the tree fell over together with Squirrel. Now Squirrel ran around, he climbed up onto another tree. He broke them all (with his body), the Rock. He broke all the trees with his body, striking against them.

They kept running around in this way. He kept running up onto big firs. He had no difficulty with any of them whatever, the Rock. He broke any big firs whatever.

7. When evening came on, they ran down by the water. There, now, Squirrel crawled up onto a sugar pine. Having crawled up onto it, Squirrel (said), 'So be it. Don't break this tree.' Now Rock kept pushing against it (with his body), the tree. Running (at it) from far off, he kept pushing against it. Now, that tree didn't break. He had trouble with it.

Having done so, he sat down near the tree. He put his legs around the tree. Having done so, he hugged the tree. Squirrel perched above, Rock sat below.

8. Having done so, Rock went to sleep. He having done so, when he snored, Squirrel, having crawled down to the ground—Rock turned his face upwards—shot him in the soft spot between the collarbones, Squirrel (did it) to Rock. Only there was there no rock, that place being there. He killed him outright.

9. He having done so, Rock died. Having done so, he turned into (the) rocks all over on the coast, Rock having cracked up.

NOTES

Preface

1. Some of the work reflected here was funded by a Documenting Endangered Languages Fellowship from the National Endowment for the Humanities and National Science Foundation (grant number: FN-230222-15). Any views, findings, conclusions, or recommendations expressed in this work do no not necessarily reflect those of the National Endowment for the Humanities and the National Science Foundation.

1. Sociolinguistic Context

1. Southern Pomo speakers have also been referred to as the Gallinomero, a term of uncertain origin with numerous attested variants, including Cainameros, Cainemeros, Calajomanes, Calle-namares, Calle-Nameras, Canaumanos, Canimares, Gallinomeros, Gallonimero, Gallynomeros, Kainamares, Kanimares, Kanimarres, Kianamares, and Kyanamara; three additional variants likely come from this term: Kainama, Kai-mé, and Kalme; and the Southern Pomo communities from the Cloverdale region were also known by a host of variants based on the native name *mus:a:la-hkon* (snake-long) 'Longsnake', a mythical creature (McLendon and Oswalt 1978: 279).
2. The Southern Pomo cognate for the -: 'at' morpheme would be length on the second consonant of the stem, though it is not clear whether the word *hi:mo* 'hole' in Southern Pomo may occur with this morpheme.
3. See McLendon and Oswalt (1978: 277, 286) for a discussion of these two names' meanings; see Walker (2016) for a detailed discussion of Northeastern Pomo (the *čʰéʔe: fóka:* 'Salt People').
4. Here is the actual quote:

p[ʰ]al[:]aʔčey	huʔ:u:=t̪on	. . .	ʔay[:]a:kʰe	čahnu	ʔa:lhok̓o:=t̪ʰot̪̓
white.people	face=on	. . .	1PL.POSS	speech	sev.speak=NEG

'We didn't speak our language in front of whites.'

5. This confusion is not limited to non-linguists. I have been told by at least one linguist with significant experience with a Pomoan language that he assumed Southern Pomo would be little different from its closest Pomoan neighbor. He was therefore surprised to find it a completely different language. Though this scholar knew that all seven Pomoan languages were mutually unintelligible,

I believe the unfortunate geographical designations for the Pomoan languages prejudiced his mind.

6. It is possible, of course, to compare Merriam's transcriptions of otherwise unattested Southern Pomo words with possible cognates in other Pomoan languages. It is generally the case that neighboring Pomoan languages agree in the choice of dental versus alveolar plosives, and in certain positions, it is often possible to determine whether other obstruents should be considered ejectives (i.e., if Central Pomo shows an ejective stop in a cognate word, it can generally be assumed that the under-differentiated form in Merriam's records must share that feature).
7. This is possibly a word for 'bat' (Ramón Billy, pers. comm.).
8. The form *ʔo:ṭʰiy* 'eagle' is recorded from the Dry Creek and Cloverdale dialect region, but I have not heard it pronounced, nor can I testify to the accuracy of the palatal-glide final transcription. I cannot understand why the word for 'eagle' is seemingly swapped in these data: Merriam records from Healdsburg the form known from later records based on the Cloverdale and Dry Creek speech forms, but he records an otherwise unknown form for Cloverdale.
9. Southern Pomo shared with Wappo a handling of cross-cousins that is otherwise unattested in California: "In the case of the xc [=cross-cousins], the nomenclature [of Southern Pomo] (together with that of the neighboring Wappo) is unique for California. F[ather's] s[i]s[ter's] d[aughter] is called by the term for f[ather's] s[i]s[ter] and all of her ♀ descendants through ♀ are similarly designated. F[ather's] s[i]s[ter's] s[on] is called by the term for f[ather's] y[ounger] b[rother], a term applied to all ♂ descendants of f[ather's] s[i]s[ter] through ♀. The reciprocal term applied by a w[o]m[an] to her m[other's] b[rother's] ch[ild] is that which should normally apply to her b[rother's] ch[ild], since her m[other's] b[rother's] ch[ild] calls her by the term for f[ather's] s[i]s[ter]. A m[a]n, however, reciprocates to his m[other's] b[rother's] ch[ild] with the terms for s[on] and d[aughter] which he would normally apply to his o[lder] b[rother's] ch[ild], since they address him as f[ather's] y[ounger] b[rother].

   "We therefore have with the Southern Pomo a grouping of xc [=cross-cousins] with paternal u[ncle] and a[unt] and with fraternal n[i]e[ce] and n[e]p[hew]" (Gifford 1922: 114).
10. Note that Webb (1971) has inexplicably aberrant transcriptions for all Pomoan languages, including badly transliterated Southern Pomo data taken from Halpern's fieldwork.
11. See Barrett (1908) for an extremely detailed list of Southern Pomo place names. Though there is not much extant data on the westernmost Southern Pomo communities, two of the five Southern Pomo consultants from whom Stewart obtained his data were the children of Indians from Southern Pomo

villages to the west of the known Dry Creek dialect villages (Stewart 1943: 30, 51–54). These two consultants, Dan Scott, whose mother was from the village of <Makauca> [clearly *ma:k*^{h}*a-wša* 'Salmon-ridge'], and Sally Ross, whose father was from somewhere named Rock Pile near the coast, appear to have self-identified as being Southern Pomo, and there can be little doubt that Southern Pomo territory did, in fact, extend to the Pacific coast and did divide the Central Pomo from the Kashaya.

12. The correct phonemic transcription for the villages of <Amalako> and <Ahkamodot> cannot be uncovered with complete confidence; however, the first is likely ʔa:ma:la-k:o 'jackrabbit-field' and the second clearly contains the word ʔahk^{h}a- 'water' as its first element.
13. This happened in 1811 according to Oswalt (1961: 6). Bernard Comrie (pers. comm.) suggests that the discrepancy in dates might be due to Russia's continued use of the Julian calendar during this time and the possibility of a mismatch with the Gregorian year.
14. It is also known as Mission San Francisco de Solano.
15. Termination was the government policy whereby Indian tribes could give up their sovereign status (and thus free the government from obligations to the tribes) in exchange for full integration into American society and certain services. In reality, however, termination resulted in little more than the political annihilation of native communities: formerly sovereign lands became taxable lands (i.e., lands subject to fines and confiscation).
16. The original word for deer was *behše* (from Proto Pomo *bihxe), but the word came to mean 'meat' at some point, and the Spanish word *gentil* 'gentile; heathen' was later added to distinguish 'deer' from 'meat' (*hint̪ilku behše* is therefore 'the heathens' meat').
17. Oswalt (pers. comm.) reported that his consultants translated *ce:me:wa* as 'lion', but he was sure it must have been the word for the then already extinct wolf, on the basis of cognates in other Pomoan languages. Oswalt almost surely got this form from C. Hart Merriam's transcription of <Tsā-meu´-wah> 'Big wolf', and this word is all the more problematic because so few Southern Pomo words begin with /c/ [ts].
18. This is the word for the animal only; Coyote, the supernatural trickster, is called *do:wi*, though *do:wi* was not restricted to sacred usage. Reg Elgin, Dry Creek Elder, recalls dollops of dough being called *do:wi-hp*^{h}*a* 'coyote-excrement'.
19. Halpern notes that the people traveled eastwards (*ʔaš:onhk*^{h}*ay*) to obtain fish, which is surely a reference to Clear Lake (H VI; see table 5 in chapter 1, this volume, for citing conventions for unpublished data).
20. The smoke hole (*ho:popon*) was more than simply an opening. Kroeber writes: "One entrance was at the south end, through a long, descending tunnel; an-

other, probably used only in certain ceremonies, was the smoke hole directly over the fire" (1925, 242). And the smoke hole as an entrance through which to converse is a conspicuous part of the story of *nup*^{h}*:e baʔ:ay* 'Skunk Woman': "They looked down in by the smoke-hole. 'My mother is sick, grandfather. Having done so, my mother had me call you.' One of the Elk men (said), 'Say Oh!, say oh! Go, her mo. fa., go. Look at your grandchild'" (H V: 4).

21. I have seen and handled a large *dok:o* which was shown me by its maker, Olive Fulwider of the Dry Creek Band of Pomo Indians. Mrs. Fulwider related how she and her grandmother traveled to the coast (most likely between 1928 and 1935) to find a rock of appropriate size and quality. The two of them, Mrs. Fulwider and her grandmother, spent approximately two years working the rock till it became perfectly smooth and almost cylindrical. I have also handled an ancient *k*^{h}*aʔbet̯̓le* which was uncovered by construction crews and brought into the Dry Creek Rancheria's Santa Rosa office. It was about 12–14 inches in diameter and made of gray stone.
22. Kroeber referred to them as "the principal purveyors of money to central California" (1925, 248–49).
23. Dry Creek would appear to be the more conservative of the two; *ʔač:ay* is cognate with Central Pomo *ča:č̓* and Eastern Pomo *ka:k*^{h}, all of which descend from a Proto Pomo form which McLendon reconstructed as *ʔaká:kʔ (McLendon 1973: 81).
24. My wife and her brother learned four Southern Pomo words as children, three of which had Anglicized pronunciations: *šaʔk̓a* 'black' (Anglicized to [ˈʃakə]); *si:li* 'buttocks'; *ʔahp*^{h}*a* 'excrement' (Anglicized to [ˈʌpə]); and *ʔehp*^{h}*eṭ* 'fart' (Anglicized to [ˈɛp^{h}ɛt]).
25. There is a separate word for a sucking doctor, and this appears to be native. Thompson and colleagues (2006: 43) record the Wappo phrase for 'I am a doctor' as <i ceʔeʔ yomtoʔ>, where <yomtoʔ> is glossed as 'doctor'. It is unclear whether Wappo is the source language for *yomṭa* in Pomoan or whether this word was borrowed into both language families from an outside source at the same time.
26. Thus Central Pomo shares the h-initial form for 'dog' though all other h-initial words in Southern Pomo correspond to Central Pomo forms without the h-initial syllable (compare Southern Pomo *hiʔbu* 'potato' with Central Pomo *bu* 'potato'). Note that neighboring Wappo also has the word <háyu> (Sawyer 1965: 31).
27. The Northeastern Pomo speakers used the word *boʔláw-ka:* 'dog', and this word is not an obvious borrowing from any non-Pomoan language. It does, however, share its first syllable with their verb *bó-n* 'to hunt', which probably bears some relationship to *bóʔo-ka:* 'elk', the most important animal hunted in pre-European times. It is possible that dogs, once introduced into Pomoan culture,

were used in the tracking and hunting of game, and a partially transparent name for the animal might be evidence that dogs arrived more recently.

28. Russian бутылка 'bottle' was borrowed into Kashaya Pomo as *put̪ilka* 'bottle' before entering Southern Pomo as *pʰot̪:ilka*.
29. Halpern notes on the facing page (H EA: 12b) that Elsie Allen knew no other word for 'teacher' beyond the English borrowing.
30. Bibby (1996: 105) gives Laura Somersal's birth date as 1892; Thompson and colleagues state that she was "born before 1890" (2006: xiii).
31. Olive Fulwider's daughter, Dorothy, was told that Olive's mother died young due to poisoning by a local Indigenous elder.
32. Tim Molino has an undergraduate degree in linguistics from the University of California at Berkeley and has worked extensively with the Kashaya Pomo language; he continued his study in a non-linguistics-related discipline at Berkeley at the graduate level.

2. Word Structure

1. Southern Pomo has complex phonological alternations, which can obscure the fundamentally agglutinative nature of the language. When there is no need to draw attention to these alternations, I prefer to show morpheme breaks within phonemic transcription. Thus *hwadun* might be broken down phonemically as /hw-ad-un/ go$_2$-DIR-SG.IMP 'come!'. When these alternations do not allow easy phonemic divisions, I resort to morphophonemic transcription, as in *hwademʔdu* ||hu:w-aded-wadu|| go$_2$-DIR-HAB 'always going about'. However, glossing only follows the morpheme breaks of the phonemic transcription.
2. Spanish words were borrowed, and some of these included non-native phones (such as [f] and [ɾ]), but the extent to which such sounds were an actual feature of monolingual Southern Pomo speakers' pronunciation of the language is unknown.
3. Buckley's symbols <t t̓ tʰ s̓ c c̓ cʰ> have been converted to <t̪ t̪̓ t̪ʰ c̓ č č̓ čʰ> throughout this work.
4. Buckley's prose explanation of this rule is as follows: "a glottalized nasal becomes a nonnasal, nonglottalized consonant in an onset; the voicing of the resulting stop is derived from the fact that nasals are voiced by default" (Buckley 1994: 49).
5. These examples should not be taken as an exhaustive list of sonorant+glottal+consonant combinations.
6. The same can be said for most kinship stems (save those in the vocative or prefixed with the third-person non-coreferential possessive prefix *miy:a-*); it cannot be said for pronouns or most common nouns.
7. This is one of the phonological phenomena which lead to my treating /:/ as the third laryngeal increment and a pseudo-consonantal segment within the pho-

neme inventory. The letter <:> is listed on current Southern Pomo language-teaching posters as the last letter of the alphabet and has been dubbed 'the doubling sign' for oral spelling games in language classes held by the Dry Creek Rancheria Band of Pomo Indians.

8. Oswalt lists this as coming from Annie Burke (AB), the mother of Elsie Allen (EA), in June 1940, which is more than a decade before he began working with Pomoan languages; it must therefore come from Halpern's unpublished notes.
9. The directional *-madučʼ-* means 'as far as'; the directional *-adučʼ-* means 'away'.
10. *hi:lá is the reconstructed word from 'nose' (McLendon 1973: 83). The *-mʔda* portion of the modern word is almost certainly a fossilized morpheme that lost the vowel of its first syllable due to post-compounding syncope processes; the glottal stop might have been the original laryngeal increment (i.e., *mVʔda), or it might have been inserted between the [m] and the [d] post compounding, which is the case for the second form in (a), *hwademʔdu* 'always going about'.
11. This is because *l, *n, *ṅ, *m, and *ṁ all collapsed into [n] word-finally. Thus the cognate forms for Kashaya words with word-final [ṁ] and [ṅ] show [n] in Southern Pomo.
12. This morpheme may also be represented morphophemically as ||-V:meṭ||.
13. This was said of Nathan Reed Kha'be [=*k^haʔbe* 'rock'] Walker not long after his birth in 2006.
14. Later in this work I choose to transcribe the conditional as ||-V:ba|| and treat it as though it has a synchronic initial vowel; this vowel, as discussed later in the section on vowel harmony, originated as an epenthetic vowel, and the conditional therefore originally began with /:/. Oswalt does not view it as synchronically vowel-initial (1976a: 25).
15. (H I) is one of Halpern's earlier texts, and the chance that he misheard the coronal plosive (or that Annie Burke had an idiolectal pronunciation different from that of other speakers) cannot be dismissed. Regardless of whether 'lungs' and 'flour' are a true minimal pair or a near-minimal pair, there is no way to predict the length of the vowels in either word, and the contrast must therefore be acknowledged as phonemic (though on a less than robust level; the functional load is akin to /ʃ/ and /ʒ/ in English).
16. Oswalt does record one example of a stem with the root *-:hmič-* where the [h] increment is lost. The stem *p^hi:hmiy* '[to visually] inspect [something] well' is recorded twice in (O D), both times from Elizabeth Dollar, once with [h] and once without [h]: *p^hi:hmičiʔma* 'Did you inspect it well?'; *na:p^hiyow ham:u čaw:an hoʔdod:u ʔa p^hi:miy* 'Everything he does, I watch carefully.'
17. The computer files in which Oswalt's dictionary (O D) is stored have not transferred to modern operating systems without difficulty; the symbols Oswalt used in these files were idiosyncratic, and some, such as the one for length,

have not survived in their original forms in my copies of (O D); I have therefore chosen to use * as a place holder for Oswalt's length sign in these computer files. Note also that the superscript schwa has no specific value separate from a full one in terms of phonetic quality. I use the supersrcipt to show that schwa in Ps is not a phoneme—it does not have the same phonological status as the other five vowel qualities which are written in full. Where it is written in full, it is present in the original transcriptions or is clearly a close phonetic notation.

18. *ši:ba:t̪ʰi/a* is irregular; either vowel (/a/ or /i/) may surface as the stem-final syllable nucleus, and the consonants and two examples of /:/ within the word defy current attempts at further morphemic segmentation. The symbol ^ is the original one present in the electronic version of Oswalt's dictionary files on which I based much of this work. Oswalt was using this idiosyncratic symbol to show that two symbols should be joined as one in a later stage of the dictionary that never happened.
19. It is not clear that the *-ma-* in this word is the essive, which is homophonous with at least two other suffixes (a directional meaning 'across' and a plural act suffix). I am not familiar with the word, and Oswalt does not provide much detail in his entry.
20. The phoneme /l/ does occur (remain?) in two known words: *ċahkil* 'blue' and *baw:ol* 'lamprey', forms for which I cannot offer an explanation beyond the possibility of their being very recent borrowings from languages with which I am not familiar.
21. The verb stem *ʔahpʰi-* 'carry' is irregular: it takes the forms *ʔahpʰi-*, ~ *ʔapʰ:e-*, and ~ *ʔapʰ:a-*, which can be predicted on the basis of suffix choice. It is possible that the root in this stem (in at least some of the forms) lacks any vowel at all, which is the analysis I have chosen for this example.
22. This knowledge might, however, prove quite valuable should a polysyllabic word be found in which the third post-consonantal vowel from the left precedes a voiced consonant and does not match with the expected allomorphs. In such a situation, a cautious reappraisal of the underlying segments might treat this vowel as a schwa and omit it from the analysis.
23. Buckley (2014) suggests that Southern Pomo penultimate stress arose via contact with Coast Miwok speakers.
24. Though he never stated it in print, in May 1962 Halpern gave a lecture at Berkeley on the reconstruction of the prosodic system of the parent language of Pomoan, in which he stated that the regular penultimate stress system of Southern Pomo could be changed to antepenultimate for rhetorical purposes (an audio recording of this lecture is archived at UC Berkeley in the Survey of California and Other Indian Languages as LA 202.012). As mentioned by Halpern in this lecture, rhetorical antepenultimate stress can be seen in

(H V:27) in *mi:hakan*, which Halpern records as [ˈmi:.ha.kan] instead of [mi:.ˈha.kan]:

[ʔ]á:maya	[ʔ]úhkʰaċda	mí:hakan	čuh:úle
ye	tripe	brought in	eat ye

'You, bringing home the tripe, eat (that).'

25. The data in Walker (2008) were originally recorded using an analog tape recorder before being converted to a WAV file and analyzed using Praat, and all data come from only one speaker, Olive Fulwider.
26. The data collection and analysis done for this section were first presented as Walker (2010).
27. For example, these versions of the texts record [ŋ] and [ŋ̊], the pre-velar allophones of /n/ and /nh/, whereas later versions omit any evidence of assimilation.
28. It is important to note that use of a comma in Halpern's text does not necessarily mean there was a pause.
29. This tally includes both words Elsie Allen spoke as part of her discourse and Halpern's notes on these words on the facing pages. It is therefore likely that some words are written more times than they were spoken. The total number of pages surveyed for this count is roughly one hundred, though many of the facing pages have large blank spaces. The totals in the table should not be taken as absolute values; rather, they demonstrate that Halpern heard more word-initial glottal stops than in his earlier work.
30. It should be noted that these words were spoken without any break or pause.
31. The word for 'inside the house' could also be analyzed as ||ʔahča-Ø|| where -Ø is a suffix with no phonological form of its own that causes a sort of consonantal ablaut pattern of CVXCV- → CVC:V- (X= /h/, /ʔ/, /:/) and gives the word to which it has been affixed an adverbial or oblique meaning. This is a regular process (it commonly applies to words such as 'foot' and 'up'), and case-marking enclitics with similar semantics (adverbial or oblique meanings) cause the same change in word stems (compare *kʰa:ma* 'foot' and *kʰam:a* 'on foot' with *t̪ʰa:na* 'hand' and *t̪ʰan:a=wi* 'with the hand').
32. In fact, I am not entirely sure that *hla:li-* and *dahla:li-* are semantically distinct; *hla:li-* might be nothing more than a truncated version of *dahla:li-* synchronically. Also, the -:li component of each does not appear to be segmentable, though it is homophonous with other attested morphemes.
33. I am not sure of the meaning of *=ʔwen* at this time, but it appears to be similar to the enclitic *=ʔwa* COPULA.EVIDENTIAL.
34. The morphemes in this word are not completely understood at this time, but a

possible breakdown is as follows: hiṱ̓:a-ad-ka-č̓-Vn 'think/feel-?-CAUS-REFLEX-SWITCH.REFERENCE'.

35. As already mentioned, there is evidence that a small number of verbs (for some speakers) may take the shape CV:CXV(C)- if the root consonant is a sonorant; a handful of function words and a few content words do not conform to this shape and are monosyllabic (e.g., *ceṭ'* 'how', *he:č̓* 'nail, claw'). Also, a very small number of verbs may take the prefix *-:lV-*PLURAL.ACT between the instrumental prefix and the root (e.g., the verbs for 'break'), and they therefore do not have the root as the second syllable of the stem.
36. Exceptions to this statement include the common verb *ċiʔ:i-w ~ ċi-w* 'make-PFV', which has no prefix; certain combinations of the verb stem *hu:w-* 'to go (about, toward here)' in combination with some directional suffixes (e.g., *h-may-ʔdu* ||hu-:w-mač-wadu|| 'go inside'), which have lost the root; and the hortative forms which use the bare verb stem, such as *ho:li=ʔya* [leave=1PL.AGT] 'let's go!'.
37. The case of kinship terms is a bit more complex, as is explained in later sections: all kinship stems must contain a possessive prefix unless they are in the vocative; some case suffixes are indicated by the absence of a suffix (i.e., -Ø). Also, the case-marking morphemes on plural kinship terms might be enclitics rather than suffixes.
38. I cannot now assign clear semantics to the root of this form.
39. I do not provide glossing for every morpheme between || || because the semantics of these root plus prefix combinations are not straightforward when each morpheme is taken separately.
40. *=wi* has idiosyncratic semantics: it carries a true instrumental meaning when attached to body part terms or tools like 'string'; it carries a locative meaning (roughly 'at') when applied to place names (e.g., *baṭʰ:inkʰlehča=wi ~ baṭʰ:inkʰleʔčawi* 'at elderberry tree (house?)' [= 'Sebastopol']); it carries a different locative meaning (roughly 'in') when applied to the word *čʰeʔ:eṱmay* 'basket (general term)'.
41. Compare Southern Pomo *ʔač:ay* 'man' with Central Pomo *čá:č̓* 'man', both of which ultimately descend from Proto Pomo *ʔaká:kʔ (McLendon 1973: 81).
42. One possible reason for this asymmetry (beyond idiolectal variation) is the existence of a derived verbal form *huʔ:u-ṱ-* 'to face', a stem that includes at least one as yet inexplicable variant where the /č/ appears to resurface where it is not expected: huʔ[:]ú:čin *huʔ:u:čin* 'look!' (H VI, 3) At this time, I can neither account for the /:/ of the penultimate syllable nor explain the /č/ which surfaces.
43. This is obviously a simplification: clitic variants of English auxiliaries surely carry some subtle sociolinguistic information. But such differences between

[=l] and [wɪl] are trivial in comparison to the types of clitics, many of which do not have phonological word counterparts, which qualify as special clitics.

44. This [ʔ] is most likely cognate with *ʔe* COPULA of neighboring Central Pomo (a glossed example of which can be found in Mithun 1990: 375). It likely underwent the following development: (1) *-wa* FACTUAL.EVIDENTIAL, *-yo* AUX (perhaps a verb for 'go' in the distant past), and *-ka* INTERROGATIVE could be added to *ʔe (e.g., *ʔe-wa, *ʔe-yo, *ʔe-ka); (2) these morpheme combinations came to combine with preceding grammatical words into phonological words (e.g., CVXCV(C) *ʔe-wa → CVXCV(C)=*ʔe-wa); (3) regular syncope rules deleted the [e] of *ʔe in such combinations, and avoidance of C+[ʔ] clusters across grammatical word boundaries within a phonological word deleted all traces of *ʔe when it followed a consonant-final grammatical word (e.g., CVXCVC=*ʔe-wa → CVXCVC=*ʔ-wa → CVXCVC=wa), but [ʔ] was preserved if the grammatical word which preceded it was vowel-final (e.g., CVXCV=*ʔe-wa → CVXCV=ʔwa); (4) speakers, who would have no traces of the old copula morpheme when it came after a consonant or when the morpheme to which it was once attached was not bound phonologically to a preceding vowel-final word, must have reanalyzed the occurrence of the glottal stop in such a tightly constrained environment as an allomorphic phonological alternation akin to the *a/an* proclitics of English; the weak semantics of the COPULA combined with its disappearance from two of the three environments in which it once occurred would effectively have erased it as a distinct morpheme.
45. This verb for 'to wake up' appears to be a part of the paradigm for 'to fly', and its stem is actually composed of the stem for 'to fly' plus the suffix -čiy ||-čič̓|| INCEPTIVE (a suffix that appears to include the suffix *-y* ||-č̓|| REFLEXIVE and sometimes has that meaning).
46. In fact, the distributional data I use to bolster my assertion that these case-marking morphemes are clitics is at odds with Dixon's opinion on clitic-hood; he specifically rejects arguments for clitic-hood for case-marking morphemes that are based on such morphemes attaching at the level of a NP and suggests such morphemes are more appropriately analyzed as affixes that attach to a whole NP rather than individual members of it (Dixon 2010a: 223). Whatever the merits of such an approach, the subset of enclitics in Southern Pomo that might be susceptible to it do not behave like other affixes in the language in their ability to combine with various word classes and their unique phonological properties (sandhi triggering with verbs; no sandhi with nouns), and an assignment to clitic status seems most appropriate.
47. Halpern records this species as *kʰaʔbekʰačʰ* 'fish hawk' (presumably the osprey); Oswalt records it as *kʰaʔbekʰač̓* 'sharp-shinned hawk', a very different species. I follow Oswalt's transcription, but neither translation seems sure, and the gloss 'raptor.species' must therefore suffice till more data are found.

48. When case-marking clitics are applied to verbs the resultant forms translate into English as gerunds or obliques.
49. The /:/ preceding the NEG enclitic might be a part of that clitic or represent a consonant (perhaps the perfective *-w*) or it might be a mistake made by Halpern.
50. For example, *behše* '(deer) meat' underwent vowel lowering at some point during its descent from Proto Pomo *bihxé (compare Kashaya *bihše*) (McLendon 1973: 72). Common nouns, unlike verbs, kinship terms, and pronouns, do not participate in any synchronic phonological alternations that would allow modern speakers of Southern Pomo to uncover the original *i vowel.
51. Vowel assimilation across syllable boundaries has been a recurrent process in the history of Southern Pomo. A review of Proto Pomoan reconstructions is outside the scope of the present work, but note that sometime in the distant past a different type of vowel harmony rule operated to raise and round /a/ in some words with /o/ in the second syllable (compare Southern Pomo *do:lon* 'bobcat' and Kashaya *do:lom̓* 'bobcat' with Central Pomo *da:lom* 'bobcat' [McLendon 1973: 95]).
52. This is also true of /u/ → [o] when the next syllable has [o].
53. The suffix *-či:-* ||-čič̓-|| includes the reflexive ||-č̓-|| but generally has an inchoative meaning on verbs; however, it clearly has a simple reflexive meaning when applied to the root ||-hkʰe-|| 'to move'.
54. The fact that two of these three nouns are trisyllabic makes it much more likely that the first element is a separable part in what was once a compound. Most nouns are disyllabic in the language, and several trisyllabic nouns can be reconstructed as compounds (e.g., *hi:lamʔda* 'nose', which descends from the older word for nose **hi:la* plus an unknown element).
55. The stem for 'to name' is *ʔahši-*. Oswalt lists the forms <?a*$im?du> *ʔa:šimʔdu* 'to call off names' (O D: ED) and <?a*$im?dun> 'Name them!' (O D: AB), but he provides no glossing. I am unsure of the meaning contributed by the morpheme(s) *-mʔdu- ~ -mʔd-*, though the sequence is strikingly similar to /-med-/, the post-vocalic allomorph of the DURATIVE in Kashaya Pomo (Buckley 1994: 249–50). If it is cognate with the Kashaya morpheme, then there is a strong case to be made that the [u] in *ʔa:šimʔdu:ba* 'he should name' is part of the conditional suffix and not the preceding morpheme.
56. Buckley posits that these variants have diverse origins: the ||V|| → [a] / /ak/__ and ||V|| → [o] / /ok/ (which Buckley handles in a different way) are assimilatory; the ||V|| → [a] / /m/__ and ||V|| → [u] / /d/__ arose at different times, but both developed from phonological changes where final vowels were deleted at some point in the past and only resurfaced when another morpheme was suffixed, thus * . . .-ma > [. . .-m]/__# but * . . .-ma-C . . . remained [. . . ma-C . . .] (the same later for [u] after /d/), and, because of the frequency of

the suffixes with the segments /ma/ and /du/, speakers reanalyzed the resurfacing vowels on the basis of the preceding phonemes and not the morphemes of which they were a part (Buckley 2004).

57. This suffix is probably composed of the semelfactive and the reflexive and has either an inchoative meaning, as it does here, or a purely reflexive meaning.
58. There is additional allomorphy with the addition of the plural act affix, but such allomorphy is built upon the allomorphy given in the table (i.e., the various plural act allomorphs cannot be predicted unless the prefixes have already been attached to the verb).
59. This is a simplification. There is a great deal of morphologically conditioned verb stem allomorphy, such as *ʔahṭ̯i-* vs. *haṭ̯:a-*, that complicates the picture for some verbs.
60. This is the evidential suffix that Oswalt transcribes as *-ŵa-* and which he identifies as the factual-indicative/visual evidential suffix in Southern Pomo (1976a, 25). Oswalt's symbol <ŵ> stands for a [w] that only surfaces after vowels. I believe this is the same suffix that was originally applied to an ancient verb 'to be' (which might be reconstructed as *ʔe) and thus took the [w]-initial allomorph [*ʔe-wa] before the vowel of this verb was lost to syncope and the resultant combination ([=ʔwa] after vowels, [=wa] after consonants) was reanalyzed by speakers as a single morpheme with both 'be'-like and evidential-like properties, hence the gloss EVIDENTIAL.COPULA for this enclitic.
61. Kashaya /q/ corresponds to Southern Pomo /k/.
62. Oswalt notes that most of the directional suffixes are probably compositional in nature (i.e., built up of a subset of independent affixes), but that it is not useful to attempt synchronic segmentation of these affixes along such historical lines. In the case of ||-mok-|| the second part probably originated as a combination of ||-ok-|| preceded by a bilabial nasal with semantics for 'in' (compare modern ||-mač-|| 'in (speaker outside)', which shares the same initial consonant). However, the glosses I use do not quite line up with such a diachronic origin, and they also differ from Oswalt's broad glosses (given for Southern Pomo and sister languages). I follow Halpern's glossing of ||-ok-|| and ||-mač-|| as being reserved for use by a speaker who is outside, and ||-ak-|| and ||-mok-|| as being used by a speaker who is inside; Oswalt pairs ||-ok-|| and ||-mok-|| together as being 'hither' (as in 'out hither' and 'in hither') and ||-ak-|| and ||-mač-|| as 'hence' (as in 'out hence' and 'in hence'), a glossing that might be true for Kashaya or etymologically correct; however, it is at odds with all of Halpern's handwritten glosses as he worked with Annie Burke (Oswalt 1976a, 23).
63. This is quite unlike the case for neighboring Kashaya Pomo. Buckley states that "Root Elision . . . changes a sequence of two vowels to a single long vowel"

in Kashaya, and his examples include /a/-initial suffixes cognate with those of Southern Pomo (Buckley 1994: 184).

64. The only heavy and light syllable patterns which are not to be found in verbs are the following: L (restricted to grammatical words); H (some grammatical words and a tiny number of nouns), HL (perhaps the commonest shape of common nouns); and LL (a possible combination for the vocative of some kinship terms, though these forms might actually be HL~LH, and the evidence is unclear).
65. A few very frequent verbs, such as *ċiʔ:i- ~ ċi(:)-* 'to do, make' allow an optional monosyllabic form with a suffixed coda in rapid speech (e.g., *ċi-w* make-PFV).
66. In other words, my databases have not been coded for this phenomenon, and it is quite possible that the verb paradigms I have consulted do not contain all of the possible five-syllable combinations of heavy and light syllables, though my analysis makes strong predictions that no five-syllable words should allow two light syllables, neither of which is the final syllable, to surface adjacent to each other. I expect to find HHHHH, HLHLH, HHHLL, HHHLH, HLHHH, HLHLL, and HHLHH forms as I continue to search my data.
67. These four verbs have been selected because I have found fairly full paradigms for them in which they show many of the same suffixes.
68. This verb has an irregular root, as shown earlier in table 21 of §2.6.1.2, and I have chosen to represent this irregular root as ||-ht̪-|| despite its always occurring with a transcremental suffix and therefore surfacing without /h/ as /-t̪:-/; the same is true of the root ||-hpʰ-|| in *ʔapʰ:almeč̓in* '[carry] down from above[!]'
69. One of these forms, *ʔapʰ:eywačin* 'carry right up to', is not straightforward. Oswalt lists the directional suffix for '[a]gainst, into contact with, onto' in Southern Pomo as *-Xayway-* in Southern Pomo (Oswalt 1976a: 24). The rest of Oswalt's form for this suffix is more problematic: the final /y/ of the suffix is actually ||č|| and surfaces as such before a vowel-initial suffix (as in this example); the first /y/ of the suffix might also be ||č||, in which case the underlying form of this suffix might be ||-ačVwač-||, in which a vowel separates the palato-alveolar stop from the next consonant, or ||-čVwač-||, in which there is no morpheme-initial vowel to be deleted. For this table, I treat this form as though there were an underlying vowel between the first and second consonants of the surface form /-ywač-/.
70. The form *pʰal:a* 'each, also' is derived from *pʰa:la* 'also, too'.
71. The combination *mihyok̓=wa* 'woodrat=COP.EVID', if it were to be found in the records, would presumably provide the same semantics as the Kashaya form and mean roughly 'it is a woodrat'.
72. The switch-reference suffix ||-en|| has the allomorph [-wen] after vowels;

I treat the form without the labiovelar approximant as basic. The [w] that surfaces after vowels is a fossilized allomorph of the perfective suffix. At one point this switch-reference suffix attached after TAM suffixes. Later, speakers reanalyzed the perfective suffix that only surfaced between a vowel-final stem and the switch-reference suffix ||-en|| as a part of the switch-reference morpheme. Because the switch-reference suffix ||-en|| was originally only vowel-initial, it behaves as an underlyingly vowel-initial suffix. Thus the palato-alveolar affricate of 'cry' may surface before it.

73. Note that the [l] or [m] which surface before vowels do not necessarily correlate to *l or *m; rather, they are in free variation in this context.
74. The morphophonemic forms and morpheme breakdowns are my own.
75. Oswalt notes that this is "a hoop and stick game" and records this stem as /mu:k^{h}elh-/ in Elizabeth Dollar's speech (O D: ED). One wonders whether final /-lh/ would vary in the same manner as Annie Burke's final /-l/ does in these examples.
76. This is true of morphemes of more than one segment. As already mentioned, ||-m-|| ESSIVE and the two suffixes with which it is homophonous do not alternate with [l] in prevocalic position.
77. Note that by nasals I mean all true nasals and the archiphoneme ||N|| (which can surface as the lateral [l] in prevocalic position).
78. Compare the forms with the nasal allomorphs with [-le] allomorph of ||-le|| that occurs elsewhere:

    čuh:úle (H V: 27)
    čuh:ule ||čuh:u-le|| → [ʧuh.ˈhu.le]
    /čuh:u-le/
    eat-PL.IMP
    'eat ye'

79. This is true of the nasal allophone of /d/ in morpheme-final position, but it might be true of other nasals as well. Note that the /d/ of this example, after becoming a nasal and assimilating in place to the /w/ (which then is lost), becomes creaky (or a glottal stop is inserted) before another /d/. This pattern of glottal insertion before a voiced or ejective consonant after a sonorant is common, and in the case of the voiced stops /b/ and /d/, it might be residual evidence of their former glottalized status as *m̓ and *n̓ in an earlier stage of the language. Outside these frozen instances of creakiness/glottal-insertion, there is no synchronic evidence that the voiced stops are inherently creaky.
80. This is a most unusual form for two reasons: (1) it was recorded as the first word in a breath group (it is post-comma in Halpern's transcription) yet has lost its first syllable to syncope, a process that is generally expected for the

encliticized version of the pronoun; and (2) I know of no other record of this morpheme showing voicing assimilation. However, it appears that Halpern heard it in this instance.

81. In order to read table 24 correctly, locate the laryngeal increment along the left side and scan across the top for the second (non-increment) consonant of the stem: the cell where the left row and the top column converge contains every permissible glottal-initial syllable that may precede that combination of laryngeal increment and consonant. For example, if /h/ is chosen from the left-hand side of the table, and C (=sonorants and voiceless unaspirated stops) is chosen from acros the top, the cell where these two overlap contains only ʔV-; a stem of the shape ʔV-hCV . . . is therefore permissible, but one of the shape ha-hCV . . . is not permissible.
82. Halpern notes the following exceptions: *ʔa:ʔa* 'I', *ʔa:čʼen* 'my mother', and *ho:hon* 'nettle' (1984: 7–8).
83. The verb ||ʔihči-|| is extremely irregular and has several unpredictable stem allomorphs. However, productive alternations in glottal initials are seen in equally irregular verbs.
84. The voiced stops /b/ and /d/ may only surface in coda position before a transcremented glottal stop (see §2.6.6 for a discussion of transcremental affixes).
85. Halpern (1984) uses the term 'augment'.
86. These terms are based on my earlier use of 'pre-augmented' and 'post-augmented' (Walker 2008).
87. The plural act affix has unpredictable allomorphs, some of which are infixes rather than suffixes.
88. There is at least one exception to this distribution: Halpern records the stem *haʔt̪ʰi-* 'to sneeze' (Halpern 1984, 8).
89. Oswalt (O D) employs a different division of words into semantic classes, which leads him to create a large number of nominal subgroups, each with unique abbreviations: A (adjective), B (adverb), V (verb), N (noun), Nah (animate human), Nam (animate mammal), Nab (animate bird), Naf (animate fish), Nar (animate reptile), Nai (animate invertebrate), Nap (animate body part), Np (plant), Nap (plant part), Nk (kin term), Nf (noun fragment), I (atactic forms = onomatopoeic words and interjections), Ii (inanimate imitative), Ia (animate imitative), Ij (interjection).
90. The verb *ʔiš:a-* means to take a spouse (man or woman) either for the first time or to go after the wife of another man. It is a transitive verb. This clause shows unusual word order, and Halpern's free translation supports an interpretation of 'man' as something other than a normal S argument of a transitive verb. Possible interpretations notwithstanding, the noun *ʔač:ay* 'man' is clearly free of any bound morphemes.
91. This morpheme is ancient and appears to be descended from the Proto Po-

moan suffix *-áya that McLendon reconstructs as having been applied to animates (McLendon 1973: 55).

92. Oswalt postulates that *-č^hma* descends from *yac . . . ma, though he does not provide a semantic reconstruction (Oswalt 1978: 17).
93. The extant texts only show this suffix in combination with 'water'. The current casino on the Dry Creek Rancheria, known as River Rock Casino, has been given the Southern Pomo name ʔak^h:a-:na k^haʔbe water-LOC rock 'river rock' by Olive Fulwider. In her speech at least, it seems the combination of 'water' and this ancient locative morpheme is fixed and now means 'creek, river'.
94. McLendon used the graph <N> for the voiceless coronal nasal of Eastern Pomo.
95. Halpern terms this phonological alternation one of "lightness~heaviness of the root"; for convenience, he treats the second (non-increment) consonant of noun stems as the root consonant (1984: 18).
96. Halpern reconstructs this as *-ahk^hači (1984: 18).
97. The morpheme *=win:a* LOC is an enclitic; however, in this compound it has undergone syncope, which suggests its having been treated as part of a compound with 'water' in the past, and I therefore do not treat as an enclitic in the gloss. This morpheme might be cognate with the Southeastern Pomo *-win-* in *x̣awinmfo* 'on the water people' (name for the Southeastern Pomo), as recorded by Moshinsky (1974: 96). (Southeastern Pomo *x̣a* 'water' is cognate with Southern Pomo *ʔahk^ha*, and *mfo* 'human plural' is cognate with Southern Pomo *noph:o* 'village'.)
98. O'Connor's transcription system has been converted to the one used throughout this study.
99. Oswalt did record several names from Elsie Allen in his handwritten notes, but many of these notes are difficult to reconcile with other records. They include the name *šo:ṭ^h*, which seems to be a unique case of final aspiration and is glossed as having no meaning. Borrowing must be suspected in this case. He also lists Elsie Allen's name and several other names of Elsie Allen's relatives and others. I do not include these here because the records are not all clear and because I am not sure that they were all meant to be shared. At present they may be accessed at the Survey of California and Other Indian Languages at UC Berkeley in the file Oswalt.001.002.0068.
100. Robert Oswalt postulated that this might be an ancient form of *hi:no* 'ash' (pers. comm., approx. 2003).
101. This name is very similar to the Kashaya kinship term *ṭ^haʔméń* 'my wife (agent case)', a word that does not have a synchronic counterpart in Southern Pomo but that did have a cognate in at least one speaker's idiolect at the time of Gifford's research: <witakamde> 'address . . . [form for] W[ife]' (1922: 115).
102. One of the names in the table, that for Elizabeth Dollar's mother's father's father, might have been given by a native speaker to a non-Southern Pomo

person. Elizabeth Dollar was reputed to have a Russian ancestor. If this kinsman were the Russian, the name 'curly haired man/one' might make more sense.

103. I should note that Olive Fulwider recalls that her grandmother, Rosa Bill, who is known to her descendants as 'Grandma ṭʰe:ṭʰe' (the child-speech vocative form of 'mother') and is Elizabeth Dollar's mother, was named *ša:kʰedo* [ʃa:.ˈkʰe.ɾo], a name which does not fit well into either of the types in the table: it has no known meaning and does not include the feminine suffix.
104. I have heard Olive Fulwider talk often about her mother calling her *na:ho*.
105. Buckley refers to the agent case suffix as the nominative (1994, 375).
106. At an earlier stage in my research I went through Halpern's notes in an effort to find as many kinship terms as possible. I recorded this form for '[her own daughter]' at this time, but the specific source was not marked. I have not been able to locate the original; however, I believe this form can be parsed in one of the following ways: (1) *ma-hṭ̭ikmed-en* 3C-daughter-PAT; (2) *ma-hṭ̭ik-med-en* 3C-daughter-FEM-PAT; (3) *ma-hṭ̭i-k-med-en* 3C-daughter-GS-FEM-PAT.
107. Gifford gives several glosses for this term (with its two variants), but he uses abbreviations which do not line up with his key (e.g., Gd and gd are both listed, and each of these should equate to 'granddaughter' according to his key to abbreviations) (1922: 113).
108. In this instance, this morpheme is specifically said by Buckley to have "special case-marking properties" as a marker of the "subjective" case, which is equivalent to the agentive case in the terminology of this work (1994: 383).
109. Halpern regularly records a final glottal stop on vocative forms; I have not heard this final glottal stop in Olive Fulwider's speech, however. Final length might also be possible here.
110. Gifford records this form as 'H[usband]' and provides a different form for 'wife'; however, the modern speakers of Southern Pomo (and perhaps all speakers of the Cloverdale and Dry Creek dialects) used the root in Gifford's word for 'H[usband]' for 'spouse' (Gifford 1922: 115). The forms Gifford records for 'W[ife]', <witakamde> (noted by Gifford as for 'address') and <awitckamen> (noted by Gifford as for 'reference'), are clearly cognate with the Kashaya word *ṭʰaʔmeṅ* '[my] wife'; however, note that even in Kashaya the paradigm for 'wife' is only differentiated in the first-person-possessed form, and all other possessive prefixes combine with the same root as seen for 'husband' in Kashaya (Buckley 1994: 377). The unusual words for 'wife' recorded by Gifford appear to be very old and might be Healdsburg dialect forms. They show the feminine suffix *-md-* ~ *-men* already discussed, and the fact that the distinct feminine form 'wife' was lost (together with its feminine suffix) in the modern dialects of Southern Pomo might be evidence that the feminine suffix was becoming obsolete outside proper names.

111. McLendon reports that the kinship prefixes "cannot as yet be completely reconstructed" for Proto Pomo (1973: 56).
112. The kinship root for 'older brother' is irregular: it is *-mi-ki-* (*-ki-* is a generational suffix) after the first-person possessive prefix *ʔa:-*; it is *-ki-* after all other possessive prefixes.
113. These forms can all be found in Halpern's notes, (H I–IX and O I). They have been chosen for inclusion herein because of the high level of confidence I have in these researchers' abilities to transcribe these forms correctly.
114. I have not been able to confirm the final glottal stop that Halpern records on such vocatives, and it might be possible that some speakers used /-e/ or /-e:/ in place of the /-eʔ/ vocative suffix, as can be seen the variants in the tables in appendix I of Walker (2013).
115. The forms throughout this subsection come from a database I created years before I began writing; they are almost all from Halpern's notes, but they do not show his accent marks. Because they were not carefully sourced in my original database, I cannot assign them all to Halpern's notes with complete confidence. They are therefore simply listed in italics. One form definitely does not come from Halpern's notes: *šiki* 'auntie!' ('mother's younger sister') comes from Olive Fulwider and several other Dry Creek members' memories.
116. In Kashaya Pomo informal first-person-possessed forms these changes are more widespread: /q/ is replaced by /k/, /č/ by /t̪/, and /ṭʰ/ by /t̪ʰ/ (Buckley 1994: 381–82).
117. I know of at least one example of the *-y-* allomorph of ||-ya-|| PLURAL occurring after a generational suffix. This form, *mi:ki:čo:kʰe* /mi-:ki-:-čo-:kʰe/ 2-older.brother-GS-PL-OBL-POSS 'your older brothers', should probably have the apparent /-:-/ allomorph of ||-ya-|| corrected to /-y-/.
118. This section focuses on the forms of the kinship terms. The actual usage of the agentive and patient cases in connected speech is discussed in chapter 3.
119. The records show variation between /t̪/ and /t̪:/ in this patient case allomorph when it follows the generational suffix ||-ċ-||; this form might have been mistakenly recorded as a singleton (thereby hiding all traces of ||-ċ-||), or any /:/ manifestation of ||-ċ-|| in this environment might be optional. I have chosen not to represent ||-ċ-|| in this form because of the complete lack any surface manifestation of the suffix in this record.
120. The vocative suffix ||-deʔ|| is often preceded by /:/ in some records, but this might be the result of transcription errors on the part of English speakers who expect greater duration in open, stressed syllables (especially with a voiced consonant as the following segment).
121. For example, the vocative forms for ||-ču-ċ-|| 'mother's brother' include the formal *ču-ċ-eʔ* and the informal *t̪u:-t̪u* ~ *t̪u:-t̪u-deʔ*; see appendix I in Walker (2013) for a partial paradigm.

122. The informal vocative affix ||-:ř-|| is omitted from this table and is not considered further in this section.
123. This comes from the saying *ʔay=t̪o ka-c̓-e* Oh=1SG.PAT mother's.mother-GS-VOC 'Oh grandmother!', an idiomatic exclamation said when feeling a chill.
124. I gloss the morpheme ||-čo-|| as VOCATIVE unless it is followed by other case-marking suffixes or clitics, in which case I gloss it as OBLIQUE.
125. The status of the comitative as an enclitic on kinship terms is unclear, and further inquiry might find it to be a suffix. It is also unclear whether this morpheme is /:/-initial in the kinship system; the transcription record is unclear.
126. The length on ||-čo:-|| is not recorded consistently, and I have chosen the long form here because it is the form most frequently encountered in appendix I of Walker (2013).
127. These are only attested in combination with the prefix ||miy:a-|| 'his/her/their'.
128. I have converted Buckley's symbols to the orthography of this work. Buckley actually uses the terms 'subjective' and 'objective'; however, these terms are meant to convey an agent/patient case distinction in Kashaya and have therefore been converted to the terminology of this grammar to avoid distraction or confusion. Note that *-yač* may appear as *-yaʔ* after debuccalization in Kashaya.
129. I have converted O'Connor's symbols to the orthography of this work. O'Connor actually uses the terms "A case" and "P case"; terminology has been regularized to avoid distraction and confusion.
130. I do not treat agentive case in the pronouns as a *-Ø* morpheme as I do for the kinship terms. Only one pronoun, *ʔat̪:iyey*, shows overt agentive case marking and it is also the only one with the *-:čon* allomorph for patient case. I view it as irregular within the pronominal paradigm, and it is the only non-kinship term to combine case and number by means of *-yey* and *-:čon* (probably ||-ya-čon|| → *-yčon* with /y/ becoming /:/ after the high front vowel).
131. There is a reflexive suffix on verbs that handles most things for which English would use 'self'. This emphatic reflexive morpheme is apparently optional with pronouns.
132. This table is a based on one from Oswalt (1978); kinship prefixes have been removed, terminology and orthography have been changed, clitics have been overtly indicated, and a few forms have been updated.
133. Note that this pronoun is not exclusively masculine and can be translated as 'it', 'her', 'he', etc.
134. Halpern records this species as *k*^{h}*aʔbek*^{h}*ač*^{h} 'fish hawk' (presumably the osprey); Oswalt records it as *k*^{h}*aʔbek*^{h}*ač̓* 'sharp-shinned hawk', a very different species. I follow Oswalt's transcription, but neither translation seems sure, and the gloss 'raptor.species' must therefore suffice till more data are found.
135. I have preserved Oswalt's terminology, though it should be noted that 'objec-

tive' and 'subjective' equate to 'agent' and 'patient' in the terminology of this grammar. Also, Oswalt uses an empty square before certain forms to symbolize a lost syllable that still interacts with stress. (The lost syllable is not lost in Southern Pomo, thus Southern Pomo *ham:u* = Kashaya □*mu:* in Oswalt's transcription.)

136. Perhaps this *-mʔdu* is ||-ad|| IMPERFECTIVE + ||-wadu|| HABITUAL. It might also be a single allomorph of either that I have not yet identified as such.
137. The symbol H stands for the laryngeal increment and is placed before the second consonant of the stem in this schematic regardless of whether it is preconsonantally incremented or post-consonantally incremented because of the transcremental and decremental processes that affect verbs (i.e., CVHCV ... is equivalent to CVhCV ..., CVChV ..., CVʔCV ..., CVCʔV ..., CV:CV ..., CVC:V ...).
138. Many disyllabic verb roots no doubt descend from earlier prefix+root combinations.
139. Oswalt (1976a) reconstructs only twenty prefixes.
140. Oswalt's definitions of the instrumental prefixes of Kashaya are the guides I have used as I encounter unfamiliar verbs. Oswalt notes the principal differences between Kashaya and Southern Pomo instrumental prefixes, and any meanings which are clearly not a part of Southern Pomo have been omitted in the headings; those which Oswalt reports are unique to Southern Pomo have likewise been included.
141. I am using the root definitions of (O D) whenever these are available.
142. Oswalt notes that much of the semantic range of *da-* in Southern Pomo is handled by *pʰa-*, and *da-* "is of rarer occurrence" in the language (1978, 19).
143. The root ||-ʔṭ̪a-|| does not translate well as 'perceive' in this stem.
144. This prefix does the duty of ||da-|| in sister languages.
145. Oswalt adds the note "(only after sug.)", but it is unclear whether this refers to the entire entry or just the final translation of 'feel draft' (O D).
146. Full translation of entry from: "(sounds like to taste; but /bihnat'/ is more common)" (O D).
147. This is my own definition.
148. This evidential suffix has the allomorph [-wa] after vowels.
149. Halpern records these forms with /:/ to the left of the sonorant and the glottal moved to the right; Oswalt's records are less clear (see §2.2.2 of the present work for discussion).
150. Plural forms are also commonly recruited for such functions (e.g., earlier English 'ye' versus 'thou'), and it might be the case that the older conditional first became a plural imperative before being used as a token of respect in addressing in-laws.

151. In one of the digital databases I have made for this project, the number of entries for this suffix stands at two, both of which show it suffixed to the same stem.
152. Oswalt defines this root as 'catch' when it does not take the reduplicative affix ||-R-|| and as 'give many quick jabs' with the reduplicative affix ||-R-||; however, these two root entries seem to be semantically related and translatable as 'contact' or 'intercept and contact one thing with another'. I have chosen 'contact' for its brevity in the gloss.
153. Verbs of motion which otherwise must appear with a directional suffix may also appear with only the perfective suffix, in which case a completive meaning is indicated by the perfective. (In some of his notes, Oswalt glosses this use of the perfective as 'terminate'.)
154. These are in free variation (see §2.6.3.2).
155. The verb stem ||dak̓:aṭ-|| is listed in Oswalt's dictionary manuscript under the root ||-k̓aṭ-|| 'to rub' in combination with the instrumental prefix ||da-|| 'with the palm'; however, if this verb stem does have this root, it is the only instance of this root combining with an instrumental prefix to form such an idiosyncratic meaning. I treat it as an irreducible verb stem for this reason.
156. I treat the verb stem as irregular with a final /a/; however, the plural act affix in this form might alternatively be analyzed as in infix splitting the directional suffix.
157. ||ʔihč-|| is an irregular verb stem.
158. This is an irregular verb.
159. ||k^{h}at̪:-|| is an irregular verb.
160. The verb stem ||ha-hča-|| 'fly' may translate as 'arise' or 'flee' when suffixed with ||-bič-||.
161. It is possible that the zero allomorph of the perfective is actually present after the semelfactive in this form. Because the semelfactive may be followed by at least some TAM suffixes, it cannot be assumed that it and the perfective are mutually exclusive. In the absence of any persuasive evidence, I choose to treat the semelfactive as the final affix.
162. As discussed later (§2.8.3.3.6), there are two suffixes which appear to indicate first and second person, though they are not obligatory when first and second person arguments are overtly present or implied, and I suspect they might have some sort of evidential meaning and might not be true person-marking affixes.
163. I have converted Mithun's orthography to the one used in this work.
164. Oswalt reports no Central Pomo cognate for the future intentive suffix ||-t̪i-|| (1976a, 25). If Central Pomo lacks a reflex of the old future intentive to use for purposive complementation strategies, this might explain its use of the future

where Southern Pomo uses ||-t̪i-||. However, it is also possible that my database is deficient, and Southern Pomo does use the simple future ||-k^h:e-|| for purposive complementation strategies, in which case the choice of ||-t̪i-|| or ||-k^h:e-|| might be lexically determined.

165. Oswalt transcribes this as <-ti+ʔd> without discussion of the second element.
166. I am glossing /-t̪iʔd-/ as FUT.INTENT.
167. The final consonant of ||šu:k^{h}ač-|| ‘breathe’ might be the semelfactive.
168. This collocation is clearly idiomatic; it does not literally mean ‘breathe asking’. Oswalt provides an alternate translation: “to hurt my feelings, perhaps ‘try my patience”’ (O D: ED).
169. The morpheme *=ʔwen* is problematic. It is quite common in some of the records, but the English translations do not elucidate its function.
170. This form is drawn from an early database I made in which I did not keep Halpern’s accent marks.
171. I am unsure of the identity of this morpheme. If it is the singular imperative, it as an unexpected use of that morpheme.
172. Oswalt glosses this verb stem as “go (of sev. in a group),” though it is clearly being used of one person in this instance.
173. This combination of ‘there’ and ‘-ward’, when suffixed with verbal suffixes, means ‘to face’.
174. This epenthetic [w] is a fossilized perfective suffix from a period when the different subject switch-references were enclitics which followed TAM suffixes; the Central Pomo cognates are still enclitics in that language, and the Central Pomo perfective may still precede different event-dependent clause markers which are cognate with the Southern Pomo forms (Mithun 1993).
175. This is actually a verb (or was one, hence the perfective suffix *-w* on the end) that serves as an adjective.
176. This probably meant blue-green, but the living speaker reserves it for ‘blue’. It is likely present in truncated form as the second syllable of ‘green’.
177. This has the feel of a borrowing; perhaps it comes from Spanish *amarillo* ‘yellow’.
178. There is also the less common form *hi:li,* which Halpern glosses as ‘where’ and translates as “anywhere” in (H VIII, 6). On the basis of shared phonology with *ma:li* and *wi:li, hi:li* seems like the natural candidate for the slot for ‘there’ in table 45, but *ha:mi* is the ususal form for ‘there’ in the texts.
179. The adverb *p^{h}a:la* is peculiar: it is sometimes recorded as *p^{h}al:a,* in which case it is not entirely clear whether transcremented /:/ signifies a difference in meaning; it may be reduplicated, *p^{h}al:ap^{h}la,* to mean ‘each; various’.
180. ||čaht̪i-N|| is an existential verb. Oswalt records the root with the meaning ‘existential verb for plural objects or uncountable noun’, and with the final

nasal he records the meaning 'continue being in a place, there is, there are' (O D). In this example it is unclear whether the <mu> portion is a unique allomorph of the ||-:mu|| SECOND.PERSON suffix on ||čahṭ̑i-|| or a combination of the final nasal of ||čahṭ̑i-N|| and unknown [u] portion.

181. The locative suffix ||-:na|| is probably frozen in this form. Olive Fulwider uses the word *ʔakʰ:a:na* for 'river' with no obvious locative meaning. She has used it to translate the name of the River Rock Casino as *ʔakʰ:a:na kʰaʔbe* 'river rock' (as opposed to a meaning like 'river-ward rock').
182. The form and translation for the reconstructed copula and verb 'go' are based on forms that retain this shape and meaning in Central Pomo.
183. This word is an adjective in this sentence; as a verb, it means 'to pity'.
184. The word *ʔam:a* means both 'earth, dirt' and 'thing'.
185. This is the truncated form of *ʔam:a* 'earth, thing' and not the encliticized version of the second-person agentive pronoun *ʔa:ma*.
186. The word *ʔam:a* means both 'earth, dirt' and 'thing'.
187. It is unclear how inalienable possession is marked on full NPs or proper names.
188. This form comes from Halpern's notes; however, I cannot locate the original. This phrase was lifted from his notes for use in the Southern Pomo classes being held by the Dry Creek Rancheria, and it is familiar to the tribe's students. The free translation is probably identical to his, but I have bracketed it to show that it is from my memory (and therefore possibly of my own creation).

3. Sentence Structure

1. Ditransitives, of course, can alternatively be considered to consist of only two core arguments plus an additional non-core argument.
2. Note a counter example of *=ʔwam:u* in (H VIII: 7), where the prohibitive form 'do not break this tree' has 'tree' marked with the subject form *=ʔwam:u* rather than the expected object form *=ʔwan*. This might have something to do with prohibitives; there are not enough data to clarify the unexpected usage.
3. Transitive in the sense that if all understood core arguments of the verb were to be overtly expressed within the clause, there would be both an A and an O argument.
4. I have also seen /-ṭ̑ʰi/ as a negative morpheme, which I believe is used in questions of the sort 'do you *not* want . . . ?' I cannot locate examples of this in my current database, however.
5. See footnote 180 to chapter 2 for a discussion of ||čahṭ̑i-N||, a positive existential verb.
6. Halpern habitually records length before the comitative enclitic *=k̓o*. This

could be speaker variation or a mistake on his part. The length before the negative enclitic *=t̯^{h}ot̯* might hide an unidentified inflectional suffix or be the product of speaker variation or linguist error.

7. Except Central Pomo *=da*.
8. Oswalt uses the term *agent* rather than *subject*; however, this usage is due to Oswalt's analysis of the agent/patient case-marking system of Kashaya as subject/object and his desire to avoid analyzing the switch-reference system of Kashaya as one that tracked the same thing as the case-marking system found on animate arguments. Thus Oswalt's terminology is the mirror image of that used in this work: Oswalt's subject = agent; Oswalt's agent = subject.
9. Historically, the switch-reference markers ||-:li|| *-:li ~ -:ni* and ||-en|| *-en ~ -wen* were both applied after the perfective suffix *-w*, so that in an earlier stage of the language they would not have been amenable to the definition of dependent clause and main verb given here. In fact, the /:/ of ||-:li|| and the /w/ of the *-wen* allomorph of ||-en|| that occurs after vowel final morphemes are actually the phonologically obscured remnants of the perfective suffix.
10. It is possible that there is not semelfactive ||-č-|| suffix in this form and it is simply the stem ||huʔ:uč-|| 'face' followed by the denominalizing suffix ||-t̯-||; however, the expected outcome from such a combination would be /huʔ:uč:-/ or /huʔ:u:t̯-/, and the semelfactive, if it is present, would explain the surface form.
11. ||duw:e|| is the noun 'night', and ||duw:eč-|| is the verb for 'night falls'.
12. This combination of 'there' and '-ward', when suffixed with verbal suffixes, means 'to face'.
13. The verb ||ʔehč^{h}e-|| 'dig' appears to consist of the instrumental prefix ||hi-|| and a root ||-hč^{h}e-||; however, Oswalt does not parse this word in his dictionary manuscript, and I can find no evidence of this root in use in any other words. I have therefore chosen to treat this verb as a stem.
14. This is the expected distribution. The agent/patient case markers are restricted to animate arguments (sentient beings, including insects), and the use of these morphemes to nominalize a verb with no nominal component (and thus no sentient argument) would be unexpected.
15. This example proves this in two ways: (1) the geminate /w/ in Halpern's transcription is clearly the perfective allomorph *-w* followed by the initial /w/ of the *=wan* allomorph of the object-marking determiner; and (2) this is a vowel-final verb stem, and the post-vocalic *=ʔwan* allomorph of the object-marking enclitic would surface here if the perfective allomorph *-w* did not come between this stem and the enclitic.
16. What is glossed as DIFFUSE here is simply the pattern whereby the laryngeal increment /:/ moves to the right of the root consonant of 'lie' to indicate a stative meaning on a handful of verbs, including this one; on nouns this same pat-

tern can indicate location in or over an area rather than a single point. Halpern does not distinguish between /i:/ and /iy/, so it is possible that the /:/ is, in fact, /y/.

Appendix 2

1. The base form is ||ku:lu-|| 'outside, wilderness'. The DIFFUSE suffix ||-Ø|| causes the laryngeal increment to transcrement (thus ||ku:lu-Ø|| surfaces as /kul:u/; see §2.8.1.1.1). In this case this suffix seems to provide a locative meaning. Halpern's free translation of *kul:u* as "in the outside" might be the best literal translation. I have omitted the preposition in my free translation because it is not good colloquial English and, though technically accurate, fails to carry the real meaning of the Southern Pomo form. In Pomoan villages, the distinction between the village and 'outside' was actually the distinction between non-wilderness and wilderness. To be *kul:u* implies that someone or something is away from permanent human habitation, which makes sense in the case of lonely anthropomorphized squirrels and rock men.
2. This word came to mean 'Indian person(s)' after European contact.
3. This is bimorphemic with the final syllable most likely coming from *de:le* 'mid(dle)', but it means 'in (the) morning'. *kʰaʔ:aškʼaden* is the general word for 'morning'; *kʰaʔ:a-* is the verb for 'to dawn'.
4. *ho:li-* means 'go' and generally indicates movement away; *h(u)w(:)a-* means 'go' and generally indicates movement toward or movement about without a particular endpoint. *ho:li-* has no singular vs. plural or collective vs. distributive meaning, but in neighboring Central Pomo, the verb *hli-*, which is cognate to Southern Pomo *ho:li-*, is reserved for multiple agents.
5. ||ʔahča-Ø|| → /ʔač:a/; the DIFFUSE suffix -Ø here indicates a state of being within the house.
6. I use 'were to' to translate the future suffix *-kʰ:e* in this sentence in order to give it the proper feel in English. Halpern's free translation is "Squirrel went . . . where they will meet each other," which is more literal.
7. When 'watch' takes the REFLEXIVE, it means 'wait' or 'watch out'.
8. Halpern's translation is more literal; see note 6.
9. Halpern glosses *bedʔeṭway* as 'they handle' and translates it as 'they kept stretching them'; Oswalt records the verb stem *bedʔe-* 'give several' (O D). As discussed in §2.8.3.3.8, the suffix *-ṭway* has not been positively identified but likely indicates plural agents. If, as chosen here, it is a bow that was tried by pulling throughout the story rather than an arrow, then Halpern's translation of *bedʔeṭway* as 'handle' or 'stretch' is best. However, if, in fact, it was an arrow that was tried by pulling (as the text overtly says), then it is possible that 4.1 should be translated freely as 'now they gave (their bows to) each other'. Halpern's reading has in its favor his intimate knowledge of the story when he

chose both the gloss and translation, and the fact that the verb šuhnaṭ̯- means specifically 'to try by pulling', and it is hard to imagine how an arrow shaft might be productively pulled for gambling. An alternate reading of the entire text would be required if Oswalt's gloss for this verb is followed, namely, that something was given instead of stretched. In favor of this alternate reading is the fact that the speaker consistently used *ċu:ʔu* 'arrow' prior to the sentence with *bedʔeṭway* and thereafter uses *šiʔmi* 'bow'. On the basis of the likelihood that arrows can be pulled competitively and Halpern's gloss and free translation, I have chosen to interpret 'arrow' in the first sections of the narrative as a mistake for 'bow' and translate *bedʔeṭway* as 'handle ~ stretch' rather than 'give'.

10. Halpern glosses *wi:minhk*ʰ*ayʔden* as 'when every time he (turns) this way' and his free translation has "While this Rock was facing towards there." It is clear that gray squirrel gnaws the bow while rock is looking away, and the 'there' toward which rock man was looking cannot have been the place where gray squirrel was gnawing.
11. It is possible that the /č/ in *huʔ:učwaden* is an unidentified suffix; however, the only suffix that might fit the phonological shape is the semelfactive, and that suffix does not fit the semantics here. There is regular variation between /y/ and /č/ in stem-final position, and it is most likely that /huʔ:uč-/ is just an irregular allomorph of *huʔ:uy* 'face'.
12. The gloss 'now' is based on Halpern's gloss and free translation. It might be more of an exclamation (e.g., 'hey').
13. This gloss is based entirely on Halpern's gloss and free translation; I am not otherwise familiar with this verb.
14. Gray squirrel gnaws the bow while rock is looking away; see note 10.
15. Halpern notes that this form was in free variation with *biʔk̓ipk̓íbak*ʰ*má:yow*.
16. Halpern has 'where?' in his gloss and "anywhere" in his free translation.
17. This verb root *mihyana- ~ mihyanh-* means 'beat up' in general and can mean 'kill' (presumably in the sense of 'beat to death').
18. Halpern has *heʔbe:ba*, but I see no evidence that the length before *-ba* represents a missing consonant; I therefore omit it as an analogical error on Halpern's part due to *-:li*, the sequential switch-reference suffix that is truly length-initial.
19. Oswalt records this stem with the meaning 'act on a long object' (O D).
20. The verb 'to fly' means 'run ~ flee' with certain suffixes.
21. Though Halpern consistently places length before *-ba*, I am not sure this length was truly there. It is possibly an error due to analogy (in his efforts to transcribe) with the length of *-:li*, the other switch-reference marker in the pair indicating sequential temporal ordering. In the case of *-:li*, there is comparative evidence to suggest that the length masks an earlier *-w* PERFECTIVE

(cf. Central Pomo, where the cognate is the enclitic *=li*, which attaches to the Central Pomo *-w* PERFECTIVE).

22. The verb *ʔahčˣʰa-* 'to fall' is intransitive, but the use of the DET.OBJ enclitic on 'the tree with the squirrel' might suggest a transitive reading, such as '(Rock man) felled the tree with squirrel (in it)'.
23. This word also shows the same laryngeal increment movement pattern that I treat as the result of the transcremental suffix DIFFUSE elsewhere (e.g., *ʔahča* 'house' and *ʔač:a-Ø* house-DIFFUSE 'in (the) house'). In this case, *pʰa:la* 'too', when changed to *pʰal:a*, seems to mean 'again' (Halpern's gloss) or 'another' (Halpern's free translation). When reduplicated as *pʰal:apʰla*, the meaning changes to 'various'.
24. The root in this verb means 'to bump ~ hit', but the prefix in this stem, ||mu-|| has multiple meanings, including 'by heat' and 'non-long object through air'. It is unclear what semantics this prefix+root combination holds, but it is likely that the ||mu-|| prefix emphasizes rock man's striking trees with the mass of his body.
25. I am unsure of the meaning of *-duway-*. It does not break down into obvious component parts, and it is not clearly a unitary morpheme. Perhaps it is related to another mysterious morpheme, *-ṭway-* (as in 4.1 in this narrative), which might be a plural agent suffix of some sort. If so, this would be the only affix-internal alternation between [duw] and [ṭw] in the language of which I am aware. The verb stem *nu:hat̪-* already carries a meaning with more than one agent, and it seems unlikely that an additional plural agent suffix would be suffixed here and not elsewhere.
26. The ablative *=t̪ow* generally means 'from', but it appears to have a conventionalized meaning in the combination *ʔakʰ:at̪ow* of 'at the water'.
27. Halpern leaves this unglossed and seems to translate it as "So be it." It shows unexpected phonology, and it is possible that it is mistranscribed.
28. The use of *=ʔwam:u* is unexpected; perhaps the use of the prohibitive is influencing the case marking of 'tree'.
29. It is unclear what this means. It is likely composed of two affixes, but those matching the shape do not seem appropriate. Halpern glosses the verb as 'always running', and his free translation is "Running (at it)." Perhaps the *-ak̓-* position of *kʰat̪:ak̓dun* is the directional suffix ||-ak-|| 'out (speaker inside)' and the *-du-* might be the imperfective suffix ||-ad-||.
30. The *-:-* is common before *=t̪ʰot̪̓* in Halpern's transcriptions. It likely represents the former presence of the perfective suffix ||-w||, but it might also be a consistent mistranscription (see example (53) in chapter 2 and its note 49, this volume).
31. *sa:ma* is generally an enclitic ||=sa:ma|| meaning 'near, beside'. It carries the same semantics here, but it is affixed with morphemes that do not provide any

obvious additional meaning and are therefore difficult to identify. It is possible that *sa:ma* has been verbalized by the addition of ||-ṱ-||, a suffix known to denominalize body part nouns. If this is correct, then the *-in* might be the same subject sequential switch-reference suffix. This seems unlikely, however.

32. Oswalt records this verb's definition as "one nonlong object be sitting on something up off the ground" (O D).
33. This also means 'to sit on ground'.
34. The stem for 'snore' is ||mi-kʰ:oṭ-||.
35. I am retaining Halpern's free translation of this body part. Though it is not clear from the text, rock man had a vulnerability known to all Russian River drainage Pomoan people. His rocky exterior did not protect a soft spot of flesh near his collarbone over which he wore abalone. In the neighboring Kashaya language Oswalt recorded a story about rock man in which the narrator makes this fact clear: "All of Rock Man's body was rock, only by his collarbone was there a spot of flesh. An abalone shell hung down covering that place" (Oswalt 1964: 73).
36. Oswalt translates this verb stem as "continue being in a place, there is, there are" (O D).
37. This is a polymorphemic form, but whatever the origins of the *-wʔduy*, its addition to *čohčʰi-* results in an idiosyncratic meaning. Oswalt defines this meaning as "hit forcefully, often so that it hurts or causes damage, often to unconsciousness" (O D). It is therefore herein treated as a single verb stem.
38. Oswalt recorded this form as meaning "to be sick (usually, though sometimes 'dead') (for one only)" (O D).
39. I treat *muhlam-* as the stem here, but it is possible that the *-m-* should be segmented off as a separate morpheme. Oswalt does not record the form *muhlam-*, but he does record *-hlabaṱ-* "split off sev." with the semelfactive form in *-hla:či-*; the example he provides is *muhla:-či-w* "rock to split off by self (from cliff)" (O D).

REFERENCES

Allen, Elsie. 1972. *Pomo Basketmaking: A Supreme Art for the Weaver.* Ed. Vinson Brown. Healdsburg CA: Naturegraph Publishers.

Barrett, Samuel. 1908. *The Ethno-Geography of the Pomo and Neighboring Indians.* University of California Publications in American Archaeology and Ethnology, vol. 6. Berkeley: University of California Press.

Bean, Lowell J., and Dorothea Theodoratus. 1978. "Western Pomo and Northeastern Pomo." In *Handbook of North American Indians,* vol. 8, *California,* ed. Robert F. Heizer, 289–305, Washington DC: Smithsonian Institution Press.

Bibby, Brian. 1996. *The Fine Art of California Indian Basketry.* Sacramento: Crocker Art Museum.

Buckley, Eugene. 1994. *Theoretical Aspects of Kashaya Phonology and Morphology.* Stanford CA: Center for the Study of Language and Information.

———. 2004. The Origin of a Crazy Rule: [du] in the Southern Pomoan Group. Meeting of the Society for the Study of the Indigenous Languages of the Americas, Boston, January 8–11.

———. 2014. Pomoan Stress: Change, Contact, and Reanalysis. Presentation given at the Microconference on Metrical Structure: Acquisition and Processing, Utrecht Institute of Linguistics OTS, April 2014.

Campbell, Lyle. 1997. *American Indian Languages: The Historical Linguistics of Native America.* Oxford: Oxford University Press.

Comrie, Bernard. 1976. *Aspect: An Introduction to the Study of Verbal Aspect and Related Problems.* Cambridge: Cambridge University Press.

———. 1989. *Language Universals and Linguistic Typology: Syntax and Morphology.* 2nd ed. Chicago: University of Chicago Press.

Dixon, R. M. 2010a. *Basic Linguistic Theory,* vol. 1: *Methodology.* Oxford: Oxford University Press.

———. 2010b. *Basic Linguistic Theory,* vol. 2: *Grammatical Topics.* Oxford: Oxford University Press.

Fredrickson, Vera Mae, David W. Peri, and Richard N. Lerner. 1984. *Mihilakawna and Makahmo Pomo: The People of Lake Sonoma.* Sacramento CA: U.S. Army Corps of Engineers.

Gifford, Edward Winslow. 1922. *California Kinship Terminologies.* University of California Publications in American Archaeology and Ethnology, vol. 18. Berkeley: University of California Press.

Halpern, Abraham. Field notes on Southern Pomo. Survey of California and Other

Indian Languages, University of California at Berkeley California Language Archive.

———. 1962. "The Reconstruction of Proto-Pomo" (lecture, University of California at Berkeley, May 3, 1962). Audio recording, Survey of California and Other Indian Languages, University of California at Berkeley California Language Archive, LA 202.012.

———. 1964. "A Report on a Survey of Pomo Languages." In *Studies on California Linguistics*, ed. William Bright, 88–93. University of California Publications in Linguistics 34.

———. 1984. "Southern Pomo h and ʔ and Their Reflexes." *Journal of California and Great Basin Anthropology*, Papers in Linguistics 4: 3–43.

Kroeber, Alfred. 1925. *Handbook of the Indians of California*. Bureau of American Ethnology Bulletin 78. Washington DC: Smithsonian Institution.

Maddieson, Ian. 1984. *Patterns of Sounds*. Cambridge: Cambridge University Press.

MacDonald, Lorna. 1990. *A Grammar of Tauya*. Berlin: Mouton de Gruyter.

McLendon, Sally. 1973. *Proto Pomo*. University of California Publications in Linguistics 71.

———. 1975. *A Grammar of Eastern Pomo*. University of California Publications in Linguistics 74.

———. 2009. "Pomoan Languages." In *Concise Encyclopedia of Languages of the World*, ed. Keith Brown and Sarah Ogilvie, 878–82. Amsterdam: Elsevier.

McLendon, Sally, and Robert L. Oswalt. 1978. "Pomo." In *Handbook of North American Indians*, vol. 8: *California*, ed. Robert F. Heizer, 274–88. Washington DC: Smithsonian Institution Press.

Merriam, C. Hart. 1979. *Indian Names for Plants and Animals among California and Other Western North American Tribes*. Assembled and annotated by Robert F. Heizer. Ballena Press Publications in Archaeology, Ethnology and History, no. 14.

Mithun, Marianne. 1988. "Lexical Categories and Number in Central Pomo." In *In Honor of Mary Haas*, ed. William Shipley, 517–37. Berlin: Mouton.

———. 1990. "Third-Person Reference and the Function of Pronouns in Central Pomo Natural Speech." *International Journal of American Linguistics* 56, no. 3: 361–76.

———. 1991. Active/Agentive Case Marking and Its Motivations. *Language* 67, no. 3: 510–46.

———. 1993. "'Switch Reference': Clause Combining in Central Pomo." *International Journal of American Linguistics* 59, no. 2: 119–36.

———. 1999. *The Languages of Native North America*. Cambridge: Cambridge University Press.

Moshinsky, Julius. 1974. *A Grammar of Southeastern Pomo*. University of California Publications in Linguistics 72.

———. 1976. "Historical Pomo Phonology." In *Hokan Studies: Papers from the First Conference on Hokan Languages*, San Diego, California, April 23–25, 1970, ed. Margaret Langdon and Shirley Silver, 55–75. Janua Linguarum, Series Practica 181. The Hague: Mouton.

O'Connor, Mary Catherine. 1987. *Topics in Northern Pomo Grammar*. Dissertation, University of California, Berkeley.

Oswalt, Robert. [1930s–1980s.] Field notes on Southern Pomo. Survey of California and Other Indian Languages, University of California at Berkeley California Language Archive.

———. 1958. Russian Loan Words in Southwestern Pomo. *International Journal of American Linguistics* 24: 245–47.

———. 1961. A Kashaya Grammar (Southwestern Pomo). Unpublished dissertation, University of California, Berkeley.

———. 1964. *Kashaya Texts*. University of California Publications in Linguistics 36.

———. 1971a. "Inanimate Imitatives in Pomo." In *Studies in American Indian Languages*, ed. Jesse Sawyer, 175–90. University of California Publications in Linguistics 65.

———. 1971b. "The Case of the Broken Bottle." *International Journal of American Linguistics* 37: 48–49.

———. 1976a. "Comparative Verb Morphology of Pomo." In *Hokan Studies, Papers from the First Conference on Hokan Languages*, San Diego, California, April 23–25, 1970, ed. Margaret Langdon and Shirley Silver, 13–28. Janua Linguarum, Series Practica 181. The Hague: Mouton.

———. 1976b. "Baby Talk and the Genesis of Some Basic Pomo Words." *International Journal of American Linguistics* 42, no. 1: 1–13.

———. 1978. "Retribution for Mate-Stealing: A Southern Pomo Tale." In *Northern California Texts*, ed. V. Golla and S. Silver. *International Journal of American Linguistics, Native American Texts Series* 3: 71–81.

———. 1981. *Southern Pomo Word List and Map of Native Place Names in the Warm Springs Area*. San Francisco: U.S. Army Corps of Engineers.

———. 1983. "Interclausal Reference in Kashaya." In *Switch-Reference and Universal Grammar*, ed. J. Haiman and P. Munro, 267–90. Amsterdam: John Benjamins.

Oswalt, Robert L., trans. 2002. "The Trials of Young Hawk." In *Surviving through the Days: A California Indian Reader*, ed. Herbert W. Luthin, 311–23. Berkeley: University of California Press.

Payne, Thomas. 1997. *Describing Morphosyntax: A Guide for Linguists*. Cambridge: Cambridge University Press.

Powell, John Wesley. 1891. *Indian Linguistic Families of America, North of Mexico*. Washington DC: Government Printing Office.

Roberts, John R. 1988. "Switch-Reference in Papuan Languages: A Syntactic or Extrasyntactic Device?" In *Australian Journal of Linguistics* 8: 75–117.

Sawyer, Jesse O. 1965. *English-Wappo Vocabulary*. University of California Publications in Linguistics 43.
Silliman, Stephen W. 2004. *Lost Laborers in Colonial California: Native Americans and the Archaeology of Rancho Petaluma*. Tucson: University of Arizona Press.
Stebbins, Tonya. 2003. "On the Status of Intermediate Form Classes: Words, Clitics, and Affixes in Sm'algyax (Coast Tsimshian)." *Linguistic Typology* 7, no. 3: 383–416.
Stewart, Omer. 1943. *Notes on Pomo Ethnogeography*. University of California Publications in American Archaeology and Ethnology, vol. 40. Berkeley: University of California Press.
Theodoratus, Dorothea J., David W. Peri, Clinton M. Blount, and Scott M. Patterson. 1975. *An Ethnographic Survey of the Mahilkaune (Dry Creek) Pomo*. Sonoma County CA: U.S. Army Corps of Engineers.
Thompson, Sandra A., Joseph Sung-Yul Park, and Charles N. Li. 2006. *A Reference Grammar of Wappo*. University of California Publications in Linguistics 138.
Vihman, Eero. 1976. "On Pitch Accent in Northern Pomo." In *Hokan Studies: Papers from the First Conference on Hokan Languages*, San Diego, California, April 23–25, 1970, ed. Margaret Langdon and Shirley Silver, 77–83. Janua Linguarum, Series Practica 181. The Hague: Mouton.
Walker, Neil Alexander. 2008. A Description of the Morphophonology of Southern Pomo (A California Indian Language). Master's thesis, University of California, Santa Barbara.
———. 2010. "The Phonemeic Status of Word-Initial Glottal Stops in Southern Pomo." In *Proceedings of the 6th Annual Conference on Endangered Languages and Cultures of Native America*, ed. K. Matsumoto-Gray and N. A. Walker. Salt Lake City UT: Center for American Indian Languages.
———. 2013. A Grammar of Southern Pomo: An Indigenous Language of California. Unpublished dissertation, University of California, Santa Barbara.
———. 2016. "Assessing the Effects of Language Contact on Northeastern Pomo." In *Language Contact and Change in the Americas: Studies in Honor of Marianne Mithun*, ed. Andrea Berez-Kroeker, Diane M. Hintz, and Carmen Jany, 67–90. Amsterdam: John Benjamins.
Webb, Nancy. 1971. *A Statement of Some Phonological Correspondences among the Pomo Languages*. Indiana University Publications in Anthropology and Linguistics, Memoir 26. *International Journal of American Linguistics* 37 (supplement).
Zwicky, Arnold M. 1977. *On Clitics*. Bloomington: Indiana University Linguistics Club.
———. 1985. "Clitics and Particles." *Language* 61, no. 2: 283–305.
Zwicky, Arnold M., and Geoffrey K. Pullum. 1983. "Cliticization vs. Inflection: English *n't*." *Language* 59, no. 3: 502–13.

INDEX

Page numbers in italics refer to illustrations or tables.